American Popular Music

Second Edition

David Joyner
Pacific Lutheran University

McGraw-Hill Higher Education

A Division of The **McGraw-Hill** Companies

AMERICAN POPULAR MUSIC
Published by McGraw-Hill, a business unit of The McGraw-Hill Companies, Inc. 1221 Avenue of the Americas, New York, NY, 10020. Copyright © 2003, 1993 by The McGraw-Hill Companies, Inc. All rights reserved. No part of this publication may be reproduced or distributed in any form or by any means, or stored in a database or retrieval system, without the prior written consent of The McGraw-Hill Companies, Inc., including, but not limited to, in any network or other electronic storage or transmission, or broadcast for distance learning.
Some ancillaries, including electronic and print components, may not be available to customers outside the United States.

This book is printed on acid-free paper.

1 2 3 4 5 6 7 8 9 0 QPD/QPD 0 9 8 7 6 5 4 3 2

ISBN 0-07-241424-3

Vice president and editor-in-chief: *Thalia Dorwick*
Exccutive sponsoring editor: *Christopher Freitag*
Freelance developmental editor: *Kassi Radomski*
Senior marketing manager: *David Patterson*
Project manager: *Diane M. Folliard*
Production supervisor: *Carol A. Bielski*
Coordinator of freelance design: *Mary E. Kazak*
Photo research coordinator: *Judy Kausal*
Photo researcher: *Elsa Peterson*
Cover design: *John Resh/Viper Press*
Cover photos: *Photofest*
Compositor: *UG / GGS Information Services, Inc.*
Typeface: *10/12 Palatino*
Printer: *Quebecor World/Dubuque*

Library of Congress Cataloging-in-Publication Data

Joyner, David Lee
   American popular music / David Joyner. — 2nd ed.
     p. cm.
   Includes index
   ISBN 0-07-241424-3 (alk. paper)
   1. Popular music—United States—History and criticism. 2. Popular music—United States—Analysis, appreciation. I. Title.

ML3477 .J7 2003
781.64′0973—dc21

2002016695

www.mhhe.com

This book is dedicated to my son "Fletch," an aspiring rock musician striving to bring a positive message to his audience and who keeps my finger on the pulse of current popular music. Fletch, you are always in my heart.

About the Author

David Joyner is an associate professor of music and director of Jazz Studies at Pacific Lutheran University in Tacoma, Washington. From 1986 to 2000, he was an associate professor on the faculty of the renowned Jazz Studies division at the University of North Texas in Denton. Dr. Joyner holds a BM and PhD from the University of Memphis, and an MM from the University of Cincinnati College-Conservatory of Music.

Dr. Joyner has done extensive research on ragtime composed and published in the southern United States. He has contributed articles for *The Cambridge History of American Music*, *Contemporary Music Review*, *Dictionary of American Biography* and a number of other books and periodicals. He has also done extensive research on the Gil Evans and Gerry Mulligan arrangements for the Claude Thornhill Orchestra. He has lectured on a variety of subjects at The Society for American Music, The International Association for the Study of Popular Music, The Society for Ethnomusicology, and The College Music Society. He has been a freelance jazz and popular music pianist, vocalist, composer, and arranger for over twenty-five years in the Memphis, Cincinnati, Dallas/Fort Worth, and Puget Sound areas.

Contents

Listening Guides

Preface

This book is intended for instructors and students with the task of surveying the history of a number of styles of American popular music in a one-semester or one-quarter time frame. As arduous as this task would be anyway, it is made more difficult by the relative lack of a single text of reasonable length that covers a wide range of styles. With that predicament in mind, I have written this book.

I have attempted to cover the major genres in popular music history—Tin Pan Alley, musical theater, ragtime and blues, early and more popular phases of jazz, country, and rock—while restricting the length of the chapters so that a couple can be covered in approximately one week of class meetings. Within each chapter I have tried to give the reader a balanced perspective of cultural and historical context, an insight into the development of the music industry and music technology, biographies of significant artists and producers, and an appreciation for the formal and stylistic design of the music itself. Each chapter includes "play-by-play" verbal analyses of recorded performances and an elapsed time chart for easy following of the recording. Suggestions for additional listening are given at the end of each chapter; instructors and students are encouraged to do their own analyses with these or with their own recordings.

Another feature of this book is an "active" discography. Rather than relegating a list of recordings to the end of the book, I have chosen to make citations within the context of the subject matter. This means that, based on its nature, a discographical entry may appear in the body of the text, in an endnote, or at the end of the chapter.

I have chosen recordings that are practical and relatively easy to obtain. The series of fine collections from the Smithsonian Institution, covering popular song, musical theater, blues, jazz, and country, are a primary source for this book and provide their own extensive and authoritative annotations. Unfortunately, since the first edition of this book, the Smithsonian has discontinued production of these recording sets, including its relatively profitable jazz collection. This publisher and I trust that many educational institutions already have many of these collections in their libraries. Rock music collections are somewhat more problematic, mostly due to copyright restrictions inhibiting general anthological sets of rock music. Different series from Time-Life Records have made the gathering of a comprehensive rock audio anthology easier, though they are certainly limited as well. For those recordings not covered by the Time-Life series, I have chosen other recordings that were in print at the time of this publication. I have only fallen back on LP format recordings when they offered a unique example worthy of mention and not currently available in CD format. I have also included, at strategic places in the book, references to video documentary sets on jazz, country, and rock.

The first edition ceased preparation in the early 1990s. Obviously, much has happened in popular music since then. Therefore, the chapters on American musical theater and contemporary country music have been updated. Chapter 22, dealing with rock in the 1980s, has been drastically overhauled, and a new chapter has been added to cover rock music of the 1990s. There have also been revisions to or expansion of discussions of popular styles in jazz since the Swing Era, heavy metal and progressive rock, and earlier pop music history and technology. In many cases I have also updated recording citations to reflect current CD issues.

It is important to understand what this book is and is not. It is comparatively economical in price and size. For both editions, the publisher and I have been committed to keeping this book accessible. This means saving space and cost with a paperback format and reduced number of pages, making it manageable to buy and to digest for both instructors and students. For economic reasons, there is no companion CD collection. The book is not a revisionist history, meant to usurp extant histories of the various styles of popular music; the package is more of a carefully selected compilation of American popular music style profiles. This book is certainly not exhaustive. To keep a survey of so many styles within a manageable length for a one-semester course, the material contained herein had to be broad in scope but selective in detail. There is not enough space to address every style or artist or to justify the inclusion of and elaboration on those who are addressed. This study, therefore, ultimately reflects my own sense of scholarly balance and priority.

Instructors new to teaching a survey course in popular music may be unfamiliar with the large body of scholarship on any one of the styles in this book; or they may lack the expertise, the time, or the inclination to design their own teaching materials. This book will give such instructors a workable solution to their teaching dilemma. Seasoned instructors and knowledgeable students will no doubt take issue with some of the artists, styles, and representative recordings I have chosen for this text. I encourage you to prepare alternative or augmenting materials, making the teaching and learning experience in the class all the richer.

I would like to express my gratitude to everyone who helped with the preparation of this second edition. First of all, my heartfelt thanks to freelance developmental editor Kassi Radomski, who worked with me so closely via e-mail and telephone for the last year and a half, and to publisher Chris Freitag, who made the second edition a reality. Second, a general thanks to everyone who developed the Internet. I don't know how I ever got the first edition done without e-mail, e-mail attachments, and the Internet's research resources. I certainly would not have gotten the second edition ready in the time I did without it. A particularly noteworthy inhabitant of cyberspace is the incredible website www.allmusic.com, one of the most valuable tools for my research and one I encourage students and instructors alike to take advantage of while using this book. Thanks to my mentor, Dr. David Evans at the University of Memphis, for his continued guidance and support. And, of course, thanks to my family—Maria, Garrett, and Reed— and to my students and colleagues at Pacific Lutheran University for my neglect during the preparation of this text.

Finally, I would like to thank the prepublication reviewers of the second edition for their valuable comments and suggestions: Guy Cantwell, Cabrillo College; Teresa Davidian, Tarleton State University; Maria V. Johnson, Southern Illinois University; Paul Laird, University of Kansas; Vance E. Larsen, Snow College; Ed Macan, College of the Redwoods; John A. McKinnon, Eastern Oregon University; and Mary A. Wischusen, Wayne State University.

Part 1

Tin Pan Alley and the Theater

Chapter 1

Tin Pan Alley and American Popular Song

Popular music is one of the most pervasive forces in our lives. By its very nature, it entertains us and relates to us. There are as many varieties and levels of sophistication in popular music as there are tastes among its listeners. Yet popular music has always been the great homogenizer of culture, searching for a common bond between us and capitalizing on it. Popular music is ever-changing, subject to the whims of the general public; but its various styles also experience periodic revivals generated by those who are discovering what is, to them, a new style.

The study of popular music highlights human cultural diversity. It is a journey through time, locale, and ethnicity that documents our values and our concerns. It also celebrates human ingenuity through the craft of music, an exacting and demanding discipline. In this increasingly pragmatic world, music is often seen as a mere luxury. In reality, it helps us to cope with and to express life's experiences; it touches our innermost beings in a way shared by no other art form.

The United States has impacted the world of popular music like no other country. With its young history and pluralistic culture, America's unique gift to the world has been distinctive and compelling forms of popular music. To understand how this phenomenon occurred, we must look back hundreds of years and follow popular music to the shores of the New World.

The earliest history of popular song is elusive and poorly documented. Until the sixteenth century most of the literate people in the Western world were the clergy and students of universities run by the church. By the ninth century A.D. notation had developed to the point that posterity could accurately re-create composed music, but the vast majority of the music preserved was religious. The prose and music of the common people was largely confined to oral tradition, dependent upon the memory of its performers for survival.

The written tradition of European popular song begins in the twelfth century with the song collection *Carmina Burana,* compiled by carousing, male university students (*goliards*). The songs are tales of love, drinking, and good times. (Much of this collection can be heard in a modern chorus and orchestra setting by the twentieth-century composer Carl Orff.) In the twelfth and thirteenth centuries written popular song flourished in the courtly compositions of the *troubadours* and *trouvères* of France and the *minnesingers* of Germany. For all these aristocratic songwriters the dominant subject matter was love. Their songs idolized women and romance, but with decorum and nonsensuality suitable for presentation to the upper crust of society. With love songs popular music found the subject that has dominated its history into the present time.

At the beginning of the seventeenth century, Italy developed the opera, a sophisticated, dramatic, theatrical context for singing that required an equally sophisticated technique from its performers—*bel canto*, literally "beautiful singing." This Italian penchant for vocal specialization spread throughout Europe, appealing mostly to learned aristocrats and royalty. England, the dominant culture of colonial America, absorbed some of the Italian opera influence as well, epitomized in the work of Henry Purcell. England, however, was remarkable among European countries for the musical attention it gave to the common-class consumer. This is most apparent in the output of published music for purchase and performance by amateurs. Simple *airs* and *glees* were the rage, establishing music publishing as a profitable business. Another published song type in England was the *broadside* ballad, the precursor of popular sheet music. Broadsides were topical songs employing a casual language style; they served as the gossip tabloid and lampoon magazine of their day. Usually printed without a musical line, they could be sung to familiar popular and folk melodies.

A popular pastime in eighteenth-century England was dining and strolling in vast, landscaped public gardens. Some, like the famous Vauxhall Gardens, offered musical entertainment among other appointments. The songs of these pleasure gardens were simple and strophic in form; that is, one melody is repeated over and over with a changing lyrical verse. The popularity of these songs prompted their publication for home use, and their popularity as sheet music led to the production of other *parlor songs* specifically tailored for the amateur market. Parlor songs were sentimental and easy to perform. The standard form was usually ABA: a short first theme, a second theme of equal length, and a return of the first theme. The harmonic scheme rarely exceeded three chords. Parlor songs remained popular for English and American audiences throughout the nineteenth century.

THE BEGINNINGS OF AMERICAN POPULAR SONG

America imported most of its fashion, art, and entertainment from Europe, particularly from England. In the popular realm, parlor songs and pleasure garden songs reigned supreme. English parlor song composers and performers like Henry Russell, who wrote "Woodman! Spare That Tree!" and "The Old Arm Chair," successfully concertized and sold sheet music in the New World. America's demand for parlor songs was further stimulated by the introduction of affordable, domestically manufactured upright pianos around 1830.

The primary output of American composers and publishers of the eighteenth century was sacred music, exemplified by the hymns of William Billings and

Lowell Mason. Americans tried their hand at art music and popular music but without much success. American music historian Charles Hamm cites 1789 as a turning point for the production of American secular music. In that year the newly ratified Constitution of the United States made provision for a national copyright act, protecting printed materials for 14 years, renewable for another 14 years. It was also in 1789 that a wartime ban on theatrical activities was lifted, opening the market for performing and publishing popular songs.[1]

The greatest American song composer of the nineteenth century was Stephen Foster (1826–1864). In Foster's later songs we see American popular music take a decided turn toward establishing a distinctive character, breaking away from the tradition of English parlor songs and Scottish Irish folk songs. Foster's earliest works, such as "Beautiful Dreamer" and "Jeannie with the Light Brown Hair," were parlor songs in the Scottish and Irish style known so well by his audience. Foster was, in fact, of Irish descent and profoundly influenced by Irish composer Thomas Moore, whose music was extremely popular in the United States and certainly found in the Foster household. Foster's most significant pieces, however, were those he wrote later in his career for the blackface minstrel theater (discussed in the next chapter). Songs such as "Massa's in the Cold, Cold Ground," "Old Folks at Home," and "Camptown Races" demonstrated Foster's unique ability to integrate the dual influences of British parlor songs and black American folk songs. Other minstrel composers of the day used this practice, but Foster took it to a greater height than his contemporaries. The influence of dance and dance rhythms, particularly from the American black tradition, marks Foster's best work and vividly forecasts popular song of the twentieth century.

After the Civil War sentimental parlor songs continued to sell briskly, though they were of much poorer quality than before the Civil War. Most parlor songs of the post–Civil War period were serious and vapid to a fault, exploiting the moral bent of Victorian Americans who combined the qualities of hearty frontiersmen and sentimental moralists. Tearful songs were considered songs of good conscience, related closely to hymns. There were images of old rocking chairs where a dear departed mother once held her children, letters of pardon that came too late, barefoot orphans standing in the snow, and soldiers lying dead in a rain-soaked trench.

A lively theatrical alternative to the minstrel show and the parlor song came to the United States in 1878, when the Gilbert and Sullivan operetta *H.M.S. Pinafore* was first performed. William Gilbert's lyrics were witty and beautifully fashioned, and their interaction with Arthur Sullivan's melodies went on to influence many of the finest American lyricists. While Gilbert and Sullivan's operettas demonstrated England's continuing influence on American popular entertainment, that influence would never again be as strong as it was in the first half of the nineteenth century.

The 1880s saw the rise of a new form of entertainment—vaudeville. It was inspired by the English music hall and eclipsed all other styles of entertainment by the beginning of the twentieth century. The use of the French term *vaudeville* was first applied by one of the genre's most successful producers, Tony Pastor, to describe the variety show at his theater at 14th Street and Union Square in New York. Whereas minstrel shows had an established ensemble of performers, vaudeville shows featured a playbill of individual performances that had never before appeared on the same stage. Vaudeville was also considered more appropriate for family entertainment than the minstrel show. Every vaudeville bill contained a performance by a singer of sentimental ballads. With a constant flow of new and established talent on the vaudeville stage, this new theatrical format continually demanded more music to present to the public; thus the new "pop" song industry was created.

THE BIRTH OF TIN PAN ALLEY

In the 1880s American sheet music publication began to gravitate around the theater district in New York, in order to provide vaudeville acts with the abundant number of songs they required. The first successful theater district publisher was the T. B. Harms, who specialized in songs only, which was a unique position to take in publishing at that time. Harms aggressively solicited vaudeville singers and producers to feature his company's songs in their shows. "Singing stooges" were planted in theater audiences to stand up and lead the crowd in the chorus of the new song. Before phonographs, radio, or television, live performances were the only means of demonstrating new music to the public. If the new song was well received, it was immediately printed and sold through various music retailers for amateur performance at the home piano.

In no time other publishing firms sprang up in New York near the theater district. Many of the early pop song publishers had been salesmen: Edward Marks sold buttons, Joseph Sterns sold neckties, Leo Feist sold corsets, and Isadore Witmark sold water filters. Typically, these songwriters and publishers did not sing and could not read or write music; notation and performance of their wares was left up to professional arrangers on staff for the company, many of them recently arrived European immigrants.

The song publishing neighborhood became known as Tin Pan Alley, a name attributed to *New York Herald* journalist Monroe Rosenfeld who described the collective cacophony of tinkling pianos issuing from the open windows of the publishing houses on a hot summer's day. The community of New York music publishers continued to grow and prosper. In 1914 this exclusive fraternity created the American Society of Composers, Authors, and Publishers (ASCAP), a licensing organization intended to enforce payment of royalties to composers and publishers for public performances of their material.

The background of Charles K. Harris is typical of many Tin Pan Alley songwriters and exceptional in that he had the first runaway Tin Pan Alley hit. He was one of the first popular music publishers to move to New York from the hinterlands—in his case from Milwaukee—where he had a "songs written to order" service. At a price of up to 20 dollars he composed songs on his banjo for weddings, birthdays, funerals, or any other occasion. Harris's break came when he had his three-verse story ballad "After the Ball," written and published by him in 1892, inserted into the hit musical *A Trip to Chinatown*. The song became America's first million seller; in fact, in 20 years it sold 10 million copies, and after its first year it was bringing in $25,000 a week.

"After the Ball" was a thoroughly Victorian, nineteenth-century waltz. A little girl climbs on her old uncle's knee to ask him why he has no children and no home. He replies that he had a sweetheart but caught her kissing another man at a ball. He would not forgive her or listen to her explanation and years later, after her death, learned that the man in question was only her brother.

"After the Ball" was followed by such hits as Charles Lawlor and James Blake's "Sidewalks of New York" (1894) and Arthur Lamb and Harry Von Tilzer's "A Bird in a Gilded Cage" (1900). Triple meters such as 3/4 and 6/8 were the most successful, and a conventional form arose: an introductory verse, followed by a chorus that offered the main melody. This verse-chorus form was conducive to the storytelling type of narrative song in this era.

The national success of Tin Pan Alley's popular music in no way indicates its immunity to criticism. The development of symphony orchestras and fine arts support groups accompanied the growth of cosmopolitan cities during the post–Civil War years. European classical music had a strong voice in the American cultural world, backed by the power of America's wealthy aristocrats. It was imposed on the often resentful public, and the imposition went beyond the concert hall. Music education, from elementary school to the conservatory, mandated the exclusive study of European art music styles. Music critics writing in the popular press and music journals preferred and defended European concert music. They reviled the commercially successful popular music and, by implication, its mass audience.

Yet the same urban social phenomena that brought about the art music contingent also led to an assertion of popular music culture in the latter nineteenth century. The moral restraint of provincial Victorian culture began to crumble as a more freethinking and more dynamic urban social style took over. America realized, as it pulled away from its European origins, that its emerging identity was comprised of African-American as well as European-American cultures. The dominant white society was both captivated and repelled by the openness and exuberance of African-American culture. White America struggled between the pressures of its own mores, emphasizing poise and expressive reserve, and individual expressive needs that found fulfillment in the adoption, to whatever extent, of African-American culture.

THE TWENTIETH CENTURY AND THE EMERGENCE OF AN AMERICAN STYLE

Popular music historian James R. Morris calls the twentieth century "the American century."[2] Significant cultural and stylistic changes took place toward the end of the nineteenth century, shaped by the American literature of Mark Twain and by the art of Winslow Homer and Frederic Remington. Great waves of European immigrants came to America. The ebullient high life of wealthy urban society set the pace for the style of American leisure. The character of American popular song and the style of its presentation in the twentieth century changed to reflect this more relaxed social outlook.

The new setting for public song presentation was the cabaret. Theaters present entertainers on an elevated stage, separated from the audience that sits in a darkened house. Though the actors may address the audience directly, there is still that physical threshold that severs the entertainer from the audience. Cabarets bridged the gap between performer and patron by bringing them into closer proximity, creating a more intimate and casual form of entertainment. After an evening at the theater, patrons would gather at cabarets for a late dinner and a show, appropriately called a *floor show*. Dinner tables were placed along the perimeter of a floor space designed both for dancing by the patrons and for performances by headliner entertainers. A new style of patter with the audience was developed as was a new and more risqué type of song and act.

The undisputed queen of the cabaret was Sophie Tucker (1884–1966). Rather than portraying the typical demure maiden, Tucker portrayed the tough street vamp. She specialized in music with black themes and songs by black composers, especially songwriter Sheldon Brooks, who penned her big hit "Some of These Days." Tucker's sassy songs and daring cabaret routines set the tone for future entertainment in night clubs and movies.

Another important factor in the growth of American song and entertainment was the development of ballroom dancing, which can be attributed to Vernon and Irene Castle. In the 1910s this handsome couple became the darlings of New York high society and fashion plates for the entire nation. They created new dance steps and adapted folk dances from blacks in the United States and from Latins in South America. They legitimized a more casual form of couples dancing that could be applied to the emerging American songs and dance music.

In 1897 vaudeville performer and songwriter Ben Harney introduced several of his compositions, which he called *ragtime songs,* a type of minstrel song that featured curious broken rhythms of African-American origin. (Elements of African-American music and ragtime will be discussed in later chapters.) *Ragtime* became a catchword in popular music and the force that would guide music and society to a more carefree attitude. Popular songs became more casual, using distinctive American slang and employing African-American derived melodies and rhythms. The culmination of the process that Harney started was Irving Berlin's "Alexander's Ragtime Band." Berlin's song turned the public's taste toward lively duple-rhythm songs and away from the sentimental waltz songs and operettas. After "Alexander's Ragtime Band" anything current and peppy was termed *ragtime,* just as in the 1910s and 1920s every song that was melancholy and sultry would be called *blues.*

Irving Berlin

Irving Berlin was the most resilient of the Tin Pan Alley writers and truly represents the American dream. He was born Israel Baline in 1888 in Russia. Soon after his family immigrated to New York his father died, leaving the eight-year-old to sing in the streets and work as a singing waiter. Typical of many popular songwriters at the turn of the century, he was musically illiterate and could only play the piano in the key of F-sharp; but he could pick out effective melodies, modeling himself after another songsmith of the day, George M. Cohan. Berlin achieved his biggest initial success with "Alexander's Ragtime Band," published in 1911. In 1919 he founded his own publishing company and became a star composer for the Broadway stage, yielding hits like "A Pretty Girl Is Like a Melody," for Florenz Ziegfeld's *Follies of 1919,* or "Say It with Music." Berlin helped bring about a revival of the love ballad with "Always," "All by Myself," and "What'll I Do?"

In the 1930s, like many Alley composers, Berlin moved to Hollywood to write for movie musicals, particularly for song-and-dance man Fred Astaire. Hit songs from this era included "Cheek to Cheek," "Puttin' on the Ritz," and "Change Partners." His film career culminated with the introduction of the

Irving Berlin, circa 1925, poses at the piano. He was one of America's most enduring songwriters.

song "White Christmas" in the Bing Crosby and Fred Astaire movie *Holiday Inn*. By the 1940s Berlin returned to writing musicals for the Broadway stage. Even at an advanced age, he not only kept up with current trends in theater and popular song but surpassed most of his peers. Such was the case with the 1946 musical *Annie Get Your Gun*, featuring his favorite singer, Ethel Merman, and the runaway hit "There's No Business Like Show Business."

By the time of his death in 1989 at the age of 101, Irving Berlin had been long established as an American institution. He was an astoundingly prolific composer, able to transcend decades of stylistic changes and to touch the hearts of millions. It can be said that he single-handedly wrote *the* Christmas Song ("White Christmas"), *the* Easter song ("Easter Parade"), and *the* patriotic song ("God Bless America"), a powerful testimonial to his importance not only in American popular music but also in American cultural life.

Going into the 1920s Tin Pan Alley was progressively infiltrated by highly skilled composers trained in the European tradition—such as Jerome Kern, who was the inspiration for George Gershwin, who in turn was the mentor of Vernon Duke. Soon came Richard Rodgers and other conservatory-trained songwriters. Berlin was able to survive this infiltration by sheer talent alone.

Analysis of "Puttin' on the Ritz" (*American Popular Song, LP format, Smithsonian R031 P7 17983, 2/6*)

"Puttin' on the Ritz" was written by Irving Berlin in 1929 and premiered in a film by the same name, but Fred Astaire's version is the definitive one. The song's form is a 32 measure AABA song form. The lyric describes the fashionable custom (in the 1920s) of Manhattan whites visiting the black clubs of Harlem.

The most intriguing aspect of the song, however, is the rhythm of the melody. The accentuation given by the word-phrasing and the peak of the climbing melodic phrases constantly disorient the listener from the steady pulse of the meter. With four beats per measure, the beat accents of the melody are **1** 2 3 **4**& / **1** 2 3 4 / **1** 2 3& 4 / **1** 2 3 4 / **1** 2 3 4 / **1** 2 3 4 / **1**. The pattern works beautifully with the clever rhythm sequences in Berlin's lyric. This displaced type of rhythm is very similar to an earlier song by George and Ira Gershwin, "Fascinating Rhythm," written in 1924. It was recorded in London in 1926 by Fred and Adele Astaire (his sister) with George Gershwin at the piano (*American Popular Song*, 2/1).

Fred Astaire is regarded primarily as a dancer, but most all Tin Pan Alley composers sought to have him premiere their songs. Though he did not have remarkable vocal technique—or perhaps because of that deficit—he rendered the songs simply and gracefully and true to the composer's intentions. Notice in this performance that he is carefree and swinging with the unusual rhythm, and his own background as an innovative rhythmic dancer only enhances the performance.[3]

The accompaniment on the record is a jazz band made up of English session musicians. The introduction evokes the style of black Harlem jazz bands in the 1920s. Astaire enters with the verse with piano accompaniment only, cast in a happier sounding *major* key. The rhythm of the melody at this point is quite straightforward. Its climbing chord progression builds up to the chorus. The chorus is in a *minor* key, usually reserved for dramatic or sad songs, giving this lively number an urbane, bluesy quality. The band enters and keeps a steady four-beat pulse to anchor the wild rhythmic accents of the chorus melody. For the *instrumental* break, the band softly accompanies Astaire's dancing. One might ask, Why have dancing on an audio recording? It is important to understand that *audible*, rhythmic, specialty dancing from the black tradition, such as tap and buck-and-wing, made significant contributions to jazz rhythm and influenced many jazz drummers such as Warren "Baby" Dodds and "Papa" Jo Jones. Astaire was famous as a pioneer of this type of *syncopated* dance rhythm, particularly in the white mainstream. His own feet become an important featured percussion instrument in this arrangement. When his vocal reenters to sing the chorus a second time, Astaire sings with a much freer rhythm, similar to the approach of jazz singers like Louis Armstrong. The jagged rhythms heard in the first chorus are therefore not as apparent.

Listening Guide   1.1
"Puttin' on the Ritz" *4 beats per measure*

ELAPSED TIME	FORM	EVENT DESCRIPTION
:00	Intro	Full band (8 measures)
:09	Verse	Voice, piano only (16 measures: 8 + 8)
:26	Chorus 1	Band enters (32 measures: AABA, 4 groups of 8 bars)
1:01	Chorus 2	Dance solo A, dialogue 2nd A, band/dance B, A (32 measures)
1:35	Chorus 3	Vocal; more improvised melody and rhythm (32 measures)
2:10	1/2 Ch. 4–1	Begins at B, piano and dance (8 measures)
2:19	1/2 Ch. 4–2	Vocal (8 measures)
2:28	End	

By the 1920s a new song form had emerged. The storytelling concept of the verse/chorus waltz ballad gave way to a more concise 32-measure chorus that merely captured a moment's feeling. One division of the 32 measures was two halves with nearly identical melodies, as in George and Ira Gershwin's "But Not for Me." The other division formula for the 32 measures was four groups of eight measures. This form involved an eight-bar melody (A) repeated with a new set of words (A), a contrasting eight-bar melody called a *bridge* or *release* (B), and a return of the first melody with new words (A). An example of this AABA chorus form would be the Gershwin brothers' "Oh, Lady Be Good."

This form proved most effective for the mass production of songs from the 1920s to the 1950s, requiring only 50 to 75 words from the lyricist. The repetition of the A melody with one refreshing bit of contrasting B melody helped to drill the song into the mind of the listener and to create an immediate identification with the song.

The large majority of Tin Pan Alley's 32-bar songs were love songs, and most of them were slow ballads. They were, however, a far cry from the character of popular love songs before 1920. Major Tin Pan Alley lyricists such as Cole Porter, Lorenz Hart, and Ira Gershwin expressed love without the formal poetic character and sentimentality of old ballads. Reflecting their urban New York toughness, the songs were less distant and nostalgic and more immediate and confrontational, expressing love in second person rather than third person ("I love you" rather than "I loved her").

Analysis of "It Never Entered My Mind" (*American Popular Song, 5/6*)

The singer on this recording is Shirley Ross, who introduced "It Never Entered My Mind" in the unsuccessful 1940 stage musical *Higher and Higher*. The performance is quite straight, true to the original sheet music. This recording does offer the rarely heard second chorus lyric.

Richard Rodgers's melodies are often constructed from an almost relentless repetition of short melodic or rhythmic fragments. Such is the case with "It Never Entered My Mind," where five of the eight measures in the first A section (measures two through six) use the same three- and four-note descending scale pattern. Likewise, on the bridge, or B section, the **1 2 3 4** rhythmic pattern occupies six measures of the eight-measure section (measures 1–4 and 7–8). In this particular song, the harmony is equally repetitive. The A section regularly oscillates between two chords every two beats. The form of the song is a 34 measure AABA song form. The last A section has one additional two-bar phrase spliced between the usual six and seventh measures.

Lyricist Lorenz Hart always wrote words to Rodgers' completed music, not before or while the music was written. Influenced in large part by the repetitiveness of the song, Hart had a penchant for frequently occurring rhymes, especially triple rhymes. He was famous among his peers for the clever way in

One of the great songwriting teams in American music, composer Richard Rodgers (left) and lyricist Lorenz Hart.

which he aligned his rhymed stresses with those created by the melodic contour or rhythmic emphasis in the music. Technical matters aside, Hart was also at the vanguard of the urbane, sophisticated style of lyric that gave a cynical, aloof flavor to even the most tender of heartache songs. Here again, "It Never Entered My Mind" is exemplary. The protagonist is abandoned and hurt by her lover. But instead of saying it with poetic utterances, Hart uses mundane and decidedly unromantic images, such as single orders of orange juice. In this way, Hart immediately reaches listeners with unglamorous, common associations we all make in our own experiences.

Listening Guide   1.2
"It Never Entered My Mind" 4 beats per measure

ELAPSED TIME		FORM	EVENT DESCRIPTION
:00		Intro	Full band (4 measures)
:10		Chorus 1	Voice enters (34 measures: AABA 8 + 8 + 8 + 10)
1:34		Chorus 2	New lyric, two-bar extension of last A (humming), last two measures
			elongated to four for ending
3:07		End	

American Song and the Media

For many years music could only be presented in print and in live performance. American music is fortunate that, in its relatively brief history, much of it has benefited from the technology of mass media. The first medium to widely disseminate music and music performances was the phonograph, invented by Thomas Edison in 1877. He intended the phonograph to be a dictation machine, but it began to be used for commercial entertainment at the turn of the century. In the early years of recording, sound entered a megaphone that vibrated a stylus that cut grooves into the record disc or cylinder. Only loud sounds could be recorded, usually brass bands and opera singers. Also, phonographs were very expensive and available only to the rich. After about 1908 phonographs lowered in price and found their way into more homes, increasing the demand for popular music to be recorded. In 1909 federal legislation mandated a two-cents-per-record royalty payment to music publishers for the right to perform a copyrighted composition.

In the mid-1920s acoustical recording was abandoned in favor of electric recording, using microphone technology originally developed by radio. It suddenly became possible to capture on records a wide range of subtle sounds, affecting the sound and style of singers and their backup orchestrations. Vibrato could be subtler and used more sparingly as an ornamental device. Electrical recording also allowed for natural pronunciation of the text. Earlier singers like Al Jolson had an exaggerated singing pronunciation that facilitated being understood in a large performance hall. Later singers adapted to the microphones, singing in a conversational and intimate manner that brought them closer to their audience. Older style "belters" became obsolete almost overnight, supplanted by a new generation of more intimate "crooners." Mellow alto and baritone singers became favored over the bright sound of sopranos and tenors. No one exemplified the new crooning sound better than Bing Crosby (1904–1977). The sensitive electronic microphone was an extension of his vocal instrument, and he set the standard for a natural, conversational, intimate style more befitting the living room than the theater.

The first commercial radio station began broadcasting in 1920. In 1926 the National Broadcasting Company began daily network programming. After the initial cost of purchasing a radio set the medium offered essentially free entertainment to its listeners, giving stiff competition to recordings and film. In fact,

Singer and actor Bing Crosby, circa 1945, the first of the great crooners who revolutionized popular singing in the late 1920s.

during the Great Depression, beginning in 1929, radio actually flourished while other media struggled for survival. Because radio traveled over the airwaves, entertainment could reach the most remote parts of the country, an aspect of importance to the growth of country music, since many of its devotees lived in isolated rural settings.

In the early 1940s, ASCAP tried to double its licensing fees to the National Association of Broadcasters. The NAB responded by banning all ASCAP material from the airwaves and forming its own licensing organization, Broadcast Music Incorporated (BMI). This event became important to the music industry outside of the closed fraternity of Tin Pan Alley writers and publishers, particularly to country music writers and publishers (see Chapter 14).

The late 1920s saw the introduction of the sound film, highlighted by Al Jolson's performance in *The Jazz Singer* in 1927. Suddenly there was a demand for movie musicals, which reached their earliest zenith in the 1930s with lavish films by choreographer-director Busby Berkeley and the movies of Fred Astaire. The film musical became a major medium for the introduction of new songs, and great Tin Pan Alley songwriters and lyricists began to divide their time between New York and Hollywood.

The 1930s and 1940s saw the rise of big swing bands. These bands often featured a singer, who rendered a vocal chorus in the middle of a mostly instrumental arrangement. In August 1942 members of the American Federation of Musicians went on strike against the major recording companies, but nonunion singers suffered no such restrictions. By the time the strike was settled in 1944, popular taste had shifted to the singers, including Perry Como, Peggy Lee, Dick Haymes, Helen Forrest, and Jo Stafford. The most influential voice of the 1940s and the most important link between Tin Pan Alley and the rise of rock and roll was Frank Sinatra (1911–1998). Sinatra was influential in that he was the first real "heartthrob" sex symbol in American popular song. He developed a style with daring phrasing that allowed for dramatic and intensely personal rendering of a song. His style made each member of the audience feel as if the song were just for him or (in most cases) her. Sinatra inspired and, in some cases, promoted a series of male singers who closely copied his style: Dean Martin, Vic Damone, Steve Lawrence, Bobby Darin, and Jack Jones. Early rock artists such as Elvis Presley also used Sinatra's sexy and emotive style as a model for their own.

Sinatra continued to produce tremendous hits from the 1960s until his death in 1998. The onset of Elvis Presley, the Beatles, and other newer stars could not diminish his position as "chairman of the board." Though younger artists were now the youthful heartthrob he had once been, Sinatra maintained his position as an authoritative song stylist, hit maker, and now, elder statesman. In the 1970s he tapered off of recordings, films, and television in favor of live shows. Then, in 1980, he covered the theme song from the 1977 movie musical *New York, New York* in a

Singer and actor Frank Sinatra performs with trumpeter Harry James's orchestra for American servicemen in California on August 16, 1947.

three-LP set *Trilogy: Past, Present, and Future.* It became a tremendous hit. In 1993 he recorded *Duets,* on which he rerecorded old favorites with other popular singers as far ranging as Tony Bennett, Bono (of the group U2), and country singer George Strait. (The latter was omitted from the released album but was later included on a George Strait box set.) It became his biggest-selling album, selling over 3,000,000 copies, and was followed the next year by *Duets II,* which won the 1995 Grammy award for traditional pop performance.

Analysis of "I've Got You Under My Skin" (*Songs for Swingin' Lovers,* CD format, Capitol C2-46570)

Frank Sinatra's earliest major exposure was with the big bands of Harry James and Tommy Dorsey. In the mid-1940s he was signed to Columbia Records as a solo artist and was also pursuing live concerts, the fledgling medium of television, and film acting. By 1952, however, he was without a record, film, radio, or television contract. He then signed with Capitol Records, founded a decade earlier by songwriter Johnny Mercer. He entered into a long-term contract, collaborating on a series of theme albums with the great arranger Nelson Riddle. A high point of this period was the 1956 album *Songs for Swingin' Lovers,* which went gold and almost made number one on its release.

"I've Got You Under My Skin" is one of the most memorable Riddle arrangements and Sinatra vocal performances of all time. The song was composed by Cole Porter. Typical of Porter, it is not a conventional 32-measure AABA song form. The first section is 16 measures in length (twice the usual length); the second is a variation of the first. The third section is 8 measures long, then, instead of repeating the first section again, there is a fourth section 16 measures in length, making the chorus an unusual 56 measures in length.

Nelson Riddle's arrangement opens with a low repeated figure, called a *vamp,* played by a bass clarinet, punctuated by high bell-like sounds from a celeste (a small keyboard instrument). This vamp will be a recurring and prominent feature throughout the arrangement and manages to get as much attention as Sinatra's vocal.

Sinatra's vocal begins with an easy and dreamy demeanor. He carefully shapes the sound of each word to accommodate his vocal quality; notice the striking way in which he sings through the "ooh" sound of "you," the closed "n" sound of "skin," both in the opening line and in the resonant low note he sings in the fourth line. In the second A section of the song Sinatra uses a bouncier, more swinging phrasing that adds lilt and aggressiveness to the line. But notice when he comes to the word "baby" he brings back a moment of tenderness appropriate to the affection expressed in that name.

The vocal and the arrangement continue their logical climb along with the shape of the melodic line and the nature of the lyric. At the end of the first chorus Sinatra's voice dies away, handing the spotlight over to the band. The vamp figure is now a chatter among the lower instruments of the band, while the string section's long notes climb higher in register, almost to a squeal. The brass section now enters with a pounding, swinging rendition of the song's second A section while a forceful trombone solo wails over the band. Sinatra reenters at the B section of the song, more forcefully than his rendition of the same section in the previous chorus. In the last C section the brass come in behind Sinatra with almost the same ferocity that they had when they were playing alone. At the end Sinatra again fades away, and the vamp goes out as gently as it began the arrangement. There is a brief pause, then a shimmering chord held by the strings with the chime of the celeste over the top.

Listening Guide   1.3
"I've Got You Under My Skin" *4 beats per measure*

ELAPSED TIME	FORM	EVENT DESCRIPTION
:00	Intro	Vamp with bass clarinet, celeste (6 measures)
:10	Chor. 1, A1	Soft vocal enters; strings enter halfway through (16 measures)
:41	A2	Add baritone sax and trombone to vamp, strings go higher in range
1:11	B	Vocal swings more, insistent saxophone section figure and smooth strings
1:26	C	Intensity is maintained
1:53	Interlude	Vamp figure is heard expanded among the trombones, string climb higher
2:15	Chor. 2, A 2	Brass play the melody in a swing style; loud trombone solo mixed in, intense
2:45	B	Similar setting as previous B but stronger
3:03	C	Brass stabs help push to the end
3:27	Ending	Vamp is reduced to bass clarinet and celeste once more; pause; string chord with celeste.
3:40	End	

After World War II television became the dominant medium for the mainstream music industry. Television programming included variety shows hosted by singing stars from the swing era. In the late 1950s and early 1960s, however, Tin Pan Alley began to lose ground. It had always catered to the tried-and-true audience of white, middle-aged, middle-class urbanites; but the burgeoning youth audience began to demand rock and roll.

The golden age of Tin Pan Alley did not end abruptly. Though rock was coming on as a major popular music force in the 1960s, the industry could still count on recordings by crooners like Frank Sinatra, Andy Williams, or Jack Jones to sell as well as most rock artists—and this type of artist still dominated television musical variety shows. Columbia's artist and repertoire head, Mitch Miller, resisted rock in favor of easy listening musical acts until the late sixties and still did quite well with sales.

By the 1970s the "Great American Songbook" was considered a thing of the past. Over the years, there have been younger artists who keep songs from the 1930s to the 1960s alive. Artists like Michael Feinstein, Barbra Streisand, Whitney Houston, Natalie Cole, Maureen McGovern, Diana Krall, and Harry Connick, Jr., may be categorized as cabaret, musical theater, or jazz, but all have championed the great Tin Pan Alley songs of the past. At the same time a spirit of Tin Pan Alley has remained in more recent music. The nature of that spirit is lyrical, carefully crafted music and lyrics by professional composers and lyricists that emphasize a beauty and elegance that hearkens back to the aesthetic of earlier popular song. This is found prominently in pop substyles such as adult contemporary and power ballads and refers to great songwriters of the last 40 years such as Burt Bacharach, Paul Williams, Jimmy Webb, or Diane Warren. To many, the so-called young country style, dating from the 1980s on, is one of the last bastions of the songwriter's craft. Indeed, music cable network VH1 began mixing contemporary country music into its adult contemporary offerings, allowing country artists like Shania Twain and Faith Hill to easily cross over to the mainstream adult pop market.

The standard songbook of the past has a remarkable universal appeal, able to capture the imagination of young people with no memory of or sentimental tie to the songs' golden age. Even in an age of aggressive music and frank lyrics, there will always be someone with a taste for the romanticism and sophistication of what could arguably be considered America's art songs.

Chapter Summary

The written tradition of early European popular music is not as extensive as that of religious music because most folk and popular music of the common people existed only in oral tradition. The written popular music that does exist deals overwhelmingly with the subject of romantic love. England was conspicuous among European countries in that it produced a large amount of music for amateur performance. This is the music that shaped the popular music of America through the late nineteenth century.

The European style of sentimental parlor songs and hymns was challenged in the mid-nineteenth century by the minstrel songs of Stephen Foster, inspired by the folk music of African-Americans. The development of vaudeville theater in New York in the 1880s prompted the popular sheet music industry. Early Tin Pan Alley products were sentimental, triple meter songs, but the continuing influence of the black culture led to a distinctive American style of song, one that used lively duple meter and informal American speech. The distinctive 32-bar song form aided in turning songs away from narrative ballads toward elaborated moments of love.

The twentieth century saw the emergence of media technology that would not only effectively disseminate American popular song but actually affect its style. The acoustic recording method required loud instruments and singers that were better suited for large performance halls. Electronic microphones allowed more subtlety and expressivity both in vocal technique and in orchestration. Radio was the most effective means of getting music to the masses. It was a medium that was essentially free after the purchase of the radio set, and its use of airwaves transmission reached listeners in the most remote locations. The radio industry also created Broadcast Music Incorporated, the music licensing organization that rivaled Tin Pan Alley's American Society of Composers, Authors, and Publishers. With the advent of sound, motion picture musicals provided another effective outlet for songwriters, rivaling the New York musical theater.

The recording strike by the musician's union brought swing band vocalists to prominence in the mid-1940s. The age of mellow-voiced crooners was epitomized with the singing of Frank Sinatra. The emergence of rock and roll in the mid-1950s brought an end to Tin Pan Alley's existence as a sheet music industry, but the sophisticated urban music of the Alley's glory days continues to inspire new generations of musicians.

Additional Listening

Sophie Tucker, "Some of These Days" (1911) (*American Popular Song*, Smithsonian R031 P7 17983, 1/1). Words and music: Shelton Brooks (1910). Listen to the limited fidelity of this acoustic recording and the loud orchestration and vocal quality required to overcome it. The form is ABCD, which contrasts with earlier repetitive story ballads, as does the less formal character of the song's lyrics.

Bing Crosby, "Out of Nowhere" (1931) (*American Popular Song*, 2/8). Music: John Green; lyrics: Edward Heyman (1931). Listen for Crosby's subtlety and intimacy afforded by the electronic microphone process of recording after the mid-1920s. This is particularly apparent in the second chorus. The form is two 32-bar choruses (16 + 16) with the verse placed between them, acting as an interlude.

Nat "King" Cole, "Stardust" (1956) (*American Popular Song*, 8/8). Music: Hoagy Carmichael (1927); lyrics: Mitchell Parish (1929). Listen for the peaceful majesty that Cole brings to the song, the difficult leaps in this melody, which was originally a medium-tempo instrumental number, the lushness of Gordon Jenkin's arrangement. The form is verse (16 bars: 8 + 8)/ chorus (32 bars: 16 + 16).

Other Songs for Additional Listening (all tracks from *American Popular Song*)

Jerome Kern, Oscar Hammerstein II: "All the Things You Are" (12/7)
George Gershwin, Ira Gershwin: "But Not for Me" (6/4)
Harold Arlen, Ted Koehler: "Stormy Weather" (5/8)
Arthur Schwartz, Howard Dietz: "Alone Together" (6/7)
Harold Arlen, Johnny Mercer: "Blues in the Night" (9/6)

Review Questions

1. Why has it been difficult to research the earliest popular music?
2. What were English forms of popular music that came to America?
3. How did Stephen Foster make the transition to a distinct American style?
4. What were American forms of theater that encouraged popular song?
5. Contrast Tin Pan Alley songs before and after "Alexander's Ragtime Band."
6. Describe the two types of 32-bar song form.
7. Describe recording technology's impact on singing and arranging practices.

Notes

1. Charles Hamm, *Yesterdays: Popular Song in America* (New York: W. W. Norton & Company, 1979), p. 2.
2. James R. Morris, Introductory essay to the recording set *American Popular Song: Six Decades of Songwriters and Singers* (Smithsonian P7 17983).
3. Public television has aired a remarkable program dealing strictly with Fred Astaire the singer, *The Fred Astaire Songbook.* It is often shown during their fund-raising campaigns.

Chapter 2

American Musical Theater

Tin Pan Alley was inextricably linked to the theater. Until the advent of mass media technology, the theater was the most effective means of introducing songs to the public; and the music industry's focus was on record and sheet music sales. Of course, American musical theater was much more than an effective marketing tool for sheet music publishers. Rich in tradition, it is a genre worthy of study for its own intrinsic value.

American musical theater takes a variety of forms, employing music in many ways. In some cases there is little or no plot to the program, just a series of songs. In other cases music and dance are carefully woven into the fabric of the story. The stories range from the comic and farcical to the dramatic and tragic.

America's first attempts at musical theater date back to at least 1735. Most musicals were modeled after British ballad operas, particularly the highly successful *The Beggar's Opera,* by John Gay. Philadelphia and New York were the centers of this activity. High society in these cities preferred European grand opera, but the majority of middle-class Americans preferred a simpler and more garish form of musical entertainment. In the course of the nineteenth century, America would start to find its own distinctive form of musical theater.

The United States spent the majority of the late eighteenth and early nineteenth centuries fighting for its independence from England. In 1803 President Thomas Jefferson purchased the Louisiana Territory from France, opening the way for expansion westward. America gradually began to hone its own culture and slowly move away from the traditions of Europe. The establishment of a distinctively American character in music was due to the cross-influence and continuing dialectic between two diverse cultures.

As we will see in Chapter 3, enslaved blacks from Africa took the European-based musical system and modified it in performance to bring it closer to the realm of their own musical sensibilities. The unique religious music, work and play songs that emerged were soon capitalized on by white entertainers.

THE MINSTREL SHOW

The first significant entity in the commercialization of African-American music was the minstrel show, the forerunner to American musical comedy. Minstrelsy was the product of a common man's culture that arose shortly after the War of 1812, a culture that acknowledged the tastes and values of the average American white rather than the upper-class aristocracy. Urban centers were growing rapidly, and rural migrants required entertainment that they could understand, entertainment that gave them a sense of worth and replaced the folk culture they left behind.

Minstrelsy adopted the image of the American black, catering to the fascination whites of that day had for them. In lampooning any ethnic group, performers exaggerate its characteristic of appearance, speech, movement, and behavior for comic effect. This practice was the trademark of minstrelsy.

The shows centered around white actors characterizing blacks. The performances attracted huge audiences, revealing the national fascination with black culture. This was especially so in the Northeast where blacks were comparatively scarce and therefore somewhat of a curiosity. Minstrelsy, unfortunately, fostered black stereotypes. Some images even carried over into the entertainment media of the 1960s.

The music used in the minstrel shows was not of black origin, but was based on the simple folk songs of England, Scotland, and Ireland. Common Americans, who were often recent immigrants from those countries, strongly identified with these songs.[1] Using black dialect in lyrics, the themes were transposed from "my bonnie lass from Ireland" to "my old plantation home" with little loss of sentimental impact.

White men in blackface portrayed blacks well before the American Revolution but primarily in solo performances. Minstrelsy was finally organized into ensembles in February 1843, when the Virginia Minstrels premiered in New York City. This group included Dan Emmett, believed to be the composer of "Dixie." The most famous minstrel troupe, however, was Christy's Minstrels, founded by E. P. Christy and featuring the compositions of Stephen Foster.

Despite the racist overtones of minstrelsy, it was the most significant genre in the early development of popular American entertainment. Some results of minstrelsy's impact were economic, while others were of an artistic nature. After the Civil War, minstrelsy provided one of the few employment opportunities to blacks, who soon competed with their white imitators. Creative opportunities also arose for black songwriters such as James Bland who wrote "Carry Me Back to Old Virginny" and "Oh, Dem Golden Slippers." From the artistic standpoint, minstrels, both black and white, introduced a new singing style. The communication of words became more important than refined singing. Spoken word and singing came closer together, and melody gave way to a more heightened rhythmic sense. Singing changed from a trained *bel canto* style to a more strongly projected declamatory style.

Minstrelsy also influenced theatrical programming. The standardized portion of a minstrel show known as the *olio* was the second half of the show. It consisted of a variety of acts, a farce or burlesque opera, and a song and dance finale with the entire troupe on stage. Many theater and film musicals, as well as many television variety shows, used the olio as a model for their format.

OTHER MUSIC THEATER FORMS IN THE NINETEENTH CENTURY

Many minstrel shows and other theater environments were considered too rough for family entertainment. The shows often featured immodestly dressed chorus girls, and audiences consisted primarily of men severely lacking in manners. One writer complained of the "incessant spitting" and the audience's ill-dressed appearance. Shows were held anywhere a crowd could gather, including tents, boats, and saloons. Tony Pastor, a former saloon owner, was one of the first to legitimize theater as family entertainment when he opened his own theater in 1881. He developed the concept of *vaudeville,* a variety show featuring both new and celebrated talent. The evening's bill of fare could be quite varied: singers, dancers, comedians, animal acts, and acrobats.

Theater forms derived from European traditions also continued to appear. The first music show sensation of this type was *The Black Crook,* which played in New York's Niblo's Garden in 1866. A French ballet troupe was used to supplement a nonsensical plot by Charles Barras. The play was peppered with songs and dances that held the audience's attention for over five hours. It ran for 474 performances, was performed off and on for the next 25 years, and indicated to future producers America's taste for the spectacular.

The legacy of European lyric theater and operetta continued with the works of Gilbert and Sullivan. Their operettas, such as *H. M. S. Pinafore* and *The Mikado,* enjoyed such success with American audiences that American producers were forced to develop similar comic operas. The greatest of the American operetta composers was Victor Herbert, creator of *The Fortune Teller, The Red Mill,* and the famous *Naughty Marietta.* Herbert's style was very European, drawing upon the Viennese waltz and French and German opera. The plots and settings were usually also European. This style of American theater peaked in 1907 with the premiere of Franz Lehar's *The Merry Widow,* at New York's lavish Hippodrome theater. This operetta satisfied the American public's hunger for big production. Thoroughly Viennese, *The Merry Widow* also spawned a craze for dancing the waltz, which may account for that era's dearth of popular songs in triple meter.

Excluding blackface minstrelsy, the first distinctly American musical comedy was pioneered by Edward Harrigan and Tony Hart. Their productions depicted scenes of everyday American life and presented comic sketches of Irish and German urban immigrants. The *Mulligan Guard* plays were such shows, presented between 1873 and 1885. In 1891 Charles Hoyt's *A Trip to Chinatown* continued this tradition of comedy with music. Ethnic comedy continued with the Jewish dialect routines of native New Yorkers Joe Weber and Lew Fields. Beginning in 1896 their shows were a combination of vaudeville and parodies of recent theater hits. In 1899 Weber and Fields added the lovely soprano Lillian Russell to the cast to provide the glamorous relief from their comic routines.

This American style of musical theater was climaxed by the work of George M. Cohan (1878–1942). He began his career at age four, with his family vaudeville group, and went on to become not only a fine songwriter but also a versatile actor, producer, and playwright for some 20 musicals. *Little Johnny*

Victor Herbert, composer of many popular operettas in the late nineteenth and early twentieth centuries.

Jones was his first Broadway hit, opening in 1904. It snubbed every vestige of European operetta with American colloquialisms and settings; and it yielded a number of songs that have now become classics, including "Yankee Doodle Dandy" and "Give My Regards to Broadway." Cohan, like his disciple Irving Berlin, was musically illiterate. His creations were simple, singable, and memorable songs that were more down to earth than the esoteric songs of the operettas. Both Cohan and Berlin were masters also of the American patriotic song. Cohan's "Over There" and Berlin's "Oh, How I Hate to Get Up in the Morning" became the virtual anthems of World War I. The American flavor of Cohan's musicals set the tone for American theater in the twentieth century and contributed greatly to the demise of European-styled theater. The extreme anti-German sentiment brought about by World War I also precipitated the decline of waltz musicals and operetta.

Jerome Kern

Jerome Kern (1885–1945) was born to a prosperous New York family. After showing little aptitude for his father's merchandise business, he was given thorough musical training in New York and Europe. Kern settled in London and began writing for the musical theater. In 1905 he had his first Broadway success, *The Earl and the Girl,* co-written with Edward Laska. Six productions and six years later, Kern received his first major assignment, collaborating with Frank Tours on *La Belle Paree.* The next year he wrote his first complete original score, *The Red Petticoat.* The four numbers he composed for the 1914 musical *The Girl from Utah* got the attention of his peers, particularly the song "They Didn't Believe Me."

Kern, with writers and lyricists Guy Bolton and P. G. Wodehouse, revolutionized American musical theater with the "Princess Theater musicals," which began in 1915. More intimate than the European-inspired spectaculars like the Hippodrome's *A Yankee Circus on Mars,* the musicals used American characters and settings. They were light and whimsical, employed small orchestras and casts, and had a minimum of set changes. Premiering in 1917, *Oh, Boy!* is the most notable of the Princess Theater musicals. A farce about mistaken identity, the show featured a number of hit songs, including the lovely "Till the Clouds Roll By."

Jerome Kern in 1928, composer of some of the most sophisticated songs in American popular music.

Jerome Kern further transformed American musical theater with the production of *Show Boat* in 1927. Whereas most musicals to this date had comic plots or no plots at all, Kern and lyricist Oscar Hammerstein II based their musical on a literary work by Edna Ferber. This show was the first example of serious drama in American musicals. It addressed socially sensitive topics such as racism, gambling addiction, and marital difficulties. The artfulness and sobriety of the music and the narrative qualified the musical as operetta to many, and *Show Boat* was considered a significant advancement in the genre. The show also yielded a number of classic songs, including "Can't Help Lovin' That Man of Mine" and "Old Man River."

Kern continued to write Broadway musicals into the 1930s—musicals that yielded song hits such as "The Song Is You" (*Music in the Air*, 1932), "Smoke Gets in Your Eyes," and "Yesterdays" (both from *Roberta*, 1933). In the 1930s Kern, like many other Alley composers, moved to Hollywood to write music for movie musicals. This period yielded two Oscar-winning songs, "The Way You Look Tonight" (1936) and "The Last Time I Saw Paris" (1945). Kern remained active in the music theater arena. Oscar Hammerstein, however, could not persuade Kern to base a musical on the bucolic story *Green Grows the Lilacs*. Hammerstein later pursued the project with Richard Rodgers to produce *Oklahoma!* At the time of his death Kern was venturing into a musical based on the life of Annie Oakley, and the assignment went to Irving Berlin. The result was *Annie Get Your Gun*.

Analysis of "Smoke Gets in Your Eyes" (*American Musical Theater*, CD format, Smithsonian RD 036 A4 20483, 1/23)

"Smoke Gets in Your Eyes" is from Kern's musical *Roberta*, his last big Broadway venture. Based on the Alice Duer Miller novel *Gowns by Roberta*, it is a sophisticated comedy about an American football player and a Russian princess. The song that carried the show was "Smoke Gets in Your Eyes," which, in earlier incarnations, had been intended as a fast tap dance number in *Show Boat*, then as a march for an NBC radio series. It was lyricist and librettist Otto Harbach's idea to slow the song down and to add a lyric based on an old Russian proverb.

Beautiful Ukranian-born Tamara Drasin was chosen to play the part of Princess Stephanie and to sing "Smoke Gets in Your Eyes," and it is she who we hear on this recording. In the show Tamara accompanied herself on guitar, but on this recording she is accompanied by a dance orchestra. Since Harbach's staging called for a jazz band onstage, the dance band accompaniment may not be totally out of place here.

Listening Guide   2.1
"Smoke Gets in Your Eyes" 4 beats per measure

ELAPSED TIME	FORM	EVENT DESCRIPTION
:00	Intro	Orchestra (4 measures)
:08	Chorus 1	(32 measures: AABA, 4 groups of 8 bars) A: sax, A: flute, B: violins, A: violins and sax, 2-bar tag
1:13	Chorus 2	Vocal enters (32 measures)
2:15	Chorus 3	Orchestra (partial chorus AA + Coda: 16 + 2 measures)
2:51	End	

Blacks in Musical Theater

Black American culture had an impact on the evolving style of American musical theater through its influence on white American composers. But black composers and performers were also making direct contributions to the main body of musical shows. *The Creole Show* opened in 1893 at the World Columbian Exposition in

Pianist and songwriter James P. Johnson, composer of "The Charleston," the veritable anthem of 1920s dance and popular music.

Chicago. Featuring Lillian Russell, it was the first black musical review to break with the minstrel format. The emerging popularity of ragtime in the late 1890s led to *Clorindy—The Origin of the Cakewalk*, with music by black composer Will Marion Cook and lyrics by Paul Lawrence Dunbar. This team went on to write *In Dahomey* in 1903, starring Bert Williams, the first black theater star to enjoy fame within the milieu of white theater.

Ragtime evolved into jazz by the 1920s, and black musical producers in New York injected it into their shows. Most of the black musical activity was centered in Harlem; but in 1921 the musical *Shuffle Along* established itself on Broadway. The music for the show, written by composer Eubie Blake and lyricist Noble Sissle, resulted in a number of hits, including the ever-popular "I'm Just Wild about Harry." Other black musicals included *Runnin' Wild,* with music by Harlem jazz pianist James P. Johnson. "The Charleston" was one of the songs from the show and became the anthem of the 1920s flapper scene. Some of the musical revues, such as the *Blackbirds* series that begin in 1928, starred black performers but contained songs by white composers such as Jimmy McHugh and Dorothy Fields. The popularity of black musical theater, along with Harlem night spots such as the Cotton Club, helped to establish black artists and bring them into the mainstream of the entertainment world. These artists would include Louis Armstrong, Fats Waller, Bill "Bojangles" Robinson, and Lena Horne.

George and Ira Gershwin

The jazz influence eventually made its way into white musicals, most notably the musicals of the Gershwin brothers, George and Ira. George Gershwin, born in New York in 1898, was largely a self-taught pianist and composer. At the age of 15 he dropped out of school to become a song *plugger*—one who demonstrates sheet music at the piano for potential customers—for the Jerome Remick music publishing company. He wrote his first complete score for a musical in 1918, but his first significant work was *Lady, Be Good!* Lyrics for this song, which premiered in 1924, were written by his brother Ira Gershwin (1896–1983). It was also in 1924 that Gershwin first performed his immortal piano and orchestra work *Rhapsody in*

The Gershwin brothers, composer George (left) and lyricist Ira. They created songs for popular musicals and the opera *Porgy and Bess*.

Blue. Throughout the 1920s and until George Gershwin's death in 1937, the Gershwin brothers composed a number of jazz-influenced Broadway scores comprised of rhythmically intriguing melodies and cleverly rhymed lyrics.

The Gershwin musicals also demonstrated the continuing quest in musical theater for meaningful social commentary, a trend begun by Kern and Hammerstein's *Show Boat*. *Strike Up the Band* (1930) addressed issues of war; *Of Thee I Sing* and *Let 'Em Eat Cake* dealt with politics and power. In fact, *Of Thee I Sing* became the first musical play to win its authors, Ira Gershwin, Morrie Ryskind, and George S. Kaufmann, the Pulitzer Prize. The climax of Gershwin's career was his *Porgy and Bess* (1935). Based on a book by DuBose Heyward, the musical setting is Catfish Row, South Carolina. The entire cast was black, and most of the dialogue was sung rather than spoken, a practice usually associated with opera. Many historians and critics have, in fact, upgraded the status of *Porgy and Bess* from musical to full-fledged opera.

Richard Rodgers, Lorenz Hart, and Oscar Hammerstein II

No one has endured in the realm of musical theater better than songwriter Richard Rodgers (1902–1979). A native of Long Island, Rodgers was educated at Columbia University and began his career in 1920 as a composer of musicals. That same year he began his association with lyricist Lorenz Hart (1895–1943). Inspired by the lyrics of William Gilbert and P. G. Wodehouse, Hart developed a sophisticated, witty, but sometimes ribald and sardonic style of lyric that would set the mood for musicals and popular songs for years to come. This is typified in Rodgers and Hart's *Pal Joey* from 1943. The story is inundated with unsavory characters and its cynicism is matched by Hart's frank, almost risqué lyrics.

In 1943 Rodgers began his collaboration with Oscar Hammerstein II, who had previously worked with Jerome Kern on the pivotal musical *Show Boat*. Hammerstein's first effort with Rodgers would prove to be another milestone in the history of musical theater. *Oklahoma!* was an adaptation of a 1931 folk drama *Green Grows the Lilacs*, a cowboy play set around the time of Oklahoma's entry into statehood. *Oklahoma!* was a giant leap forward for musicals on several counts. Firstly, it was conspicuous for its cowboy theme and western setting. Second, reflecting the simplicity of the original play, *Oklahoma!* diverged from the pageantry and irrelevant digressions of song and dance that characterized so many American musicals. Third, *Oklahoma!* was the first musical to make the dance sequences advance the characters and plot, thanks to the sensitive choreography of Agnes De Mille. Finally, *Oklahoma!* made history as the first musical to appear in its complete form on an original Broadway cast recording.

Rodgers and Hammerstein went on to write a string of the most successful musicals to date. These include *Carousel* (1945), *South Pacific* (1949), *The King and I* (1951), and *The Sound of Music* (1959). The gentility and elegance of Hammerstein's lyrics and the integration of music, dance, and plot in the Rodgers and Hammerstein shows brought back the flavor of European operetta.

Musicals and the Classics

Over the years there have been a number of musicals based on classic plays and literature. *The Golden Apple* (1954) was based on Homer's *Iliad* and *Odyssey*. *My Fair Lady* (1956) was based on George Bernard Shaw's *Pygmalion*. Two musicals of this type were the products of Leonard Bernstein (1918–1990) the prodigious American composer and longtime conductor of the New York Philharmonic. The first musical was *Candide*, written in 1956 and based on Voltaire's eighteenth-century classic. Lillian Hellman transposed the European social commentary to include stabs at Senator Joseph McCarthy's infamous communist trials in the 1950s. Bernstein's score at once precisely re-created and parodied comic operetta, an accomplishment that is possible only through a thorough knowledge of the genre.

Bernstein's second work was *West Side Story*, based on Shakespeare's *Romeo and Juliet*. Rival Anglo and Hispanic gangs in New York's West Side portray the tragic lovers' warring families. Bernstein and master choreographer Jerome

Robbins nurtured the idea over several years. In the early stages, Bernstein intended to write his own lyrics, a notion he eventually abandoned. Instead, he recruited 25-year-old Stephen Sondheim, a protégé of Oscar Hammerstein II. This was Sondheim's first major production project. In the tradition of *Oklahoma!* the dance numbers in *West Side Story* are an integral part of the narrative rather than a digression from it. Bernstein's score is one of the most complex in the history of musical theater and seamlessly integrates jazz and classical music idioms.

By the late 1950s rock was becoming the dominant force in American popular music, drawing public attention away from the musical. Ironically, instead of employing the new rock music into its style, musical theater chose to end a long period of stylistic experimentation and fell back on more tried-and-true formulas—formulas that still proved successful.

Musicals such as *Mame, Hello Dolly, The Music Man,* and *Bye Bye Birdie,* all from the early 1960s, were popular and long-running. One of the more unusual musicals of this time was *Fiddler on the Roof,* a story set in a Jewish peasant village in Russia. The music is by Jerry Bock, the lyrics by Sheldon Harnick, and the choreography by Jerome Robbins, his last venture before devoting himself entirely to ballet. The story is a touching account of the disintegration of tradition and the fading hope of an oppressed people. Actor Zero Mostel played the lead character, Tevye, and created one of the most memorable male roles in the history of musical theater. *Fiddler on the Roof* marked the end of an era in musical theater.

Analysis of "Sunrise, Sunset" (*American Musical Theater,* 4/18)

"Sunrise, Sunset," from *Fiddler on the Roof,* is sung during the wedding of Tevye's oldest daughter, Tzeitel. In this song, we hear the musings of Tevye, his wife Golda, and other characters attending the wedding. They sing about how fast the years pass and children blossom. It is a touching moment that counters the boisterous "To Life" that is heard earlier in the action.

The song is in a minor key. The melody and the instrumentation of the accompaniment capture the culture flavor of the Russian Jewish peasants and the traditions depicted in the story. Zero Mostel is a perfect Tevye, possessing the expressive range to depict both the rowdy jubilation and the deep pain his character experiences. Golda is played by Maria Karnilova.

Listening Guide   2.2
"Sunrise, Sunset" 3 beats per measure

ELAPSED TIME	FORM	EVENT DESCRIPTION
:00	Intro	Orchestra (4 measures)
:06	Verse 1	Mostel (Tevye), Karnilova (Golda) (32 measures)
:52	Chorus 1	Men, women (32 measures + 2 measures tag)
1:45	Verse 2	Cast members in turn (32 measures)
2:32	Chorus 2	Ensemble vocal (32 measures)
3:32	End	

Off-Broadway and New Experimentation

In the last half of the 1960s a new age of experimentation dawned. It hailed the infiltration of rock music into musical theater. The 1960 musical *Bye Bye Birdie*, with a story based on teen rock idols, made an attempt at rock music; but there was little real rock and roll music in Charles Strouse's score. The first musical to reflect the youth culture of the sixties was *Hair*. The show utilized the music, dance, art, attitudes, and fashion of the hippie counterculture. *Hair* also represented a new phenomenon—the off-Broadway musical. The experimental and sometimes renegade musicals that were outside the more conservative Broadway milieu challenged old conventions and injected new life into the musical theater.

Among other experimental subject matter in the American musical was religion. In 1971 Andrew Lloyd Webber and Tim Rice created the rock-opera recording *Jesus Christ, Superstar,* which was soon adapted for the stage. The musical depicted the Passion and death of Jesus Christ, but it portrayed Christ as a mere man, struggling with his earthly mission and inevitable death. While the score was an undeniable artistic achievement, both Jewish and Christian organizations were deeply disturbed by the implications of the story. Yet musicals with unconventional interpretations of religious themes continued unabated. Webber and Rice had previously written *Joseph and the Amazing Technicolor Dreamcoat.* About the time of *Jesus Christ, Superstar* came Stephen Schwartz's *Godspell,* based on the book of St. Matthew, as was the black musical *Your Arms Are Too Short to Box with God.*

Stephen Sondheim and the 1970s

American musical theater in the 1970s was dominated by Stephen Sondheim, the lyricist who had an auspicious beginning collaborating with Leonard Bernstein on *West Side Story.* Sondheim was born in New York in 1930 and grew up in rural Pennsylvania. His childhood friend was the son of Oscar Hammerstein, who at the time was working on the story and lyrics to *Oklahoma!* Young Sondheim began writing his own musicals, with Hammerstein as his mentor. He went on to major in music at Williams College, concentrating in composition.

After *West Side Story* Sondheim collaborated with composer Jule Styne on *Gypsy* (1959), based on the life of stripper Gypsy Rose Lee. Sondheim's first significant production as lyricist *and* composer was *A Funny Thing Happened on the Way to the Forum* (1962), based on the ancient Roman comedies of Plautus. Other musicals followed in the sixties, but it was in the seventies that Sondheim produced a consistent string of theatrical hits. His first musical of the decade was *Company* (1970), which introduced the *concept musical,* a show built around a single theme but without a narrative story line. *Company*'s theme was loneliness, centered around a

Composer and lyricist Stephen Sondheim in 1962. Sondheim collaborated with composer and conductor Leonard Bernstein on the enduring musical *West Side Story* and solely composed great musicals such as *A Funny Thing Happened on the Way to the Forum* and *Sweeney Todd.*

bachelor musing over marriage and relationships. The show was also unusual in the austerity of the set design, made up of just a few stainless steel frames and glass.

Company was followed by *Follies* (1971), the story of a reunion of show business has-beens reminiscing about their golden days and facing their shattered dreams. *A Little Night Music* (1973) was a stage adaptation of an Ingmar Bergman film, *Smiles of a Summer Night*. Sondheim captures the atmosphere of the musical's turn-of-the-century setting by casting all of the music in triple meter. One song from the musical became a sensational single hit. In 1975 Judy Collins (who was not in the show) recorded "Send in the Clowns," dispelling critical comments that Sondheim's songs could not stand apart from the musicals in which they originated. Sondheim's most daring musical, in terms of plot, was *Sweeney Todd* (1979), based on a story dating back to 1847. *Sweeney Todd, The Demon Barber of Fleet Street* tells of a mad barber who cuts the throats of his customers and has his downstairs neighbor, Mrs. Nellie Lovett, put them into her meat pies. The macabre tone of the story was enhanced by Sondheim's extensive use of the *Dies Irae*, the medieval chant of the dead. He also integrated extensive sequences of combined dramatic progression and music, similar to the operas of nineteenth-century German composer Richard Wagner.

Analysis of "The Ballad of Sweeney Todd" (*Sweeney Todd*, RCA 3379-2-RC)

Stephen Sondheim wrote *Sweeney Todd* as a macabre, yet playful musical based on a popular English nineteenth-century story. Sondheim wanted the music to have the effect of a score to a horror movie. To that end he used the sound of a pipe organ, often associated with Gothic horror, and dissonant chords. To show the underlying lighthearted nature of the musical, Sondheim has pointed out that he kept using a certain chord in the music throughout the show, a chord borrowed from the movie music of Bernard Herrman, who wrote for such movie thrillers as Alfred Hitchcock's *Psycho*. There is also extensive use of the *Dies Irae*, the music used in the Mass for the Dead (see Figure 2.1) in the Roman Catholic Church, which Sondheim found both moving and frightening. (French composer Hector Berlioz used the *Dies Irae* to great effect in his chilling *Symphonie Fantastique* from 1830.)

"The Ballad of Sweeney Todd" is the opening of the show. The setting is a graveyard, and two gravediggers are unceremoniously dumping a wrapped body into the hole in the ground. Members of the company begin to come on stage and sing a prologue describing the character Sweeney Todd and his deeds.

The opening melody sung by the first two members of the company is in a fast triple meter, reminiscent of the rhythm of a British folk jig. Then the entire company admonishes Todd to swing his razor wide to a melodic variation of the *Dies Irae*. It is done in grand, full choral style. The first melody comes back, passed around to various members of the company as they sing about how calculated and inconspicuous Todd was as he carried out his sinister deeds. There follows a

FIGURE 2.1

Portion of the *Dies Irae* from the Mass for the Dead

Portion of the *Dies Irae* from the Mass for the Dead

musical bridge, a climbing section. Sondheim begins playing around with the accents and rhythm of the meter, creating jagged and agitated effects in the music. Added to this, the company begins climbing in their vocal range and increasingly singing different music on top of each other. This climaxes with the group practically screaming the name "Sweeney," a cue for the dead Sweeney Todd to appear from the grave and join the chorus for the last verse before the first act. The orchestra ends the selection with the brittle sound of the xylophone over the orchestra, a mallet instrument with wooden bars struck with hard mallets. In many Halloween and horror settings its sound has been associated with the clattering bones of skeletons dancing. The piece closes with low trombones and percussion, suggesting the slamming of a coffin's lid.

Listening Guide   2.3
"The Ballad of Sweeney Todd" 3 beats per measure

ELAPSED TIME	FORM	EVENT DESCRIPTION
:00	Intro	Organ chords, sudden whistle, strings
:47	Verse 1	First male singer
1:14	Verse 2	Second male singer
1:41	Chorus	Full chorus, based on *Dies Irae*
2:01	Verse 3	Melody sung by different members
2:24	Bridge	Builds to climax through range; manipulation of rhythm; busy layering of parts
2:58	Verse 4	Todd answered by chorus
3:34	End	

Andrew Lloyd Webber and the 1980s

In the 1980s Stephen Sondheim was overshadowed by Andrew Lloyd Webber, the composer of the religious rock operas *Joseph and the Amazing Technicolor Dreamcoat* and *Jesus Christ, Superstar*. The musicals of this English composer use very little dialogue but integrate music and narrative much like opera. *Evita*, Webber's first hit musical of the eighties, was based on the life of Eva Peron, wife of Argentine dictator Juan Peron. *Evita* found renewed popularity in 1996 with the film version starring pop star Madonna, who had campaigned tirelessly for the role in her attempt to recast herself as something other than a vampy teen idol.

English musicals composer Andrew Lloyd Webber in 1979. From *Jesus Christ, Superstar* and *Phantom of the Opera*, he came to dominate the genre of musical theater.

The most popular Webber musical in the 1980s was *Cats*, based on poet T. S. Eliot's *Old Possum's Book of Practical Cats*. The production featured a musical blend of opera, rock, jazz, and traditional Broadway styles. The cast, costumed as cats, are put in the setting of an urban junkyard. Ramps run into the audience, allowing the characters to scamper into the crowd. The most moving segment of the musical is when Grizabella, a faded beauty, recalls her youth before ascending into heaven. "Memory," the song in this segment, became a much-requested popular hit. As the 1980s drew to a close, Andrew Lloyd Webber once again dominated musical theater with a new setting of the classical story *The Phantom of the Opera.*

While Stephen Sondheim and Andrew Lloyd Webber have been the most consistent hit makers in the last 20 years of musical theater, there were a number of other hit shows presented in a variety of ways. One prominent format was the musical review. This consists of a modest setting, no plot, and a small cast singing the music of a particular artist or composer. The most popular review was *Ain't Misbehavin'*, a musical tribute to Harlem pianist, singer, and composer Thomas "Fats" Waller. The all-black cast consisted of three women, two men, and a pianist; the set resembled a posh hotel lobby. The immense success of this review led to tributes to other great black musical artists of the past. *Bubblin' Brown Sugar* paid homage to the music and entertainers of Harlem in the 1920s and 1930s. *Eubie* was a tribute to black pianist and composer Eubie Blake, the composer of the smash 1921 all-black musical *Shuffle Along* mentioned earlier in this chapter. Blake was 95 years old when *Eubie* opened.

There were other successful musicals with black casts and subject matter in the 1970s. *Purlie, Your Arms Are Too Short to Box with God* and *Ain't Supposed to Die a Natural Death* all dealt with the pain and pride of the black experience, past and present. One of the most successful musicals of the seventies was *The Wiz*, a black version of the literary and movie classic *The Wizard of Oz*. There were even all-black versions of *Hello, Dolly* and *Guys and Dolls.*

One of the longest-running shows in the history of musical theater was *A Chorus Line* (1975), a musical about rehearsing a musical. The premise for the show is an audition for positions in a chorus line. Young hopefuls interview with the intimidating director, spinning out various tales of tragedy and hope. "What I Did for Love," composed by Marvin Hamlisch, became a hit single from the musical, as did "One," the song from the show's finale.

At the dawn of the 1990s musical theater was in serious trouble. An extremely small segment of the population patronized the genre, including tourists to New York, wealthier middle-aged adults, and a significant representation from the gay community. Ticket prices and production costs were prohibitive, and the garish elegance and throwback style did not connect with much of the public, nor did dark, serious new musicals that threatened the light nature of the musical everyone had come to expect.

New productions continued to follow the trend of revivals or new works on older themes. Dancer/singer/producer Tommy Tune brought about *Will Rogers' Follies* in 1991, featuring an affable characterization of the Oklahoma cowboy and humorist by Keith Carradine. *Jelly's Last Jam* was a musical based on the life of Creole jazz pianist and composer Jelly Roll Morton. There were musical versions of the movies *Kiss of the Spider Woman* and *Sunset Boulevard*, the latter starring stage and film actress Glenn Close, who later found work portraying Cruella Deville in a live action version of Walt Disney's *101 Dalmatians* and its sequel *102 Dalmatians.*

Disney, in fact, turned out to be the primary voice of the musical in the 1990s. Whereas the majority of the public had lost interest in the genre of live musical theater, musicals found acceptance in animated motion picture features from Disney studios and, later, from former Disney animator Don Bluth and Dreamworks.

The Little Mermaid was an overwhelming success. Energized by its good fortune, the Disney animation studio followed up with *Beauty and the Beast* and *Aladdin.* These and other animated film musicals employed top-notch songwriting by composers and lyricists such as Alan Menken, Tim Rice (who worked with Andrew Lloyd Webber on *Jesus Christ Superstar*), pop singer Elton John *(The Lion King)*, and former Genesis drummer Phil Collins *(Tarzan).*

With all of its success with musicals in the film medium, Disney then made its move to dominate Broadway. It bought a theater in the famous New York district and staged a live version of its animated film *Beauty and the Beast.* Seen by Broadway veterans as an extension of Disney's theme park shows, *Beauty* benefited from the seemingly limitless financial resources of the Disney company. Like a traveling circus or ice show, it enjoyed tremendous marketing and family appeal, while insisting on the status of a legitimate Broadway musical. Disney followed up with a stage version of *The Lion King.*

Expense and corporate sponsorship squelched creativity and experimentation in musicals, and it seemed that animated films would eclipse live musical theater. In 1996, however, Broadway was revived with Jonathan Larson's *Rent.* Adapted to the economic realities of musical production, *Rent* used a sparse set design that made it easier to stage and to replicate in performances around the country. Composer/lyricist Larson died on the night of the off-Broadway dress rehearsal, so the musical became as much a cause as a production. Curiously, while proving immensely popular, it produced no hit songs.

In 1997 a stage musical version based on the true story of the sinking of the Titanic was produced. As well worn as the story has been through film and television dramatizations and documentaries, the concept was well received by audiences. (It appears only coincidental that the hugely popular James Cameron film *Titanic* came out at the same time. The film was inspired by the 1985 discovery of the Titanic wreckage at the bottom of the Atlantic Ocean. It was not a musical, though the soundtrack, with its love theme "My Heart Will Go On," sold well.) The musical focused on the immigrants in the lower-class holds of the ship. It featured a number of ethnic styles representing the various characters in the play.

Moving into the twenty-first century, Broadway seems to be relying still on revivals and adaptations of movies to the stage. *Annie Get Your Gun,* for instance, with songs by Irving Berlin, premiered in 1946 and was first revived in 1966. In 1999 it featured Broadway musical veteran Bernadette Peters, but it later marked a triumphant invasion of Broadway by popular Oklahoma-born country singer Reba McEntire. *A Funny Thing Happened on the Way to the Forum* was revived in 1996, featuring the successful actor of stage, screen, and television Nathan Lane. Musical versions of the popular movies *Saturday Night Fever, Ragtime,* and *The Full Monty* were also produced. In 2001 a staged musical version of Mel Brooks's zany 1960s film *The Producers* premiered. The film was the story of a group of hucksters attempting to stage an unsuccessful musical. It was certainly a triumph for Mel Brooks, but at the time of the musical production, Brooks was in his late seventies, leaving us to wonder if the musical will die with him. It will be interesting to see if the musical takes a new course or continues formulaically with animated musical films, theme park show–type productions, and revivals. Will it become a cloistered genre appealing only to its few loyal followers (affluent social elite, the gay community) or attempt to redefine itself for a larger, contemporary audience? Like any other endeavor it will probably exist as both tradition and change, reminiscent of its glorious and glamorous past, and recasting itself to stay viable in the ever-changing world of popular entertainment.

Chapter Summary

Tin Pan Alley and American musical theater were interdependent; composers created music for the stage, and their publishers used that exposure to sell hit songs from the show to the public. American musical theater is a unique form of entertainment that combined the tradition of middlebrow European lyric and comic theater with the emerging distinctiveness of American music.

The first distinctive innovation for American musicals was blackface minstrelsy. This singing style and show format would influence musicals and variety shows for years to come. In later years formats employing urban ethnic humor and American settings continued in the shows of Harrison and Hart and in the shows of Weber and Fields. Meanwhile, the penchant American audiences had for European operetta continued with the music of Gilbert and Sullivan and Victor Herbert.

George M. Cohan, Irving Berlin, and the Jerome Kern/Oscar Hammerstein Princess Theater musicals carried the American musical further away from European-styled shows. The country was entering the jazz age of the 1920s. The musicals of George and Ira Gershwin displayed the mainstream's growing affinity for jazz music and themes addressing social issues. In the meantime black composers and entertainers from Harlem were creating their own significant productions, such as *Shuffle Along* and *Runnin' Wild*.

The musical continued to evolve with Rodgers and Hammerstein's *Oklahoma!*, the musical that integrated song and dance into the dramatic narrative. This trend was epitomized in the late 1950s with *West Side Story*. That show started the career of Stephen Sondheim. Dominating the 1970s, Sondheim continued to experiment with format in the concept musical.

Off-Broadway productions also contributed to new styles of musicals, incorporating rock music and addressing controversial issues of religion and society. One of these musicals, *Jesus Christ, Superstar*, was composed by Andrew Lloyd Webber, a British composer who would dominate musical theater in the 1980s.

In the 1990s the musical theater found itself losing much of its audience and struggling with high ticket prices and production costs. Revivals and adaptations of movies seem to be the order of the day. Once in a while a hit like *Rent* came along, but dominance of the 1990s musical belonged to the Walt Disney company. It not only made a series of hit animated film musicals but brought them to Broadway in lavish, high-tech productions.

Additional Listening

"Baltimore Buzz," from *Shuffle Along* **(1921)** (*American Musical Theater*, 1/8). Music: Eubie Blake, lyrics: Noble Sissle (1921). *Shuffle Along* represents one of the most significant early efforts by black songwriters for the mainstream musical theater. "Baltimore Buzz" is sung on this recording by Noble Sissle, the show's lyricist and star. The instrumentation and the rhythms of the song's melody place the work in a stylistic time frame between late ragtime and early jazz.

"I Get a Kick Out of You," from *Anything Goes* **(1934)** (*American Musical Theater*, 2/1). Music and lyrics: Cole Porter (1934). This recorded performance features the distinctive and commanding voice of Ethel Merman, a singer greatly in demand by songwriters for the Broadway stage. The song is typical carefree, sophisticated Porter and demonstrates his knack for unusually lengthy song forms—in this case, 64 measures. It also shows Porter's penchant for risqué and daring lyrics; many radio stations banned this song because of its reference to cocaine in the second A section of the chorus.

"Some Enchanted Evening," from *South Pacific* **(1949)** (*American Musical Theater*, 3/7). Music: Richard Rodgers, lyrics: Oscar Hammerstein II (1949). This tremendously successful musical was based on James Michener's book *Tales of the South Pacific*, set in the Pacific Islands during World War II. The show's plot centers on the love affair between American nurse Nellie Forbush, played by Mary Martin, and wealthy French planter Emil de Beque, played by opera singer Ezio Pinza. "Some Enchanted Evening" perfectly captures the exotic setting of the story, the passion of the characters' sentiments, and the dramatic majesty of Pinza's clear bass voice.

"Comedy Tonight," from *A Funny Thing Happened on the Way to the Forum* **(1964)** (*American Musical Theater*, 4/14). Music and lyrics: Stephen Sondheim (1964). This burlesque version of the ancient Roman comedies of Plautus was initially a failure. Necessary revisions included a new opening number, "Comedy Tonight." The song features Zero Mostel as the play's *prologus*, the narrator of ancient drama who introduces the characters and the plot. Sondheim's music and lyrics adeptly combine stylistic elements of the big Broadway opener, stereotypical movie score Roman fanfare, Shakespearean poeticism, and circus barking. One of the most charming features of the song is the closely spaced rhymes in the verse ("appealing"/"appalling," "convulsive"/"repulsive").

Review Questions

1. Where were the centers of musical theater activity in America during the eighteenth and nineteenth centuries?
2. What were the reasons given for the significance of blackface minstrelsy in American music and musical theater?
3. Explain the format and style of vaudeville and cabaret theater.
4. How did George M. Cohan and the Jerome Kern Princess Theater musicals lead America away from European theater models?
5. What were some significant black musicals in the 1920s?
6. What sets George Gershwin's *Porgy and Bess* apart from earlier musicals?
7. What sets Rodgers and Hammerstein's *Oklahoma!* apart from earlier musicals?
8. What musicals are based on classic literature?
9. How did rock music influence American musical theater?
10. How did Stephen Sondheim and Andrew Lloyd Webber impact musical theater in the 1970s and 1980s, respectively?
11. How has the "corporate musical" affected creativity and innovation in the Broadway musical, and what has been the role of the Walt Disney company in recent musicals?

Notes

1. A good example of this Anglo-Celtic identification with the black characters on stage is the portion of the show that featured the sentimental plantation song. An Irish tenor in blackface sang a ballad about homesickness, longing for the paternal care of his white master and serenity of rural plantation life. This was a period when many of the Irish in the audience had recently fled a devastating potato famine in their home country. They saw the minstrel character's plight as analogous to their own.

The African-American Tradition

Part 2

Chapter 3

African Origins and Acculturation in the New World

As stated in the two previous chapters, American popular music and culture are a distinctive hybrid of African and European cultures. It is one of the tragedies of human history that Europeans brought people from west Africa to the New World against their will over 350 years ago. However, like the pain of the oyster that yields the pearl, that experience has led to a body of music that has influenced the world. The institution of slavery was not unique to the United States, but the resulting cultural products are.

It is a fascinating study to trace the history of black culture from its African roots to America. Moreover, such a study helps to explain why the Euro-African cultural hybrid that occurred on American soil is unique to that which occurred in other countries.

WEST AFRICAN MUSIC AND SOCIETY

The majority of black slaves brought to the New World came from the western part of Africa—the Gold Coast, the Ivory Coast, and the savannah region. Africa is a diverse continent, made up of many ethnic groups and hundreds of languages. For this reason, it is necessary to generalize west African cultural and musical practices in order to examine how and to what extent the west African slaves retained these practices in America.

Within any village-based culture there is an atmosphere of communalism, a team spirit that deemphasizes individual achievement and instead stresses individual activity toward the common good. Music is likewise a communal activity, with everyone participating to some extent.

There are occasions when west African musicians play music for their own pleasure, but much of west African music is linked to some activity in the lives of the community members. In this case, the music is not an artistic end in itself. Therefore, the beauty of a piece of music may not be judged strictly on its aural

This photo shows social drumming among members of the Kassena-Grunshi tribe in Ghana, Africa.

merits but on its effectiveness in achieving the goal of the activity that it accompanies. There is music for births, puberty rites, hunting trips, harvests, and marriages. Particularly important are ceremonies that invoke one or more of the multiple deities in west African religions, such as the ceremony for healing the sick and the funeral ceremony. Many west Africans believe in the necessity of ancestor worship and the appeasement of spirits to ward off bad luck and illness.

West African music is also linked with dance and body movement. In fact, most west African master drummers are also master dancers and insist that their students dance as part of their drumming instruction. The integration of repetitive movement and music also accounts for the comparative formlessness of west African music. Over many years European art music has developed musical forms such as the sonata or the fugue. These structures divide a piece of music into sections delineated by different melodies, different chord progressions, modulation to a different key, or a change of tempo. The impetus for the development of sectionalized music is that it is primarily intended for listening. Since west African music is primarily for dancing, it is more seamless and repetitive in its structure. The hypnotic effect of west African music and the dance it accompanies also facilitates entering trancelike states for religious or medical purposes. Nonparticipatory listeners would find the music merely monotonous and boring.

The fundamental form that is used in west African music is *call-and-response*. In this form the leader performs a portion of music and the group performs a response. This form is not unique to west African music; call-and-response is found in many musical cultures around the world.

West African Rhythmic Concept

The hallmark of west African music is its rhythmic concept, which is among the most complex in the world. The basic premise for west African rhythm is a steady, basic pulse that other rhythmic elements play off of. The practice of emphasizing notes that do not align with the pulse is what Western music practice calls *syncopation*. This is a term that implies an exception to the rule of usually playing *with* the beat, a rule not shared by west Africans.

In a west African drum ensemble four to six drummers play several simple rhythms simultaneously. The individual patterns are often of different lengths and do not begin and end at the same time. Though each part has its own distinctive rhythmic design, they interweave into a complex whole. The composite effect of the different rhythmic lines is called *multilinear rhythm*. To non-African ears multilinear rhythm may sound like confusion, but African music is actually a tightly structured music. Improvisation is practiced to a limited extent. It takes the form of variations on a given musical pattern; it is not just an unrelated extemporization. The master drummer and a couple of the drummers in the ensemble commonly engage in an improvised dialogue. But the manner of improvisation is very controlled by tradition and practice, and is always related to the overall musical event.

West African melody and rhythm are closely linked with the spoken word; they are, in fact, inseparable. In many languages, a syllabic sound uttered at different pitch levels can vary its meaning. In a rudimentary way, meaning can be imparted by the pitches or rhythms of musical instruments alone. This manifests itself in "talking drums" or talking ivory trumpets that can transmit communication over long distances. It is also necessary that the musician be careful with the melodic shape of a text, so that the meaning is not altered.

In west African musical aesthetics, coloring a sound by "dirtying" the tone is desirable. It is a way to enrich and bring life to the sound. To this end, vocalists intentionally color their vocal sounds with bends, growls, and rasps. Many west African instruments that would be pure of sound are modified to make them rattle or buzz when vibrating. For example, the *mbira*, a handheld resonating box with metal tines that are played with the thumbs and forefingers, usually produces a clear, pure tone. It is a common practice to loosely attach several beverage bottle caps to the instrument so that its vibration produces a buzzing sound.

AFRICAN ACCULTURATION IN THE NEW WORLD

The extent to which African slaves retained their folkways depended largely on where they were brought in the New World. One factor for determining African cultural retention was how isolated their locale was from other cultures. For instance, blacks living on the chain of swampy islands off the coast of South Carolina and Georgia retained more African language and cultural traits than blacks that were in constant contact with whites and other cultures.[1]

Another factor in the degree of cultural retention was the ethnic background of the slave owners. The islands of the West Indies were settled mostly by Latin-Catholics—the French and Spanish. The mainland south was dominated by British-Protestant colonists. The Latin-Catholics, while interested in converting the slaves to Christianity, were more tolerant of African traditions. Slaves were allowed to continue their African customs as long as their duties were fulfilled. Also, the Catholic faith, with its invocation of various saints and its use of icons, was similar to the multiple-deity religious practice of the Africans. The *vodun* religious practice of black Haitians is a good example of how the Dahomey, Yorubaland, and Kongo peoples from Africa synthesized European Catholicism with worship of a number of spirits from their own religious traditions. The sacred and secular music of the West Indies, Cuba, and Central and South America all display a higher degree of African retention than is found in black music from the mainland United States.

The British-Protestant colonists of the southeastern United States felt that they were responsible for the slaves not only in body but also in soul. Their fervent evangelistic tendencies made them highly intolerant of African folkways. Southern slave owners considered African culture and religion to be savage and heathen, and sought to stamp out every vestige of the slave's former culture. In regard to music, native African instruments were forbidden, especially drums; slave owners feared the slaves would signal each other from one plantation to another and organize an uprising. But the slaves proved to be highly resourceful and improvised instruments out of the materials available. If there were none, they would just stamp their feet or beat their chests and thighs—what one former slave called *patting juba.*

In early colonial days slaves were taken to churches to learn Christianity and the music that went along with it. Few people in the congregations read music, and music in the hymnals was taught by itinerant singing teachers. These teachers would sing the hymns to the congregation a line at a time, a practice called *lining out* a hymn. Thus blacks and whites together learned the hymns of Lowell Mason, Isaac Watts, and others.

With the growing sentiment against slavery in the early nineteenth century, the South isolated itself to shut out the disrupting influence of the abolitionists. White slave owners also took defensive measures from within. Blacks were cast out of the churches, forcing them to form their own churches. Many slaves were forbidden to read and were given only limited instruction in the Christianity that had been forced upon them. Left to their own devices, latent African musical practices flowered in the creation and interpretation of black spirituals. Much of the African-American religious music was highly rhythmic, repetitive, and chantlike. It often involved dance or some form of coordinated body movement. The music used call-and-response, gruffness in the vocal sound, pitch bends, and a fervent shouting style, musical practices reminiscent of their African origins.

Analysis of "Kneebone" (*Georgia Sea Island Songs*, New World NW 278)

This African-American spiritual is performed by a group of singers from Georgia's swampy coastal sea islands. Because these islands could only be reached in small boats, the inhabitants remained fairly isolated from the mainstream culture of the South. As a result, there was a high degree of African retention in their language, culture, and music. "Kneebone," recorded by folklorist Alan Lomax in the early 1960s, is an excellent example of a primitive black spiritual.

"Kneebone" is repetitive (*strophic*) and utilizes the call-and-response pattern between the group leader and the group. The group's responsorial part in the song never changes ("Aah, kneebone" and "O Lord, kneebone bend"), while the leader's lines vary from verse to verse. This changing verse and static refrain form is typical of many ballads, group chants, and popular songs. It is unclear what the leader, 90-year-old Joe Armstrong, is referring to with lines like "Kneebone in the morning," "call you in the evenin'," or "Kneebone, didn't I call you." Sea Island scholar Lydia Parrish said there was a rowing-song version of "Kneebone" and

African-American field workers picking cotton in the South around 1900. From this context came many black laboring songs such as field hollers and work songs.

that the knee-bending action of group rowing was the basis for the song. Lomax speculates the singers are evoking the bones and spirits of their ancestors.[2] In any event, the singers did perform a knee-bending choreography as they sang the spiritual. The only clear religious reference is "Knee-bone, Zacharias," Zacharias (also Zechariah) being the father of John the Baptist, the biblical character who prepared the way for the coming of Jesus Christ.

The group is singing without instrumental accompaniment, but they do clap an accompanying rhythm with their hands. There are two rhythmic patterns being clapped. When combined they have the disjunct compositive effect of many African group rhythm patterns. This hand-clapping pattern was prevalent in the sea islands and was the inspiration for the rhythm of "The Charleston." Notice also the loose, syncopated rhythms in the sung melody, particularly the soloist's part.

Because of the repetitive nature of the spiritual and its static dramatic shape, we have not included a timed listening guide to this recording selection.

Both during and after slavery, blacks continued to create music that was integrated with everyday tasks, as did their African ancestors. Indeed, the characteristics of the music were shaped by the nature of those tasks. The *field holler* was a nonrhythmic chant sung by a solitary worker, usually while plowing or harvesting. The words were sometimes preplanned and sometimes whatever came to mind. The *work song*, on the other hand, was a song that took its rhythm from synchronized group tasks such as cutting trees or driving railroad spikes. It was a steady, rhythmic song, utilizing call-and-response between the task leader and the other workers.

Analysis of "Arwhoolie" (*Folk Music of the United States,* LP format, Library of Congress AAFS L8, 1/6)

This field holler, performed by Thomas Marshall, was recorded in Edwards, Mississippi, in 1939 by folklorists from the Library of Congress. Arhythmic and chantlike, the field holler has a sad, wailing quality to it that is similar to many solo songs heard in Africa. Many field hollers are melancholy songs about the hard work or other unfortunate aspects of the worker's condition. This holler, however, is sung late in the evening, as the worker looks forward to quitting for the day: "I won't be here long," "Dark gonna catch me here."

Even though this is a solo performance, there is clearly a verse/refrain or call-and-response pattern to "Arwhoolie." The song opens with a highly ornamented melody on the word "Oh." This acts as the refrain or response. It is sung in the singer's upper range, giving the melody an emotional, pained quality. Alternating with this refrain is a line of lyric, sung in the lower part of the singer's range and providing a low-key expressive contrast to the refrain.

Analysis of "Hammer, Ring" (*Folk Music of the United States*, LP format, Library of Congress AAFS L8, 2/2)

This recording was made by folklorists John and Alan Lomax at the State Penitentiary in Huntsville, Texas, in 1934. This work song differs from the field holler in that it is sung to a strict rhythmic pulse by a group of workers—in this case, prisoners hammering spikes to fasten train rails to the wooden ties. It is a classic example of the integration of music with the task it accompanies. The tempo of the song and the melodic and rhythmic embellishments are all dictated by the steady pulse created by the falling hammers.

As in "Kneebone," this is a strophic repetitive song that alternates between a changing verse sung by the soloist and a static refrain sung by the group. The leader blends two themes in the verse lyrics. The first theme is the hammer: "Won't you ring, old hammer?" and "Broke the handle on my hammer." He then relates wood, hammers, and building with the Bible story of Noah, who built the ark to save his family and the animals of the world from the flood.

As much as any function, the work song, with its hypnotic repetition, serves as a sort of anesthetic for the laborers. Carried by the insistent rhythm of their hammering and the song that works within it, the workers achieve a euphoric state that numbs them to the backbreaking and boring work. Each time the soloist goes into the upper range of his voice (about every fourth verse) there is a noticeable increase in intensity among the other singers. They began to whoop and shout in ecstasy and to embellish their static refrain line.

Elements of African-American Music

In our narrative of African music and its acculturation in America, we have cited a number of stylistic tendencies that prevail in the music. To study this acculturation is to witness how displaced Africans took the scales, melodies, harmonies, rhythms, and sound aesthetics of European musical practice and altered them to fall in line with their own musical traditions. This hybridization resulted in a music that was neither European nor African, nor was it an Afro-Euro blend that occurred in any other country. Spirituals, labor songs, game songs, and ballads are the primordial soup that shaped America's distinctive musical style. From musical theater to rock and roll, the stylistic traits of African-American music have shown their influence. Because these stylistic elements are present in all of the styles discussed in this book, we should look at them in greater detail.

Blue notes: *Blue notes* are named such because of their association with the feeling and sound of the African-American style called the *blues*. One of the parent styles of jazz, the blues developed in the southern United States at about the same time as jazz.

In the musical *The Sound of Music*, Maria sings the song "Do-Re-Mi" to the von Trapp children to teach them the *major scale*. Thousands of melodies in the European musical tradition are based on this seven-note scale (find middle C on the

FIGURE 3.1
C Major Scale

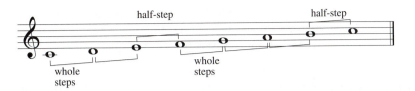

piano and play the next seven white keys to hear this familiar scale, also shown in Figure 3.1). You will also notice that there are black keys separating each of the white keys, with the exception of the third and fourth and the seventh and eighth white keys. (The eighth white key is, of course, another C and denotes the *octave*, "oct-" indicating *eight* notes from the previous C.) The distance between adjacent notes on the piano, as is the case with the third and fourth white keys and the seventh and eighth white keys, is called a *semitone* or *half-step*. The distance between the other notes that are adjacent to each other but separated by black keys is called a *whole step*.

If we took a tuning hammer to the strings inside the piano and slightly lowered the pitch of the third and seventh notes in this scale (the notes E and B in the key of C), we would have *blue notes*. These pitch adjustments were made by African-Americans because the tuning of the European major scale sounded foreign to them. To European ears, however, a lowered third and seventh note sound like a *minor scale*, a scale often associated with sad or dramatic music. Even though blue notes are used in the most joyous of music, they are often considered the device that gives African-American music a melancholy, moaning expression (in a Western cultural context). That is the hallmark of the blues.[3]

Unique tone production: One of the greatest contrasts between European art music and African-American music is found in their concepts of tone production, or *timbre*. The European art music tradition established an aesthetic of tone production best characterized as pure, a sound that is consistently maintained throughout the duration of a particular note. For any given instrument, there is a timbral standard that all who play that instrument are expected to achieve with a minimum of variation.

In African-American music, however, individual character of timbre is accepted, even encouraged. In addition, the African-American aesthetic makes use of nasal sounds, growls, and hoarseness in the timbral quality of the voice or instrument to add expression to the musical line. As much as the use of blue notes, it is the rough quality of timbre that characterizes African-American music. Therefore, someone singing low-down blues with "correct" European operative vocal technique would sound as ludicrous as a gravel-voiced bluesman singing a Verdi aria.

Motor rhythm: Motor rhythm means the presentation of a steady rhythmic pulse at a consistent tempo. This type of rhythmic usage is most commonly found in music that facilitates coordinated body movement such as dancing, marching, rowing, or hammering. An audible steady pulse lays the foundation against which rhythmic devices such as syncopation and swing feeling work.

Syncopation: The lilting, sometimes jagged feeling that many people associate with African-American music is due to a rhythmic technique called *syncopation*. If you count aloud 1–2–3–4 with a steady pulse, say 120 beats per minute, but accent the 2 and the 4 with a louder voice, you will create a simple syncopation. In a four-beat rhythmic group, the first and third beats tend to be the strong beats. By accenting the weak beats, or displacing the accents, we create a lighter feel that is the basis of syncopation.

Swing feeling: Probably the most nebulous concept in African-American music is its *swing* feeling. Simply stated, music swings when a relaxed rhythmic feeling and softer articulation of individual notes in a musical line are superimposed over the more tense rhythmic drive of the underlying steady pulse of the motor rhythm. This is achieved by two basic means.

First of all, the musician uses a softer articulation to begin each note than would be played for a more rigid rhythmic feel. For instance, if you sang a march melody, you would probably use a deliberate and crisp articulation, saying "Ta—ta ta—tata." On the other hand, if you were imitating a swinging jazz melody, you would use a softer articulation singing "Da—da da . . ." or "Doo—doo doo. . . ."

Second, and perhaps more important, musicians playing with a swing feel play three subdivisions of the beat instead of two. Therefore, in a pattern of two notes per beat the note that begins on the beat is twice as long as the note that occurs off the beat (1–2 3). This lopsided, bouncy feeling between beats combined with the softer articulation work gives African-American music a relaxed character in the midst of the even, driving motor rhythm of the steady pulse, even at fast tempos.[4]

Improvisation: *Improvisation* is the spontaneous creation of a performer reacting to the musical environmental situation of the moment. The range of freedom used in musical improvisation is wide. At one extreme, improvisation involves a free rendering of the existing melody of a song only, altering the original rhythms of the melody or adding some extra notes in an ornamental fashion. This is called *paraphrasing* the melody. From about the mid-1920s on, musicians moved toward spontaneously creating entirely *new* melodies assembled from their personal repertoire of well-practiced musical phrases, or *licks*. These new melodies were constructed to fit the preexisting succession of chords. From about the 1950s, musicians began to create even freer improvisations that were not obligated to follow a set of chord changes or even a particular key or scale.

Like syncopation, improvisation is not a technique peculiar to jazz. In the history of European art music, many of the great composers such as Bach and Mozart improvised instrumental pieces and cadenzas with great success and frequency. In the Baroque era (c. 1600–1750) solo singers improvised ornamental passages in their *recitatives*. In more recent history, however, the practice of improvisation seems to have faded away within the European art music tradition, with the notable exception of the organ.

On the other hand, African-American music, among other musical traditions, has always placed a high priority on the development and execution of improvisational skills. This places the center of responsibility on the individual musician, who is at once composer and performer. It is rather risky to extemporize a dramatically satisfying series of musical ideas with all the integrity and effect of someone who composed a piece at leisure. But when the improviser is successful—and there are *many* successful efforts on recordings—it is a rewarding experience for both performer and listener.

Since improvisation is the musicians' reaction to a time and place, a particular improvised performance can never be re-created exactly the same way again—even by the same performers on the same day. Once an improvised performance has passed through time, it is gone forever. By virtue of this fact, improvisation has a fragile and rather elusive nature. This is precisely why recordings are the only way in which improvised performances exist in any permanent form. It is easy to see why the recorded body of jazz, folk, blues, country, and rock performances is so highly valued by enthusiasts. How fortunate we are that much of America's African-American music and recording technology came into existence at the same time.

Chapter Summary

The music of African-Americans has been influential worldwide and has defined music of a truly American character. To understand what the distinctive characteristics of African-American music are, we must first look at the context and content of African music itself.

Music-making, like most other activities in African cultures, tends to be communal and integrated into everyday life. Music is not always judged on its own merit, but on how it serves the function it accompanies. It is highly rhythmic music, repetitive and conducive to dance. Groups play simple multilinear rhythmic lines that interlock in complex ways. Dirtying the sound of the voice or an instrument is considered aesthetically desirable.

The degree of African musical and cultural retention in the New World depended upon the cultural makeup of the slave owners. Latin-Catholic colonies allowed slaves to retain more African traditions than did the British-Protestant colonies of the mainland South. The musical training of most Americans, black and white, was in the church singing schools where hymns were lined-out by music teachers. Blacks were eventually forced to establish their own churches and sacred music styles, employing latent African characteristics to the worship and the songs. Laboring songs, such as the field holler and the work song, carried on the tradition of functional music from Africa.

From this acculturation process, African-American music has given us a number of stylistic elements that are now applied to most of our musical styles. These elements include blue notes, unique tone production of the voice or an instrument, an overt and constant motor rhythm, swing feeling, and unique applications of syncopation and improvisation.

Additional Listening

Refer to citations in the footnotes of this chapter.

Ba Benzélé Pygmies, *An Anthology of African Music: Ba Benzélé Pygmies* (Baren Reiter Musicaphon BM 30 L 2303). The Ba Benzélé Pygmies are from central Africa, and this collection of recordings demonstrate vocals, drumming, wind, and string instruments. The *hindewhu* (whistle) solo on this LP was re-created on the Herbie Hancock album *Headhunters* (Columbia 32731). The Ba Benzélé recordings are available in CD format as *Anthology of World Music Ba Benzélé Pygmies* (Rounder, 1998).

Various Performers, *Roots of the Blues* (New World Records NW 252). This is a collection of African and African-American recordings selected and annotated by eminent folklorist Alan Lomax.

Various Performers, *Roots of Black Music in America* (Folkways 2694). This is a collection of African and African-American recordings selected and annotated by folklorist Samuel Charters.

Review Questions

1. In what ways is music functional in African everyday life?
2. What is the relationship between African music and dance forms (or structures)?
3. What are syncopation and multilinear rhythm?
4. In an African drumming ensemble, who is allowed to improvise and to what extent does that drummer improvise?
5. What is the relationship between melody and meaning in African music?
6. What were the geographical and cultural factors that determined how much African musical and social culture was retained in the New World?
7. What is the difference between a field holler and a work song? How do the tasks they accompany impact their musical character?
8. Describe blue notes and tone production in African-American music.
9. What musical elements create a swing feel in African-American music?
10. What is improvisation?

Notes

1. An excellent study of the black inhabitants of the Georgia Sea Islands is *Slave Songs of the Georgia Sea Islands,* by Lydia Parrish (New York: Creative Age Press, 1942). A follow-up to Parrish is the field recordings made by folklorist Alan Lomax in 1960–1961, available on New World Records, LP format, NW 278.
2. Alan Lomax, liner notes to *Georgia Sea Island Songs* (New World Records, NW 278). These recordings have also been released in CD format in the "Southern Journey" series from Rounder, Volumes 12 and 13 (Rounder, 1998).
3. A good example of blue notes and pitch and timbre manipulation is Bessie Smith and Louis Armstrong's performance of "St. Louis Blues," from the *Smithsonian Collection of Classic Jazz* (referred to hereafter as *SCCJ*) (LP format, Smithsonian Records R 033 P7–19477).
4. An example of swing feeling, motor rhythm, and syncopation is Fletcher Henderson and his orchestra performing "Wrappin' It Up," on *SCCJ*. This piece will be analyzed in some detail in Chapter 8.

Chapter  4

Early Commercialization of African-American Music

Over the course of some 300 years, African-American folk music evolved in the kitchens, fields, and prisons of the southern United States. This evolution took place in the arena of the common people rather than the professional stage. The music was incorporated into everyday activities to make chores more bearable. It was an integral part of worship. At leisure times, the music was performed for small audiences by amateurs and itinerant professionals in intimate settings such as homes, picnics, and small taverns.

While the music was confined largely to the cultural context from which it came, others were watching and listening. Many white Americans could not resist the unfettered and down-to-earth expression of black music and culture. Throughout the nineteenth century, white minstrel entertainers created facsimiles of black music, dance, and culture to the delight of white audiences all over the country.

Blacks themselves eventually formed minstrel ensembles and, later on, moved into vaudeville. These theatrical settings and the burgeoning sheet music industry provided an entrée to the commercialization of authentic African-American music. By the early twentieth century, black composers and entertainers became more prevalent in clubs, stage acts, film, and the publishing houses of Tin Pan Alley. They presented their own musical wares to the public and established trends that the music industry was eventually forced to follow. The style of music that provided the catalyst for this commercial growth was ragtime.

RAGTIME

As noted in Chapters 1 and 2, minstrelsy began to give way to vaudeville by the 1880s, due in large part to the pioneering efforts of theater producer Tony Pastor. One of Pastor's acts was a white Kentucky songwriter, Ben Harney, who used the term *ragtime* in print to describe his own songs, although in form and rhythm they did not resemble instrumental rags at all. The songs of Harney, Ernest Hogan, and others actually grew out of the minstrel tradition and were called *coon songs.* The immense popularity of these songs, along with the employment of the term *ragtime,* led popular music away from the vapid sentimental repertoire of nineteenth-century Victorian style and paved the way for the popularity of instrumental ragtime. The crowning achievement of the ragtime song's impact occurred in 1911 with Irving Berlin's "Alexander's Ragtime Band."

The World's Columbian Exposition of 1893 was a major tourist event. Musicians, including black itinerant pianists, came to Chicago to play in the speakeasies on the periphery of the fairgrounds for the enjoyment of Exposition patrons. By this time, the pianists were playing what we now know as ragtime; this is the first time the music was heard by a large mainstream audience. Most of the pianists were from the Southwest and the Mississippi Valley. They had developed the music over a number of years, playing in the male-only environs of the saloons, pool halls, and bordellos of the red-light districts of various cities. Through the medium of sheet music, piano rags eventually appeared in middle-class homes and in the more respectable dancing establishments.

In the middle-class home, the parlor piano was a status symbol; and the sale of pianos in the 1890s was at an unprecedented high. Playing the piano was an accomplishment primarily of the young lady of the house. It was considered a trait of her refined finishing, and she was expected to provide intimate recitals of respectable classical works and to act as accompanist for parlor hymn-singing with family and friends. (Boys did not take piano lessons; it was considered effeminate.) Given the usual bill of fare in the piano bench, ragtime offered a lively alternative; and a young lady and her friends could dance to the lively syncopations of the piano rags—when her parents were not at home.

However the appetite for piano rags got started, publishers and performers were soon compelled to supply the public with the product. Beginning in 1897 several instrumental rags appeared. An immediate predecessor of the rag was the *cakewalk,* a lightly syncopated slow march that accompanied a high-stepping dance of the same name. The dance got its start on the stage and became *the* dance craze of the 1890s. Many cakewalks were performed by military bands like John Philip Sousa's, and it was he who was most responsible for taking the cakewalk craze to Europe.[1]

Another catalyst for popularity of piano ragtime was the advent of the automatic player piano. The following explanation describes the operation of a player piano. A piano roll (a roll of paper perforated with holes) unwinds on a mechanism in the piano, passing over a *tracker bar* with 88 air holes that align with the perforations on the paper roll. When the hole of the roll passes over the hole of the tracker bar, air is taken in that triggers a pneumatic lifter to make the corresponding hammer strike a string on the piano. The only contribution by the "pianist" is to work the vacuum bellows by pumping two pedals under the piano. Before the widespread use of phonographs, the player piano was the only form of recorded music available for the home. Since many households did not have a pi-

Scott Joplin around 1899. Joplin was the greatest composer of ragtime music. He composed around 60 works for piano, a ballet, and two operas.

anist to fill their home entertainment needs, the purchase of a player piano and a library of piano rolls provided a satisfying alternative. There were even *word rolls*, where the lyric was printed on the perforated paper, allowing everyone to sing along as the words rolled by.

The most famous of all ragtime pianists was Scott Joplin (1868–1917). Joplin was born near Texarkana, Texas; and, unlike the majority of black itinerant pianists, he had a fair degree of formal training. His skills as a pianist were quite modest, but his ragtime compositions are the pinnacle of that art form. Scott Joplin provided the catalyst for piano ragtime's popularity when he composed "Maple Leaf Rag," published in 1899 while he was playing at the Maple Leaf Club in Sedalia, Missouri. He wrote 37 rags in all; but most were too ambitious for consumption by the general public, and he never again achieved the popularity he had with "Maple Leaf Rag."

Analysis of "Maple Leaf Rag" (*SCCJ*, 1/1)

This recording of "Maple Leaf Rag" features a player piano roll of a performance by Scott Joplin himself. He performed the rag on a special piano that placed dotted marking on the paper, which was punched out later and duplicated. The roll was made in 1916 when Joplin was suffering from the effects of syphilis, one being the gradual loss of his motor ability. For this reason, the piano roll performance is rather stiff and clumsy, but we can still see how Joplin would interpret his most famous piano rag.

"Maple Leaf Rag," like all rags, is a multithematic form; that is, it is a composition made up of a succession of three or four melodic sections. It shares this form with the march, its primary model. (Listen, for instance, to John Philip Sousa's "Stars and Stripes Forever" and note its three distinct themes.) "Maple Leaf Rag" has four themes, and like the march and other rags it changes key after the second theme.

The rhythmic relationship between the left and right hand is typical of all rags. The left hand alternates an even bass/chord accompaniment to the syncopated melody in the right hand (see Figure 4.1).

FIGURE 4.1

Excerpt from *Maple Leaf Rag*

The concept of this compositional form and texture would provide the basis for many rag and jazz compositions and performances until around 1930.

It is interesting to note that Joplin does not play "Maple Leaf Rag" note for note from the printed music. His use of improvisation is minimal, with just a few embellishments. It was a common practice for piano roll editors to add extra notes to "live" performances to give the piano a bigger, orchestral sound. Ragtime researchers and interviews with Joplin's contemporaries have confirmed that this type of improvisatory embellishment was also a common practice in ragtime.

Listening Guide 4.1
"Maple Leaf Rag" 2 beats per measure

ELAPSED TIME	FORM	EVENT DESCRIPTION
:00	A	Piano (16 measures: 8 + 8)
:23	A	(16 measures 8 + 8)
:45	B	(16 measures)
1:07	B	(16 measures)
1:30	A	(16 measures)
1:52	C	New key (16 measures)
2:14	C	(16 measures)
2:37	D	Back to original key (16 measures)
2:59	D	(16 measures)
3:21	End	

COMMERCIALIZATION OF THE BLUES

In Chapter 5 we will trace the origin and characteristics of the folk blues. What is notable, however, is that commercial recordings of the raw folk form of the blues came *after* its polished, urban commercialized form. Twelve-bar blues strains began appearing in published piano rags as early as 1904,[2] but the real popularity of the commercial blues began with the work of W. C. Handy (1873–1958). Handy was a formally trained black musician from Florence, Alabama. As the son and grandson of prominent Methodist preachers, he was not exposed to the class of blacks that sang the blues. Instead, he pursued a career as a concert band cornetist and conductor. While working in Mississippi, he began to see a commercial potential for the blues. He made an effort to clean up what he considered its rough character and still retain its melancholy essence.

Handy's first blues composition was "Memphis Blues," written as a campaign song for the Memphis mayoral race in 1909. He had it published in 1912, and it triggered a blues craze for the remainder of the decade. It was not the first blues song in print, but it was the first to achieve national notoriety, rivaled only by his later blues song "St. Louis Blues" in 1914. In 1918 Handy moved his publishing company from Memphis to New York and continued to compose blues songs.

Soon other black blues composers and publishers joined Handy in New York to cash in on the craze that he had started—composers such as Clarence Williams, Spencer Williams, and Perry Bradford. They joined the ranks of Tin Pan Alley songsmiths and were founding members of ASCAP. It is through the ingenuity of

Blues songwriter W. C. Handy (left) shaking hands with the great American composer Duke Ellington in 1945. Handy's sheet music was an important vehicle for popularizing the blues and standardizing its form.

black songwriter Perry Bradford, however, that recording took a decided turn.

From the time that popular music was first captured on records until 1920, black singers were excluded from recording. Instrumental groups, such as W. C. Handy's or James Reese Europe's orchestras, were allowed to record because instrumental music was not as likely to reveal the race of the performers. Though black-influenced forms of music such as rags, blues, and jazz were being recorded, the majority of the instrumentalists and singers were white. Handy's blues songs were recorded by white comedians specializing in black material, such as Al Bernard, May Irwin, Sophie Tucker, and others. Major record companies catered to the white urban upper and middle class.

Around the time of World War I, however, blacks (and poorer whites) began a mass migration out of the South. They were seeking better-paying wartime industrial jobs in northern cities such as Chicago, Detroit, and New York. Perry Bradford recognized this burgeoning black consumer market and appealed to the General Phonograph Corporation to record a black singer performing the blues. The company finally consented and allowed Bradford and a black cabaret singer from Philadelphia, Mamie Smith, to record Bradford's "Crazy Blues" in 1920. The recording was a tremendous success and kicked off a deluge of recordings by black singers for the black record-buying public. This was a historically significant event for several reasons.

1. This was the first recording of a blues song by a black singer and targeted primarily to a black audience.

2. With the success of Bradford and Smith's effort, a succession of black cabaret singers—mostly women—were recorded extensively over the next 15 years. They were accompanied by many of the pioneering jazz instrumentalists of the twenties, who saw their own individual careers launched, musicians such as Fletcher Henderson, Coleman Hawkins, and Bubber Miley (see Chapter 8). This style of blues performance became known as *vaudeville blues, cabaret blues, urban blues,* or *classic blues.*

3. By proving the viability of targeting records to special interest groups, subsidiary *race record* labels such as Okeh and independent labels such as Gennett (see Chapter 6) mushroomed in the entertainment industry. This helped nurture not only the recording of blues but also of jazz, country, and various other ethnic music.

4. The popularity of published and commercially recorded blues led to the recording of genuine southern folk blues singers. Thus one of America's most unique oral traditions was preserved in its most authentic form.

Many of the female blues singers recording in New York in the early 1920s were from the Northeast. They were not as familiar with blues singing as they were with the Broadway material they sang in New York musical revues. The first authentic blues voice on record was heard in February 1923, with the premiere of Bessie Smith (1894–1937) singing "Down Hearted Blues" for the Columbia label. Smith was born in Chattanooga, Tennessee, and grew up singing the blues in tent shows and minstrel shows throughout the South. Fortune brought her to New York in the early twenties, and there she began her fruitful recording career. She preferred the accompaniment of the jazz bands in New York, and it was she who was most responsible for molding a significant jazz-blues type of performance.

There were many reasons for Bessie Smith's uniquely prominent position among the blues divas of her day. Growing up in the South, she was closer to the source of the blues than many of her peers in classic blues. Her early career was spent performing with Gertrude "Ma" Rainey, a Georgia-born blues and vaude-ville singer (1886–1939), historically considered The "Mother of the Blues." Some historians state that Smith was a blues pupil of Rainey's; others feel that Smith was a mature blues stylist when she met Rainey. In any event, her association with Rainey would have influenced Smith. This authenticity of style lent an honesty and authority to Smith's recorded performances.

Bessie Smith's persona transcended just her blues singing. There was new pride in the black audience that there were finally black performers available on records, but Smith took it to the next level. She had an assertive personality, de-

A glamorous publicity photo of blues diva Bessie Smith from around 1923. She recorded around 150 songs for Columbia and was one of the most influential singers of all time.

manding deference and submission from all those around her, including whites. She recorded with some of the most prominent jazz and blues musicians in New York and Chicago. Her lifestyle was excessive and reck-less. Her voice was powerful and, teamed with some of the lyrics in her songs, projected a defiance and self-assertiveness that must have been an inspiration to her black listeners, particularly black women. Equally inspiring would have been her commercial success. Her first release in 1923 sold more than 750,000 copies that year, lifting her to equal status with Mamie Smith's (no relation) ground-breaking blues record "Crazy Blues" in 1920. She had a sizable income in her heyday, al-though opportunistic businesspeople and love interests bled much of it away from her.

Smith's songs lifted up the less fortunate, and her 1929 recording "Nobody Knows When You're Down and Out" is cited by blues historian William Barlow as a "personal epi-taph and a Depression-era classic." Unfortu-nately, the Depression era had also yielded to a more polished vocal style that rendered Smith's style passé. For the next few years she was reduced to the small-time, performing mostly in the South, where audiences still identified with her earthy style. She was on the verge of a comeback in 1935, thanks in part to the efforts of producer and longtime admirer John Hammond (discussed in Chapter 8). While riding through Clarksdale, Mississippi, Smith's car struck an oncoming truck. She later died from injuries incurred in that accident.

Time has proven Bessie Smith's dominant influence over that of any other classic blues singer of the 1920s. Her legacy can be found in the music of jazz singer Billie Holiday, gospel singer Mahalia Jackson, and even female rock artists like Janis Joplin. She was truly the "Empress of the Blues."

Analysis of "St. Louis Blues" (SCCJ, 1/3)

This recording is by the greatest of the classic blues singers, Bessie Smith. It was made in 1925 and features W. C. Handy's most popular published blues song, "St. Louis Blues." This session is of particular interest because Smith is accompanied by a young Louis Armstrong on trumpet. As we shall see in Chapter 7, Armstrong was a consummate interpreter of the blues, as a vocalist and as an instrumentalist. He posed somewhat of a threat to Bessie Smith's performance, with a wonderful musical rivalry being captured on the recording.

The other instrument on the record is a reed pump organ played by Fred Longshaw. Even though these urban blues recordings were slicker in their production than recordings of folk blues artists, there were occasional attempts made to capture a rustic, down-home sound; hence the pump organ, creating the image of the old country church. Other classic blues singers, such as Gertrude "Ma" Rainey, occasionally sang to a *jug band*, where the musicians hummed through kazoos, blew into glass jugs, and scraped on washboards.

Bessie Smith's voice is robust and powerful, well suited for the acoustic method used for this recording. While the range of her voice rarely exceeds an octave, her command of blues vocal mannerisms more than compensates. On this particular recording listen for the exaggerated blue notes in the melody. In most cases a blue note is a result of the singer sliding into or out of a particular note. Armstrong matches her blues inflections with his trumpet note for note.

Handy's "St. Louis Blues" is actually a formal blend of ragtime, verse/chorus song, and 12-bar blues. There are three distinct melodic themes in this song. The first is a 12-bar blues form. The second theme is a 16-bar bar in a minor key; in the original sheet music, a tango rhythm was written in the accompaniment. The third theme is a 12-bar blues form with a repetitive bluesy melody dominating it.

Listening Guide   4.2
"St. Louis Blues" 4 beats per measure

ELAPSED TIME	FORM	EVENT DESCRIPTION
:00	Intro	Organ chord followed by trumpet
:03	A1	Vocal with trumpet fills (12 measures)
:49	A2	Vocal with trumpet fills (12 measures)
1:33	B	Vocal, shift to minor key (16 measures)
2:29	C	Vocal, back to major key (12 measures)
3:10	End	

Along with the premiere of Bessie Smith, 1923 also saw the first recordings of folk-blues artists (mostly male) recorded on location in the South. With the growing demand for blues records, record companies sought to inexpensively record folk material that would be exempt from royalty payments to a composer and his publisher. Talent scouts were stationed in southern cities such as Dallas, Atlanta, and Memphis to acquire local black blues talent for recordings. Portable recording machines were set up in hotel rooms or other makeshift studios in these cities. Singers were recorded and paid a flat fee, and the wax masters were sent back North for mass production and distribution. Even though this was strictly a commercial venture, these companies preserved the performances of musicians that had been, for the most part, ignored by folklorists of the day. These recordings give us a more realistic picture of the blues in its unfettered form; they have inspired generations of musicians and leave us with a valuable testament to black art and performance practice.

With the commercial distribution of ragtime and blues, the process of oral tradition changed among musicians. No longer was it necessary for a folk musician to come into intimate contact with another to learn his style and repertoire; he only needed to purchase a record and a piece of sheet music. Also, the artist could assume that the music encountered in mass media was music that should be learned by local folk musicians for their particular audience. In this way many commercial performances entered or, in some instances, *re*entered the folk tradition. This can be seen in folk blues performances of W. C. Handy compositions as well as folk country performances of ragtime, minstrel, and Tin Pan Alley songs.

Ragtime died (coincidentally) with Scott Joplin in 1917, the year the first jazz record was made. Ragtime had succeeded in turning America's tastes toward lively syncopation. A new-found freedom expressed itself in styles of dress, dancing, and night life that forever abandoned the rigid formality of nineteenth-century Victorian ritual.[3] In the cabarets and dance halls of America, the appetite for black-based styles of music—however commercially watered down—continued unabated.

Chapter Summary

After a long and unself-conscious incubation period, African-American music began to be imitated and commercialized by white entertainers. Minstrel and vaudeville theater provided the setting for black and white entertainers. In the late nineteenth century, ragtime proved to be the genuine force to radically change the mainstream of American popular music. On the stage, ragtime songs entertained audiences, while piano rags were popularized in sheet music form for home amateur performance. The real turning point in ragtime's popularity came when Scott Joplin's "Maple Leaf Rag" was published in 1899, and the style flourished until it was supplanted by jazz in 1917.

During the age of ragtime, traces of 12-bar blues occasionally could be found in the strains of vocal and instrumental rags. W. C. Handy was the first to make the blues fashionable with his lyrical and polished adaptations of folk blues. Through the success of songs like "Memphis Blues" and "St. Louis Blues," blues sheet music began to show up in Tin Pan Alley. Eventually, black blues composers and record producers managed to get a black singer recorded singing blues. This marked the emergence of the race record industry and led to a proliferation of *classic blues,* an urban musical product usually featuring black female cabaret singers. By 1923 the popularity of blues recordings led record companies to seek out folk-blues singers for field recordings in the South.

Additional Listening

Richard Zimmerman, *The Collector's History of Ragtime* (LP format, Murray Hill Records, M-60556/5). This five-LP set contains 71 piano rags composed between 1897 and 1939 by various musicians. It is performed by Richard Zimmerman, ragtime authority and president of the Maple Leaf Club. There is also an informative eight-page booklet included. The set may be obtained by writing to the Maple Leaf Club, 105 Ricky Court, Grass Valley, CA 95949.

Bessie Smith, "Down Hearted Blues" (1923) (*The World's Greatest Blues Singer*, LP format, Columbia GP 33, 1/1). This is the first in a 10-LP series of rereleases by Chris Albertson. *The Essential Bessie Smith* (Columbia/Legacy 64922, 1997) is a good one-volume CD. Smith's complete Columbia recordings are available in a five-volume CD set, *Bessie Smith: The Complete Recordings* (Columbia/Legacy C2K-47091, 1991).

Gertrude "Ma" Rainey, "Hear Me Talkin' to Ya" (1928) (*Folkways Jazz Vol. XI: Addenda*, LP format, Folkways FJ 2811, 1/4). Also see volumes 2 and 4. Ma Rainey is considered by many to be Bessie Smith's mentor. In her recordings we hear her with jug bands, pianists, and jazz bands, including one led by Thomas A. Dorsey, the father of black gospel music (discussed in Chapter 19).

Katharine Handy, "Memphis Blues" (1958) (*W. C. Handy Blues*, LP format, Folkways FG 3540, 1/2). Katharine Handy, W. C.'s daughter, did this recording project to set the record straight on how her father intended his blues compositions to be performed. She sings several of Handy's blues compositions, accompanied by James P. Johnson. Her style is subdued and pleasant, striving to bring out the melodic beauty and refinement that W. C. Handy sought.

Various Artists, *Let's Get Loose* (LP format, New World Records NW 290). This album is a collection of folk and popular blues performances from the 1920s.

Review Questions

1. How did the *coon song* usher in the popularity of ragtime?
2. How did the home piano market help popularize ragtime?
3. How does a player piano work?
4. Describe a typical piano rag in terms of what each hand does and the form (structure) of the melodies.
5. What was H. C. Handy's role in the commercialization of the blues?
6. What was the historical significance in Perry Bradford and Mamie Smith's recording of "Crazy Blues" in 1920?
7. How did record companies come to record folk-blues singers in the South, and what was the procedure for recording them?
8. How did recordings change the way folk musicians learned their music?

Notes

1. This is evident not only from newspaper reports of cakewalking in the courts of England, France, and Germany but in subsequent early nineteenth-century art music works such as Debussy's "Golliwog's Cakewalk" (1908), from his *Children's Corner* piano album, and Igor Stravinsky's "Ragtime for Eleven Instruments" (1911).

2. This blues strain appeared in the piano rag "One of Them Things" by James Chapman and Leroy Smith, published by Joseph Placht and Son in St. Louis in 1904.
3. Credit for this new social attitude can be attributed solely to Vernon and Irene Castle, who initiated a wave of popular ballroom dance steps in the 1910s. They were the darlings of upper-class society and served as models of elegance and respectability, introducing ethnic-based dance steps and the syncopated music that accompanied it.

Chapter 5

American Blues Traditions

In the late nineteenth and early twentieth centuries, many black musicians throughout the South were day laborers; only a few played music full-time. Some of the musicians were blind; music was the only way they could make a living. In their travels searching for work, itinerant black musicians encountered a variety of audiences and had to maintain a diverse repertoire. In addition to ballads, chants, and spirituals, black musicians played songs they heard at minstrel tent shows. Closer to the turn of the century, they played ragtime and even Tin Pan Alley sentimental songs and waltzes. They also had a repertoire of simple country songs similar to what poor rural whites were playing. These versatile black folk musicians were called *songsters*.

As will be restated in Chapter 10, there was free interchange of folkways between poor blacks and whites, including music. The southern whites brought a rich tradition of British folk and broadside ballads to the New World; before long, southern blacks created their own version of the epic story song. Blacks sang about legendary heroes and villains, about notable events and deeds. Many of these songs like "John Henry" or "Frankie and Albert" (also known as "Frankie and Johnny") have a strophic form comprised of a two-line verse followed by a one-line refrain. Like many verse-chorus and call-and-response patterns, the words to the verse changed from stanza to stanza, while the words of the refrain remained constant, reinforcing the central idea of the ballad—"He was her man, but he done her wrong."

In the 1900s a new black musical form arose that borrowed from the spiritual, the field holler and work song, and the three-line ballad. It was the blues, and its simple, resilient form and poignant, direct expression has been a continual inspiration for many forms of music. Where the blues ballad was made up of a two-line verse with a one-line refrain, the blues was a three-line stanza comprised of an opening statement, a repeat of that statement, and a consequent *punch line*. Usually, the last word of the last line rhymes with the last word of the first line. The dramatic plan for the blues stanza is to state a condition or sentiment, such as "I'm gonna lay my head on some lonesome railroad line." The repetition of this line emphasizes the first line, creates dramatic tension by anticipation and delay of the punch line, and then follows through to resolve the tension—"And let that 5:15 train pacify my mind."

The harmonic framework for the blues is derived from the simple hymns of the church. The progression from the *tonic* chord in the key, to the intermediate tension of the *subdominant* chord, to the maximum tension of the *dominant* chord is the most fundamental chord progression in Western functional harmony. It is to chord progressions what primary colors are to painting. In the blues the tonic is played under the first line, the subdominant under the second line, and the dominant back to the tonic is played under the third line. The dramatic design of the chord progression and that of the stanza structure coincide exactly. See the diagram in Figure 5.1.

When formally trained musicians such as W. C. Handy heard the blues and attempted to notate it, they standardized it into a set number of measures and a fixed harmonic progression. Their standardization is illustrated in Figure 5.1. Folk-blues musicians, however, did not perform blues in three even four-bar sections; their blues were flexible and of varying length, basically going to the next line when they felt like it.

Another important component of the blues form is the use of call-and-response. Notice in Figure 5.1 that the vocal line only occupies the first two measures of the four-measure phrase. The rest of the phrase is filled in with an *answer* by an instrument or by humming or by an "Oh, Lawdy" from the singer. This dialogue between blues vocalists and instrumentalists was important in the nurturing of African-American stylistic elements in instrumental music.

Subject matter in the blues was predominantly sorrowful, as singers and their audiences came to grips with the bleak conditions of their lives: social injustice, failed love, a nomadic life. But blues could also be a celebration of good times or show a sense of humor, even in the face of tragedy and despair. Look at this blues stanza again and note the humorous way it expresses itself.

> *I'm gonna lay my head on some lonesome railroad line.*
> *(Repeat)*
> *And let that 5:15 train pacify my mind.*

Unlike blues ballads, blues stanzas do not necessarily relate to each other thematically. The blues performer draws from a common stock of stanzas and strings them together on the spur of the moment. Blues lyrics are peppered with black slang and sexual double entendre meant to thwart the understanding of audiences outside the culture. Words and phrases like "easy rider," "hot

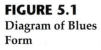

FIGURE 5.1
Diagram of Blues Form

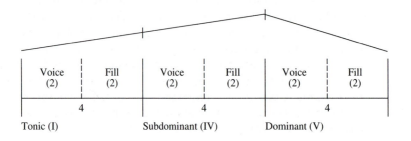

foot powder," even "rock and roll" and "jazz" were part of the lexicon of black poetry whose meanings were not understood by the majority of the white public.

The 1890s is a convenient decade to cite for the emergence of the blues, not because a conspicuous single musical event occurred but because of increasingly frequent reports of the blues' existence.[1] The blues was witnessed by folklore scholars in the workplace and in the bars. It originated in the Deep South, from Mississippi east to Georgia and the Carolinas. There was also significant early blues activity west of the Mississippi River, in Texas and Louisiana. Rural folk blues exhibit regional stylistic differences; some aspects of these differences are more obvious than others.

MISSISSIPPI DELTA BLUES

The Mississippi Delta is an area of flatland that stretches from Memphis, Tennessee, to Vicksburg, Mississippi, a distance of approximately 200 miles. After the Civil War many blacks in the Delta and elsewhere in the South remained on Delta plantations as sharecroppers, outnumbering whites by as many as seven to one. In the early twentieth century other labor opportunities came about for blacks in the Delta. Forests of hardwood trees were being cleared for lumber and land development. In the woods that remained, remote turpentine camps were established. The Army Corps of Engineers began building levees to keep the Mississippi River from flooding the Delta lowlands. There were also riverboats that moved harvested cotton upriver to market in Memphis, Tennessee. Black workers could be found in all these labor settings, and each occupation developed its own folklore and music.

Mississippi Delta blues is arguably the most pervasive of the regional styles. The earliest known blues musicians, certainly the most influential, came from the Delta; and their stylistic lineage has been well documented. From studies by David Evans, Paul Oliver, and others, we can narrow the genesis of Delta blues down to Dockery's Plantation in Sunflower County, Mississippi. From there came the "father of the Delta blues," Charley Patton.

Charley Patton was born around 1881 near Jackson, Mississippi. He began learning the guitar at the age of 14 and played music in the Jackson area. His family moved to Dockery's Plantation in 1897, where he lived until 1928 or 1929. With Dockery's as a home base, for over 30 years Patton made music throughout the Delta. He made his first recording for the Paramount label when he was over 40 years old.

Patton's vocal quality was rough, growling, and intense. He often deliberately slurred his words, a practice that became an identifying trait of the Delta blues style. He also tended to let his voice melt into his guitar playing, never finishing the line of lyric—or perhaps letting the guitar finish it. Historian Robert Palmer says Patton obscured or altered the syllabic accent of words strictly for musical reasons, so that his voice could contribute to the rhythm of the guitar accompaniment. He (and friends in the recording studio) would interject comments, not only for entertainment effect but also as rhythmic fills between lines of the song. Common to the African-American vocal tradition, Patton would slide around on his vocal notes, employing "blue" third and seventh degrees of the scale.

CHARLEY PATTON

The only known photograph of Delta bluesman Charley Patton, as seen in recording catalogs of the day.

Patton's guitar accompaniment was simple; but it created a strong dance rhythm, accented by his slapping the guitar with his hand or snapping the guitar's strings against its neck. He also used the blunt end of a knife or the neck of a glass bottle to slide up and down the neck of the guitar, allowing it to imitate the sliding pitch of his voice. The *bottleneck* guitar technique is also characteristic of Delta blues.

Charley Patton taught many blues singers, and many more were influenced by him. Some of the more famous names among blues fans are Tommy Johnson, Sam Chatmon (Patton's half brother), Son House, Willie Brown, and Howlin' Wolf (Chester Burnett). But Robert Johnson was the most famous bluesman to encounter Patton.

Robert Johnson

Robert Johnson was born in Hazelhurst, Mississippi, in 1911. In his early teens he took up the Jew's harp, then moved on to the harmonica. In the late twenties he made the switch to guitar. In searching for a mentor, Johnson found Willie Brown, a close friend and colleague of Charley Patton. Johnson was also heavily influenced by both Patton and Son House, whom he saw perform frequently. Later on, Ike Zinnerman became his teacher; and it was at this time, in the midst of the Depression, that Johnson's own style matured.

He took to the road, determined to make a living in music to avoid sharecropping. He was appreciated for his musical abilities but was viewed with suspicion and contempt by the sharecropper men. He was a small man but quite handsome; and, like many blues musicians, he had a way with women. This would often start fights that his size kept him from finishing. He spent the rest of his short life running after women and away from their men.

Johnson, like most of the Delta bluesmen, had a vast repertoire other than blues songs, including polkas, country and western songs, sentimental ballads, and Tin Pan Alley pop songs. After his initial apprenticeship with Son House and some time on the road, Johnson's ability improved markedly, so much so that many in the Delta believed he had sold his soul to the devil in exchange for his musical prowess. He played a full-sounding and rhythmic style of guitar, being adept at slide guitar and picking a solid lead line on the high strings. Johnson established himself as the best and most influential of the second-generation bluesmen.

He was quite popular in the Delta; but he longed to make recordings, as Charley Patton and Son House had done. He finally came to the attention of the American Record Company through a Jackson, Mississippi, music store owner and talent scout. Johnson's first recording session was in San Antonio, Texas, in 1936, where he recorded, among other songs, "Terraplane Blues." It was his biggest seller and prompted the record company to schedule another session for the following June, though they produced nothing that equaled its success. With the passage of time, however, all 41 of Robert Johnson's recordings have been cherished by generations of jazz, blues, and rock enthusiasts.

Analysis of "Hellhound on My Trail" (*The Complete Recordings*, CD format, Columbia C2K, 46222)

The blues performance by Robert Johnson was recorded in a Dallas hotel room on June 20, 1937. Johnson's style is characterized by a sense of foreboding, of always being unsettled and on the run. Some of his lyrics had him in league with the devil ("Me and the Devil Blues," "If I Had Possession over Judgment Day"), and his mysterious demise in 1938 (poisoned whiskey from a jealous husband) only added to his enigmatic historical image. His recorded performances have inspired countless young blues and rock musicians.

"Hellhound on My Trail" is a blues that demonstrates some sort of thematic relationship between the stanzas, combining to form, if not a narrative, then a unified idea. Johnson uses potent imagery to describe his wandering, a sense of paranoia, of being pursued by something not quite known or seen, and a longing for true love's comfort.

The drama is heightened by Johnson's strained, nasal tone quality. His enunciation is slurred (many times deliberately) and combined with black slang to hide the underlying meaning of the lyric. "Hot foot powder" refers to someone forcing him to move on for some reason; "little sweet rider" is a lover.

Johnson renders his blues stanzas in the flexible manner described before. Some parts have a driving rhythm while others are suspended in time. His guitar phrases closely emulate the inflections in his vocal.

Other Blues Regions in the South

Delta blues is the best documented and romanticized of the blues strains, but the blues was active and regionally distinctive all over the South. Alabama had an active blues scene in the cities of Birmingham and Montgomery, as well as in rural areas, but was overlooked by recording expeditions from the North. Georgia fared much better in recording and popularizing of its blues.

Atlanta was the focal point of the Southeast. Its rapid growth and prosperity drew rural blues singers from all over the region, making it a prime target for blues talent scouts and record producers. In the recordings of Atlanta blues singers we hear certain general stylistic tendencies. A number of Atlanta bluesmen, including Charlie Lincoln, Robert Hicks ("Barbecue Bob"), and Blind Willie McTell, preferred the 12-string guitar, with its rich two-guitar sound. Atlanta blues features a more delicate fingerpicking style on the guitar, as opposed to the more forceful rhythmic feel of Delta blues guitarists. Atlanta singers used more distinct pronunciation and lighter vocal tone quality.

Another major center for the blues was Dallas, Texas. Blues singers traveled the 180-mile stretch of Highway 80 (now Interstate 20) from Shreveport, Louisiana, to Dallas, gathering at the railroad stations and clubs in the "Deep Ellum" section of Elm Street. Two such traveling bluesmen were Huddie Leadbetter ("Leadbelly") and Lonnie Johnson, both Louisiana natives who were drawn to the better prospects in Dallas. (Johnson will be mentioned in the analysis of jazz recordings in Chapter 7; Leadbelly will be discussed in Chapter 16.)

The most legendary Texas blues singer, on a par with the best of the Delta blues singers, was Blind Lemon Jefferson, born about 80 miles south of Dallas. He

The only existing photo of Texas bluesman Blind Lemon Jefferson, circa 1925, taken from a Paramount Records catalog.

was a nomadic singer and known to musicians throughout Texas, Louisiana, and the Mississippi Delta. He began recording for Paramount in 1926 and sold well throughout the southern market. His voice had a high, strained sound and a haunting, urgent quality. He had a tough, defiant character, both in his personality and in his music. His lyrics were often tragic and violent and at times had sexual nuances, as in his famous "Black Snake Moan." Jefferson's style was close to the chantlike field holler; concomitantly, his guitar style lacked a steady rhythm, prompting bluesman Son House to comment that there "couldn't nobody never be lucky enough to dance by his music."[2] He was a major influence on the blues styles of Leadbelly, Son House, Aaron "T-Bone" Walker, and many others. Jefferson died in a Chicago snowstorm in 1930.

Country Blues Leaves the Country

Record companies from the North began recording folk-blues singers in the South in 1923, bringing them out of obscurity and homes and entertainment spots all over the country. However, there were other factors that changed both the styles and careers of blues musicians. The first step was migration to the city, and for many southern blacks the first city was Memphis, Tennessee.

Blues historian Giles Oakley writes, "Memphis was for many a launching pad for the journey to the North. . . . Roustabouts, boatmen, levee workers—who had to keep the levees built up to protect the city from the river—railworkers, pull-

The corner of Beale Street and Main in downtown Memphis, Tennessee. Beale was a black enclave of commerce and entertainment and a legendary haven for the delta blues.

man porters, cotton farmers, drifters, gamblers, musicians, hustlers and prostitutes, all mingled on Beale Street in Memphis."[3]

Memphis lies on the eastern bank of the Mississippi River in the southwest corner of Tennessee, bordering Mississippi and Arkansas. It is the largest river city between New Orleans and St. Louis and is the commercial axis for a rural area that stretches approximately 150 miles in any direction. It was a major stop for the Illinois Central Railroad, the artery that ran from New Orleans to Chicago. Highways 51 and 61 led from the heart of the Mississippi Delta to downtown Memphis. For many rural dwellers who came by boat, rail, and road, Memphis was the first taste of city life.

For blacks, the action in Memphis was on a five-block stretch of Beale Street that extended from the river to

4th Street. Beale was lined with stores and pawnshops run by Jewish merchants and saloons and theaters run by Italian entertainment promoters. City and country blues musicians could be found everywhere, playing in the streets, in railroad stations, or in the rough-and-tumble bars, performing at local theaters, or even playing at elegant parties for white socialites. It was on Beale Street that W. C. Handy first found fame and fortune.

One of the most popular blues formats in Memphis was the jug band. Louisville, Kentucky, is credited with having the first jug band (c. 1905), but it became a standby in Memphis by the 1920s and continued into the 1930s. The use of such primitive instruments as the jug, kazoo, or washboard was as much for novelty effect as for any other reason. (Recall classic blues singer Ma Rainey's use of the jug band instrumentation from the previous chapter.) A more significant part of their instrumentation was the addition of the harmonica, which eventually would become a staple lead instrument in urban blues bands. Jug bands usually performed outdoors for mixed audiences, so by necessity their repertoire was varied.

Besides being a major field recording center for folk-blues, Memphis also provided the catalyst for live performance tours of blues artists. Major theater chains, such as the Orpheum, Keith, and Loew's, had booked white vaudeville acts for some time; but in 1909 Anthony Barrasso organized the Theater Owner's Booking Agency (TOBA) to book black acts for his chain of southern theaters that catered to black patrons. The TOBA—the entertainers said it stood for "Tough on Black Actors"—grossly underpaid its talent and provided squalid working conditions; but throughout the 1920s it did provide employment and exposure for hundreds of blues singers and black vaudevillians from Jacksonville, Florida, to Chicago.

The 1930s brought a significant change in the style and context of blues performances. The Depression decimated the record industry, and race records took a particularly hard blow. Field recording of rural blues singers was reduced to a minimum; Memphis, for instance, was totally ignored until the 1940s. Radio, however, not only survived but flourished during the Depression; but it was not until the 1940s that black blues entertainers began to appear on southern radio. The first significant radio blues show started in 1941 when a white-owned radio station, KFFA, went on the air in Helena, Arkansas, which was downriver from Memphis. *King Biscuit Time,* sponsored by a local flour mill, featured a staff blues band playing at midday, five days a week. The show catered to the large black population in the locale. Its success encouraged the station to send the band on performance tours in the area, playing everywhere from grocery stores to outdoor political rallies. Other radio stations in the South followed suit, but the most noteworthy station was WDIA in Memphis. Beginning in 1948, WDIA totally dedicated its programming to the Negro market in the region, which was comprised of about 1.25 million people. It not only provided significant radio exposure for black blues but also rejuvenated Memphis as a blues center, and blues recording started up once again.

Chicago

Memphis remained a significant blues center going into the fifties, thanks largely to the recording studio of Sam Phillips, who continued to feature local black blues artists until he went in pursuit of rockabilly music (discussed later in Chapter 15). For many blacks, though, Memphis was only a stopover on the way to

Chicago. A strong magnet was the black newspaper *The Chicago Defender*. In the 1910s the paper told its southern subscribers of bountiful job opportunities in the city, especially during World War I when industry was booming and the flow of competing European immigrants was reduced. Many blacks from the Mississippi Valley seized the opportunity to escape the sharecropping system and took the Illinois Central Railroad to Chicago. Some moved on to other industrial midwestern cities such as Detroit and Cleveland. In the Southeast, blacks from Virginia, Georgia, and the Carolinas moved up the eastern seaboard to Philadelphia and New York.

As Chicago's South Side filled with black migrants, so came the musicians. During the 1910s and 1920s many of the blues musicians in Chicago maintained the style and format they brought from the rural South. The Depression, however, created a cleft in the evolution of the blues, and the city blues that emerged in the mid-thirties was markedly different. It was more intense in its performance style and much less ambiguous in its sexuality. One new strain of city blues was called *hokem blues*, lighthearted and naughty double-entendre songs that did not leave the audience guessing about the content for long. The first successful hokem blues was Georgia Tom and Tampa Red's "It's Tight Like That," recorded in the late 1920s. It led to other hokem songs with equally outrageous titles: "Selling That Stuff," "Let Me Feel It," and "Let Me Play with Your Poodle." (Ironically, Georgia Tom eventually devoted himself to religious music and became the virtual creator of modern gospel music.)

One of the hokem musicians who worked with Georgia Tom was Big Bill Broonzy. He was from Mississippi, had come to Chicago early on, and generously helped newly arrived blues musicians get established. His first recordings were of country reels played by duo guitars. He then recorded guitar-piano duets. By the mid-thirties he altered the instrumentation of his band to what would become a standard for urban blues groups. The new electric guitar was implemented; and one or two horns, piano, bass, and drums were added. A more insistent dance beat and a louder sound were used, so as to be heard over the noise of the South Side clubs. Another important addition to the new Chicago blues sound was the harmonica, played through a microphone as a powerful frontline instrument. John Lee "Sonny Boy" Williamson was the single artist that brought the harmonica from its southern jug band context into the standard lineup of electric, urban blues bands.

The 1940s saw the reign of many influential urban blues musicians in Chicago. Elmore James, Howlin' Wolf, Junior Wells, and many others enjoyed great popularity in clubs as well as on records. Blues recording in Chicago got a boost in the mid-thirties. Music publisher and agent Lester Melrose began working with Victor and Columbia record companies to provide them with talent for jukeboxes in urban black clubs. Between 1934 and 1951 Melrose recorded most of the available blues talent.

By the late 1940s *Billboard* updated its "race" record category to "rhythm and blues." At the same time, two bar owners, brothers Phil and Leonard Chess, took on Melrose with their own R&B labels, Chess Records and Checker Records. Chesses' talent lineup was every bit as stellar as Melrose's, but Muddy Waters was the company's brightest star. He was born McKinley Morganfield in 1915 and came from the Stovall plantation near Clarksdale, Mississippi. He knew Robert Johnson, and Waters's style was a vivid reflection of the legendary bluesman's. He eventually made the train trip to Chicago and in 1944 got his first electric guitar.

Urban bluesman Muddy Waters performing around 1979. Waters was one of the first postwar artists to create an electric blues sound that influenced a host of American and British rock and blues musicians.

In 1948 he recorded "I Can't Be Satisfied," which was an early success. He soon formed an important electric blues band featuring himself and harmonica player Little Walter Jacobs. Robert Palmer wrote of this band, "Muddy and his associates can't claim to have invented electric blues, but they were the first important electric band, the first to use amplification to make their ensemble music rawer, more ferocious, more physical, instead of simply making it a little louder."[4] Muddy Waters took the hard-driving, shouting style of the Delta blues and brought it to full fruition in electric urban blues. Waters provided the link from rhythm and blues to rock and roll, and Chess Records signed young Chuck Berry to finish the process. Waters and his fellow urban blues artists had particular influence with young British blues musicians. Some groups evolved into the Rolling Stones, John Mayall's Bluesbreakers, and Cream.

Analysis of "I'm Your Hoochie Coochie Man" (*Rock and Roll: The Early Days*, CD format, RCA PCD1-5463)

By the time this blues was recorded in 1954, Muddy Waters was consistently placing on the R&B national charts. "I'm Your Hoochie Coochie Man" and his other hits from that year, "I Just Want to Make Love to You" and "I'm Ready," were written by Chess bassist Willie Dixon. Dixon, through Muddy Waters, pioneered a more upbeat, lively style of blues song that stood apart from the more lugubrious blues that prevailed at the time. These livelier songs, no doubt, are what caught the attention of young listeners in the 1950s and helped usher in rock and roll.

Other personnel on this recording session included blues harpist Little Walter and pianist Otis Spann. "Hoochie Coochie Man" opens with a stop-time riff that has become an urban blues signature. It was conceived at the session and was not part of Dixon's original composition. It is also used on the other two songs from that session. When the steady beat finally enters, we hear a strong, slow shuffle, provided by the drums and piano. The bass plays a constant *walking* pattern, and the harmonica keeps a constant supply of fills and commentary with the vocal. Muddy Waters's voice is powerful and gruff, and there is occasionally a deliberate slurring of the pronunciation.

After the mid-fifties blues was more or less absorbed by rock and roll. Artists such as B. B. King and Bobby "Blue" Bland have remained favorites, and there are occasional revival concerts by surviving urban blues masters; but the heyday has passed. Young black audiences embraced the northeastern black vocal groups in the late fifties, and the soul styles of Stax and Motown were the rage in the sixties. Blues still remains at the root of many styles of American popular music; but in its purest form it has become an esoteric music enjoyed more by successive generations of young whites.

Fortunately, since the late fifties there have been a number of international scholars dedicated to researching and recording folk and urban blues. Events like the successful reissue of Robert Johnson's complete recordings by Columbia indicate that this type of research and preservation is sorely needed. There will always be the necessity for American music and culture to rejuvenate itself by experiencing the legacy of the blues.

Chapter Summary

Folklorists wrote about the folk blues from its beginning; but it was not documented on recordings until 1923, riding the wave of popularity generated by a Tin Pan Alley polished version of the blues. From that time until about the mid-thirties, folk blues singers from the South (mostly men) were recorded for sale to black audiences.

The blues derived from spirituals, laboring songs, and the blues ballad. The latter was fashioned after British balladry and usually had a two-line verse and a one-line refrain. The blues form was a modification of the ballad form: a repeated line and a consequent punch line. Though loosely adhered to by the folk musicians themselves, the general form of the blues—as it was standardized later in sheet music—was a 12-bar form comprised of three groups of four measures. Lyrics were often, but not always, sad. Verses were usually strung together in performance and did not necessarily relate to each other.

Rural blues styles are distinguishable by region, but we are most aware of styles represented in the field recordings from Memphis, Dallas, and Atlanta. Mississippi Delta blues has yielded the most influential artists and style. The music came out of rural obscurity in the course of the twentieth century through its exposure on race records, black theater tours, and radio. The music changed both its style and its context with the mass migration of blacks to northern cities, particularly Chicago. The music became electrified and louder, employing a more insistent dance beat. By the mid-fifties the blues became overshadowed by rock and roll.

Additional Listening

Various Artists, *The Story of the Blues*, Volumes 1 and 2 (LP format, Columbia 66218, 66232). This collection was compiled by noted British blues historian Paul Oliver. It is the most convenient single source for a variety of blues performances by men, women, pianists, guitarists, and groups from the 1920s through World War II.

Various Artists, *Wizards from the Southside* (LP format, Chess Records, a division of Sugar Hill Records, Ltd. CH 8203). A collection of performances by Chicago blues artists between 1950 and 1963, including Howlin' Wolf, Muddy Waters, and John Lee Hooker.

Various Artists, *The Blues: A Smithsonian Collection of Classic Blues Singers* (CD format, Smithsonian RD 101 A4 23981, A4 23986). This collection was issued in 1993 and was selected and annotated by blues scholar W. K. McNeil. There are 93 recordings dating from the 1920s to the 1980s. It is very comprehensive, with the only glaring omission being B. B. King (due to contractual problems). The 93-page book is brilliantly done. While this set is out of print along with others from the Smithsonian, it is worth knowing about and seeking out in libraries or used book and record stores.

Review Questions

1. What type of music could be found in the repertoire of black songsters?
2. How did the form of the black blues ballad change to the form of the blues?
3. What are the three chords usually used in the blues, and how do they correlate to the dramatic shape of the lyrics?
4. What are common topics and slang terms found in blues lyrics?
5. What are the stylistic traits of Charley Patton and other Delta blues singers?
6. How does the Atlanta blues style differ from the Delta blues style?
7. Describe the style of Texas bluesman Blind Lemon Jefferson.
8. What importance did Memphis, Tennessee, and the Theater Owners Booking Agency have for black blues musicians?
9. After World War II, what radio show featured the blues?
10. How did blues styles evolve in Chicago?

Notes

1. David Evans, *Big Road Blues* (Berkeley: University of California Press, 1982), p. 32.
2. Arnold S. Caplin, liner notes to *Son House–Blind Lemon Jefferson* (Biograph BLP 12040).
3. Giles Oakley, *The Devil's Music* (New York: Harcourt Brace Jovanovich, 1976), p. 145.
4. Robert Palmer, *Deep Blues* (New York: The Viking Press, 1981), p. 16.

Chapter 6

Jazz in New Orleans and Chicago

African and European musical elements in the United States blended in a way that was unique to the rest of the world. There were also unique blends within different regions of the United States. In the case of jazz, no music could be more distinctive, as is its city of origin. Jazz is also singular in the way it progressed through the twentieth century. Its stylistic siblings—blues, country, rock, and so forth—remained within the realm of commercial music over the years; whereas jazz eventually took the road of high art and lost most of the popular audience.

Jazz enjoyed its share of success within the larger scope of popular music throughout the 1920s and 1930s, although most white listeners considered it to be no more than a rather quaint, even rude, fun type of music. Yet among musicians and a smaller, more faithful segment of the listening public, jazz was something more than novelty entertainment. It was a significant musical concept; and from its beginning it would be scrutinized and modified by talented musicians, black and white, American and international.[1]

Traditionally, New Orleans is renowned as the birthplace of jazz. Some scholars argue that the attribution is too clean-cut, that long before jazz was first recorded in 1917 it could be heard in cities throughout the South and Midwest. This is countered by New Orleans advocates who tell us that jazz musicians from New Orleans had wandered through other cities and exposed various local musicians to the style. In any event there is a strong case for crediting New Orleans with the birth of jazz: It is unique among southern cities, and the musical and cultural events that forged jazz into a distinct entity are characteristically New Orleans.

In this chapter we will examine the musical and cultural traditions of New Orleans to determine how jazz came about and why it is peculiar to that city. We shall also see how the music came to leave New Orleans, see how it was first presented commercially, and meet some of its earliest artists.

THE CULTURAL HISTORY OF NEW ORLEANS

New Orleans was founded in 1718 by Jean Baptiste LeMoyne, Sieur de Bienville, and was alternately under French and Spanish rule, although the French culture has always remained the most dominant. The fine arts were highly treasured in

New Orleans society, and the number of French opera houses and orchestras was unusual for a city of its size. There was an Old World vigor and zest for life, a high degree of permissiveness, a tolerance for cultural pluralism, and a general laissez-faire attitude that encouraged free and open expression by many people in many ways. Like the West Indies, New Orleans was a Latin-Catholic colony and, as mentioned in Chapter 3, was more lenient toward cultures outside the mainstream.

The New Orleanians of French and Spanish descent who were born in the New World were called Creoles. The French culture, which was the most dominant, was a point of pride, and Creoles maintained their cultural ties with the motherland. One custom held by Creole men was the open practice of having a second household or, in simpler terms, keeping a mistress. This was an accepted practice in New Orleans society, bound by a contract with the mistress's parents and the provision of living quarters in the downtown area. These women were often of mixed blood.[2] From these relationships emerged a subclass called Creoles of Color, which we will refer to as Creoles, superseding the original designation of strictly white French descendents.

Creoles, being of mixed blood, were tolerated by the dominant white New Orleans culture as a unique class of people, higher in the social hierarchy than darker blacks but not quite to the level of whites. They were permitted to work and live in the downtown area, known today as the *Vieux Carré*, or "French Quarter," which was predominantly white. The Creoles were careful to accentuate the European rather than the African part of their ancestry, lest they be associated with the darker black population of uptown New Orleans. This kind of racial and cultural tolerance would have been unthinkable elsewhere in the South. Creoles continued to follow French culture; those who could afford it sent their children to France for their education.

Music was encouraged, but only on an amateur basis. To play music professionally was to plunge to the social depths reserved for gypsies, actors, and prostitutes. Those who pursued music did so in the European tradition, often studying with orchestra musicians at the opera houses. The Creoles neither knew nor cared about the musical traditions that were being developed by their blacker cousins uptown.

Blacks in New Orleans had no problem with playing music professionally, since they had no social position to defend anyway. Many rich musical traditions were present within the black milieu. There was the repertoire and performance practice of the black church. There was an Afro-Latin contingency, as blacks from Latin-Catholic Caribbean settlements, such as Haiti and Cuba, came to New Orleans. Until 1855 blacks routinely performed traditional African dances and music on a public green known as "La Place Congo." Even after it was officially banned, the practice continued underground for another 30 years; and we can assume that some of the earliest jazz musicians witnessed it in their childhood.

Brass Bands and Jazz Bands

One of the strongest musical and cultural traditions in New Orleans was the black social clubs, similar to Masonic lodges or Shriners. These civic organizations acted as social meeting places for the community, vehicles for charity, and, especially, funeral arrangers. The concept of ancestor worship, spirit appeasement, and elaborate funeral rites was a throwback to African customs. By belonging to one or more of these societies one was ensured of a proper funeral.

One of the societies' amenities was a parade band that escorted the funeral procession from the church. Typically, these bands would play a slow dirge, usually an appropriate hymn, on the trip to the cemetery. After the grave-side ceremony, the band would play a hymn, up-tempo and syncopated, in "hot rhythm" as they called it.

These bands played for other functions as well—dances, citywide parades such as the Mardi Gras, outdoor picnics, and backyard garden parties. This multiplicity of performance settings required the bands to maintain a versatile and wide-ranging repertoire. Many black musicians had the opportunity to study formally to varying degrees, and they could (at least at one time) read music. In general practice, however, the musicians had long ago memorized the music and were compelled to add a little touch of their own to the arrangement.

Let us again consider our model march, John Philip Sousa's "Stars and Stripes Forever." In examining the general texture of the band, we hear the "oom-pah" bass rhythm and the independent horn lines over it. Traditional marches have three basic components: the melody played by the cornets, a fluttering countermelody played above the melody by the woodwinds, and an embellished bass counterline played by the trombones. The black parade band musicians, always men, approximated this textural effect by ear; although once a musician had worked out his part, he probably stuck pretty close to it from one performance to another.

Once in a while a smaller band was needed, one that would fit in the backyard of a private residence or on the back of a wagon. The band was then trimmed to one clarinet, one cornet, one trombone, a banjo or piano (depending on the setting), and a drummer. This became the basis of the instrumentation and the function of the individuals in early jazz bands.

Another way the parade band heritage nurtured jazz was through an institution called the *second line*. The second line was essentially the people who followed the band along its route. This would include spectators, dancers in the street, and other groupies. Among these were young black boys who acted as personal errand boys for the band members and carried instrument cases or whatever. In return, the band members were obliged to teach the youngsters how to play the instruments. Band members were further obligated to pass along, orally, the band repertoire and the accepted manner in which to improvise embellishments. This is how the earliest jazzmen received much of their training.

Meanwhile, fate had turned against the Creoles. At about the time of the Louisiana Purchase in 1803, when France sold its territory to the United States, the dominant white society began to systematically chip away at the fragile social position held by the Creoles. By the mid-nineteenth century Creoles had begun to flee New Orleans; by the late-nineteenth century the remaining Creoles had been almost completely disenfranchised. A Louisiana Legislative Code was passed in 1877 that effectively obliterated the ambiguous policies over the social treatment of people of mixed ancestry. Anyone with any black blood would henceforth be considered black. Creoles lost their downtown businesses and their social positions and were eventually little better off than blacks. They were forced to live and to interact with the uptown blacks and, among other things, to learn to play music with them on a regular basis.

Black musicians taught the Creole musicians how to play in hot rhythm (syncopating a melodic line and playing eighth notes unevenly), how to add tonal and timbral manipulations, and how to "fake" music. The Creoles, in turn, brought European traditions, including their music, to the black community. Along with the repertoire of marches, spirituals, and hymns they already played, the black bands added the European set dances played by the Creole orchestras, dances such as the polka, the mazurka, the waltz, and the quadrille. Like the march and, soon after, ragtime, these dance forms were usually multithematic.

Another element in the development of jazz was the emergence of ragtime and blues as popular forms of music. These band units played in many contexts, including dances; and, like any dance band, these groups were expected to play popular requests of the day. Ragtime numbers have a lighter oom-pah 2/4 feel, whereas blues were played with a slow, thumping 4/4 feel. Eventually, the rhythmic feels combined and a hybridized and distinctive rhythm emerged. The string bass or tuba may have played on the first and third beats while the banjo played on all four beats.

By the turn of the century, the new music was firmly in place. It had developed slowly and naturally, and its practitioners were probably unaware that something unique had grown out of the multifaceted New Orleans music tradition. The music flourished within the confines of the black community, but it went virtually unnoticed by white New Orleanians.[3] Local stars began to emerge, those musicians most revered by other musicians and those most requested by the listening public. Charles "Buddy" Bolden (1877–1931) was one of the first notable musicians. Others of his generation included cornetists Joe "King" Oliver (1885–1938) and Freddie Keppard (1889–1933), trombonist Edward "Kid" Ory (1886–1973), and pianist Ferdinand "Jelly Roll Morton" Le Menthe (1890–1941). It is unfortunate that there are no recordings of the music from these formative years. We can only listen to the first recordings made in Chicago and New York in the late teens and early twenties—no doubt already affected to some degree by the popular music industry—to determine how these musicians played in New Orleans.

Storyville

One of the old legends linked with early jazz is its connection with Storyville, New Orleans' infamous red-light district. Because New Orleans was a major river port and distribution center, many merchants and transport workers came to the city for business *and* pleasure. Prostitution had gotten so out of hand that the city fathers, in an attempt to control it, designated a legal prostitution district in 1898. It was unofficially given the name Storyville, to the chagrin of Alderman Sidney Story who was the author of the legislation that established the district.

The edge of "Storyville," New Orleans' infamous red-light district. In the foreground is the saloon of Tom Anderson, the unofficial mayor of Storyville.

It was once purported that Storyville provided employment to many of New Orleans' jazz musicians. Upon the district's demise in 1917, so the story goes, the musicians' livelihood perished with it and they left New Orleans to seek work in Chicago. In fact, very few bands worked in Storyville. Most of the bordellos' parlors were small and quite inappropriate settings for a loud six- or seven-piece band; it was pianists who most readily found work in the district. The closing of Storyville by the Navy Department during World War I had little effect on the migration of band musicians out of the city.

Jazz Leaves New Orleans

Musicians had trickled out of New Orleans all along. Jelly Roll Morton left town around 1907 and wandered through Mobile, Memphis, Chicago, and California. (When in Memphis, he frequented W. C. Handy's haunt, Beale Street, and wrote one of his most famous compositions, "King Porter Stomp.") Kid Ory, King Oliver, and others also had gone to California, targeting the red-light districts in Los Angeles and San Francisco. This is probably when black musicians in other cities first heard the new music and copied it.

White musicians copied the new music too. In New Orleans, a few enterprising white musicians had formed ragtime bands and were soon engaged to play in cabarets in Chicago. The most successful of these was the Original Dixieland Jazz Band (ODJB), with "jass" being the original spelling of the word. *Jazz* was not originally a word applied to music; it was street slang with sexual connotations. The term was first used by an irate Chicago music establishment in an attempt to denigrate the origins of the music and repel potential customers. As is usually the case, designating jazz as the forbidden fruit only intrigued the public, and the music became a hit.

After an engagement in New York, the ODJB made the first jazz record at Victor Studios in 1917. The historical irony is that a white New Orleans band introduced a black music to the world. While the quality of the ODJB performance is debatable, the fact remains that through a mass medium and their live performances in the United States and Europe, they introduced a startling new sound to the public. The domain of jazz recording was ruled by this band until at least 1922, when another white New Orleans band, the New Orleans Rhythm Kings, began recording in the Chicago area.

Black jazz musicians had been moving into Chicago as well. Black newspapers such as *The Chicago Defender* had told of better-paying factory work in northern urban centers, initiating a mass migration of black and white southerners. Chicago's black section was its South Side, and it was there jazz would flourish.

A studio portrait of the Original Dixieland Jazz Band from 1917, the year they recorded the first jazz record. Left to right: pianist Henry Ragas, clarinetist Larry Shields, trombonist Eddie Edwards, cornetist "Nick" LaRocca, and drummer Tony Sbarbaro.

Joe "King" Oliver came to Chicago in 1922 and formed his Creole Jazz Band. The band was made up of New Orleans veterans, with the exception of Memphis-born Chicago pianist Lillian Hardin. Oliver's band was unusual in that he had a second cornet, a position filled by young Louis Armstrong. After playing for a time at

Studio photo of King Oliver's Creole Jazz Band in 1923. Almost all the members of the band were from New Orleans and greatly influenced many later jazz musicians through their recordings and live appearances in Chicago. Left to right: trombonist Honore Dutrey, drummer Warren "Baby" Dodds, cornetist Joe "King" Oliver (standing), trumpeter Louis Armstrong (kneeling with a novelty slide trumpet), pianist Lillian Hardin (the only non–New Orleanian and later wife of Armstrong), banjoist Bill Johnson, and clarinetist Johnny Dodds (brother of Baby Dodds).

Chicago's Royal Gardens, the Oliver band made the trip to Gennett Records in Richmond, Indiana (where many of these Chicago jazz artists recorded), to make a series of records that would be the first significant performances by a black jazz band. The most influential recording of the series was Oliver's own "Dippermouth Blues."

Analysis of "Dippermouth Blues" (*SCCJ*, 1/5)

"Dippermouth Blues" is multithematic like a rag piece, whereas blues are typically strophic. The ensemble portions are collectively improvised, though this practice of improvisation comes closer to prearranged playing without music. Of particular note is the well-coordinated work between the two cornets, an atypical combination in a New Orleans–style jazz band.

The rhythm section is playing a 4/4 feel rather than a lighter 2/4 feel typical of ragtime. Baby Dodds plays rhythms reminiscent of a syncopated march or tap-dance rhythm. He is not playing the drums but the woodblocks, a standard instrument in his live performances. They were necessitated also because of the older acoustic method of recording that did not record drums well.

The most outstanding feature of this 1923 performance is the cornet solo by Joe Oliver. The fact that it is covered somewhat by the doodling of the other wind instruments and was worked out, for the most part, in advance does not detract from its brilliance. It is an essay in economy, effectiveness, and formal balance. In one neat package, this 1923 performance summarizes the major features of jazz music and has become an influential model for generations of jazz musicians.

The opening gesture is straightforward enough: a blue (lowered) third to the tonic note B-flat (see Figure 6.1). The entire solo rarely exceeds an octave and only involves five or six notes; the same can be said for most of blues singer Bessie Smith's recorded performances. What Oliver and Smith do with those few notes is remarkable, proving the adage from an old song title "It Ain't What You Do,

FIGURE 6.1

A Blue (lowered) Third to the Tonic Note B-flat

It's the How What You Do It." Between the blue third and the tonic, for instance, Oliver applies several types of manipulation to achieve expressive tension and release: (1) The pitch smoothly rises then falls from the first pitch to the second. (2) Vibrato is delayed until just before he stops the second note, so that vibrato is used not for general tone production but as an expressive device. (3) Oliver uses a mute on his cornet, a plunger or his hat. He places it over the bell of his cornet and quickly fans it immediately after starting each note, giving the cornet a wah-wah articulation, a common product of timbral manipulation.

In the first four measures of Oliver's second solo chorus he plays a three-note motive in a free rhythm that would be virtually impossible to put into music notation accurately. While this is not an example of swing in the strictest sense, the fluidity of Oliver's rhythm is an example of a relaxed rhythm over the tension of the insistent quarter-note pulse in the rhythm section.

The third chorus of Oliver's solo begins with a two-note repeated figure at the high end of the solo's overall range. The combination of repetitiveness and range is the perfect choice here, demonstrating a plan whereby the beginning of each successive solo chorus becomes more dramatically tense. Additionally, the banter of the other instruments gradually moves toward the foreground, almost engulf-ing the last third of Oliver's solo; the tension he creates seems to simultaneously egg the band on and fight to maintain command of the moment.

The final chorus of the piece is the same as the first; the band plays a collective improvisation. The performance ends with a two-bar extension of the last chord, a typical New Orleans practice.

Listening Guide   6.1
"Dippermouth Blues" 4 beats per measure

ELAPSED TIME	FORM	EVENT DESCRIPTION
:00	Intro	Trumpet duet (4 measures)
:05	A	Ensemble (12 measures)
:21	A	Ensemble (12 measures)
:37	B	Clarinet solo by Johnny Dodds, stop-time (12 measures)
:54	B	Clarinet solo by Johnny Dodds, stop-time (12 measures)
1:11	A	Ensemble (12 measures)
1:27	Solo (C)	Cornet solo by Joe Oliver (12 measures)
1:44	Solo (C)	Cornet solo by Joe Oliver (12 measures)
2:00	Solo (C)	Cornet solo by Joe Oliver (12 measures)
2:16	A	Ensemble (14 measures: 12 + 2 extension)
2:35	End	

There are other wonderful recordings by transplanted New Orleans musicians, such as cornetists Freddie Keppard and Henry "Red" Allen or clarinetist Jimmie Noone, but the series of Creole Jazz Band recordings certainly represent some of the best music these musicians had to offer.

Jazz had been in a constant state of evolution from the time it became jazz until these recordings, although we have no way to monitor its progress other than from the testimony of participants and eyewitnesses of the music. The evolution process continued even after jazz was first recorded. We have to remember that although jazz was something radically new to much of the world in the late teens and early twenties, it was at least 20 years old to those who introduced it. It was time for the music to move on. New Orleans musicians were being affected by the music around them as much as the music around them was affected by jazz. Likewise, musicians from outside the New Orleans milieu wanted to try their hand at jazz but had not grown up with the musical traditions that were second nature to New Orleans musicians. This had a great deal of bearing on the development of jazz and produced offshoots of jazz and new facets to the music. Its days as a well-kept secret with a certain regional and ethnic context were coming to a close.

In the next chapter we will profile three significant jazz figures who produced some of their most important work in the Chicago setting. Two are youngsters who forged a new path for jazz, and one is a jazz musician who epitomized the older New Orleans style.

Chapter Summary

Jazz is a unique form of African-American music in its cultural origin, its blend of musical traditions, and its eventual move toward high art rather than commercial pursuit. It evolved in its native city of New Orleans, Louisiana, a city laden with the Latin-Catholic culture it shared with the islands of the Caribbean. New Orleans' relaxed social codes allowed for tolerance and free intermixing of different ethnic groups. This was exemplified by the middle-class status afforded to the Creoles of Color, light-skinned blacks who continued the customs of the dominant French culture and were musically trained in the classical manner.

Darker blacks in New Orleans played music primarily by ear, and they freely embellished the melody and rhythms of preexisting hymns and marches. Circumstances finally brought the Creole musicians and the black musicians together, and they created a distinctive syncopated march music derived from rags, blues, spirituals, and African-Caribbean music. Its instrumentation, repertoire, and texture came from the black parade bands.

Throughout the first 20 years of the twentieth century, musicians from New Orleans took their music around the country; but its greatest commercial impact initially was in Chicago. It was here that the white New Orleans band, the Original Dixieland Jass Band, first lit the fire of commercial success for jazz. It culminated in their recording the first jazz record in New York in 1917.

The first significant black band to record was King Oliver's Creole Jazz Band, a group of New Orleanians based in Chicago, who made their recordings in 1923. King Oliver's straightforward solo on "Dippermouth Blues" taught the world the beauty of the jazz style.

Additional Listening

Jelly Roll Morton, "King Porter Stomp" (1939) (*SCCJ*, 1/9). This is a demonstration of Morton the solo pianist. The piece follows the form of a rag. Morton plays a highly embellished style reminiscent of the texture in the early jazz bands, with several musical lines going on simultaneously. Notice how each improvised variation on the third theme gradually builds the performance to an exciting climax.

Various Performers, *Jazz Classics in Digital Stereo, Volume 1: New Orleans* (BBC Enterprises Ltd., BBC CD 588). This is the first CD in a 1986 edition featuring early jazz entertainers, including group performances by New Orleans greats such as King Oliver, Louis Armstrong, Jelly Roll Morton, and the New Orleans Rhythm Kings.

Various Performers, *Riverside History of Classic Jazz* (Riverside SDP 11). This five-LP set includes jazz performances from New Orleans and early Chicago jazz musicians as well as performances by classic blues singers, folk-blues singers, ragtime piano rolls, and prejazz genres. The Riverside collection is available on CD in a three-volume set from Fantasy/Riverside (1994).

Video Source

Jazz: A Film By Ken Burns (VHS and DVD format, 10-volume set, PBS Home Video, 2001). This engaging series was originally aired on PBS television in January 2001. It was produced by Ken Burns, celebrated documentary filmmaker of films on the Civil War, baseball, and others. Heavily biased toward earlier jazz, due to the influence of some of the film's participants, most notably trumpeter Wynton Marsalis, it is still a fine achievement and well worth checking out.

The Story of Jazz (VHS format, BMG Video, 1997). In the 1990s, BMG released a series on jazz and blues, most produced by filmmaker Toby Byron. **The Story of Jazz** is a 90-minute overview of jazz, informative and delightful. As with the Ken Burns series, it shortchanges jazz from around 1970 on, but is very well done as far as it goes. **The Story of Jazz** is also included in a six-volume box set that contains biographies of Count Basie, Thelonious Monk, Sarah Vaughan, and John Coltrane, and a fine blues documentary, **Bluesland,** that can be effectively used for Chapter 3–5 of this book.

Various Performers, *Ken Burns's Jazz: The Story of American Music* (CD format, Columbia/Legacy C5K 61432). This five-volume set is the companion to the PBS film documentary series broadcast in January of 2001 (see Video Source above). Since the demise of the *Smithsonian Collection of Classic Jazz,* this set has taken up the slack. It includes most of the important recordings found in the *SCCJ* and updates its collection to more current artists and recordings.

Review Questions

1. What was the cultural atmosphere in New Orleans that encouraged the development of jazz?
2. What were the functions of black brass bands in New Orleans and what kinds of music did they play?
3. What was the form and texture of the march, and how do these relate to the early New Orleans jazz bands?
4. How did the New Orleans musicians use improvisation in their jazz performances?
5. What was the second line in the New Orleans brass band tradition?

6. When the Creole musicians were forced to live and play with the darker musicians of uptown New Orleans, what did the two groups contribute to each other musically?

7. What was Storyville, and which jazz musicians did it employ? What impact did its closing have on jazz?

8. What events led to the recording of the first jazz record?

9. What elements of Joe "King" Oliver's solo on "Dippermouth Blues" demonstrate the jazz stylings of his day?

Notes

1. An excellent, if somewhat dated (1956), introduction to jazz is Leonard Bernstein's lecture *What Is Jazz?* (LP format, Columbia CL919, reissued on CD in 1998 by Sony Classical), featuring many prominent jazz stars.

2. Interracial marriage and the bearing of children of mixed blood were common occurrences in New Orleans. Popular events were the quadroon and octoroon balls, where wealthy businessmen were escorted by women of mixed blood.

3. For instance, in researching the scrapbooks of Werlein's, New Orleans' oldest music store, it seemed as though the New Orleans music establishment was oblivious to the musical occurrences in the black community. Attention was focused more on recitalists appearing at the opera houses. Jazz seemed to be a total mystery to Werlein's when they advertised the first jazz record in 1917.

Chapter 7

Jazz Pioneers in Chicago

Jelly Roll Morton (1890–1941) was a Creole pianist and composer from New Orleans. In his youth he played piano in the bordellos of Storyville. Morton's recorded solo piano performances demonstrate that he (and perhaps other New Orleans pianists) was using some of the same musical innovations as the New Orleans bands: an embellished bass (like the trombone), a syncopated melody with uneven eighth notes (like the cornet), and high decorative fills (like the clarinet). He also used improvisation to about the same degree as New Orleans band musicians. Compare Scott Joplin's performance of his own "Maple Leaf Rag" with Morton's interpretation (*SCCJ*, 1/1, 1/2).

After extensive traveling around the United States between 1907 and 1923, Morton arrived in Chicago and recorded some piano solos (mostly his own compositions) and made some piano rolls for player pianos. His body of compositions includes rag and blues numbers, all well organized and balanced in their melodic and textural variety and in their integration of prescribed and improvised material.

New Orleans pianist and composer Ferdinand "Jelly Roll" Morton. Morton was an early and prolific composer of jazz and blues, including "King Porter Stomp."

Morton's most famous activity began in 1926, when he formed a studio band called the Red Hot Peppers. The band was made up primarily of ex–New Orleans musicians who were appearing with different bands in Chicago. In this setting Morton proved to be an inventive and thoughtful arranger. He combined the instruments of the standard New Orleans–style band in various ways that complemented the contrasting themes in his compositions. It is unlikely that many of Morton's arrangements were written out; yet he insisted that his musicians improvise in such a way as to serve the composition instead of stealing the moment from the band.

Analysis of "Grandpa's Spells" (*SCCJ*, 1/8)

"Grandpa's Spells," originally a piano rag written by Jelly Roll Morton, was recorded by him in 1924 as a piano solo. For our analysis we shall study the arrangement Morton did for his Red Hot Peppers band in 1926.

Typical of a rag, the piece has three 16-bar strains, with the third strain modulating up a fourth. Typical of the jazz treatment of a rag, the first two strains are repeated once apiece and the third theme is repeated four or five times, devoted to improvised variations by the different soloists. In this manner the first two strains act almost as introductory material or as a prologue to the third strain. The form of "Grandpa's Spells" is illustrated in Figure 7.1.

Morton's arrangement shows his characteristic variety of instrumental combinations that perfectly complement the composition. Following the four-measure introduction, the first A strain is played in stop-time rhythm by solo guitar in the low register answered by the ensemble. The second A is played in stop-time by the cornet and answered by the ensemble. It is not an exact repetition of the melody played by the guitar, but it is related to it rhythmically and in the design of its phrasing.

The presentation of the B strain compares *and* contrasts with the A strain in two ways. First, the full ensemble plays all the way through the strain, contrasting with the call-and-response format of the A strain. It compares with the A strain in that it continues the format of four bars of stop-time followed by four bars of steady rhythm. The repeat of the B strain is played by solo clarinet, balancing the ensemble presentation of the previous B.

The A strain appears once more; and Morton chooses, on this third time through, to fragment the music orchestrationally. Instead of one soloist versus ensemble, as in the first two A strains, Morton has two soloists. The trombone and bass, the two low instruments, play two measures apiece, followed by four measures of ensemble.

We now come to the C strain. The key moves up a fourth; and the solo cornet, playing with a mute this time, introduces the theme. To contrast with the fragmented orchestration of the previous strain, the cornet solo continues for the duration of the 16-bar strain. The second time through, C is a clarinet solo. In contrast to the cornet solo, the band plays stop-time accents behind the clarinet. The third time through, the C strain is shared by the piano and clarinet. The piano plays the first half unaccompanied by the rhythm section; the clarinet plays the second half accompanied by a calypso-flavored guitar rhythm. The fourth and final repetition of the C strain is played by the entire ensemble as a rousing finale.

FIGURE 7.1

Diagram of the Form of Jelly Roll Morton's "Grandpa's Spells"

```
            Part 1              Part 2
         ┌─────────┐        ┌─────────┐
         A A I B B I A I    I C C C C
Key: I                      IV
```

Listening Guide   7.1
"Grandpa's Spells" 4 beats per measure

ELAPSED TIME	FORM	EVENT DESCRIPTION
:00	Intro	Ensemble (4 measures)
:04	A	Guitar solo vs. ensemble, stop-time (16 measures)
:23	A	Cornet solo vs. ensemble (16 measures)
:41	B	Ensemble, piano solo break (16 measures)
1:00	B	Clarinet solo (16 measures)
1:18	A	String bass and trombone solos vs. ensemble (16 measures)
1:37	C	New key, muted trumpet solo (16 measures)
1:56	C	Clarinet solo, stop-time (16 measures)
2:15	C	Piano solo, clarinet solo (16 measures: 8 + 8)
2:33	C	Ensemble (16 measures)
2:51	Coda	Guitar solo, ensemble (2 measures)
2:54	End	

Louis Armstrong

Louis Armstrong (1901–1971) was born in New Orleans and from infancy heard the myriad forms of black music in that city. He sang in a quartet of street urchins as a young boy. When he was 12 he was impounded in the Colored Waif's Home for shooting a pistol during New Year's festivities. It was at the home that Louis took up the bugle—later the cornet—and upon leaving at the age of 16, he began playing professionally. Joe Oliver, Kid Ory, and the other elders of the jazz scene gave young Armstrong guidance and employment. After Oliver's travels brought him to Chicago to form his Creole Jazz Band, he sent for Armstrong to play second cornet.

During his nine-month tenure with Oliver's band, Armstrong was little more than a team player. His first recorded solo—the only one allowed him during this time—was on "Chime Blues." It was quite preplanned and not characteristic of his later style. He married the group's pianist, Lillian Hardin, who prepared him

Louis Armstrong's Hot Five in 1925. Many members were veterans of the King Oliver and Jelly Roll Morton bands. Left to right: trumpeter Louis Armstrong, banjoist Johnny St. Cyr, clarinetist Johnny Dodds, trombonist Edward "Kid" Ory, pianist Lil Hardin.

to leave Oliver and go on his own as a freelance artist. From 1924 on, Armstrong appeared with many bands in Chicago and New York and accompanied several classic blues singers, including Bessie Smith. (Refer to "St. Louis Blues" in Chapter 4.) During this period Armstrong became the Johnny Appleseed of jazz, profoundly influencing his musical constituency wherever he went. He taught musicians, primarily by example, how to play effective blues and hot-style jazz, concepts that were shared by many other New Orleans players but relatively unknown to northeastern white and black musicians.

Something else was evident in Armstrong's music, something unique and startling. He had a rare technical and creative talent, which emerged in his performances, that would set a new standard in jazz performance and redefine its very concept. These unique qualities included the following:

1. Louis Armstrong redefined the trumpet. His technical prowess far exceeded his predecessors or contemporaries. Whereas King Oliver's melodic lines rarely exceeded the range of an octave, Armstrong's range routinely covered at least two and a half octaves. The realm of the high C was almost exclusively his own. By extending the range of the trumpet, Armstrong expanded the melodic vocabulary of jazz. He set a new technical standard that future generations of musicians were expected to attain, if not surpass.

   His tone was bright and exciting. (He was one of the first jazz musicians to switch from the cornet to the trumpet, favoring the latter's brighter timbre.) He pioneered unique effects on the trumpet, such as sliding up to a high note while pressing the trumpet's valves halfway down. This produces a squeezed effect that adds to the tension of the upward slide. Armstrong had a distinctive and intense vibrato—more of a lip trill—with which he placed emphasis on the key structural notes of his phrases.

2. Armstrong changed the context of solo improvisation whereby the solo became an event in itself, without necessarily being subservient to the arrangement. He was a rare creative genius, making him the likely pioneer of jazz improvisation as a soloist's art. Prior to Armstrong, jazz was usually improvised in a collective fashion. As evidenced in our discussion of Jelly Roll Morton, solo improvisations did not draw much attention to themselves; they were more a contributing factor to the overall arrangement. Under the influence of Armstrong, for that few moments the arrangement gives way to the individual performer, whose musical creation may indeed eclipse the arrangement in quality. (With Armstrong, this was often the case.) By the 1940s the freedom to improvise solos became the most treasured attribute in jazz, and New Orleans–style collective improvisation became outmoded. It takes a soloist of exceptional creative ability to spawn such a context, and Louis Armstrong possessed that ability.

3. Louis Armstrong possessed the unique creative gifts necessary for effective improvisation. In any type of composition, the creator of the music must take stock of those elements that generate tension and release and arrange them in such a way as to design a satisfying dramatic event. Those elements include: **melodic range** (how high or how low for how long), **rhythmic velocity** (a fast succession of notes, a long static note, or silence), **rhythmic displacement** (the degree to which the rhythms of the melody align with the underlying beat), **timbral manipulation** (adding vibrato, growls, or any variable to the degree of brightness or darkness in the sound of the instrument), and **the degree of consonance and dissonance** (from one melodic pitch to another *and* as the melody relates to the chords which accompany it). To effectively distribute these elements in a spontaneous manner is a remarkable feat. Couple these aspects of composition with the more intangible aspects of how they are executed in performance (simultaneously, in the case of improvisation) and you have the essence of a distinct and personal style.

Louis Armstrong pioneered the concept of *chorus-phrase,* or spontaneous improvisation. In our discussion of Jelly Roll Morton and other New Orleans musicians we observed that improvised playing was usually quite preplanned and that from one performance to another you could anticipate hearing many of the same ideas. Armstrong maintained that practice as well. (Compare his solos on "S.O.L. Blues" and "Gully Low Blues" from 1927.[1] They are the same piece with different lyrics, and his solos are almost identical. Comparing the small differences between them is an excellent illustration of how the older improvisational practice worked.) In addition, however, Armstrong made it a common practice to devise entirely new melodies on the spot, stringing phrases together to create an effective musical architecture. The exceptional thing about Armstrong, in this respect, was that he fulfilled this design without sounding the least bit calculated.

4. Louis Armstrong was also a formidable force in American popular singing. One of the marked advantages Armstrong had as a musician was a fine ear for singing. His concept of melody and phrasing in singing and trumpet playing were the same, even inseparable. He did not invent *scat singing* (the practice of using nonsense syllables instead of words to imitate the articulation of an instrument), but he was its first notable practitioner. His phrasing and flexibility of rhythm influenced many popular singers, most notably Billie Holiday.

Analysis of "Hotter than That" (*SCCJ*, 1/16)

This recording was made on Columbia's Okeh race record subsidiary. It was part of a series recorded between 1925 and 1928 by a studio band that was alternately called the Hot Five and the Hot Seven, under the leadership of Louis Armstrong. Though the group usually featured New Orleans veterans, such as Johnny and Baby Dodds and Kid Ory, and employed some of the stylistic conventions of the New Orleans bands, such as King Oliver's Creole Jazz Band, this was a new context for these musicians. Individual solos play a much more prominent role; arrangements are slicker and reflect the influence of popular dance bands of the day. (Armstrong greatly admired the "sweet" sound of Guy Lombardo's orchestra.)

"Hotter than That" prominently features the individual work of Armstrong, in his capacity as a vocalist and as a trumpeter, and guest guitarist Lonnie Johnson, who was also featured on Jelly Roll Morton's "Grandpa's Spells."

The piece opens with an eight-bar introduction and a statement of the 32-bar theme by Armstrong. Each succeeding chorus is preceded by a two-bar solo break. The clarinet takes the first solo, playing a full 32-bar chorus.

Armstrong follows with a scat vocal chorus, accompanied only by the guitar. Compare the lines he sings with those he plays on the trumpet. You will hear that, with the exception of a few effects and range differences that are idiomatic to the trumpet, the melodic ideas are very much the same. A particularly effective tension-building device is used in the last half of the vocal chorus. Armstrong sings a repeated figure that sounds like triple meter and superimposes it over the duple rhythm maintained by Johnson's guitar. The fact that Armstrong keeps this effect up for about six measures signifies that this was not intended to be just another dance piece, if a dance piece at all. That intention is even more doubtful in the next chorus, when the constant beat and tempo stops while Johnson and Armstrong indulge in a musical dialogue with no accompaniment. Unlike the subservient role of the New Orleans practice, these two soloists have stolen the show for two choruses.

The piano then ushers in the rhythm section to accompany a muted trombone solo that, while adequate, pales in comparison to the events of the previous two choruses. Armstrong once again takes command with a two-bar break leading into the final ensemble chorus. The break is a thrilling climbing chromatic figure, spiced with carefully placed accents and almost inaudible *ghosted notes*. Once the chorus has begun and the rhythm section reenters, the perpetual motion of the break figure is countered with a repeated note riff that serves more as a rhythmic device than a melodic one. It is the perfect choice by Armstrong for reenforcing the hard-driving rhythm required to achieve the triumphant big finish effect.

Listening Guide   7.2
"Hotter than That" 4 beats per measure

ELAPSED TIME	FORM	EVENT DESCRIPTION
:00	Intro	Ensemble (8 measures)
:09	Chorus 1	Trumpet solo, clarinet break (32 measures: 30 + 2)
:46	Chorus 2	Clarinet solo, vocal break (32 measures: 30 + 2)
1:23	Chorus 3	Scat vocal and guitar (32 measures + free tempo)
2:17	Interlude	Piano in tempo (4 measures)
2:21	Chor. 4 P1	Trombone solo, trumpet break (16 measures: 14 + 2)
2:39	Chor. 4 P2	Ensemble (8 measures)
2:48	Chor. 4 P3	Solo trumpet breaks (6 measures)
2:55	Coda	Trumpet vs. guitar (6 measures)
3:03	End	

A major turning point in Louis Armstrong's career came in 1929. He returned to New York from Chicago and performed the revue *Connie's Hot Chocolates* at Connie's Inn in Harlem. In that show he was featured on the Fats Waller song "Ain't Misbehavin'." He created such a sensation that he was soon on his way to becoming a major popular entertainment star and vocalist. He fronted the Luis Russell Orchestra throughout the 1930s before returning to a traditional New Orleans instrumental lineup in the mid-1940s. He also proved to be a convincing and charismatic actor. Given the typecasting of cinema's early years, Armstrong was often put in humiliating, minstrel-like roles, but his talent and charisma always triumphantly transcended the degrading contexts of the scripts. His appearance in the 1969 film musical *Hello Dolly* was so thrilling that he practically stole the scene from its star, Barbra Streisand.

The theme song from *Hello Dolly* was a testament to Armstrong's longstanding ability as a chart-topper. In 1964, at the height of Beatlemania in the United States, Armstrong's recording of "Hello Dolly" was the only American popular recording to compete with the Beatles for the top spot on the *Billboard* charts. He rose to posthumous popular heights with the black war comedy *Good Morning, Vietnam,* starring Robin Williams and featuring Armstrong's 1968 recording of "What a Wonderful World." His recordings have appeared in romantic comedies such as *Sleepless in Seattle* (1993) and *French Kiss* (1995). In the late 1990s his voice could still be heard on television commercials selling everything from tourism to cosmetics and allergy medications. He took the lion's share of the historical coverage in Ken Burns's exhaustive public television documentary *Jazz* (2001), released the year marking the centennial of his birth. He is truly a timeless musician and entertainer, honored even today by both the world of jazz artists and the popular audience.

Bix Beiderbecke

Leon "Bix" Beiderbecke (1903–1931) was born in the Mississippi River town of Davenport, Iowa. He was of German ancestry, and was raised in a cultural milieu that was midwestern middle-class. As a boy, Beiderbecke taught himself cornet and piano. He probably heard New Orleans musicians when excursion steamboats briefly docked in Davenport, but it is hard to say how much of an impact they had on him. We can be certain that he was greatly affected by the recordings of the Original Dixieland Jass Band (ODJB) and the New Orleans Rhythm Kings (NORK).

Beiderbecke came to Chicago in 1922, and the next year he formed a band of young white musicians called the Wolverines. They modeled themselves and their repertoire after the ODJB and the NORK and played primarily for college dances in the Midwest. During that time Beiderbecke went to Chicago's South Side to hear Joe Oliver, Louis Armstrong, and other black jazz musicians. In 1924, like so many other jazz musicians in Chicago, the Wolverines went to Gennett studios in Richmond, Indiana, to make recordings of their performances.

Beiderbecke worked with several ensembles, most notably with the Jean Goldkette Orchestra, a fine but short-lived band out of Detroit, and the Paul Whiteman Orchestra. His association with the latter organization marked the zenith of Beiderbecke's career, and it was during these years that he performed some of his most influential work.

Bix Beiderbecke's significance in jazz is marked by his originality and the legacy of those who were affected by it—white and black. His was a style that bore no resemblance to either the black South Side musicians or the other white musicians in Chicago that were his age or younger. His significance can be described as follows:

1. Beiderbecke founded a *cool school* strain of jazz, a term usually applied by historians to an offshoot of the bebop style in the late forties (see Chapter 9).

Cornetist Leon "Bix" Beiderbecke around 1925. He was the earliest major influential white jazz artist.

Whereas Louis Armstrong created an exciting solo style by using a bright trumpet sound, extended high range, a robust vibrato, and adventurous rhythms, the elements of Beiderbecke's style were the antithesis of Armstrong's. This is not to say that Beiderbecke's style was dull, but it was a decided alternative to Armstrong's approach.

Beiderbecke, unlike Armstrong, never switched from the cornet to the brighter sound of the trumpet. He developed a warm, mellow sound that was exceptional even among other cornetists, a sound his colleagues say was never adequately captured on recordings. He did not make extensive use of the high register of his horn.

Behind this rich, mellow sound was an introspective and modest character in Beiderbecke's playing that has been described as cool, cerebral, romantic, and intimate. This unassuming style is subtle enough that students of jazz history often contend that Armstrong's more flamboyant style overshadowed Beiderbecke's. This should not be the case. More recently, jazz trumpeter Miles Davis displayed a similar coolness in his approach to trumpet playing without anyone feeling it was overshadowed by the hotter style of Dizzy Gillespie or Clifford Brown.

2. Beiderbecke pioneered a viable ballad style in jazz. Do not be confused by the term *ballad*, which was defined in a different way earlier in this book. Ballads are generally defined as epic folk stories set in a strophic verse form. In the parlance of jazz and popular musicians, however, *ballad* also connotes a slow number, such as "Misty" or "My Funny Valentine." We will risk inconsistency in the use of this term because it is so commonly used in both contexts. This was a time of jazz and popular music when slow tunes were not very slow and fast tunes were not very fast; this music was primarily for dancing, and moderate tempos were expected, no matter what its character. In any event, slower pieces such as romantic or melancholy songs tended to be performed in one of two ways: either as plodding dirges, such as "West End Blues" (*SCCJ*, 1/17), or as syrupy-sweet emasculated renderings of the easy-listening variety played by hotel bands of the day. Beiderbecke offered an alternative. By virtue of his soft tone and introspective style, he brought an elegant and romantic approach to jazz performances of ballads without losing the virility of the jazz style.

3. Beiderbecke was one of the first modernists in jazz. His exposure to the arrangements of the Paul Whiteman band had a profound effect on his musical development. Much of the semiclassical side of Whiteman's presentation was derived from a late nineteenth- and early twentieth-century style of French classical music known as Impressionism.[2] The striking melodic and harmonic feature of this style is the use of the whole-tone scale (see Figure 7.2), with its raised fourth that renders an exotic sound to Western ears accustomed to the half step between the third and fourth tones of the diatonic scale.

   These and other factors compelled Beiderbecke to explore a subtle use of dissonance that pervaded his improvisations. Armstrong used dissonance sparingly and more for effect, but Beiderbecke used it as a standard part of his melodic language.

4. Beiderbecke achieved stature as an individual artist who inspired many musicians of his time. Cornetists and trumpeters such as Jimmy McPartland, Red Nichols, Bunny Berigan, and Bobby Hackett were the most conspicuous descendants of the Beiderbecke style. Songwriter Hoagy Carmichael was an ardent admirer and associate of Beiderbecke. Perhaps Carmichael's most famous song, "Stardust," was inspired by Beiderbecke's style of melodic invention.

FIGURE 7.2
Whole-Tone Scale

Analysis of "Singin' the Blues" (*SCCJ*, 1/21)

This recorded performance is one of the most celebrated in jazz. It features Beiderbecke and longtime colleague Frank Trumbauer. Trumbauer played the C-melody saxophone, an obsolete instrument whose range lies between the alto and tenor saxophones. Trumbauer and Beiderbecke's solos influenced many jazz musicians, including black saxophonist Lester Young and black trumpeter Rex Stewart. This performance is also exemplary of the ballad style that Beiderbecke was perfecting.

After the introduction, Trumbauer plays the first solo. In style and character he is similar to Beiderbecke: a velvety tone, an elegant and intimate presentation, and a sound almost devoid of vibrato.

Beiderbecke takes the second chorus of the song. Notice in the first four measures that he has a straightforward and effective technique for constructing his improvised solo. He plays a line in the first measure, repeats it in a slightly altered version in the second measure (to fit the change of chord), then plays a two-measure idea to balance the 1 + 1 combination. In the next phrase, he plays a four-measure line that balances the previous 1 + 1 + 2 phrase. This is a technique jazz historian James Lincoln Collier calls *correlated chorus*. It is a technique that closely follows the symmetrical construction of the preexisting music, where melodic phrases begin and end when the chords change. As jazz improvisation evolved, soloists began to construct phrases that did not line up with the chord changes (see Chapter 9); but this more "boxed-in" technique served early improvisors well, and Beiderbecke used it with finesse.

Notice that Beiderbecke's note choices are slightly eccentric, creating angular contours in his melodies. His notes are not wrong, but they are approached in an atypical way.[3]

Listening Guide   7.3
"Singin' the Blues" *4 beats per measure*

ELAPSED TIME	FORM	EVENT DESCRIPTION
:00	Intro	Cornet and saxophone duet (4 measures)
:07	Chorus 1	Saxophone solo (32 measures: 16 + 16)
1:04	Chorus 2	Cornet solo (32 measures)
2:02	Chor. 3 P1	Ensemble (8 measures)
2:17	Chor. 3 P2	Clarinet solo (8 measures)
2:32	Chor. 3 P3	Ensemble with guitar break (16 measures)
3:02	End	

Chapter Summary

Much significant music was recorded in Chicago, but the work of Morton, Armstrong, and Beiderbecke represents the best of Chicago jazz.

As mentioned at the end of Chapter 6, Morton was not so much an innovator in jazz as a culminator. He was about 20 years older than Armstrong or

Beiderbecke and was too set in the older New Orleans jazz practice to keep up with the innovations of his younger peers. Similar to Johann Sebastian Bach's role in culminating the Baroque style, Morton brought the New Orleans style to its most refined state, both within the realm of composition and in jazz arranging. While Morton was considered old-fashioned in his lifetime—again like Bach—we can look now with clear historical retrospection at the contributions Morton made to the *art* of jazz. His creative efforts forecast the compositional and coloristic traits of jazz musicians such as Duke Ellington, Thelonious Monk, and Gil Evans.

Armstrong and Beiderbecke represented a second generation of jazz musician, those whose innovations were fresh and exciting in this significant time (the 1920s) when the majority of the world was just coming to grips with the style of jazz. While differing markedly in their styles and musical personalities, Armstrong and Beiderbecke were equally influential in the jazz world, establishing the pillar and post of a new approach to improvisation and the hot and cool strains of jazz that would prevail for years to come.

Additional Listening

Jelly Roll Morton's Red Hot Peppers, "Black Bottom Stomp" (1926) (*SCCJ*,1/6). This is another fine example of Morton's arrangements and probably the most celebrated of the Red Hot Peppers' sessions. This piece contains only two themes. Notice the rhythmic variety in the rhythmic section: two-beat, four-beat, a Charleston or "Spanish tinge" rhythm, and a strong drum backbeat at the end.

Jelly Roll Morton's Red Hot Peppers, "Dead Man's Blues" (1926) (*SCCJ*,1/7). In this arrangement there is the addition of a clarinet trio section.

Louis Armstrong and His Hot Seven, "Potato Head Blues" (1927) (*SCCJ*,1/14). The highlight of this performance is the series of two-measure solo breaks in the last third of the performance. Armstrong continually builds through his improvisation and triumphantly leads the band back in.

Frank Trumbauer and His Orchestra, "Riverboat Shuffle" (1927) (*SCCJ*,1/22). This recording is a more up-tempo setting of Bix Beiderbecke's cooler style.

Louis Armstrong and His Hot Five, "West End Blues" (1928) (*SCCJ*,1/17). This is considered by many to be Armstrong's most memorable recorded performance. He opens with an intricate cadenza, all alone. His solo covers a tremendous melodic range and is rhythmically quite dramatic.

Review Questions

1. How was Jelly Roll Morton's jazz piano approach similar to the New Orleans jazz band approach?
2. What was Morton's composing and improvising approach?
3. What was Morton's orchestrational approach?
4. What are the four important aspects about Louis Armstrong's contribution to music listed in this chapter? Familiarize yourself with the boldface terms.
5. How did Bix Beiderbecke compare to Louis Armstrong in his cultural background and musical style?
6. What are the four important aspects about Bix Beiderbecke's contribution to music listed in this chapter?

Notes

1. Both selections can be found on the album *Hot Fives & Sevens, Vol. 3* (CD format, Columbia CK44422).

2. The musical characteristics of French Impressionism are the only aspects of the style that concern us here. If you listen to exemplary pieces such as Debussy's "Prelude to the Afternoon of a Faun," Maurice Ravel's "Pavane for a Dead Princess," or Paul Dukas's "The Sorcerer's Apprentice," you will hear the melodic and harmonic characteristics discussed in this chapter.

3. A good barometer of melodic eccentricity is its singability. Hoagy Carmichael wrote his famous song "Stardust" based on Beiderbecke's style of improvisation. It began as an instrumental number, and lyrics were added later by Mitchell Parish. It is very beautiful but a difficult song to sing.

Chapter  8

Big Bands and the Swing Years

The years from about 1935 to 1945 encompassed the most popular period for jazz and are usually referred to as the *Swing Era*. Through the efforts of some jazz musicians during the 1920s and early 1930s—Louis Armstrong, for instance—jazz moved away from the rhythmic and improvisational practice of its New Orleans days.

In New York a new kind of jazzman and a new sound were emerging. These musicians played as accompanists for classic blues singers during recording sessions. They also formed dance orchestras to play at various clubs in Manhattan and Harlem.

Fletcher Henderson and Don Redman

One of the most significant of these fledgling big bands, as they would be called, was the Fletcher Henderson Orchestra. Henderson (1897–1952) was a pianist who assembled his band from musicians he had led in blues recording sessions. Although he was a fine arranger, Henderson left much of the early arranging to his lead saxophonist, Don Redman (1900–1964). Many of these musicians had a good deal of formal training, which enabled them to write complex arrangements and to read them in performance once they were written.

In the beginning the Henderson band was not really a jazz band. The musicians played a lively syncopated dance music that was closer to ragtime. As it evolved, influences came from two distinct sources.

Louis Armstrong played with Henderson for about nine months in 1924 and 1925, and he brought his innovative, hot, swinging style with him. Armstrong's more relaxed rhythm and exuberant style was infectious, and it was absorbed by Henderson's players and arrangers alike.

The other influence was the Paul Whiteman Orchestra. Many early big bands modeled themselves after this highly successful band. This orchestra was the most popular dance band of the day and was quick to identify itself with the new catchword *jazz*. The impressive arrangements of Ferde Grofé, Lenny Hayton, and Bill Challis, with their liberal use of classical music elements as well as jazz, inspired the writing of other arrangers and led them to new heights of sophistication within the jazz idiom.

Jazz big band composer and pianist Fletcher Henderson around 1940. He was a pioneer of the swing big band concept, and his arrangements launched the career of Benny Goodman, the so-called King of Swing.

The instrumentation of these jazz big bands was significantly different from their New Orleans predecessors. Instead of the frontline horn section of a clarinet, trumpet, and trombone, bands like Henderson's were larger. They used a section of three (later four or five) saxophones, two trumpets (later three or four), and one trombone (later from two to four). The saxophone's appearance in dance orchestras came from the idea of using a section of them to reinforce or replace a section of strings, since they were louder but had a similar timbre. The family of saxophones (soprano, alto, tenor, baritone, and bass) corresponds neatly with the family of string instruments (violin, viola, cello, and double bass). Redman pioneered the arranging technique of pitting the saxophone section against the brass section, usually in a call-and-response manner. Another arranging technique, necessitated by the larger number of wind instruments, was *block* writing or *homophonic* writing. This means that the horns played chords and moved along in more or less the same rhythm, rather than playing independent *polyphonic* lines like the three-horn New Orleans bands.

In the early days of big bands the rhythm section commonly used the banjo and tuba; these instruments were loud and they recorded well. The drums were still used sparingly, as much for coloristic effect as keeping the beat. By the early 1930s the softer, more subtle and relaxed sound of the guitar and plucked string bass was favored. The instrumentation of the drum set evolved to include the *hi-hat* or *sock cymbal*. A distinctive, steady rhythmic pattern was played on the hi-hat, combined with a stroke of the bass drum on every beat. The bass drum reinforced the string bass and guitar, which also played a note or chord on each beat.

Written big band arrangements and improvised solos were developing at a parallel pace, and both had to coexist within the big band format. Many of the arrangements for the Henderson band had an equitable distribution of solo space and space featuring intricate section and ensemble work. Written backgrounds behind the various solos were carefully scored to complement the particular instrument that was being played. For instance, an alto saxophone solo might have soft, sustained brass chords accompanying it. A lively trumpet solo would have the saxophones as background, playing a repetitive, rhythmic figure to maintain the excitement of that particular solo sound.

Analysis of "Wrappin' It Up" (*SCCJ*, 2/2)

This is a Henderson composition and arrangement recorded in 1934. It is instructive to compare the performing and arranging style in this recording to "The Stampede" (*SCCJ*, 3/7), a Redman arrangement played by the Henderson band in 1926. The earlier recording uses banjo and tuba and stiffer rhythms all the way around. "Wrappin' It Up" dramatically demonstrates the culmination of a smoother swing style that had evolved during the intervening years.

"Wrappin' It Up" is a 32-measure form, subdivided into two 16-measure sections. The number opens with a brass figure played in consecutive upbeats and answered in the next two measures by the saxophones. This call-and-response continues through the eight-bar introduction, with the brass and saxes alternating every two bars, then every bar, then finally coming together in the last two bars of the introduction.

The theme is stated by the saxophones and answered at the end of each phrase by a short, one-note brass figure. In the second eight measures of the theme, the brass answer with a two-note figure. The brass finally join the saxes in the last 16 bars to finish out the theme.

The next chorus is an alto saxophone solo by Hilton Jefferson. The light sound of the alto is accompanied by soft, sustained brass chords in their middle and low register. The brass figures get a little pushy rhythmically in the last eight bars of the alto solo, but they soon return to their more submissive character.

The arrangement then builds with a bold trumpet solo by Henry "Red" Allen. The excitement of his solo is enhanced by a background of saxophones playing a busy, repetitive rhythmic figure. Allen's solo is interrupted briefly in the second eight bars of his chorus by an ensemble passage. He then regains the spotlight for the second half. Notice the timbral contrasts evident in the arrangement thus far: a reed solo accompanied by brass, followed by a brass solo accompanied by reeds.

Following Allen's solo there is a two-bar brass figure that actually extends the 32-bar chorus to 33 bars. This is a lead-in to the brass playing the opening theme that had been played by the saxes. They are answered every two bars by the reed section, now all playing clarinets. With each entrance, the clarinets alternate playing their figure in the high then low register. The second eight bars of the chorus are a clarinet solo with the brass again playing a soft sustained background. The second half of the chorus features the saxophone section in a very demanding eight-bar passage followed by eight bars with the full ensemble that ends the arrangement.

Listening Guide   8.1
"Wrappin' It Up" 4 beats per measure

ELAPSED TIME	FORM	EVENT DESCRIPTION
:00	Intro	Brass vs. saxes (8 measures)
:09	Chor. 1 P1	Saxes, short brass answers (16 measures)
:28	Chor. 1 P2	Ensemble (16 measures)
:49	Chor. 2	Alto sax solo, brass background (32 measures)
1:27	Chor. 3 P1	Trumpet solo, sax background (8 measures)
1:36	Chor. 3 P2	Ensemble (8 measures)
1:46	Chor. 3 P3	Trumpet solo continues (16 measures)
2:05	Chor. 4 P1	Brass vs. clarinets (9 measures: 1 + 8)
2:16	Chor. 4 P2	Clarinet solo (8 measures)
2:25	Chor. 4 P3	Saxes (8 measures)
2:34	Chor. 4 P4	Ensemble (8 measures)
2:45	End	

Count Basie

A different approach to the big band developed in Kansas City, Missouri. During the Prohibition years of the 1920s and early 1930s, Kansas City had a lively music scene that attracted musicians from Texas to Chicago. Unlike their New York counterparts, black musicians in the Southwest were part of a long tradition of the blues

Pianist and bandleader William "Count" Basie in London, 1957. His band, founded in 1936, was the most prominent proponent of the Kansas City swing style.

and boogie-woogie styles. Generally, they also had less formal training and were incapable of writing or reading the complex arrangements in the manner of Redman or Henderson. Instead, more emphasis was placed on the individual solo, a practice that was honed to perfection in countless after-hours jam sessions.

Big band arrangements were simple affairs, many times created on the spot. Typically, a member would dictate a short melodic figure to the band. The band would then play the figure several times in succession, either in unison or with improvised harmonization. Musicians call this short, repeated phrase a *riff,* and these impromptu arrangements were called *riff charts.* As the Kansas City style of arranging evolved and more arrangements were committed to paper, the riffing tendency was retained. Audiences and musicians alike were captivated by these riff figures that possessed more rhythmic than melodic interest.

The greatest of the Kansas City bands was the Count Basie Orchestra. William "Count" Basie (1904–1984) was a pianist from Red Bank, New Jersey. He got his style from Fats Waller in New York and came to the Southwest in the 1920s. Basie played with Walter Page's Blue Devils, a band based in Oklahoma City, and with the Bennie Moten Orchestra in Kansas City. After Moten's death in 1935, Basie eventually formed a band using many of the same members.

Among other things, Basie possessed the finest rhythm section of the swing era: Basie on piano, Walter Page on bass, Freddie Green on guitar, and Jo Jones on drums. Prominent soloists included alto and baritone saxophonist Jack Washington, trumpeter Buck Clayton, trombonist Dickey Wells, and tenor saxophonists Hershel Evans and Lester Young.

Analysis of "Doggin' Around" (*SCCJ, 2/20*)

This recording was made in 1938 and is typical of the riff chart style. It is a 32-bar AABA popular song form. Note that the only prominent ensemble passages are the saxophone section melody at the beginning and the ensemble riff at the very end. The rest of the performance is involved with solo presentations accompanied by occasional ensemble backgrounds.

After a piano introduction, the saxes play the opening riff, answered by the brass. The B section has no precomposed melody but achieves its contrast from the A theme by featuring an eight-bar solo improvisation, in this case Jack Washington on alto sax; this practice is typical in riff charts. The sax riff finishes the first chorus.

The second chorus begins with a solo by tenor saxophonist Hershel Evans. Evans's sound is deep and husky, and he adds a wide vibrato to certain notes for emphasis, much as Louis Armstrong did on trumpet. This style of tenor saxophone was established by Coleman Hawkins (1904–1969), star soloist with the Fletcher Henderson orchestra. For contrast on the bridge of the chorus, trumpeter Buck Clayton takes over as soloist, accompanied by the saxes. Jack Washington returns, this time on baritone sax, to finish out the chorus.

The next chorus is a solo by Basie. Here is a marvelous example of his economical, yet effective style that proves less is more. Basie makes great use of space and silence in his solo, but the few notes he plays are strategically placed to enhance and propel the momentum and excitement of the steady pulse kept by the rhythm section.

Basie's solo is followed with a tenor saxophone solo by Lester Young (1909–1959). Young's sound was quite different from most of the tenor players of his day; it was based on the softer sound of Frank Trumbauer (Chapter 7). Basie's favorite arrangement format was to pit Young and Evans against each other in *tenor battles*. Young's cooler character is the perfect follow-up here to Basie's understated approach.

Young's solo chorus is followed with a drum solo by Jo Jones. Then the arrangement is completed by a brass riff accompanied by an ascending saxophone section line.

Listening Guide 8.2

"Doggin' Around" 4 beats per measure

ELAPSED TIME	FORM	EVENT DESCRIPTION
:00	Intro	Piano (8 measures)
:07	Ch. 1 A × 2	Saxes riff, brass answer (16 measures)
:22	Chor. 1 B	Alto sax solo (8 measures)
:30	Chor. 1 A	Saxes riff, brass answer (8 measures)
:38	Chorus 2	Evans's tenor sax solo, brass riff (32 measures)
1:10	Ch. 3 A × 2	Trumpet solo, sax riff background (16 measures)
1:25	Ch. 3 B, A	Baritone sax solo (16 measures)
1:41	Chorus 4	Piano solo (32 measures)
2:13	Chorus 5	Young's tenor sax solo, brass riff (32 measures)
2:45	Interlude	Drum solo (8 measures)
2:53	Coda	Brass vs. saxes, based on A of the form (8 measures)
3:02	End	

Benny Goodman

Swing was a fully formed style by the 1930s, but it had not been accepted into the mainstream of American popular music. The band most responsible for that acceptance was the orchestra of Benny Goodman (1909–1986). Goodman was a white clarinetist born in Chicago. A midwestern youngster, such as Bix Beiderbecke, he haunted the bars of the South Side to hear black New Orleans musicians. His style was heavily influenced by New Orleans clarinetist Jimmy Noone and Memphis clarinetist Buster Bailey. All three studied with the same clarinet teacher in Chicago.

Clarinetist and bandleader Benny Goodman performing in New England in 1953. He was most responsible for initiating the swing craze of the 1930s.

Goodman worked through the Depression years as a successful sideman and formed his first band in 1934, with the help of entrepreneur and record producer John Hammond.[1] Goodman's band purchased the Fletcher Henderson library, which provided the basis for its style.[2] (Henderson's orchestra had gone bankrupt by 1934 and disbanded.) Later, when Hammond discovered Count Basie's Orchestra, Goodman began to feature some of Basie's arrangements with his own band. The Goodman band opened the field for scores of white and black bands and initiated an unprecedented period of popularity for swing music. Eventually, bands led by trombonists Tommy Dorsey and Glenn Miller, clarinetists Woody Herman and Artie Shaw, and saxophonists Jimmy Dorsey and Les Brown took their place of prominence in the Swing Era. There were many others—too many to mention here—but Goodman is conspicuous in the history of jazz as the benchmark of its success.

More significant to the history of jazz were the various small groups led by Goodman. These groups borrowed personnel from other bands and displayed a liberal racial mixing of musicians that was uncommon for the day. One group was a trio made up of Goodman, drummer Gene Krupa (1909–1973), and black pianist (and Hammond discovery) Teddy Wilson (1912–1986). Later, black vibraphonist Lionel Hampton (b. 1909) was added to the group. Goodman also led sextets including trumpeter Cootie Williams, saxophonist Georgie Auld, Count Basie and his rhythm section, and electric guitarist Charlie Christian. This meld of great jazz musicians and the improvisational freedom afforded by the small group context produced some of the finest musical moments in jazz. (Listen to "I've Found a New Baby" or "Breakfast Feud" on *SCCJ*, 2/23 and 2/24, respectively.)

Duke Ellington

An anomaly among big bands was the orchestra led by Edward Kennedy "Duke" Ellington (1899–1975). Ellington's style of writing was like no other, and no one continually reached the ambitious level of high art within the context of popular music the way he did.

Ellington brought his band to New York from Washington in the early 1920s. His band, like Fletcher Henderson's, began as just another syncopated dance orchestra. Two significant factors shaped the early Ellington style.

The first was the hiring of trumpeter James "Bubber" Miley (1903–1932). Miley had successfully absorbed the hot New Orleans style of King Oliver and Louis Armstrong and affected Ellington and his band in much the same way that Armstrong did Fletcher Henderson's band. Additionally, Miley perfected a freakish growl effect on his trumpet, a combination of manipulating a plumber's helper, or "plunger," over the bell and a throat growl. (Listen to the 1927 version of "East

Composer, pianist, and bandleader Edward Kennedy "Duke" Ellington. The prolific number and stylistic range of his music and the longevity of his career make him stand out from other jazz bandleaders and have established him as one of America's greatest composers.

St. Louis Toodle-Oo" [*SCCJ*, 3/1] to hear Miley's style.)

The second factor was the band's tenure at Harlem's popular Cotton Club from 1927 to 1931. The Cotton Club was typical of Harlem venues at the time. It was operated by a mobster, Owney Madden, and geared to sell illegal liquor during the era of the Prohibition. The club's policy was also to offer black entertainment to a primarily white Manhattan audience. The Cotton Club shows catered to the desires and stereotypes of that white audience, featuring light-skin chorus girls doing shimmy dancing to hot jazz. There were low-down bluesy numbers, specialty dancing by tuxedo-clad acts such as the Nicholas Brothers, and even exotic African settings, featuring the cast in grass skirts and feathered head dressings.

As house orchestra, the band played behind singers and dancers for these musical revues; Ellington was required to compose and arrange prolifically. His personnel remained relatively stable, and this familiarity with his players' unique styles became the pervasive force in his compositional and arranging process.

Ellington obtained an art scholarship from the NAACP to the Pratt Institute of Art in New York. He did not, however, choose to pursue a career in the visual arts. He did, however, bring his ideas of color, texture, and mood to the manuscript page rather than the canvas. Many of his compositions show a preoccupation with correlating these ideas, with titles such as "Mood Indigo," "On a Turquoise Cloud," "Blue Serge," "Magenta Haze," and "Lady of the Lavender Mist."

As mentioned above, Ellington's compositional and orchestrational conceptions were inextricably linked with the unique stylistic properties of the members in his band. Ellington did not label his individual parts "Trombone 1," "Trombone 2," and "Trombone 3" but rather "Lawrence," "Sam," and "Juan," because he knew how distinctive these three individuals sounded and how their sound would function within the context of what he had written. There was the sweet, romantic, bluesy sound of Johnny Hodges's alto sax, the gritty forcefulness of Harry Carney's baritone sax, the dark, wooden tone quality and fluid solo lines of Barney Bigard's clarinet, the plunger growl of Cootie Williams (Miley's successor), and the solid, yet supple technique displayed in the bass playing of young Jimmy Blanton.

This individualistic tendency in Ellington's ensemble writing compelled him to write passages using unusual combinations of instruments, leading many music historians to label him one of the great orchestral "colorists" in jazz. Whereas Fletcher Henderson arrangements usually featured section writing, solos, and full ensemble passages, Ellington created exotic consorts within his bands. A favorite combination was a low-register clarinet in harmony with a muted trombone and trumpet. "On a Turquoise Cloud" features a combination of bass clarinet, muted trombone, violin, and a wordless female vocal!

Ellington's career lasted well into the 1970s. Unlike many of his peers who had big bands in the 1920s through the 1940s, Ellington wrote prolifically for his own band. And it was not just dance material. Ellington was a master composer of expansive concert music for the jazz orchestra and of popular songs that rivaled those of Tin Pan Alley's finest songwriters. Due primarily to racism, he was denied the Pulitzer Prize for music during his life in the 1960s, but in 1999, the centennial of his birth, he was posthumously given a special and belated Pulitzer award.

Analysis of "Ko-Ko" (SCCJ 3/4)

This recording was made in 1940 during a peak productive period for Ellington. It was also a time that saw the greatest combination of instrumentalists Ellington ever assembled.

"Ko-Ko" is a blues in E-flat minor, a key that creates a particularly dark quality in the voicing of the chords in the orchestra. It is classified as one of Ellington's "jungle pieces," featuring jungle-style drums by Sonny Greer, exotic chord voicings, savage, stabbing rhythms in the brass, and chantlike melodies.[3] The most notable aspect of "Ko-Ko" is that it is a programmatic concert piece, not a dance number, even though it is played with a danceable beat at a danceable tempo.

The number opens with Sonny Greer's tom-toms and a sustained bass note from Harry Carney's robust baritone sax; together they give the effect of a timpani, or kettledrum. The trombones play a dramatic introduction followed by the first theme. It is played by Juan Tizol on valve trombone; this particular instrument's musical character is plaintive and mysterious.[4] Tizol is countered by the saxophone section's aggressive answer to his chantlike melodic figures.

The next solo is also a trombone solo. Usually this would be considered a redundant and poor orchestrational choice, but Ellington knew his trombone section and how different the individuals could sound. This second trombone solo is by "Tricky" Sam Nanton. He played a trombone version of Bubber Miley's plunger style, but his sound took on a strange vocal quality, like someone singing the vowels "Ya Ya." He is playing forcefully in the upper range of his horn, and he is accompanied by two trumpets and one trombone playing short, jagged rhythms and using plunger mutes like Nanton. Beneath that is a more sustained line in the saxophones.

Ellington builds tension in the next section by compressing the individual brass and saxophone figures from the previous section. Over this he plays dissonant clusters and sweeping scalar lines on his piano, accentuating the savage character of the piece.

The intensity builds further in the next section with a climbing four-note figure layered in turn by the reeds, trombones, and trumpets, all meeting on an abrupt two-note figure. The shriek of the horns gives way to a two-measure walking figure played by Jimmy Blanton's bass, then the horns return with the same degree of ferocity. The bass and horns continue this exchange for the remainder of this section.

In the final climactic section, the brass, topped by a screeching clarinet, hold long chords while the saxophones play a busy unison line. The introduction returns, and the piece ends with one more slowly climbing figure from the horns.

Listening Guide   8.3
"Ko-Ko" 4 beats per measure

ELAPSED TIME	FORM	EVENT DESCRIPTION
:00	Intro	Trombones, tom-tom rhythms (8 measures)
:13	Chorus 1	Tizol's valve trombone solo, saxes answer (12 measures)
:32	Chorus 2	Nanton's plunger trombone solo, plunger brass (24 measures)
:52	Chorus 3	Nanton's solo continues
1:09	Chorus 4	Piano solo, long sax riff, plunger brass riff (12 measures)
1:28	Chorus 5	Trumpet riff, reeds and trombone answer (12 measures)
1:47	Chorus 6	Ensemble alternates with bass solo (12 measures)
2:06	Chorus 7	Sax melody, brass and clarinet chords (12 measures)
2:25	Coda P1	Trombones, tom-tom rhythms like intro (8 measures)
2:37	Coda P2	Ensemble rising chords over tom-toms (4 measures)
2:45	End	

An Overview of Other Big Bands in the Swing Era

Large dance orchestras were, of course, not invented with the advent of the Swing Era of the thirties. We already noted Paul Whiteman as a formidable influence on jazz musicians such as Bix Beiderbecke and Don Redman. There were other successful dance orchestras of the day as well, led by Vincent Lopez, Art Hickman, and Ben Selvin. These were white orchestras with access to the major recording labels, the finest and most prestigious ballrooms, and the most exposure on radio. The playing and writing in these bands constantly displayed the technical perfection of some of the finest musicians in the country. But they were also extremely conservative in their approach and leaned toward the sweet side of popular music.

Meanwhile, black bands were creating a bold and driving music wherever the prevailing racial customs allowed. Through the exposure that Benny Goodman eventually gave this music, it was mainstreamed into popular music, encouraging an influx of other white and black bands hoping to vie for Goodman's title as the "King of Swing." Now "sweet" and "hot" coexisted before the mass audience. Some bands remained sweet, some remained hot; some of the most successful tried to do both. Music magazines such as *Metronome* and *Down Beat* conducted readers' polls for the best band in each of these two categories. As Frank Sinatra points out:

> The big bands differed as much in personality as any random bunch of individuals you might pass on the street. Some tried for a strictly commercial style and a mass audience; sometimes the corn was as high as a piccolo's A. Others, and this was especially true when the swing era began, had objectives that reached beyond entertainment and dancing; they played for fans who wanted to listen, think, and even analyze.[5]

Glenn Miller

Perhaps the swing band most familiar to the general public—and many times the only name known to younger generations—is the Glenn Miller Orchestra. Miller (1904–1944) started as a sideman trombonist and arranger in some of the

Trombonist, bandleader, and arranger Glenn Miller. Though he did not form his band until late in the swing craze, his band became the most popular and well known throughout the years with hits like "In the Mood," "Moonlight Serenade," and "A String of Pearls."

dance orchestras of the 1920s. Riding on the wave of Benny Goodman's popularity, Miller finally made a splash with his own band in 1939. He, like Goodman, was a perfectionist; and, through his efforts as a bandleader and arranger, he developed the most commercially viable style of any of the swing bands. In the manner of Goodman and the black bands, Miller played swinging numbers such as "In the Mood," "A String of Pearls,"[6] and "Pennsylvania 6–5000." But he also knew how to blend in just the right amount of sweet, with ballads such as "Moonlight Serenade," "Sunrise Serenade," and "Elmer's Tune." A particularly identifiable element in the Miller style is the orchestrational technique of clarinet lead over saxophones. Even though Duke Ellington had used this sound for years, it had not been used by other bands, and most of the general public was not aware of Duke Ellington at the time. Also, it had not been used in quite the way that Miller presented it.

Tommy Dorsey

Dorsey (1905–1956) was an early colleague of Goodman, Miller, and Bix Beiderbecke, playing in various orchestras of the 1920s. Before considering his formidable success as a bandleader (from the thirties until his death), we should note that he was one of the finest trombonists in any style. Along with Jack Teagarden (1905–1964), Dorsey refined the technique of jazz trombone and advanced it beyond the *tailgate* style of New Orleans. Unlike the gruff, slippery jazz trombone of the past, Dorsey presented the trombone as a facile and beautiful solo instrument. In fact, his tone, sense of phrasing, and remarkable breath control was the primary influence on Frank Sinatra, who was a singer for the Dorsey band in the early 1940s.

After sharing leadership of a band in the late 1920s and early 1930s with his brother Jimmy,[7] Tommy Dorsey formed his own band. It was one of the most popular and long-lasting of the Swing Era's big bands, but it was only intermittently a jazz band. From 1935–1940 the band was alternately Dixieland and sweet oriented. Around 1940, the band acquired the arranging talent of Sy Oliver (1910–1988) and became a true jazz-oriented band. ("Opus 1" is the most famous Oliver number for Dorsey.)[8] Alternately, the Dorsey band rendered beautiful romantic ballads, performed not only by Dorsey on his supple trombone but also by Frank Sinatra and his vocal group the Pied Pipers. ("I'll Never Smile Again" is one of the most famous ballads by these singers.)

Artie Shaw

One of the most intriguing personalities in the Swing Era and the only real threat to Benny Goodman's clarinet expertise was Artie Shaw (b. 1910). His sensitive personality and conspicuous intellect ill-equipped him for the pressures of musical commercialism, throngs of adoring fans, and relentless gossip about his private life; and his band was probably one of the most unstable. The band was formed and disbanded eight times between 1936 and 1955 before Shaw withdrew from the music scene permanently, devoting the rest of his life to writing books and working the college lecture circuit.

Emerging from his sideman days with most of the bandleaders mentioned above, Shaw formed a curious group that consisted of a Dixieland band with string quartet! The violinist/arranger for the band was Jerry Gray. The band was re-formed in 1937 as a more conventional swing band. The big commercial breakthrough came in 1938 when Gray arranged Cole Porter's "Begin the Beguine," Shaw's most famous recording.[9] The band's success also was greatly enhanced by the addition of drummer Buddy Rich and vocalist Helen Forrest.

Woody Herman

Herman (1913–1987) began as a sideman in the band of popular and influential Isham Jones, a contemporary of Paul Whiteman. After its demise, Herman reorganized the band under his own name. Designated "the band that played the blues," the band met with success in 1939 with the riff chart "Woodchopper's Ball." They played other material as well, such as ballads sung by Herman, who possessed a lovely crooning voice. The band also did high-spirited novelty songs and technical showpieces, such as "Apple Honey," "Lemon Drop," and "Caldonia."

Herman himself was a clarinetist and alto sax player. While not as technically adept as Goodman or Shaw, he was a tasteful and distinctive reedman. His clarinet playing was reminiscent of Barney Bigard, a New Orleans–born clarinetist with Duke Ellington, and his alto playing was reminiscent of Johnny Hodges, the lead alto player with Ellington.

Herman's band was also one of the first bands to apply the innovations of the emerging bebop style to a big band context.[10] (Bebop is discussed in the next chapter.) His band was an all-star group that produced some of the finest jazz soloists and studio arrangers and players in the country. The following list names only a few of these stellar musicians.

Arrangers: Ralph Burns, Neal Hefti

Saxophonists: Stan Getz, Flip Phillips, Zoot Sims, Al Cohn

Trumpeters: Pete Candoli, Sonny Berman

Among other innovative products of the Herman band was "Ebony Concerto," which was expressly written for Herman and his band by the distinguished composer Igor Stravinsky in 1946.

Long after the demise of the Swing Era, Herman continued to lead innovative jazz bands, acting as a catalyst for the careers of many fine players, composers, and arrangers, until his death in 1987.

There are many, many bands from the Swing Era that cannot be covered within the scope of this book, ranging from Lawrence Welk to Stan Kenton. There are surprising and wonderful musical moments to be enjoyed in listening to some of these bands.

Though sweet and hot coexisted for a while in the Swing Era, the processes of commercialism soon prevailed. The music of the bands became more polite; the arrangements became more conservative and began to crowd the space previously reserved for improvising jazz soloists. The greatest fame, money, and exposure was again relegated to white artists. But musicians would continue to explore the furthest depths of their creative and technical abilities in intimate jam sessions, a pursuit that would eventually flower into *bebop*, the style of the forties.

Other forces worked toward the demise of the swing big bands. Many of the sidemen in the big bands became stars in their own right, demanding huge salaries that no band could support. With the outbreak of World War II, many of the sidemen were drafted for military service. Rationing of gasoline and other products curtailed touring and record production. From 1942 to 1944 the musicians' union imposed a ban on recording; singers, however, were not union members and were exempt from such restrictions. The public's attention was gradually given over to these singers, whose popularity finally eclipsed the bands they had appeared with. The heyday of instrumental jazz had ended.

Chapter Summary

The Swing Era of the thirties and forties was the most commercially successful period for jazz. This age emphasized big bands, a phenomenon created primarily in New York that grew out of the society and ragtime bands of the 1910s. Through exposure to the looser rhythmic feel of New Orleans musicians, these society bands adopted the hot style of playing.

Fletcher Henderson and Don Redman pioneered intricately written arrangements, featuring both improvised solos and dazzling section and ensemble work. They established big band arranging standards, such as block writing and saxes versus brass dialogue. In Kansas City a simpler arranging technique was used. Short, rhythmic riffs were repeated in lieu of elaborate melodies, and more emphasis was given to soloing. These two approaches were blended with the band of Benny Goodman, a white clarinetist and bandleader who, along with record producer John Hammond, popularized hot big band jazz with the mainstream audience.

With the commercial success of Goodman, the way was open for a number of black and white big bands, playing sweet and hot styles and everything in between. The orchestra of Duke Ellington, however, was unique among the other bands. While he was a success with popular audiences, Ellington also composed ambitious concert works customized to the individual styles and talents of his band members, winning the admiration of artistic audiences.

Additional Listening

Refer to citations in the footnotes and in the body of the text.

Review Questions

1. What were the two distinct sources that influenced Fletcher Henderson's band?
2. Describe the instrumentation of the early jazz big band and how Don Redman wrote for the instruments in his arrangements.
3. How did the big band swing rhythm section change in instrumentation and style?
4. How did the written arrangements accommodate improvising soloists?
5. How did the Kansas City big band approach contrast with the Fletcher Henderson/New York style?
6. What were John Hammond's and Benny Goodman's roles in the popularity of big band swing music?

7. How did specific players in Duke Ellington's orchestra affect his arranging style?

8. Ellington was known as one of the great colorists in jazz. What is it about his writing style that would bring him this designation?

9. What is the orchestrational technique most associated with the Glenn Miller Orchestra?

10. What was Tommy Dorsey's contribution to the development of jazz trombone, and what singer did he influence with his remarkable sense of phrasing?

Notes

1. John Hammond is worthy of mention in any discussion of the Swing Era. It was he who initiated the idea of the Goodman orchestra, its purchase of the Fletcher Henderson library, as well as the discovery of greats such as Billie Holiday, Teddy Wilson, Count Basie, and Charlie Christian—all of whom played with Goodman on occasion. Without Hammond, there might not have been a Swing Era.

2. The recording of "King Porter Stomp" by Goodman's band (*Big Band Jazz: From the Beginnings to the Fifties* [Cd format, Smithsonian RD 030 DMC 4–0610], 2/9) is an arrangement by Fletcher Henderson that had been done by his band.

3. A common format at the Cotton Club, where Ellington had the house orchestra, was the "jungle number." It featured exotic dancers in grass skirts and skimpy, seductive costumes. The general exoticism of these productions was reflected in the sound of the music that accompanied them, and Ellington occasionally chose to draw upon the style in his later compositions such as "Ko-Ko."

4. The valve trombone, as suggested by its name, uses three valves like a trumpet rather than a slide. This gives it a slightly different timbre and enables the musician to play certain melodic lines easier than on a slide trombone. Ellington used Tizol in unusual ways befitting the technical qualities of his instrument.

5. Frank Sinatra, forward to *The Big Bands* by George T. Simon, 4th ed. (New York, Schirmer Books, 1981), p. xii.

6. *Big Band Jazz*, 3/10 and 3/11, respectively.

7. It should be noted that Jimmy Dorsey was also a masterful technician, in his case on the saxophone. He helped set the standard for that instrument in jazz and influenced many black jazz players of note, including Lester Young and Charlie Parker (Chapter 9).

8. *Big Band Jazz*, 2/17. "Well, Get It!" (2/15) and "On the Sunny Side of the Street" (2/16) are also Oliver arrangements performed by Dorsey's band.

9. *Big Band Jazz*, 3/6.

10. *Big Band Jazz*, "Down Under" (4/7), "Four Brothers" (4/10).

Chapter  9

Popular Styles in Jazz Since the Swing Era

JAZZ TAKES THE ROAD OF HIGH ART

By the mid-1940s a new generation of musicians had entered the field, and they spawned fresh ideas about how jazz should be played. This music acquired the name *bebop*, the scat syllables used in singing the rhythm and articulation of two swing eighth notes. The primary centers for the development of this music were Minton's Playhouse in Harlem and several clubs along 52nd Street; the two major pioneers of the style were Dizzy Gillespie and Charlie Parker.

John "Dizzy" Gillespie was born in South Carolina in 1917 and moved to Philadelphia as a teenager. He came to New York in the late thirties, frequented the clubs on 52nd Street, and began to develop a new style. He and pianist Thelonious Monk began to explore upper extensions of chords and relationships between melody notes that had not been used in jazz before. These elements are featured in Dizzy Gillespie's recorded performance of "I Can't Get Started" (*SCCJ*, 7/6).

Charlie Parker (1920–1955) was born and raised in Kansas City. He had moved to New York by 1944 and soon formed a quintet with Gillespie. Parker's reputation spread quickly, and the jazz world turned to the duo as the fountainhead for its musical language. By their own testimony, Parker and Gillespie fed off of each other. What each had developed independently they now unified into the most formidable voice in the world of jazz. An exemplary recording of Parker is "KoKo" (*SCCJ*, 7/8), his improvisation of the Tin Pan Alley song "Cherokee."

The basic repertoire for bop musicians was the body of Tin Pan Alley popular songs. The selection of music and the manner in which it was performed became more challenging and abstract, as opposed to functional (say, for dancing). Tempos were often extremely fast or extremely slow. The popular songs that were singled out had more interesting chord progressions and modulations through different keys. To add to the challenge, new instrumental melodies were devised to replace the original melody. These lines were sometimes repetitive riff melodies, reminiscent of the Kansas City style; but they were often difficult lines made up of fast eighth notes in long phrases.

Alto saxophonist Charlie Parker in New York, 1949. Along with trumpeter Dizzy Gillespie and pianist Thelonious Monk, he forged jazz into the modern age with a stylistic approach dubbed *bebop*.

In the 1930s jazz was thrust into the mainstream of popular music by white bandleaders such as Benny Goodman and Glenn Miller. The residual effect was that many black bands that had played hot swing music for a number of years gained some degree of prominence as well. Of course, the mainstreaming of jazz led to its homogenization by the music industry; it acquired a sweet sound and a preponderance of vocals. Bebop counteracted this process. It was too fast and too slow to dance to. The melodies were instrumentally abstract and did not lend themselves to singing. Rhythms were irregular and complex, and they obscured the basic 4/4 pulse that the audiences relied on for dancing. The nonmusician audience has only two basic ways to actively participate in a musical performance—they can either sing along or dance along. Bebop allows neither. The only means of active participation left for the audience is to *listen*, and that is a practice audiences have always been the least willing to implement.

Therefore, jazz lost most of its audience and took the road of high art. Some fans stuck with swing music; others reassessed the situation and decided that New Orleans– and Chicago–style jazz from the 1920s was the only pure form of jazz after all. This led to a Dixieland revival movement in the forties, with many of the clubs located right across the street from the clubs where the boppers played. Also, by the 1950s rhythm and blues and rock and roll had become the music of choice for many young blacks and whites; the inaccessibility of bebop only helped to steer more listeners in that direction.

The Birth of the Cool

Not long after the maturation of bebop, an alternative style arose. Whereas the music of Parker and Gillespie was characterized by jagged rhythms, edgy tone qualities, and a fiery delivery, there were players who followed the approach that was founded by Bix Beiderbecke and continued in the playing of Lester Young. The lighter tone quality and "cool," detached, and cerebral approach, along with a reawakened interest in integrating European art music with jazz, characterized some of the jazz musicians in the latter 1940s.

Cool jazz is often considered synonymous with *West Coast Jazz* from California, but this is misleading. Both New York and the West Coast developed a cool sound in jazz, but they developed independent of each other and at about the same time. On the East Coast, the postwar big band led by pianist Claude Thornhill was a major catalyst for the cool approach. Thornhill's was primarily an easy-listening band that explored soft, pastel sounds from the instruments in the band, particularly on slow ballads. The band also included instruments not usually found in a modern jazz orchestra, including multiple clarinets, bass clarinets, two French horns, and a tuba. Inclusion of these instruments made Thornhill's big band sound more like a classical wind ensemble.

One of Thornhill's arrangers was Gil Evans (1912–1988). Evans had perfected the soft, orchestral arranging style of Thornhill but, being in tune with the modern bebop jazz developments in New York at the time, embraced the new music of artists such as Dizzy Gillespie, Charlie Parker, and Thelonious Monk. Evans adapted several bebop compositions for the Thornhill band. Later, Gerry Mulligan (1927–1996), another Thornhill veteran, began writing bop-style arrangements for the band. Evans, Mulligan, and other arrangers formed a smaller ensemble based on the Thornhill band concept. Young trumpeter Miles Davis (1926–1991) was recruited to lead the band, whose recordings over 1949 and 1950 were eventually released as an album entitled *The Birth of the Cool*. The band met with little popular appeal from either audiences or the jazz community at the time and it lasted only a short while. In retrospect, however, *The Birth of the Cool* has turned out to be a tremendously influential album. A few years later, beginning in 1957, Davis and Evans collaborated again in a series of important albums for Columbia Records, using a larger, Thornhill-inspired orchestra and featuring Davis as the primary soloist. *Miles Ahead, Porgy and Bess,* and *Sketches of Spain* have proven to be some of the most enduring albums in jazz history.

Other New York musicians who developed the cool concept include John Lewis, pianist on one of the *Birth of the Cool* sessions and veteran of Dizzy Gillespie's big band. From the Gillespie rhythm section, Lewis formed the Modern Jazz Quartet. The MJQ specialized in incorporating classical music elements into its music and presenting itself, tuxedo clad, in formal concert settings. Its music was poised and restrained, and popular to many segments of the listening public. Another pianist living in New York at the time was Lennie Tristano, who had a literal school of young musicians playing with a light sound performing complex music.

As mentioned earlier, there was a simultaneous cool development on the West Coast. As Thornhill was the big band progenitor on the East Coast, Stan Kenton had the catalytic big band in Los Angeles. Seeking to redefine the jazz orchestra as more than a dance band, he featured ambitious jazz compositions geared more toward listening than dancing. Even though Kenton's music tended to be bombastic, the band did yield many veterans who pursued a lighter, softer-sounding brand of jazz. Lennie Niehaus, Charlie Mariano, Shorty Rogers, and others are included among these veterans. And there were occasions for the two coasts to mingle their cool music. Gerry Mulligan and Lee Konitz—a Tristano pupil, Thornhill member, and sideman on the *Birth of the Cool* sessions—worked in the Kenton band for a time; he then teamed up with Mulligan and West Coast cool trumpeter Chet Baker to record for the Pacific Jazz label in the early 1950s.

Dave Brubeck: Popular Ambassador of the Cool School

Cool jazz turned out to be a hit with college-age youth in the early 1950s. It combined a soft, unimposing sound with intellectual content, allowing the consumer to either zero in and contemplate it deeply or relegate it to the background of activity without it being overwhelming. Consciously or not, it became an erudite music, often found in bohemian coffee shops and bars, frequently adjacent to college campuses, and sharing its popularity with folk music revival acts (see Chapters 16 and 18). Some jazz acts decided to court the college crowd on its own turf—on campus. While most college music departments had a dim view of jazz and would not have welcomed jazz to their recital halls, a jazz performer could book through the university's student union council, comprised of students themselves. In this way, many jazz, folk, and popular music acts made their way onto campuses, appearing in the university's main auditorium or student center.

Cool style jazz artist Dave Brubeck, one of the most popular jazz artists of all time. He consciously courted college campuses for concert appearances and set sales records with his 1959 album *Time Out*, featuring saxophonist Paul Desmond's classic composition "Take Five."

Leading the way in this marketing effort was the Dave Brubeck Quartet. Brubeck (b. 1920) had thorough classical training, and many jazz aficionados considered his music to be only marginally jazz. He formed his quartet with alto saxophonist Paul Desmond in 1951, and in the early fifties he began actively soliciting college campuses to give concerts.

Paul Desmond's sound was light and pure. His improvisations were brilliant and lyrical. To many, he was the saving grace of the group. Brubeck's piano approach tended to be stiff and overdone, and few of his jazz colleagues liked his playing. He was, however, a fine composer, particularly of ballads. The bass and drums played light, almost transparent. As palatable and mild as the Brubeck Quartet's style was, the group made innovative strides in jazz. Their most popular album, *Time Out* (CD format, Columbia 65112), featured music in unusual meters for jazz, such as 9/8, on "Blue Rondo a la Turk," and 5/4, on the perennial favorite "Take Five."

Brubeck and his quartet consistently won *Metronome* and *Down Beat* readers' polls, his records sold in the millions, he toured the United States and the world extensively, and he even made the cover of *Time* magazine, the first jazzman since Louis Armstrong to do so.

Art Blakey and Horace Silver: Funky Jazz

Funky jazz was another brand of postswing jazz that occasionally achieved commercial success. It grew out of second-generation bebop in the 1950s. Known as *hard bop,* its name distinguished it from cool bop. The funky strain was a return to a more downhome, gospel-inspired style, combining complex bebop melodic and harmonic concepts with simpler, more elemental melodies. It was a jazz version of the prevailing rhythm and blues style in the 1950s.

The pioneers of the funky approach in jazz were Art Blakey (1919–1990) and Horace Silver (b. 1929). Art Blakey, a native of Pittsburgh, started out as a pianist, then switched to drums. He played with Fletcher Henderson's band in 1939, and by 1944 he was playing with the band of Billy Eckstine, a fine singer and the bandleader of an important bebop-style big band. By 1954 Blakey established a cooperative group, the Jazz Messengers, with pianist Horace Silver.

Horace Silver, a native of Connecticut, began his career playing with jazz tenor saxophonist Stan Getz. Getz, a cool-school player, rose to fame in the Woody Herman band and went on to popularize Brazilian *bossa nova* in the early 1960s. As a young man Silver was influenced by the bop pianists of the day, but other influences became a vital part of Silver's personal style. Of particular importance was a 1940 recording of "After Hours" played by the Erskine Hawkins orchestra and featuring pianist Avery Parrish.[1] Parrish's performance was slow, earthy, bluesy, and proved influential on many funky jazz pianists, including Ray Bryant, Ramsey Lewis, Bobby Timmons, Red Garland, and Wynton Kelly.

In the early 1950s Silver began featuring his own compositions with the Jazz Messengers and with his own group. While clearly part of the bop tradition, they were also tuneful and humorous. Silver's "Opus De Funk" and "The Preacher" are clear examples of the exuberance and catchy sense of melody inherent in all of his compositions. Silver's wit shows up in his titles also; he likes to name his pieces after distinctive personalities, people real or imagined, such as "Sister Sadie" and "Filthy McNasty." On the other hand, compositions like "Song for My Father" demonstrate a Latin music influence and "Peace" displays a more introspective or serene quality.

Blakey continued combining funky jazz with hard bop after Horace Silver's departure from the Jazz Messengers. Pianist/composers for the Jazz Messengers, such as Sam Dockery, Bobby Timmons, Cedar Walton and, more recently, James Williams, Mulgrew Miller, and Donald Brown, have maintained the heritage begun by Blakey and Silver, while asserting their own personal styles.

Bossa Nova

In the 1960s another substyle of jazz found favor with the general public. This was not an American musical style, and some may not consider it jazz because the *bossa nova* came from Brazil. Brazilians have their own rich tradition of folk and art music, which combines the cultural roots of Brazil's Portuguese, African, and native South American inhabitants. In the 1950s some Brazilian musicians became enamored with the light approach of American cool jazz and incorporated elements of it into their own musical styles. The result was the *bossa nova*, or "new beat." It combined a slower version of the *samba* with complex chord progressions of bebop. Its melodies were repetitive and singable, the lyrics (in Portuguese or translated into English) were sophisticated and romantic, the tempo and rhythmic feel was danceable, and the complex chord progressions offered a stimulating challenge to jazz improvisors. In most ways, it was pleasing both to bebop musicians and to the general audience.

It was certainly pleasing to cool-style saxophonist Stan Getz, who embraced the new music from the moment he first heard it. He collaborated with Brazilian composer-singer-guitarist João Gilberto in 1963 to record the album *Getz-Gilberto* (CD format, Verve 810048–2), which became a runaway best-seller. *Bossa nova* became a cherished style in jazz clubs as well as country clubs. Other Brazilian composers rose to prominence, particularly Antonio Carlos Jobim, composer of "Wave," "Desifinado," "Meditation," and the threadbare "Girl from Ipanema."

The popularity of *bossa nova* caused it considerable damage. Many inferior imitations came forth, both from the jazz and pop circles. Stan Getz feared that he would never be asked to play any other style again. In the long run, it has endured and continues to influence jazz and popular musicians to this day.

Jazz-Rock Fusion

By the mid-1960s rock had become a significant force in music. It had passed through its folklike beginnings, had penetrated the commercial music industry, and by this time was dominating world popular music. Along with the first

British invasion by groups such as the Beatles and the Rolling Stones, the black soul music of Atlantic and Motown became a new voice for black pride, a voice that was universally appealing.

It was at this time that rock music became artistically more self-conscious and began to drift away from the compact AM radio format with its four-minute single. England led the way with the Beatles' *Sgt. Pepper's Lonely Hearts Club Band* album and continued with artists and groups such as Graham Bond, Cream, Pink Floyd, and Soft Machine. These musicians recorded albums with extended solos and interrelated pieces that gave the entire album the character of a single multimovement work. Studio editing and effects, exploitation of electric instruments, and a higher standard of instrumental technique advanced rock to a new plateau in its development. These achievements gained serious attention from jazz musicians.

The same generation of musicians that were pioneering these advances in rock were also involved in the mainstream of jazz music. Many jazz musicians born in the twenties and thirties were influenced by rhythm and blues, and many jazz musicians born in the thirties and forties had matured with rock music. Rock was as much a part of their being as bop-oriented jazz. While working within the mainstream of jazz, these musicians felt a personal need to integrate aspects of rock music into their overall musical pursuits. This idea met with considerable resistance from zealous jazz journalists and critics who viewed rock music unworthy of the jazz musician's consideration. While the rhetoric has been toned down in more recent years, there is still an underlying sentiment that "jazz that don't swing ain't jazz!" Other writers and historians at least feel compelled to try and categorize the music along a continuum with jazz at one end and rock at the other, trying to decide the extent of the music's pedigree. In almost every case, however, the musicians themselves have no need to draw clear-cut lines in their style. They evolved smoothly into an electric rock setting, some occasionally returning to an acoustic jazz setting and some never looking back.[2]

The Evolving Miles Davis Group

No one did more to legitimize the incorporation of rock in the eyes of the jazz community than trumpeter Miles Davis (1926–1991). Davis began his jazz

Trumpeter Miles Davis. Davis maintained his prominence in jazz over 40 years, beginning his career with Charlie Parker in the 1940s and exploring jazz-rock fusion from the late 1960s until his death in 1990.

career as a member of Charlie Parker's quintet in 1945. In 1949 he collaborated in a nine-piece group that helped establish the cool approach to bebop. In the 1950s he established the premier group of the hard bop style, including tenor saxophonist John Coltrane and pianist Red Garland. By the 1950s he was greatly revered in the jazz community, admired as a restless innovator and experimenter. So when he

Pianist Herbie Hancock in November 1968. A veteran of the Miles Davis Quintet, Hancock explored modern jazz, jazz fusion, and even hip hop.

embraced rock, it seemed to give the go-ahead to the rest of the jazz world.

In the mid-1960s Miles Davis formed his second great quintet, with saxophonist Wayne Shorter, pianist Herbie Hancock, bassist Ron Carter, and drummer Tony Williams, all young men born in the 1940s. The group specialized in an updated, looser style of hard bop. In the latter part of the sixties that Davis group began to experiment with rock rhythms and instrumentation.

This experimentation was not new to Hancock. About the time he joined Davis's group in 1963, he recorded his first album *Takin' Off* (CD format, Blue Note B2–46506), which included a hit single "Watermelon Man." The rhythmic feel of the piece was similar to the music of James Brown, Ray Charles, Ramsey Lewis, and the so-called funky jazz of the late fifties by artists such as Horace Silver—all heavily influenced by gospel music. While with Davis, Hancock continued to record albums as a group leader and also continued his integration of funky soul elements with jazz.

In the meantime, former Davis alto saxophonist Cannonball Adderley had formed a quintet with his brother, cornetist Nat Adderley, and featured a pianist from Vienna, Austria, Josef Zawinul (b. 1932). The Adderley group was experimenting with gospel- and soul-inspired music. Zawinul's composition "Mercy, Mercy, Mercy" became a hit single and a Grammy award winner for best instrument in 1967. In addition to being a fine acoustic pianist, Zawinul was one of the first jazz keyboardists to explore the possibilities of the electric piano.

Miles Davis heard Zawinul and became intrigued with the sound of his Fender Rhodes electric piano. Davis had embarked on a series of experimental recording sessions, where he too was dabbling in electric instruments and rock and soul music. He assigned Herbie Hancock to the electric piano and began using rock-style electric guitarists, including Joe Beck, George Benson, and John McLaughlin, in his studio experimentations.[3]

The culmination of these efforts was the 1969 Miles Davis album *In a Silent Way* (CD format, Columbia CK40580), with the title piece composed by Zawinul. Historians consistently cite this album as the first widely influential jazz-rock album, though it was not the first such album. Vibraphonist Gary Burton (b. 1943), guitarist Larry Coryell (b. 1943), bassist Steve Swallow (b. 1940), and jazz drums legend Roy Haynes (b. 1926) had recorded the jazz-rock album *Duster* in 1967. (Burton, once a contract recording session vibist for RCA in Nashville, established a "heartland" folk-country style of jazz that continued through artists such as guitarist Pat Metheny.) *In a Silent Way*, however, marked a culmination in

1960s jazz-rock experimentation. Part of the impact of this album was because it was by Miles Davis, but another reason was that it also involved personnel from other jazz-rock groups of significant historical importance.

Tony Williams, John McLaughlin, and organist Larry Young had already formed the group Lifetime, highly inspired by the progressive British blues-rock band Cream (see Chapter 21) and West Coast psychedelia. McLaughlin himself was a British guitarist in the era of British guitar greats Eric Clapton, Jeff Beck, Jimmy Page, and, by adoption, Jimi Hendrix. Being influenced by Indian music and Hinduism, as many Westerners were at the time, McLaughlin formed the Mahavishnu Orchestra, a grand jazz–progressive rock band. The high energy and majestic quality of the group, related somewhat to the sounds of King Crimson or Yes, inspired Davis veteran Chick Corea (b. 1941) to form Return to Forever in the early 1970s. After a few years' break from jazz-rock, Corea formed the Elektric Band in the mid-1980s. Herbie Hancock formed the Headhunters inspired by Sly and the Family Stone and even had an early pop chart-topper with his song "Chameleon" (from the 1973 album *Headhunters*, CD format, Columbia/Legacy 65123). In addition to funk, Hancock was influenced by African music, as can be heard in the *Headhunter* album's reworking of his "Watermelon Man." In 1983 Hancock made a huge urban contemporary hit with "Rockit" from his album *Future Shock* (CD format, Columbia/Legacy 65962) and a popular MTV video to accompany it.

Miles Davis himself came to enjoy reaching out to the rock youth and consistently produced funk-oriented jazz albums until a self-imposed sabbatical from music around 1975. The most significant album from the early 1970s was *Bitches Brew* (CD format, Columbia/Legacy 65774), his immediate and more famous follow-up to *In a Silent Way*. When Davis returned to recording and performing in 1981, he continued his jazz-R&B fusion, now working closely with pop bassist and producer Marcus Miller. Davis's music became more tightly arranged and produced. He used the latest instrumental technology, appeared on MTV, and even covered pop repertoire of the day, such as Michael Jackson's "Human Nature" and Cyndi Lauper's "Time after Time."

John Coltrane

Any discussion of jazz must include the great tenor saxophonist and jazz spiritual leader John Coltrane (1926–1967). His vast career and accomplishments are worthy of a book by itself, and though he never played jazz-rock, he does deserve mention in this discussion of jazz-rock.[4] Coltrane was a star tenor player with Miles Davis during the 1950s, but he really blossomed with his own quartet during the first half of the 1960s. Coltrane had a spiritual and musical awakening, beginning in 1957. Musically, he incorporated elements of world music into his playing as well as the emerging concept of "free" jazz, spontaneous improvising with little or no regard for prescribed form, melody, or chords. His improvisations were muscular, lengthy, probing, and, above all, transcendental. The influence of his legacy can be found in many jazz-rock artists—for instance, Michael Brecker and Bob Mintzer. But his inspiration can also be heard in the Yardbirds' "Shapes of Things," the Byrds' "Eight Miles High," and the Doors' "Light My Fire," as well as the music of guitarist Carlos Santana. If there is a single album that might properly illustrate the spirituality and musical depth of Coltrane's music, it would be his 1964 album *A Love Supreme* (CD format, Impulse 155), his four-part musical prayer.

Jazz Musicians Cross Over

Musicians with jazz backgrounds had been working within the rock/pop mainstream for some time. Frankie Valli, lead singer of the Four Seasons (a popular early sixties vocal group), attributed his trademark falsetto style to his experience with jazz male vocal groups modeled after the Four Freshmen and the Hi-Los. The staff rhythm section at Motown Records was made up of Detroit jazzmen.

In 1967 the group Blood, Sweat and Tears came on the pop music scene. Their second album, simply entitled *Blood, Sweat and Tears* (CD format, Columbia 63986), yielded three hits. One of them, "Spinning Wheel," featured a jazz solo by trumpeter Lew Soloff, which was edited out for the radio airplay version and replaced by a brief and conventional guitar interlude. The six top 40 hits that BS&T enjoyed were invariably the cuts that showed the least jazz experimentation. Nevertheless, scrutiny of the material on their first few albums reveals their powers of jazz improvisation and ambitious arranging (especially by organist Dick Halligan) within the context of the pop music mainstream.

Another horn band that emerged about the same time and one that endured much longer was Chicago. Chicago was less rhythm and blues and funk-oriented than BS&T, and a jazz concept was less evident in their style of improvisation or arranging; but their presentation was no less ambitious. Chicago featured extended compositions, ambitious rock guitar solos by Terry Kath, and a penetrating unison horn sound by trumpeter Lee Loughnane, reedman Walt Parazaider, and trombonist Jim Pankow (formerly of the Woody Herman band).

Though BS&T and Chicago are only remotely jazz, their being labeled as such brought the mainstream of pop and jazz closer together. Soon the group Dreams was formed, with future jazz-rock greats such as Don Grolnick, Randy and Michael Brecker, and Billy Cobham. Longtime jazz producer and recording engineer Creed Taylor's CTI label began to feature jazz-rock, as well as postbop performances by artists such as George Benson, Freddie Hubbard, Grover Washington, Jr., Harvey Mason, Don Sebesky, Bob James, and Eumir Deodato. The Arista label premiered the Brecker Brothers in 1975, featuring bassist Will Lee and altoist David Sanborn. Another Arista group was the Jeff Lorber Fusion, with saxophonist Kenny Gorelick (now known as Kenny G.). Columbia and other labels presented saxophonist Tom Scott.

Groups and artists who work within jazz-rock are numerous. Tower of Power, the Yellowjackets, and Spyro Gyra are among the mainstay ensembles. Tribal Tech, led by guitarist Scott Henderson, has been another remarkable group. Jazz-bluegrass group Béla Fleck and the Flecktones (see Chapter 14) married traditional bluegrass with the virtuoso funk bass of Victor Wooten, and the trio Medeski, Martin, and Wood have blended 1950s organ trio music with 1960s psychedelic music and beyond. Finally, mention might be made of experimental saxophonist John Zorn, whose groups have blended everything from rock to spy movie soundtrack music. One of Zorn's most illustrious alumni, guitarist Bill Frisell, has likewise been faithful to no one style in his fusion efforts.

For many reasons of monetary or artistic gain, jazz musicians seemed to be pouring into the pop music mainstream. Older composer/arrangers, such as Benny Carter, Oliver Nelson, and J. J. Johnson, could be found in Los Angeles scoring music for television cop shows. Jazz-rock musicians backed up pop singers like Joni Mitchell, Maria Muldaur, and Paul Simon. Jazz-rock artists such as Will Lee and saxophonists Tom Scott and Branford Marsalis have appeared in or led late-night talk show bands. These musicians have abstracted their craft beyond the point of stylistic allegiance, choosing only to do whatever they do well. Michael Brecker is one of the most in-demand musicians in the New York studio scene, both as a jazz artist and as a versatile and competent sideman for everything from pop albums to deodorant commercials. Perhaps Brecker can serve as the model of the jazz musician as the complete musician, technically flawless, infinitely creative, versatile and respectful of all kinds of music, and unquestionably dedicated to his craft.

The Diversity of Jazz Today

Today the most conspicuous form of jazz is jazz-rock, recently packaged as *smooth jazz* and offered as an easy-listening alternative to heavier rock music. Although jazz-rock is the most recent development in jazz, the other traditions have not faded into inactivity.

Ragtime and Traditional Jazz

Traditional jazz is the preferred term for the practitioners of early New Orleans, Chicago, and New York jazz that is popularly known as Dixieland jazz. All over the country, traditional jazz festivals are held featuring bands like Jim Cullum's Jazz Band, the Black Eagle Jazz Band, the Hot Cotton Jazz Band, The Sons of Bix, and others.

Ragtime, jazz's stylistic predecessor, is often featured at these festivals; but it maintains its own distinct tradition apart from jazz. The most important festival devoted solely to ragtime is the Scott Joplin Ragtime Festival, held each June in Sedalia, Missouri, the birthplace of Joplin's monumental "Maple Leaf Rag." Some of the most notable recent performers at this event are pianists Max Morath, Richard Zimmerman, Dick Hyman, and John Arpin.

Swing

The dancing public continues to demand popular commercial hits like "In the Mood" and "One O'Clock Jump" from professional big bands, and "Hooked on Swing" albums or reissues of original artists are still big sellers. There are also numerous *ghost bands,* bands officially carrying the names of their deceased leaders (Glenn Miller, Count Basie, Woody Herman, etc.), that are keeping the music alive; and these groups are staffed with musicians of all ages.

A successful movement within educational and professional circles is toward jazz repertory ensembles. Repertory ensembles specialize in re-creating the original classic big band compositions and arrangements encompassing every stylistic era of jazz, but they tend to lean on the Swing Era music of Duke Ellington, Fletcher Henderson, and others. There have been several professional repertory bands of note, such as Chuck Israels's National Jazz Ensemble in the 1970s, John Lewis's American Jazz Ensemble in the early 1980s, and the Smithsonian Jazz Masterworks Orchestra from Washington, D.C. Certainly the most successful effort in the repertory field has been the Lincoln Center Jazz Orchestra, directed by trumpeter Wynton Marsalis.

Bop

Bop is the style that prevails above all others within the jazz milieu, although it possesses little popularity with the general public. Where, to many, jazz-rock seems too compromising and free jazz too unbridled, bop has succeeded as the mainstay in education and performance, somehow striking the right balance between conservative and progressive. By staying within these boundaries, bop offers structure without stricture. It represents a system of checks and balances that allows creative freedom within certain theoretical guidelines, keeping the music from sounding too old or too new.

While many jazz musicians play this so-called postbop style, the young alumni of Art Blakey's Jazz Messengers are particularly notable. Brothers Wynton and Branford Marsalis (trumpet and sax, respectively), saxophonists Billy Pierce and Donald Harrison, trumpeter Terence Blanchard, and pianists James Williams and Mulgrew Miller are included in this illustrious company.

Free Jazz

Free jazz was a concept that came about in the late 1950s as a reaction against the rigidity of bebop music with its many chord changes. Its goal was to free the improviser from preset chords and formal design. The results, however, can be quite dissonant and rambling to the average listener. Even though free jazz is the least appreciated form of jazz, it is courageously continued by its pioneers, such as Ornette Coleman, Pharoah Sanders, Arthur Blythe, and Don Cherry.

Beginning in the 1970s a second Chicago school of jazz was born; it was committed to experimental music. The Art Ensemble of Chicago, the Association for the Advancement of Creative Musicians, and Anthony Braxton are representatives from this Chicago scene. Sun Ra (1914–1993), based in Philadelphia, and the World Saxophone Quartet, based in St. Louis, also continued the free jazz cause. These artists successfully integrated elements of world folk music, twentieth-century art music concepts, and theatrical components (for example, recitation, and costumes) into their styles.

Latin Jazz

Latin music has always been a part of jazz; in fact, it was a key ingredient in the New Orleans musical gumbo that gave birth to jazz. What New Orleans pianist Jelly Roll Morton called "the Latin (or Spanish) Tinge" came from Cuba, Mexico, the Caribbean, and Central and South America. During the Swing Era of the 1930s the Latin side of jazz faded away, only to return with a vengeance in the 1940s when Dizzy Gillespie teamed with Cuban drummer Chano Pozo to fuse Cuban music with the new bebop style of jazz. There were also non-Latin advocates of Latin music, such as Stan Kenton and vibraphonist Cal Tjader.

From the 1940s on, Latin artists such as Machito, Mario Bauza, and Tito Puente led a vibrant New York Latin jazz scene that has continued in intensity to this day. There are many substyles of Latin jazz, the most well-known being *salsa*, but all generally use a traditional percussion battery of claves, cowbell, bongos, conga drums, and timbales, give or take a few other instruments. These are combined with jazz instrumentation of different configurations, from a couple of horns to a full big band. A few of the many current Latin jazz artists are trumpeter Arturo Sandoval and Paquito D'Rivera (both veterans of the Cuban jazz group Irakere), Eddie Palmieri, and Ray Barretto. These artists represent more of the Cuban side of Latin jazz.

There is also a significant Central and South American side to jazz, particularly the music of Brazil. The advent of the *bossa nova* was mentioned earlier in this chapter, but Brazilian jazz is represented by a diversity of substyles and artists, including Airto Moreira, Flora Purim, Egberto Gismonti, and Hermeto Pascoal.

Brazilian music in particular has become a prominent feature at many of today's jazz festivals.

All of the jazz styles mentioned here are still being performed by some of their original practitioners, who continue to provide entertainment and inspiration to generations of audiences. This is one of the luxuries of a music that is less than 100 years old. But these musicians are growing older; and it is important that, after they are gone, their music live on in something other than recordings.

The exciting aspect of jazz today is that this music is being played, in schools and concerts, by musicians of all ages and backgrounds, most of them born long after these styles faded from popularity. These devoted musicians keep the traditions alive by playing with a new sense of discovery and a vigor and immediacy that were evident in the original performances of long ago. Everything old can be new again. Groucho Marx, observing the continuing popularity of Marx Brothers movies over the span of years, commented that a joke isn't old if you've never heard it before. Jazz did not "get better" with age; it did not learn from its mistakes; old and new are not synonymous with good and bad. Jazz today can be characterized as a rich, living tradition, rediscovering the past as well as discovering the possibilities of the future.

Chapter Summary

Jazz has never been as popular as it was during the Swing Era of the 1930s. Bebop was the signpost that jazz was, for the most part, leaving the realm of popular music to pursue more artistic goals. Along the way, however, certain jazz styles and artists made a brief splash in the popular music arena.

The soft, lyrical nature of cool jazz found favor with popular audiences in the 1950s. Dave Brubeck's quartet was the most widely known of the cool groups, particularly through their university concert tours. In harder styles of jazz, the funky, soul-filled style of Art Blakey and Horace Silver also found public favor. By the mid-1960s rock had been around long enough to impact every aspect of music, including jazz. While jazz artists made modest attempts at a jazz-rock fusion throughout the 1960s, it took the stature of legendary trumpeter Miles Davis to legitimize it. Many of his band members went on to form significant jazz-rock groups of their own.

Musicians trained in jazz continued to affect the world of commercial music. Today, there is some debate as to whether or not jazz-rock is now just "jazz." Rock stylings are an integral part of the jazz lexicon, and their implementation does not necessarily indicate just a musician's inclination to sell out. Jazz is young enough that it wants to keep changing and stay current, yet it is old enough to have a tradition and variety worth preserving. This is reflected in the multitude of jazz substyles that are actively practiced today by artists both young and old.

Additional Listening

Refer to citations in footnote 1 and in the body of the text.

Horace Silver, "Opus de Funk" (1953) (*Horace Silver*, CD format, Blue Note 1520). This trio performance is a fine example of the bebop/blues fusion that Silver was developing at this time.

Horace Silver, "The Preacher" (1954) (*Horace Silver and the Jazz Messengers* CD format, Blue Note 46140). This piece is from Silver's days with Art Blakey's Jazz Messengers and was tremendously popular well into the 1960s.

Art Blakey, "Moanin'" (1958) (*Moanin'*, CD format, Blue Note CDP 7 46516 2). This is the CD rerelease of Art Blakey's most popular recording. The piece was composed by pianist Bobby Timmons and is a prime example of the funky gospel-influenced style in jazz during the 1950s.

Yellowjackets, *The Spin* (CD format, MCA Records, MCAD-6304). The Yellowjackets have been a popular fusion group since the 1970s.

Chick Corea, *The Chick Corea Elektric Band* (CD format, GRP Records, GRP-D-9535). Corea has made intermittent ventures into electronic music and fusion since the early 1970s. This was the introductory album of his newest fusion group. "Rumble" and "Got a Match" are probably the most popular tracks from this album.

The Lincoln Center Jazz Orchestra, *Live in Swing City: Swingin' with the Duke* (CD format, Sony 69898). The Lincoln Center Jazz Orchestra, under the direction of Wynton Marsalis, is the premiere jazz repertory ensemble in the United States. This album of Duke Ellington's music was released in 1999, the centennial of Ellington's birth.

Tito Puente, *The Best of Tito Puente: El Rey del Timbal!* (CD format, Rhino 72817).

Review Questions

1. What are some musical characteristics of bebop? Why did it fail to become a popular style of music?
2. What alternatives to bebop did the listening audience find?
3. What musical elements defined the *cool* strain of jazz, and how are they exemplified in the style of the Dave Brubeck Quartet?
4. Define the *funky* style in jazz of the 1950s? Why was it popular?
5. What are the origins of the *bossa nova,* and how did its popularity damage it?
6. What happened in the development of rock in the 1960s that caused jazz musicians to take it more seriously as a resource for their own music?
7. Who were the sidemen that led Miles Davis toward a fusion of jazz and rock? What were some of their own fusion efforts before or during the time they played with Davis?
8. Who were some jazz-influenced musicians from the pop music side during the 1950s and 1960s?
9. Describe the various jazz traditions that are being practiced today.

Notes

1. *Jazz Piano: A Smithsonian Collection* (CD format, Smithsonian RD 039 A421010), 1/19.
2. A comprehensive overview of many of these musicians is *Jazz Rock Fusion* (New York: Delacorte Press, 1979), by Julia Coryell (wife of jazz/rock guitarist Larry Coryell).
3. It should be noted at this point that Gil Evans, Davis's perennial collaborator, was behind the scenes of jazz/rock experiments at this time and was growing quite enamored with rock. Pioneer rock guitarist Jimi Hendrix had an equally profound effect on both men, especially on their decision to incorporate rock guitar into their work.
4. The best John Coltrane biography is *John Coltrane: His Life and Music* (Ann Arbor: University of Michigan Press, 2000), by Lewis Porter.

Country Music and the Anglo-American Tradition

Part 3

Chapter 10

The Folk Origins of Country Music

Country music is one of the most formidable commercial products in the American music industry, superseded only by rock. Like the people who created it, it has spread from farms and small towns to the city, consequently taking on the city's diversity and sophistication. Throughout the years of its commercial development, country music has incorporated into its style blues, ragtime, New Orleans jazz, swing, rock, and easy-listening. Yet even though country music has become an international phenomenon and a multimillion dollar industry, it has managed to retain the basic character and values of its southern, rural, Anglo-Celtic origin.

WHAT IS COUNTRY ABOUT COUNTRY MUSIC?

One thing that makes country music "country" is that it was developed by rural dwellers. While the fact should be obvious, it is important to understand that for years country music has been produced in urban centers like Nashville, New York, and Hollywood. What *keeps* country music country is that it continues to draw from the imagery and values of rural life and the common folk who live that life.

The majority of top country stars have been Anglo-American, male, and from the poor and working-class rural South. With the development of media technology, these entertainers have become international commercial stars, but they have never lost touch with their roots. To understand the distinctiveness of country music, it is important to understand the South and the culture it reflects.

When settlers from the British Isles arrived in the New World, the warm climate and fertile soil of the American South proved more conducive to agriculture than to industry. The South was sparsely populated; the land taken up not by people but by fields of crops. Farmers were isolated; the nearest neighbor often lived miles away. Cities and towns remained small and widely separated. Farmers occasionally drove to the city to buy supplies or to bring their goods to market, but they did not reside or work there. The competition of black slave labor and the lack of job diversity discouraged new immigrants from settling in the

South, leaving it with little ethnic diversity. This inherent isolationism and restricted interaction resulted in a society that did not change as quickly as the more dynamic social system of the urban/industrial North. So as popular trends in the twentieth century became increasingly urbanized, the South lingered with the tastes and sentiments of the previous century.

The nineteenth-century popular perception of rural life was romantic and sentimental. Rural life was considered serene and pastoral, close to nature and God, a land peopled by rugged individuals who were self-sufficient, a secure and simple place that never changed. This contrasted with the perception of the urban jungle—fast-paced, decadent, dirty, and bewildering, a land of corporate subservience and anonymity. Rural life was hardly as rosy as popular entertainment portrayed it; but rural dwellers liked to think it was, in order to escape from the harsh reality of their existence.

The infrastructure of nineteenth-century southern society was built on a class hierarchy based largely on genealogy—a strong sense of "It's not what you have, it's who you are." The "blue bloods" of the plantation aristocracy, the wealthy landowners from noble European family lines, made up a very small percentage of the southern population. They were greatly outnumbered by their black slaves and the poor whites who toiled on the more inferior, leftover patches of land. After the Civil War the freed slaves and poor whites became mutually entrapped in the tenant farmer and sharecropper systems, working the land of the impersonal plantation owners for meager wages. Company stores extended credit at exorbitant rates, plunging farmers into hopelessly perpetual debt. This situation ultimately led to the mass migration of whites and blacks into the cities of the South and North in the early twentieth century.

The poor whites realized that they were little better off than the former slaves, which left them with an ingrained inferiority complex. They attempted to mask this class consciousness by conjuring up myths of their own superiority and individualism. One myth was the white's natural supremacy to blacks, an illusion that was more intense among poorer whites because of their lower class status and the threat of economic competition with newly freed black farmers and laborers.

Another myth intended to cure the poor white's self-image problem is what Latins would call *machismo* or *macho,* a condition of male strength and virility. Endurance and power is displayed in a man's proficiency at hard physical labor and sports—and in less principled acts like drinking, fighting, and seducing other women (while vehemently protecting the chastity of one's own women).

Male Victorian values saw the ideal woman as chaste and unblemished, a vestal virgin worthy to bear his children, one who reflected the perceived purity of his own mother. While possession of such a cherubic spouse (and possession is what it was considered) made the Victorian man feel more forthright and upstanding in the community, sex was infrequent and unromantic, considered a defilement of the image men had of their women. Eroticism was reserved for mistresses and prostitutes, adultery being considered a less grievous sin than sexual pleasure with one's own wife.

Fundamentalist Christianity seemed to shape and control all other attitudes in the South. The dominant religious sects of the South came about through the Second Awakening, or Great Revival, which took place at the beginning of the nineteenth century. It was a grassroots reaction by the common people to the complex doctrine and cold formality of the Church of England. This was the beginning of camp revival meetings, where impassioned evangelists preached the message

Scene of a rural church service during the Depression era of the 1930s.

of salvation for those who would seek it and hellfire and damnation for those who would not. A century later this pious and emotional style of religion was renewed in the Holiness-Pentecostal movement, propagated by untrained lay ministers preaching to small churches of various sects.

While fervent religious practice did offer hope and comfort, the weight of one's own sins often caused great inner turmoil. Historian Bill Malone points out that the southern man was an individual of extreme contradiction, characterizing the South with two antithetical but equally powerful images: "the home of both corn whiskey and Prohibition, and the land of hell-raising good old boys and God-fearing fundamentalists."[1] The end result of such contradictory behavior is a feeling that, despite leading a godly life, God is ever present and will hold humankind atonable for every transgression. So a feeling of shame pervaded the southern mind. This was most evident in the somber and melancholy sacred and secular music of the South, which laments this earthy travail and looks forward to the reward of the afterlife when the battle between good and evil will end.

One of the most cherished attributes of the southerner is the penchant for rhetoric, the "gift of gab." It is an indulgence in a manner of public speaking and storytelling that demonstrates the orator's talent for eloquence, glorification and bragging, exaggeration (even lying), passion, defiance, and verbosity in general. This is particularly evident in the charismatic delivery of southern preachers, whose programs dominate television and radio airwaves. Some of the most profound moments in the sessions of the United States House and Senate are the colorful speeches by southern senators and congressmen; many have been transcribed and published as popular literature. In the world of entertainment, some of this country's finest storytellers have been southerners like Andy Griffith, Archie Campbell, Tom T. Hall, and Jerry Clower. One of the most refreshing aspects of country songs, compared to other forms of popular music, is that they still tell a story.

How Country Music Reflects Rural Characteristics

Topics in country songs include extolment of a simpler rural life, ideal love, family ties, religious conviction, male machismo, and the pride of the working class. Country music also addresses the conflicts brought on by the darker side of human nature and the struggle of rural or working-class existence. Some of these conflicts are contradictions within the mind itself; others are the product of the protagonists' altered environment. It is through these conflicts that we derive many of the themes in country music.

Many country songs express the inner conflict between pleasure-seeking and the pursuit of religious devotion or wanderlust and the security of home. The overriding credo of country music seems to be "No human endeavor is greater than the pursuit of the pure love of God and family," a credo proclaimed by those who follow that pursuit and by those who wish they had followed it. This moralistic view can be seen in the countless remorseful songs about drinking, infidelity, and the consequences suffered from being away from home.

Why would the portrayal of conflict spell success for country music or any style of popular music? The answer: Because conflict makes for more interesting songs; and our desire to cope with it compels us to write, sing, or listen to those songs. As lyricist Sheila Davis writes, "One reason that sad love songs seem to outnumber happy ones [on top 40 playlists] is that happiness lacks conflict. The ending of a relationship generates more dramatic juice: it's much easier to find a new slant on 'You Done Me Wrong' than to find a fresh way to say 'I love you.'"[2]

Much of our popular music is about tragedy or the problems of love rather than its virtues; but it is the direct and often self-pitying way in which the problems are expressed in country music that makes it distinctive—and to many people, corny. Country music expresses emotions the way the white working class does, using plain language instead of elegant poetics. This means that country music is not concerned with cleverly disguising or squelching the level of emotion; it talks tough and displays its feelings openly and unabashedly. It is truly "white blues."

Another major conflict with rural values is the South's increasing urbanization, which significantly increased by the 1920s. As mentioned earlier, the quicker dog-eat-dog living environment of the city was considered contradictory to the romantic image of rural life, sense of family, religious communalism, and self-sufficient isolation. Yet the statistics of the past 100 years reveal the increasing shift in the southern population from farm to city. The city had an irresistible appeal for rural Americans, especially for youngsters longing for the excitement, wealth, and glamour of the city and an escape from the monotony and drudgery of farm work. That lure was probably heightened around the turn of the century when Tin Pan Alley songs made the shift from glorifying rural quaintness to glorifying urban sophistication.

The move from country to city led to a significant rise in the number of urban, lower middle class. Though they traded their plows for bulldozers and their farms for factories, rural southerners found themselves bewildered and lost in the big city. They fell victim to its pale human relationships and familial strains. This left them longing nostalgically for home, love of family, and the simple rural life—sentiments expressed in a great many country songs. However, these transplanted ruralists were unwilling to retreat to the country and settled instead for adapting the rural value system to city life. Country music adapted as the rural dweller did, identifying with the urban blue-collar worker and truck driver as well as the farmer.

THE TRADITION OF BRITISH AND AMERICAN BALLADRY

Country music developed in the southern United States out of the white Anglo-Celtic tradition of ballads, folk songs, and dance music. As recorded anthologies from the Library of Congress[3] will attest, British ballads were not the exclusive property of immigrants to the South; they existed in almost every region of the United States. It was only in the South, however, that the right chemistry of geography, social makeup and religion combined with the peculiarly concentrated proximity of blacks and whites to create a distinctive and successful form of commercial music.

Ballads are narrative songs that tell a story. Many British folk ballads are called *Child ballads,* not because they are for children, but because they were named for Francis James Child (1825–1896). He was an American scholar who collected, analyzed, and published versions of 305 English and Scottish ballads in 10 volumes between 1881 and 1894. The ballads he codified are hundreds of years old and existed purely within oral tradition. Their authors are unknown or forgotten; in fact, the ballads are probably the product of many people who added verses and altered the melodies over years of performing them and handing them down from generation to generation.

British ballads were usually simple songs in strophic form, rolling out repetitively, verse after verse. They were sung, unaccompanied, in an emotionless, plain style, usually by amateurs for their own personal entertainment or, at most, for an intimate gathering in the home. The ballad plots are usually dramatic events between people—such as family feuds and romantic encounters—with no elaboration as to time or place, making them timeless and abstract. They were often doleful and tragic, with melodies in minor modes.

Another type of ballad that came from Britain was the *broadside.* Broadsides differed from Child ballads, which existed primarily in oral tradition, in that they were composed and printed on large single sheets or in groups called songsters. They were the urban counterpart—the Tin Pan Alley—of British folk ballads. Also, unlike Child ballads, they were more journalistic and topical in nature, dealing with current or historical events such as famous battles, politics, crimes, lovers, or stories of sailors at sea. They date as far back as the sixteenth century, and most were published in London. They were no more adorned or compositionally ambitious than the Child ballads; they were, in fact, quite formulated. Their bare-bones construction, without the benefit of much artistry, clearly reflected the customs, morals, and the living conditions of the people for whom they were produced.

Once Anglo-Celtic immigrants arrived in the South, they began to modify or totally change the subject matter of their Old World ballads to fit their new American experiences. Many of the American-born ballads were topical, similar in design to the broadsides; but they depicted places and events of pioneer America: train wrecks, coal-mine disasters, famous murders, and epic journeys. A distinctive trait of American ballads was the addition of a moral at the end—a gesture the new southern fundamentalism felt compelled to make. When an account of illicit love or a fatal disaster is given, we are warned to avoid a similar fate or to get our affairs in order should it happen to us.

ETHNIC INFLUENCES ON THE ANGLO-AMERICAN MUSIC TRADITION

The Anglo-American settlers of the Southeast, especially those who lived in the isolation of the Appalachian Mountains, kept their folkways relatively intact. From colonial times until the expansion westward, the South's ethnic makeup was limited largely to African-Americans and Anglo-Americans. While there has been conflict between southern blacks and whites over the last 400 years, it would be difficult to find a more intense exchange and assimilation of folkways. It is this unique cultural interchange that distinguishes southern music, including country music, from the music of other regions of the United States. Though they would rarely mix socially, these two ethnic groups were always in close contact. Black "mammies" suckled white babies; poor blacks and poor whites worked together in the fields; they shared the same religion and had similar styles of worship. However slowly, unconsciously, or naturally, blacks and whites came to share speech patterns, cuisine, and, most of all, music.

Blacks had their own tradition of balladry; some were adaptations of Anglo-American ballads, and some were original creations by blacks themselves. Black ballads more closely matched the Old World bawdiness and violence that had been expurgated by the more puritanical southern whites. The subject matter in black ballads tended to focus on individuals who had become legendary for their bad deeds as well as for their good ones. Black ballads usually had no moral overtones, letting the subject's flamboyant acts stand on their own merit. These ballads make the best dramatic use of repetition, and the tunes are generally more interesting. Many of these ballads are commonly used in white country music, such as "Frankie and Albert" (or "Frankie and Johnny"), "Stagger Lee," and "John Henry." When the blues evolved from these black ballads, it was also readily incorporated into white country music.

As the general migration of the South followed the Cotton Belt westward, southerners took many of their folkways (food, architecture, music, and religion) with them, and a certain amount of homogeneity prevails throughout the South to this day. Yet this ethnic makeup would gradually include other groups, who also had an effect on the music.

As Anglo-American southerners migrated, they encountered German immigrants in Arkansas; Germans, Czechs, Poles, and Hispanics in Texas; French Acadians in Louisiana; and various Indian tribes.

Instruments in Early Country Music

The song repertoires of various ethnic groups were borrowed by Anglo-Americans, but more influence can be seen in the adoption of musical instruments and instrumental techniques. From the Anglo-Celtic tradition came the legacy of jigs and reels, played on pennywhistles, bagpipes, and fiddles.

A country string band. Left to right: banjo, fiddle, and Dobro guitar. The musician at right in the coat and tie is playing a cello, an instrument not usually found in folk or commercial country music.

The fiddle was the chief instrument of the Anglo-Americans. It is a common folk instrument found throughout northern Europe, and it is the backbone of the early string bands that were featured at the beginning of country music's commercial career. Fiddles were almost always used in the context of country dances and were considered by many Christians the devil's instrument. Even though the fiddle was the oldest instrumental tradition in the Anglo-American culture—and probably the most conservative—it was not immune to change. Every folk fiddler had his own degree of innovation or conservatism; and every instrument in the folk tradition, including the fiddle, seemed to demonstrate a distinctive regional style. For instance, melodic ornamentation in Scottish folk fiddling tended to be done with the bow; Irish melodic ornamentation was done with the fingers. In America around the 1920s, fiddlers, especially those in the Southwest, began to adopt jazz and blues stylings into their hoedown repertoire. (There will be more on this in the discussion of western swing.) In Louisiana, Cajuns played the distinctive "doo-wacka-doo" fiddle rhythm slower and "greasier" than folk fiddlers in other regions of the South.

The guitar is synonymous today with country music, but it did not come into common use until the turn of the century. The Spanish guitar tradition brought over from Europe seemed to have little effect on the Anglo-American tradition; instead, it was the African-American bluesmen, with their distinctive finger picking styles, that caught the attention of white country musicians. As country music moved westward, it picked up guitar techniques from Hispanics in south Texas; but an even greater influence (from around the turn of the century) was the Hawaiian style of sliding a steel bar on the neck of the guitar rather than fingering the notes—a technique foreshadowed by black guitarists who used knife blades or the necks of glass bottles to achieve a similar crying effect.

A cousin of the guitar, and an instrument that is equally identified with country music, is the banjo; again we have the African-American tradition to thank. The banjo, in its earliest form, was probably the only indigenous African instrument to survive in the United States. It was used and modified extensively by blackface minstrels in the nineteenth century, who added frets and a shorter fifth string. It is quite likely that the banjo was introduced to Anglo-American southerners by these traveling minstrel shows. By the turn of the century there was the five-string banjo, used in country music of the southeast, and the four-string tenor banjo, used in jazz and Dixieland. The instrument had an archaic, quaint, and even comical image, which would only be changed by innovative bluegrass banjoists, such as Early Scruggs and Don Reno, after 1945.

One other instrument that figures prominently in the development of country music is the mandolin. Although this instrument is usually associated with Italy, it does not seem likely that the instrument was adopted by Anglo-Americans because of contact with Italian immigrants—although we cannot rule out that possibility. It is more likely that the popularity of amateur mandolin orchestras, as a turn-of-the-century pastime, influenced its use in country music. It would become associated with the mandolin/guitar duos of the thirties and bluegrass in the forties.

Urban Influence on Precommercial Country Music

Aside from the slow, natural, and unconscious process of change that took place in folk traditions during the Anglo-Americans' migration and subsequent contact with other cultural groups, there was the process of change due to contact with the commercial products of urban culture. This proves that there was never a "pure" southern Anglo-American folk culture.

Even in colonial times, itinerant singing masters conducted *singing schools* at rural churches, teaching congregations the sacred songs in their published hymnals. This activity provided training, performing style, and repertoire to country musicians. Traveling minstrel performers and medicine shows brought the latest styles of urban music and humor to entertain rural audiences. Rural musicians adopted these songs and performing styles into their repertoires as well. The tragic sentimental songs and ballads published and performed in the nineteenth century entered the southern repertoire and have shaped the style and mood of original country songs to this day.

Urban culture did not always come to the country; rural dwellers also went to the city, making contact with the commercial music industry and art music, as well as with the red-light districts that nurtured ragtime, jazz, and the blues. If or when the country dweller returned to the country, he or she took at least some of the music and culture of the city home, influencing fellow rural dwellers.

All the factors that influenced country music went through a mysterious folk process by which they became fused with and dominated by the rural Anglo-American culture. Therefore, the general character of country music is more an Anglo-American reflection of all these diverse cultural elements rather than a direct view of them—the result of a cultural filtering process. Indicative of this Anglo-American cultural dominance is the lack of black performers in country music, despite the sizable contribution of black styles to its evolution; only De-Ford Bailey and Charley Pride come to mind. Another somewhat homogenizing effect on culture and music in the South is the general sense of conservatism that has prevailed in that region. This is due to its self-imposed isolationism, its relatively late move toward urbanization and industrialization, and its prevailing rigid fundamentalist Christian views. These are all elements that will change as the South increasingly moves away from a rural agricultural economy to an urban industrial and transportation economy, with all its inherent cultural dynamics.

In the next few chapters we shall see how this summation of country music holds up to the manipulation of the commercial music industry and its urban environment. We shall see that country musicians succeed in making the transformation from folk musician to professional entertainer, but they always manage to maintain a sense of who they are and where they come from.

Chapter Summary

Country music is a formidable force in the national commercial music industry; yet the best country music is true to the expression of the working-class people who brought about its beginnings. It reflects a number of ethnic influences but is unique in the way the primarily Anglo-Celtic culture in the southern United States assimilated them. It is a music of class consciousness and moral struggle, of pride and religious piety. It is a rich tradition of storytelling harking back to the epic folk ballads of the British Isles.

Musical forms that made up southern rural folk music include English and Scottish folk ballads (Child ballads), urban broadside ballads, and ballads adapted or composed in the New World. Black folk songs and instrumental styles influenced the Anglo-American tradition early on, and with westward migration there were influences from French, Spanish, German, and other cultures. Additionally, popular music influenced rural dwellers through the traveling shows, whose published songs entered the folk tradition.

Additional Listening

Refer to footnote 3 for ballad recordings. The citations that follow are country performances of traditional ballads, broadsides, and fiddle tunes. All are taken from the LP format of *The Smithsonian Collection of Classic Country Music*

(Smithsonian RO25 P8 15640), selected and annotated by Bill Malone, referred to hereafter as *SCCCM*. This fine eight-LP set went out of print around 1987 and has been succeeded by a second edition (the four-CD format is Smithsonian RD 042 DMC4-0914). While bringing the selections more up-to-date, the second edition is not nearly as comprehensive. In the *SCCCM* citations that follow, the letters "CD" followed by a disc and track number will indicate that the recording can be found on both editions.

A. C. "Eck" Robertson, "Sallie Gooden" (1922) (*SCCCM*, 1/1). "Sallie Gooden" is one of the staples of the old fiddle repertoire, a party song played with a number of variations. Dance fiddlers like Robertson were conditioned to play for hours at a stretch. The abrupt ending probably indicates Robertson's surprise when the wax disc ended after only about three minutes into his performance.

Buell Kazee, "Lady Gay" (Child 79) (1928) (*SCCCM*, 2/3). This is a southern mountain version of the British ballad "The Wife of Usher's Well."

Coon Creek Girls, "Pretty Polly" (British broadside) (1938) (*SCCCM*, 3/4). The Coon Creek Girls were popular in the Midwest in the 1930s and frequently appeared on the WLS National Barn Dance. The galloping rhythm of the banjo and guitar and the minor mode of the song add to the menacing character of Willie, the murderous rounder. Notice that, curiously, the verse structure is AAB, the same as the blues.

Cliff Carlisle, "Black Jack David" (Child 200) (1939) (*SCCCM*, 3/3). This is a rendition of the British ballad "The Gypsy Laddie." The ribald sexual bragging in the song fits well with the bluesy style of Carlisle's vocal and Dobro steel guitar playing.

Review Questions

1. What keeps country music country?
2. Class consciousness is one of the main themes of country music. Describe the class system in the development of southern culture that may account for this.
3. Describe the conflict between the southern social concepts of machismo and fundamentalist Christianity.
4. In what way does country music express sadness that makes it distinctive and, to many, objectionable?
5. What are the differences in a Child ballad, a broadside ballad, and an Anglo-American ballad? How do you characterize African-American ballads?
6. What were the musical contributions of other ethnic groups to the developing Anglo-American musical tradition?
7. Describe the background of the instruments used in country music. Which instrument is the oldest in the Anglo-American tradition?
8. How did professional performances and published music influence country music before radio and recordings?

Video Source

America's Music: The Roots of Country (VHS formats, 6-volume set, Turner Home Entertainment, 1996). This video set is a long overdue survey of country music. Meticulously researched and presented, it covers country from its folk roots to the music of its release in 1996. This series was originally aired on the TBS cable channel.

Notes

1. Bill C. Malone, *Country Music, U.S.A.* rev. ed. (Austin: University of Texas Press, 1985), p. 17.

2. Sheila Davis, *The Craft of Lyric Writing* (Cincinnati: Writer's Digest Books, 1985), p. 24.

3. Suggested listening (all LP format): *Anglo-American Shanties, Lyric Songs, Dance Tunes, and Spirituals* (Library of Congress AFS L2), *Anglo-American Ballads* (Library of Congress AAFS L7), *Child Ballads Traditional in the United States* (Library of Congress L57, L58). Many of the Library of Congress field recordings have been available on CD through Rounder since 1999.

11

Early Commercialization of Country Music

As important as radio was to the spread of all popular music, it was particularly crucial in the commercial development of country music. Rural isolation and comparatively lower incomes made the purchase of phonograph records difficult for southerners. Radio was as important as the railroads in linking farms with cities.

Of the more than 500 radio stations in 1922, 89 were in the South. At this point in their history, these stations were low-wattage local affairs, serving the informational needs and entertainment tastes of their immediate area. Radio gave popular local entertainers a new medium for reaching their audience. Championship fiddlers, string bands, singers, preachers, and politicians—perennial favorites at rallies, picnics, and county fairs—could now reach an entire community of households with one appearance on the radio.

Today Nashville is synonymous with country music; but at the beginning of country music's commercialization, the key city was Atlanta, Georgia. Atlanta radio station WSB went on the air in March 1922, the first radio station in the South. In the course of its daily programming, it featured favorite local acts such as Fiddlin' John Carson, Reverend Andy Jenkins, and Gid Tanner, all of whom would become the first country recording stars.

RALPH PEER AND THE FIRST COUNTRY RECORDS

In 1920 songwriter Perry Bradford persuaded the General Phonograph Company (GPC) to make the first blues recording performed by a black singer. The success of this event proved that there was a viable market outside the white, urban middle class. By the 1920s the record industry was suffering from the competition of radio and started emulating radio's efforts to serve the special entertainment interests of various regional and ethnic groups. This led to the establishment of *race record* labels and the dispatching of talent scouts to southern cities in search of folksingers.

The earliest recording expeditions to the South were conducted by Ralph Peer (1892–1960), a producer for GPC. One of his largest race record distributors was Polk Brockman, owner of a family furniture store in Atlanta and the region's most successful distributor of race records. Brockman persuaded Peer to record "Fiddlin'" John Carson (1868–1949), a champion fiddler and singer, a favorite with white Atlanta audiences for years, and a star on WSB. Peer recorded Carson performing "Little Old Log Cabin in the Lane" and "The Old Hen Cackled and the Rooster's Going to Crow" in June 1923. The recording was released on GPC's Okeh race label along with their black blues recordings and was intended solely for the Atlanta market. History repeated itself; just as the popularity of Mamie Smith's "Crazy Blues" reached far beyond the financial and demographic expectations of its producers, so did Carson's record. Carson was signed to an exclusive Okeh contract and went on to make well over one hundred records. Thus Carson became the first *commercial* country recording artist.[1] Ralph Peer continued to seek out and produce country artists, including the Carter Family and Jimmie Rodgers, and became as important a figure in the development of country music as John Hammond was to jazz and the popularity of swing.

Analysis of "Little Old Log Cabin in the Lane" (*SCCCM,* 1/2)

This is not a traditional folk song but a popular song composed by Will Hays in 1871, demonstrating once again that popular music was well known to southern musicians and performed by them in these early years. The lyric is typical minstrel fare: Sung by a blackface character, it is nostalgic and sentimental. The decaying plantation is a metaphor for the singer's own aging and loneliness.

> *Now I'm getting old and feeble, and I cannot work no more.*
> *That rusty bladed hoe I've laid to rest.*
> *Old Massus and old Missus they are sleeping side by side.*
> *Their spirits now are roaming with the blest.*
> *Things have changed about the place now, and the darkies they have gone.*
> *You'll never hear them singing in the cane.*
> *But the only friend that's left here is that good old dog of mine,*
> *And the little old log cabin in the lane.*

Chorus:

> *The chimney's falling down, and the roof's all caved in*
> *Lets in the sunshine and the rain;*
> *But the angel's watching over me when I lay down to sleep*
> *In my little old log cabin in the lane.*

> *Now the footpath is growed up that led us 'round the hill,*
> *The fences all gone to decay.*
> *The pond it's done dried up where we once did go to mill.*
> *Things have turned its course another way.*
> *Well, I ain't got long to stay here; what little time I've got*
> *I'll try to rest contented while I remain,*
> *Until death shall call this dog and me to find a better home*
> *Than our little old log cabin in the lane.*

Fiddlin' John Carson's vocal style is typical of traditional country performers; he sings in a formal, church-delivered manner and does not act out the lyric or

Listening Guide 11.1
"Little Old Log Cabin in the Lane" 2 beats per measure

ELAPSED TIME	FORM	EVENT DESCRIPTION
:00	Intro	Fiddle, based on the verse (16 measures)
:21	Verse 1	Vocal (32 measures)
1:00	Chorus 1	Vocal (16 measures)
1:19	Instr. verse 1	Fiddle (16 measures)
1:37	Verse 2	Vocal (32 measures)
2:14	Chorus 2	Vocal (16 measures)
2:32	Ending	Fiddle, partial verse (8 measures)
2:42	End	

display emotion in his rendering. (Peer did not approve of Carson's singing, but Brockman assured him that it was the style accepted by his audience.)

Instead of playing a more subordinate accompaniment on his fiddle, Carson plays the melody as he sings it. He uses the melody of the verse as an instrumental introduction, as an interlude between verses and as an ending. He does not play a rhythmic accompaniment on the fiddle, and the only harmony is provided by the droning of open strings. The final fiddle passage ends rather abruptly in mid-verse; Carson, accustomed to playing longer stretches than a 78 rpm recording allows, was apparently surprised by the producer's cue to stop.

Soon after John Carson's initial success, other companies began seeking country performers to record for commercial release. From the beginning, these musicians were aware of their race record status and the stereotyped perception of white southerners; and they accommodated the minstrel-show slant in marketing their product. They took on colorful names like Gid Tanner and His Skillet Lickers, Doc Bates and His Possum Hunters, the Fruit Jar Drinkers, and the Gully Jumpers. They sometimes dressed in straw hats and ragged clothes—*rube costumes* as they called them—and performed cornball vaudeville acts called *rural dramas*.

At first, promoters had a hard time finding a name for the music, calling it *old time music, hill country tunes,* and the like. The name that became most common typified the hick image that was most often imposed upon it: *hillbilly* music.

Gid Tanner (1885–1960) is a good example of these early country entertainers. Tanner was a hoedown fiddler and often performed with Riley Puckett, a blind guitarist and singer. They were popular entertainers on WSB in Atlanta and began recording for Columbia in 1924. By 1926 they added another fiddle and a banjo to form the Skillet Lickers. They not only recorded traditional fiddle tunes, ballads, and breakdowns but also ragtime, blues, and Tin Pan Alley songs.

Analysis of "Soldier's Joy" (SCCCM, 1/8)

"Soldier's Joy" is a traditional English fiddle tune performed by Gid Tanner and His Skillet Lickers. The form is typical of most fiddle tunes: It is in two sections, verse/chorus, with the first part in a lower fiddle register than the second. The two-part form alternates with a vocal based only on the melody of the verse.

Listening Guide   11.2
"Soldier's Joy" 2 beats per measure

ELAPSED TIME	FORM	EVENT DESCRIPTION
:00		Spoken monologue by Tanner
:13	Intro	Fiddle melody, based on 2 verses, 2 choruses (32 measures)
:44	Verse 1	Vocal (8 measures)
:51	Instr. 1	Fiddles, based on 1 verse, 2 choruses (24 measures)
1:13	Verse 2	Vocal (8 measures)
1:21	Instr. 2	Fiddles, based on 2 verses, 1 chorus (24 measures)
1:43	Verse 3	Vocal (8 measures)
1:51	Instr. 3	Fiddles, based on 2 verses, 2 choruses (32 measures)
2:20	Verse 4	Vocal (8 measures)
2:27	Instr. 4	Fiddles, based on 2 verses, 1 chorus (24 measures)
2:49	Ending	"Shave and a Haircut"
2:51	End	

The recording opens with a spoken introduction by Tanner, fashioned after the way he would announce tunes on the radio. The verse to the tune begins immediately with Tanner and fiddler Clayton McMichen playing more or less in unison. The vocal and guitar accompaniment are supplied by Riley Puckett.

We can only speculate as to how much the fiddlers adhere to the traditional melody of "Soldier's Joy," but the lyric is definitely rural South. Fiddlers often added lyrics to fiddle tunes to break the monotony of long dance sets. The lyrics were often nonsense or based on the most mundane of subject matter—in this case, the price of pole beans or "Grandpapa sittin' on a sweet 'tater vine."

Toward the end of the performance, the fiddlers move from a constant sixteenth-note rhythm to a strident doo-whacka-doo gallop on the verse. Unlike the recordings by fiddlers John Carson and Eck Robertson, who merely stopped when the recording ran out, the Skillet Lickers play a slick "shave and a haircut" ending.

Tin Pan Alley Joins in the Country Craze

The new hillbilly market soon came to the attention of the popular-music industry in New York. Ragtime, blues, and jazz were considered quaint and unmenacing musics from the hinterlands at first; but when it became apparent that they were forces to be reckoned with, the music establishment tried to imitate and formulate them. So it was only a matter of time before someone outside the southern milieu would try to cash in on the newest regional phenomenon.

The most successful of the Tin Pan Alley country artists was Vernon Dalhart (1883–1948). Born Marion Slaughter, in Jefferson, Texas, he sang light opera and popular music for Edison and Victor records in the 1910s. He took his stage name from two Texas cities. When his popularity waned in the early twenties, he began to record hillbilly material. His most successful recording was "Wreck of the Old 97" (*SCCCM*, 1/5) and "The Prisoner's Song" (*SCCCM*, 1/6), both recorded in 1924. This record became one of the top sellers in Victor's catalog, catapulted Dalhart to national fame, and, despite its artificiality, gave a tremendous boost to the fledgling country-music market. It also established two of the most enduring themes in country music: the *event song*, broadsidelike ballads of

Vernon Dalhart, a former pop singer who made a tremendous comeback in the 1920s as a country singer.

news events (usually monumental tragedies), and *prison songs*, most often a lament by someone wrongly sent to prison.

As country music progressed through the 1920s, new country songs penned by commercial composers began to compete with traditional music and nineteenth-century sentimental songs. Kansas-born Carson Robison (1890–1957), a frequent accompanist for Vernon Dalhart, became a successful writer of event songs, literally referring to the day's newspapers for ideas. Another significant early country songwriter was Memphis-born Bob Miller (1895–1955), who wrote over seven thousand songs from his publishing company in New York. His "Twenty-One Years" (*SCCCM*, 3/5) eclipsed Dalhart's "The Prisoner's Song" as *the* prison song and led to several sequels.[2]

The Solemn Old Judge and the Barn Dance

As radio grew in the early twenties, stations in the South and Midwest peppered traditional music throughout their broadcasting day, along with popular parlor music by staff orchestras and singers. As early as 1922, WBAP in Fort Worth, Texas, began featuring a lengthier program of *barn-dance* music with M. J. Bonner, a fiddler whose band had previously specialized in Hawaiian music. Other attempts at a barn-dance format were tried, but none had the success of WLS's National Barn Dance (NBD) in Chicago and WSM's Grand Ole Opry in Nashville. These two shows had a common element: an announcer from Indiana named George D. Hay. In 1919 Hay was a reporter in Memphis, and he was sent to cover a war hero's funeral in Arkansas. While there he witnessed a barn dance and gained the inspiration to showcase the music of the common people. He got his first opportunity to do so in 1924, when WLS in Chicago hired him to develop and announce a new radio barn-dance show. A year later the National Life & Accident Insurance Company in Nashville started station WSM and hired Hay to establish a barn-dance show for them.

Drawing upon the rich folk-music heritage of the hill country of Tennessee, Kentucky, Virginia, and North Carolina, the WSM Barn Dance was born. The show's original cast consisted only of Hay, "the solemn old judge," Uncle Jimmy Thompson, an octogenarian fiddler, and Thompson's niece on piano. Soon local amateur solo and group acts began to vie for a spot on the show, playing gratis, with no commercial sponsorship, solely for the thrill of appearing on the radio.

Hay created and carefully guarded the folk ideal of the show, and it was he who gave it its distinctive name, Grand Ole Opry. Once the National Broadcasting Company established network radio in 1926, the usual programming routine was to carry successive portions of radio shows from around the country, often in eclectic combinations. As a prime example of this penchant for glaring contrast, the WSM Barn Dance followed Dr. Walter Damrosch and the NBC Symphony Orchestra's Music Appreciation Hour from New York each Saturday evening. As a good-natured ad lib one night, Hay held his folksy show up to the preceding program by calling it the Grand Ole Opry, a name that stuck and gave his show an element of national distinction.

Since radio programs have come and gone and records have remained, it is easy for us to give too much weight to an artist's recorded output as a measure of his or her significance in music history. In fact, radio and live appearances were

The 1936 cast of the Grand Ole Opry. George D. Hay is standing at the extreme right, Uncle Dave Macon is seated on the second row, sixth from the left, and black harmonica player DeFord Bailey is at the right end of the back row.

the vehicles most used for an entertainer's rise to popularity; many of country music's most enduring acts crested their careers upon appearing on the National Barn Dance in Chicago and the Grand Ole Opry in Nashville. The NBD faded away some years ago; but if you haven't made it on the Opry, you haven't made it!

The Bristol Sessions

Back in the realm of recorded music, Ralph Peer had established himself as a successful freelance talent scout and producer of hillbilly music, most often supplying his product to Victor records. In July and August of 1927, Peer made a field trip to Bristol, Tennessee, located in the northeast corner of the state among the Smokey Mountains and bordering Virginia, North Carolina, and Kentucky. It was here he would discover two of the most important acts of early country music and establish its two primary strains: a conservative southeastern strain and an eclectic southwestern strain. The first was exemplified in the work of the Carter Family from Virginia and the second in the work of Jimmie Rodgers of Mississippi.

The Carter Family

The Carter Family was from Virginia and, until their retirement in 1943, preserved the traditional music of their native Appalachian Mountains. Their material included parlor songs, sacred music, and original music, all evoking memories of family stability, the godly life, human tragedy, and secure rural life. Their "God, Mom, and home" theme exemplified the conservative old-time approach of the southeast and would be one of the major influences on bluegrass music in the 1940s.

In the beginning the Carter Family consisted of A. P. Carter and his wife Sara. Born in 1891 in the Clinch Mountains of Virginia, A. P. learned to play fiddle as a child but abandoned it as an adult to devote himself to singing. He collected hun-

The Carter Family around 1937. The Carters popularized traditional Appalachian and gospel music. Left to right: Maybelle, A. P., and Sara.

dreds of traditional folk songs. He married Sara in 1915, and they played for local gatherings for the next 11 years. Sara played the guitar, banjo, and autoharp, a strummed multi-string instrument with buttons that, when depressed, stop some strings and let others ring to play different chords. Eventually, A. P.'s sister-in-law, Maybelle, joined the group. Maybelle primarily played a Gibson L-5 guitar and developed a complex style of playing the melody on the lower strings. She tuned the guitar lower than the standard, a tuning still used by bluegrass guitarists today.

After successfully auditioning for Ralph Peer in Bristol, Tennessee, in 1927, the three members of the Carter Family signed a contract with Victor Records. Over the next seven years they recorded some of their most enduring songs, including "Wildwood Flower," "Wabash Cannonball," and their signature song, "Keep on the Sunny Side." Many of the traditional songs they performed were, from then on, known as Carter Family songs. The Depression took its toll on the act, splitting them up in search of work. They often only saw each other at recording sessions. In 1935 they moved to the ARC label; later they recorded for Decca. They also resuscitated their career in a lucrative radio contract with XERF in Del Rio, Texas. With the station's vast broadcast range, the Carters found wide, newfound popularity and influence. (The significance of Decca Records and border radio "X" stations on country music, particularly that of the Southwest, is discussed in Chapter 12.)

Unfortunately, A. P. and Sara's marriage fell apart and so did the group. They made fitful comeback appearances in various combinations over the subsequent years. Maybelle formed an act with her three daughters, one being June Carter, who later married country and rockabilly legend Johnny Cash. Their daughter, Rosanne Cash, enjoyed brief celebrity status, and her former husband, Rodney Crowell, has long been an in-demand country performer and songwriter.

The Carter Family has been a tremendous influence in country music history, not only on the traditional side of country styles but on folk and rock musicians such as Woody Guthrie, Bob Dylan, Emmylou Harris, and Bill Monroe and a legion of bluegrass musicians. Maybelle's guitar set a standard in the tradition of country music guitar picking, influencing legendary country guitarists such as Merle Travis and Chet Atkins (who actually began his career playing for Maybelle and her daughters). The Carter Family's place in country music is so monumental that they became the first inductees into the Country Music Hall of Fame in 1970.

Analysis of "Wildwood Flower" (*SCCCM*, 2/7)

"Wildwood Flower" was recorded by the Carter Family in 1928 at Victor Studios in Camden, New Jersey. It features Sara Carter as vocalist accompanied by Maybelle Carter on guitar. "Wildwood Flower" came from a nineteenth-century

Listening Guide   11.3
"Wildwood Flower" 2 beats per measure

ELAPSED TIME	FORM EVENT DESCRIPTION	
:00	Intro	Solo guitar, based on verse (20 measures)
:21	Verse 1	Vocal (19 measures)
:43	Instr. verse 1	Solo guitar (19 measures)
1:03	Verse 2	Vocal (19 measures)
1:24	Instr. verse 2	Solo guitar (19 measures)
1:45	Verse 3	Vocal (19 measures)
2:05	Instr. verse 3	Solo guitar (19 measures)
2:25	Verse 4	Vocal (19 measures)
2:46	Instr. verse 4	Solo guitar (18 measures)
3:08	End	

parlor song called "The Pale Amaranthus." You will notice the archaic style of the lyric.

Sara Carter's vocal style is typical of traditional mountain singing and hails back to the vocal practice for rural English balladry. Her vocal sound is unadorned by the coloration of a vibrato and is very nasal in quality (the country "twang" you have perhaps heard about). There are also the distinctive elements of Appalachian pronunciation that affect Sara's vocal delivery, such as in the line "wavy black hair." "Hair" is pronounced "har"; and Sara chooses to hold out her note, singing through the "r" sound, which gives her vocal timbre a constricted quality on to the more open "a" vowel sound, rather than holding. The style is reserved and formal, intentionally holding back a dramatic or emotional delivery of the lyric, no matter how tragic, religiously fervent, or otherwise compelling.

The most celebrated feature of this recording is Maybelle Carter's guitar playing. Her accompaniment and instrumental verses between Sara's sung verses are the most imitated in country guitar and are the goal of all fledgling players. Maybelle picks the melody on the lower strings and strums the accompanying chords and rhythms on the upper strings with a downstroke. To achieve this effect of two guitarists (one lead and one rhythm), Maybelle must quickly alternate between picking and strumming without sacrificing smoothness or continuity in either, a goal she accomplishes most successfully.

The form is strophic, a succession of verses with no chorus or contrasting formal material. Sara and Maybelle alternate vocal and instrumental verses. The verse is actually 16 measures long, four phrases of four measures; but the Carters add an extra measure after the first, second, and fourth phrase, extending the verse length to 19 measures. This practice of giving the singer a little extra time to catch a breath for the next phrase would carry over into bluegrass.

Jimmie Rodgers

The Carter Family helped to establish the conservative southeastern style of country music. A more eclectic, blues- and pop-based music would emanate from the southwest, kindled by Jimmie Rodgers. He has rightfully been called "the fa-

Jimmie Rodgers and his family with Ralph Peer and his wife at Rodgers's Texas home.

ther of country music" and was its first superstar.

James Charles Rodgers (1897–1933) was born near Meridian, Mississippi, son of a railroad worker. He also worked the railroad, wandering up and down the line in search of odd jobs. The mythology and romance of trains and railroads pervade American music and folklore, representing freedom and the passage to a better life for some and wandering and loneliness to others. Rodgers and his music will forever be associated with the images and myths of the railroad.

Rodgers was conversant with traditional country material, ballads of the railroad workers,[3] and black folk-blues of his native Mississippi. He was also influenced by popular singers of the day such as Al Jolson and Gene Austin. Rodgers's mature style would blend all these influences and result in a distinctive presentation that redefined country music in the 1930s and 1940s and influenced many of its greatest stars.

When Ralph Peer came to Bristol, Tennessee, in 1927, Rodgers was living in Asheville, North Carolina, working as a detective and singing on local radio. He auditioned as a solo performer and impressed Peer enough to get a Victor recording contract. On his initial session Rodgers did the first in a series of *blues yodels*, subtitled "T for Texas, T for Tennessee." These songs were essentially traditional black blues verses but with a distinctive difference; between stanzas Rodgers would yodel a brief interlude. It proved to be a hit formula and established Rodgers simultaneously as "The Singing Brakeman" and "America's Blue Yodeler."

Jimmie Rodgers's repertoire and performing style was markedly different from performers such as the Carter Family and others from the southeast. Rodgers sang a wide variety of music, from risqué to religious, humorous to sentimental, all presented with equal ease and authenticity. Unlike the Carter Family's stoic formal style, Rodgers's performances were intimate, informal, and effortless. His shows were almost always solo, just him and his guitar. Though he sometimes posed for publicity photos in a brakeman or cowboy outfit, he most often dressed in the fashionable clothes of the day.

Rodgers's vocal style was characterized by a throaty, reedy quality. The relaxed effect of his vocal performances can be attributed to his blues-derived technique of occasionally sliding between pitches and employing softer pronunciation of his words.

A true mark of the distinctiveness and resilience of Jimmie Rodgers's style is how it holds its own in a variety of musical settings. On many of his recordings, he accompanies himself on guitar. He was a rudimental guitarist, and his instrumental ability is a negligible aspect of his musical greatness. He was accompanied by commercial radio orchestras ("Miss the Mississippi and You"), by trumpet and piano ("Standing on the Corner" with Louis Armstrong and Lillian Hardin Armstrong), and by New Orleans–style jazz bands, such as on his most popular recording, "Waitin' for a Train."[4]

Listening Guide　11.4
"Waitin' for a Train" 4 beats per measure

ELAPSED TIME	FORM	EVENT DESCRIPTION
:00		Vocal train whistle imitation
:06	Intro	Trumpet melody (4 measures)
:16	Verse 1	Vocal (24 measures)
1:07	Tag	Yodel (2 measures)
1:12	Instr. verse	Trumpet and clarinet (16 measures)
2:46	Verse 2	Vocal (24 measures)
3:36	Tag	Yodel (2 measures)
3:42	End	

Analysis of "Waitin' for a Train" (*SCCCM*, 2/9)

This recording was made in Atlanta in October 1928. It features a bowed string bass, Hawaiian slide guitar, guitar, muted trumpet, and clarinet, playing in a relaxed, jazzy, Dixieland style. This type of presentation demonstrates Rodgers's and Peer's tendency toward commercialism, a tendency quite distinct from the more traditional presentation and repertoire of the Carter Family. "Waitin' for a Train" was indeed Rodgers's most popular recording.

This piece begins with Rodgers's vocal imitation of a train whistle, half whistled and half yodeled. The band then enters with the introduction. Note the role and sound of each instrument. The guitar provides the rhythm; the Hawaiian slide guitar provides a fuller sound with slides and sustained chords, "padding" the texture of the band. The muted trumpet and clarinet are reserved for an instrumental section between verses and do not provide padding or fill-ins during the vocal.

The lyric is about being a hobo, wandering along the railroad line. Contrasting with the "God, Mom, and home" lyrics of the Carters, Rodgers portrays himself as a wanderer and a misfit, down on his luck.

Rodgers's vocal style is relaxed and wistful, lazily sliding from one pitch to the next and frequently employing blue notes, demonstrating that he was as much a white rural blues singer as he was a hillbilly singer.

Chapter Summary

Much of the credit for the commercialization of country music must go to Ralph Peer for realizing the potential for rural southern music. The recording period from Fiddlin' John Carson in Atlanta (1923) to the Carter Family and Jimmie Rodgers (c. 1928) was a time of discovery for the music industry. It was a time to explore the stylistic parameters for what was then called hillbilly music. As this music grew, there was a gradual shift in repertoire, from traditional vocal and instrumental music and nineteenth-century popular music to newly composed country songs by writers such as Carson Robison and Bob Miller. Northern studio singers, such as Vernon Dalhart, also tried the new style.

Meanwhile, George Hay realized his dream of a radio show featuring rural folk music, first on Chicago's WLS National Barn Dance and Nashville's WSM Grand Ole Opry.

Finally, by the end of the 1920s the Carters and Jimmie Rodgers forged the two distinctive stylistic paths for country music, the former defining the moralistic and traditional southeastern conservative style, the latter defining the more eclectic blues- and pop-oriented southwestern style.

Additional Listening

Refer to footnotes and citations in the body of the text.

Review Questions

1. What was the impact of radio on the early commercialization of country music?
2. What were the events that led Ralph Peer to record hillbilly talent?
3. What were Tin Pan Alley's earliest attempts at country music?
4. What were the two radio barn dances founded by George D. Hay? Where were they located?
5. Who were the two acts discovered by Ralph Peer in Bristol, Tennessee, that defined a conservative southeastern strain and an eclectic southwestern strain of country music?

Notes

1. In the interest of historical accuracy, it should be noted that the first country artist *ever* to be recorded was "Eck" Robertson (1887–1975), a championship fiddler from Amarillo, Texas. He recorded a traditional fiddle instrumental, "Sallie Gooden," at Victor's New York studio in 1922. The recording was a product of Robertson's own initiative and not a conscious effort by anyone to create a marketable style. That record went virtually unnoticed until years after Carson's recordings, which did lead to the commercialization of country music. "Sallie Gooden" can be heard on *SCCCM*, 1/1.
2. "Twenty-One Years" was recorded in 1928 by Mac and Bob (*SCCCM*, 2/2). Another example of a popular prison song is "Birmingham Jail" (*SCCCM*, 3/5), recorded in 1927 by Darby and Tarlton.
3. Folklorist John Lomax recorded a collection of railroad ballads sung by real railroad workers in the 1930s. They can be found on *Railroad Songs and Ballads* (LP format, Library of Congress AFS L61).
4. The other recordings mentioned here can be found on a record set, selected and annotated by Rodgers historian Nolan Porterfield, entitled *Jimmie Rodgers, America's Blue Yodeler* (LP format, Smithsonian DMM 2-0721).

Chapter 12

Country Meets Western

In 1929 Jimmie Rodgers settled in Kerrville, Texas. He was very proud of his adopted state and was fascinated by the cowboy lore that was associated with it. He performed frequently in Texas, featured western themes in his songs, and occasionally posed for publicity shots in cowboy regalia. His influence on subsequent western singers is undeniable, and he provided the catalyst for a commercial western style in country music.

The American West of the nineteenth century was already prone to a mythical image in the eyes of the popular public. The paintings of Frederic Remington, countless dime novels, and the Wild West shows of Buffalo Bill Cody helped to establish this romantic impression among patrons in the more populous eastern states. By the 1910s motion-picture dramas furthered the mythical West with silent movie cowboy stars such as Tom Mix, Hoot Gibson, and William S. Hart. Once synchronized sound technology came about, movie cowboys were required to be as quick with a guitar as they were with a six-shooter.

GENE AUTRY AND THE HOLLYWOOD SINGING COWBOY

One of the most proficient Jimmie Rodgers imitators was Gene Autry (1907–1998). A native of Tioga, Texas, he was discovered while working in an Oklahoma railroad telegraph office by the famous cowboy humorist and actor Will Rogers. He began recording in 1929 and first appeared on WLS in Chicago in 1930, billing himself as "Oklahoma's Singing Cowboy." His acclaim in the Midwest eventually landed him a job in Hollywood, acting and singing in westerns.

Autry began with a small part in the 1934 picture *In Old Santa Fe;* he then went on to star in over 90 movies, establishing himself as "America's Number One Singing Cowboy." Now, in addition to radio, live appearances, and records, country music had a new medium in which to present itself. Song themes evolved from "country" to "western." Country singers routinely dressed in western wear, a practice that is widely practiced today whether or not the singer's repertoire includes western themes. In fact, some of the most cherished possessions of country artists are the garish western movie costumes custom-designed

Singer and Hollywood western cowboy star Gene Autry on his ranch in 1951.

by Nudie of Hollywood, replete with sequined wagon wheels, ropes, and guitars.

As popular music historian Charles T. Brown points out, the movie cowboy's image went far beyond the character he portrayed; he was a symbol of the model American male. He was clean-cut, wholesome, and virtuous; but he was also virile and always triumphant in battle. Young boys in the 1930s idolized movie cowboys like Autry, and many benefited from the positive image he conveyed. There is no doubt that studio marketing also benefited from this idolatry, with brisk sales of Gene Autry guitars, songbooks, records, and other paraphernalia.

Autry bowed out of the limelight to serve in the military during World War II, but he came back to show business as strong as ever. Apart from western-themed songs, Autry scored an incredible hit with Johnny Marks's Christmas favorite "Rudolf, the Red-Nosed Reindeer." Autry reluctantly recorded it in 1949 at the end of a session, but it turned out to be his biggest seller. By the 1950s he was still a popular star but not the box-office powerhouse he had once been. America had made the move to television, and so did he. Not only did he appear in television, but he also purchased studios and television and radio stations, and he founded a production company. For the rest of his career he amassed a sizable fortune from these investments.

Another notable change Hollywood brought to the presentation of country music was a conscious effort to smooth the twangy style of more traditional hillbilly music. Hollywood geared its western movie music to appeal to the broadest possible audience and was certainly not interested in preserving or presenting "authentic" cowboy music.[1] Autry nurtured a lower vocal pitch and a crooning, relaxed delivery that would give no offense to the urban middle class. The instrumental accompaniment was likewise pastel in tone and texture, with soft guitars, violins, and Hawaiian steel guitar. Autry's 1941 Hollywood recording of "You Are My Sunshine" (*SCCCM*, 6/9) is an example of this smooth style.[2]

Movie westerns also showcased female country artists. Patsy Montana (1914–1996), a singer and fiddler from Arkansas, became the first female country star with her 1935 million seller, "I Want to Be a Cowboy's Sweetheart" (*SCCCM*, 5/4, CD 1/16). She featured virtuoso yodeling and western themes in her music; and while never reaching the star status of Gene Autry, she did become the role model for many subsequent female country singers.

Another unique musical style that developed in western movies was what could simply be labeled *cowboy harmony*. The distinctive male harmony approach to western singing can be attributed to the Sons of the Pioneers. This trio consisted of Canadian-born Bob Nolan, Missourian Tim Spencer, and Leonard Slye, born near Cincinnati, Ohio. The group was formed in California in 1934 and featured a smooth style of harmony. Their finely crafted songs included "Cool

Water" (*SCCCM*, 5/3, CD 1/19) and "Tumbling Tumbleweeds" (*SCCCM*, 5/2, CD 1/18), which exploit the romantic image of the western desert. In 1937 Slye left the group to join Republic Pictures, changed his name to Roy Rogers, and went on to rival Gene Autry as America's most popular singing cowboy.

Media, Technology, and Their Impact on Western Music

During the Depression years of the thirties, the motion picture medium had a significant impact on western artists. Meanwhile, there were also significant developments in radio and records. With record sales and production at their lowest point, American Decca was formed from its parent company in England. Under the direction of talent scout David Kapp, much emphasis was given to talent in the Southwest, particularly hillbilly talent. Decca signed now-legendary western stars to fruitful recording contracts and launched Nashville's recording industry in the 1940s.

Decca also offered a 35 cent record to its public, countering the price of 75 cents commanded by the major labels. Soon the major record companies were offering budget label subsidiaries to compete with Decca, making recordings more accessible to the Depression-weary public. Jukeboxes became common fixtures in public dance facilities during the thirties. Along with cheaper records, the industry was rejuvenated.

Another type of radio station was born in Texas. In the border town of Del Rio, station XER (later XERA) was founded in 1931. By placing the transmitter across the border in Mexico (hence the "X" in the call letters), XERA was exempt from FCC transmission restrictions and cut through the airwaves with over 100,000 watts. Soon other *X stations*, or *border radio* stations, were founded, their signals reaching as far away as Canada. They were a powerful vehicle for the exposure of country talent, particularly western country talent, as well as exposure for the many commercial products that sponsored their radio performances.

One other technological achievement is worth noting in the development of western styles: the electric guitar. Experimental electric guitars had been around since the twenties; but they did not appear in country music until Bob Dunn, guitarist with Milton Brown (mentioned later), began using an amplified steel guitar in 1934. Its immediate acoustic predecessor was the Dobro, a guitar with a large metal resonating disk beneath the strings rather than a hole. Once the electric instruments were adopted, they became the defining feature of southwestern country music; the Dobro and other acoustic string instruments remained associated with the more conservative country music of the Southeast.

Due in part to these developments, western music increasingly asserted itself on the country music tradition. The two major styles of western music that emerged during the 1930s were *western swing* and *honky tonk*.

Western Swing

Western swing is an eclectic dance music that originated in Texas, a state characterized by diverse ethnic traditions, but musical and cultural. As southerners of Anglo-Celtic ancestry migrated westward across the United States, they encountered settlers of other ethnic backgrounds: French Acadians, Germans, Czechs, Slavs, Hispanics, American Indians, and, of course, African-Americans. (The significant historical legacy of black cowboys has been largely overlooked.) The typical western road musician was required to maintain diverse repertoires to cater to the tastes of these various ethnic groups, and it seemed only natural that a musical hybrid should arise in the Southwest.

Bob Wills and His Texas Playboys are pictured on an outdoor stage in Hominy, Oklahoma, in 1940. At this time, western swing band combined full-fledged swing bands with a country fiddle band. Note that the instrumentation includes five wind instruments, two fiddles, piano, banjo, bass, drums, electric lap steel guitar, and electric guitar. Wills is the fiddler in the darker shirt.

The major figure in the development of western swing was Bob Wills (1905–1973). His career and musical background were typical of this Texas musical diversity. Wills was a third-generation hoedown fiddler, possessing a vast repertoire of traditional dance tunes that migrated west with his family. Added to that was Hispanic folk music and the influence of African-American folk blues and jazz. Wills's biographer, Charles Townsend, said that Wills worked side by side with blacks in the cotton fields, like many poor whites, and knew their folkways and music firsthand.[3] This is evident in Wills's vocal and instrumental mannerisms. He also listened to a lot of race records and was particularly impressed with vaudeville blues queen Bessie Smith. In fact, his first recording for the Brunswick label, made in Dallas in 1929, included "Gulf Coast Blues," a cover (which is a remake) of a famous Bessie Smith recording.

In 1931 Wills consciously worked toward forming an urban style of hoedown western music. He formed a band with a jazz rhythm section to provide a danceable beat, hired white blues singer Milton Brown, and began to incorporate some use of jazz improvisation. This band became the Light Crust Doughboys, sponsored by Burrus Mills in Fort Worth. Soon disputes with manager W. Lee O'Daniel led both Milton Brown and Bob Wills to quit the band and form groups of their own.

Milton Brown formed his Musical Brownies in 1932 and continued to rival Wills and his band until a fatal car accident ended his career in 1936. Brown was a fine jazz and blues singer, as his recording of W. C. Handy's "St. Louis Blues" will attest (*SCCCM*, 6/2, CD 1/12). The Brownies, in fact, recorded rags, blues, and popular numbers; they rarely performed conventional country fare.

Bob Wills moved south to Waco, Texas, and formed the Texas Playboys, the most famous of the western swing bands. The peak years for the group, 1934 to 1942, were spent in Tulsa, Oklahoma, broadcasting over radio station KVOO.

The Light Crust Doughboys, Milton Brown and His Musical Brownies, and the earliest Texas Playboys were string bands. The quintessential hoedown band was comprised of fiddle and guitar; an extra fiddle or banjo may have been added. Western swing instrumentation began to evolve with Milton Brown's band. While remaining a string band, Brown employed fiddlers who could improvise in the jazz style, used jazz-style piano, and was the first to use the electric steel guitar, which was used more like a horn than a chordal backup instrument. Leon McAuliffe, a member of Wills's band, made his contribution to the popularity of the steel guitar in 1936 with his recording of "Steel Guitar Rag" (*SCCCM*, 6/3, CD 1/21). This became one of the Playboys' most requested numbers and the staple étude learned by all students of the instrument.

As early as 1934, Wills took the next step in western band instrumentation by adding drums and horns to the band. The resulting instrumentation was essentially a Dixieland horn band (trumpet, clarinet, and trombone) combined with a country string band. By 1940 Wills had added enough horns that the group was essentially a swing *big band* with a country string band. The rhythm section was quite large, including drums, bass, electric rhythm guitar, electric steel guitar, two (sometimes more) fiddles, banjo, piano, and, sometimes, accordion. Though not as polished as northeastern swing bands, Wills's group was extremely versatile. They were able to offer southwestern audiences exactly what they demanded—everything from Dixieland to square-dance music.

Analysis of "New San Antonio Rose" (*SCCCM*, 6/8, CD 1/22)

The real turning point for Bob Wills and western swing was the 1940 recording of "New San Antonio Rose." Wills had written and recorded the tune as an instrumental in 1938, but he added lyrics for this new version. It became a huge national success and brought western swing out of its regional confines. Soon Wills and his band began appearing in movie westerns, adding a cowboy song facet to their repertoire.

This vocal version is made up of three themes, one more than the original instrumental, arranged ABCA. Since this form departs somewhat from the typical verse/chorus format of popular song, in this analysis, the letters A through C will be used to define the different themes of the song.

"New San Antonio Rose" presents the instrumentation and music styles that comprise western swing. The introduction features the horns in a typical swing dance band introduction. The horns continue with a smoother fox-trot rendering of the A and B themes. This opening instrumental omits the C theme and, instead, goes back to the swinging rhythms of the introduction to set up the entrance of the vocal.

Vocalist Tommy Duncan then presents the melody in its entirety. In the A and B themes his vocal line is reinforced by the saxophones in harmony. In the C theme Duncan's vocal melody is doubled by trumpets in close harmony, reminiscent of the trumpet section of a Mexican mariachi band. The last A theme returns to the saxophone background.

Listening Guide   12.1
"New San Antonio Rose" 4 beats per measure

ELAPSED TIME	FORM	EVENT DESCRIPTION
:00	Intro	Horns, swing dance-band style (4 measures)
:05	A	Horns continue, smoother fox-trot style (16 measures)
:23	B	Horns (18 measures, 16 + 4 overlapping transition)
:44	A	Vocal with saxophones (16 measures)
1:03	B	Vocal and saxes continue (16 measures)
1:21	C	Vocal with mariachi trumpets (16 measures)
1:40	A'	Vocal with saxes (16 measures)
1:58	C	Mariachi trumpets (16 measures)
2:16	A'	Saxes and overlapping ending (17 measures)
2:36	End	

The mariachi-style trumpets return to recap the C theme, followed by the saxophones with the A theme, this time without the vocal. The four-measure ending finishes out the arrangement.

Another signature Bob Wills trait to be heard on this recording is Wills's calling out during the course of the performance. Between phrases, or at certain points in the instrumental solos, one might hear Wills call or sing "Take it away, Leon," "Al Strickland, now," or just "yee-haw." By all accounts from his musicians, it was a bit of show business, but mostly Wills's unbridled enthusiasm during the course of a performance.

World War II brought about the end of an era in western swing. As with most bands at this time, the draft took its toll on the personnel of the Wills group. He reorganized in California in 1943 with a smaller band, essentially returning to a string-band format. Now the electric guitar and electric steel guitar had to compensate for the missing horns. Wills's string band accomplished this quite adequately. For instance, on a block chord passage Wills would combine fiddle lead, guitar, steel guitar, accordion, and, perhaps, one tenor saxophone to simulate a brass section. This technique would prove influential on early rock-and-roll bands such as Bill Haley and the Comets.

The California ballroom scene began in 1942 when the Venice Pier Ballroom opened to cater to transplanted Oklahomans, who had fled the devastating dust bowl of the 1930s. Western swing soon began to outdraw name swing bands such as Tommy Dorsey's and Benny Goodman's. One of the key figures in the California ballrooms was Donnel Clyde "Spade" Cooley (1910–1969), an Oklahoma fiddler who formed a large western swing band in California in 1942. Compared to Wills, Cooley's band was bigger, more polished, and more of a crossover into popular dance music.

Spade Cooley was the Paul Whiteman of western music. He had as many as 24 musicians, including a full string section and harp, and formal arrangements. His musicians were primarily well-trained note readers, whereas Bob Wills's musicians often faked arrangements. Also, Cooley's band was not as reliant on blues and black folk music as Wills's. While Cooley's band did not have the unfettered spontaneity and ebullience of Wills's, his band did represent the western swing style at its most refined.

Honky Tonk

Another strain of western music that emerged in the 1930s was *honky tonk,* so named for the establishments in which the music was heard. During the height of the Depression, the Texas oil boom brought many rural dwellers to remote oil towns in search of work. On the weekends these workers headed to the outskirts of town to drink and dance in the taverns that proliferated after the repeal of Prohibition in 1933.

In this atmosphere the gentle "God, Mom, and home" themes of earlier country music were lost, as were the traditional ways of performing them. Honky tonks were loud places, and people were there to dance; but to do any dancing the music had to be heard above the noise. As with western swing—honky tonk's sister music—a more insistent dance beat had to be employed, sometimes aided by the piano and, only occasionally, by drums. The electric guitar and steel guitar became distinctive features of honky tonk instrumentation. The former's role was that of lead, or "take-off," guitar, alternating solo verses with the vocal.

Themes in honky tonk lyrics took on the experiences and the sentiments of the patrons. The songs celebrated the party atmosphere of the tonks and the good times to be had, but the primarily fundamentalist upbringing of the performers and the audience added a counterbalance of morality. Self-pity and remorse lay at the heart of most honky tonk songs. This "cry in your beer" approach seemed to offer justification by guilt to those who inhabited honky tonks and an "I told you so" self-righteousness to those who would not have been caught dead in such places.

The first great honky tonk singer was Ernest Tubb (1914–1984). Born in Crisp, Texas, he began his career as a devout Jimmie Rodgers imitator. By 1940 he had signed a contract with Decca Records and recorded his first big hit, "Walking the Floor Over You." Several years later, he made an appearance on the Grand Ole Opry, serving as a potent representative of the honky tonk style and inspiring many future honky tonk singers. Tubb did not originate the use of amplified take-off guitar, but his widespread appeal influenced many others to adopt it.

Analysis of "Walking the Floor Over You" (*SCCCM,* 7/1, CD 1/23)

The first feature exemplified in this performance is honky tonk country music's distinctive instrumentation and the role of those instruments. There is no drummer; an acoustic guitarist keeps the rhythm. The prominent instrument is the electrically amplified guitar, sharing equal space in the limelight with Ernest Tubb's vocal.

The subject matter of "Walking the Floor Over You" foreshadows the scandalous and remorseful cheating and drinking songs of future honky tonk artists. Yet this early in the development of honky tonk (1941), the singer's emotional situation is not as graphically depicted. Tubb's vocal presentation is, in fact, rather pleasant and upbeat, regardless of the heartache expressed in the lyric.

Listening Guide   12.2
"Walking the Floor Over You" 2 beats per measure

ELAPSED TIME	FORM	EVENT DESCRIPTION
:00	Intro	Electric lead guitar, based on verse (16 measures)
:16	Verse 1	Vocal (16 measures + 1 measure extension)
:34	Chorus	Vocal (16 measures)
:51	Instr. verse 1	Electric lead guitar (16 measures)
1:07	Verse 2	Vocal (16 measures + 1 measure extension)
1:24	Chorus	Vocal (16 measures)
1:42	Instr. verse 2	Electric lead guitar (16 measures)
1:57	Verse 3	Vocal (16 measures + 1 measure extension)
2:14	Chorus	Vocal (16 measures)
2:31	End	

The end of the war saw a spate of popular honky tonk singers and the firm establishment of the style. Honky tonk marked the beginning of country music's dealing with the themes of jilted lover and "hanky panky," in retrospect, much like New York cabaret and urban blues singers had done 20 years before. By the late 1940s the darker side of human relationships was more graphically depicted in honky tonk songs. Texan Floyd Tillman wrote and recorded the first great cheating song, "Slipping Around" (*SCCCM* 10/2, CD 2/11) in 1949. Webb Pierce recorded the first great drinking song in 1953, "There Stands the Glass" (*SCCCM* 11/1). It was a scandalous lyric that openly endorsed drinking to numb one's heartache, and it was banned on many radio stations.

Honky tonk themes and instrumental styles evolved from the 1930s to the 1950s, as did its audience. Country music fans became increasingly urban and blue collar. They were ready to confront the realism of social ills depicted in honky tonk songs, yet they were tentative in condoning such behavior. This psychological irony sometimes manifested itself in the musical history of the song itself. A case in point: The first big hit for Roy Acuff was "Great Speckled Bird" (*SCCCM*, 4/7, CD 1/14), a religious number he recorded in 1936. Its melody was used by Hank Thompson for his 1951 honky tonk hit "The Wild Side of Life" (*SCCCM*, 10/5, CD 2/20) and its sequel "It Wasn't God Who Made Honky Tonk Angels" (*SCCCM*, 10/6, CD 2/21), recorded by Kitty Wells in 1952. The combination of a gospel song melody with a remorseful lyric about honky tonk life was a musical manifestation of the moralistic/hedonistic struggle within the psyche of the country music audience.

In the years since its beginning, most of the significant proponents of the raw honky tonk style have been from the Southwest, including Lefty Frizzell, Hank Thompson, Ray Price, Buck Owens, Merle Haggard, George Jones, and George Strait. The songs of these and other honky tonk artists have retained their basic character but have not been immune to change over the years. With today's more liberal view of women, many female honky tonk singers have been not only accepted by the public but have flourished along with their male counterparts. Minority groups, in rare instances, have also been accepted in the traditional honky tonk realm. Several examples of this are black country singer Charlie Pride and Hispanic singers Freddie Fender and Johnny Rodriguez. Increased public frankness on subjects like sex, drugs, and violence has added new and graphic intrigue to honky tonk lyrics.

The Bakersfield Sound

The Southwest has also established a couple of music production centers that, while no match for Nashville, have made significant contributions to the country music industry. Migrating Oklahomans in the 1930s and the rising ballroom scene in the 1940s helped to establish the working-class town of Bakersfield, California, as an important country music center from the 1950s to the 1970s. The most significant artists from this country scene were Merle Haggard, born near Bakersfield in 1937, and Buck Owens, a native of Sherman, Texas. While essentially characterized as honky tonk music, a distinctive "California" or "Bakersfield" sound emerged. It was a louder and more electric type of music, heavy on electric guitar and electric steel guitar and on high strident vocals, perhaps sharing more of a kinship with rockabilly or later country rock. Eventually, the burgeoning country scene in Bakersfield and Los Angeles kindled increasing rivalry with Nashville. This led to the establishment of the Academy of Country Music, a West Coast industry cooperative of country music studios, promoters, artists, and publishers.

Austin and Outlaw Country

Another important country music scene in the Southwest was Austin, Texas. As state capital and the home of the University of Texas, Austin in the 1970s had a thriving intellectual and highly eclectic music scene. College students who were devotees of urban folk music and rock were caught up in the fierce regional pride of their own native music also. This fostered a club scene, where graduate students and rednecks, rockers and honky tonkers coexisted in harmony. The music that arose from this unlikely bohemian culture was an eclectic mix indeed, ranging from the Carter Family and blues to Bob Dylan and psychedelic rock. The group Asleep at the Wheel settled in Austin in the mid-1970s, combining rock with western swing. Jerry Jeff Walker, a former New York folk artist and the composer of "Mr. Bojangles," was also an early member of the *redneck rock* scene. The growth of Austin's music eventually led to the television program *Austin City Limits*, which still airs weekly on public television.

Just as San Francisco spawned a counterculture in rock music in the 1960s, Austin of the 1970s had its own brand of rebellious imagery. It glorified the image of the ruthless western outlaw, the antithesis of the moral giant portrayed by Hollywood westerns. Artists wore black cowboy clothes, long hair and beards, blue jeans and sneakers. Some, such as Ohio native David Allan Coe, had served time in prison, which enhanced their public image rather than being detrimental to it. Coe eventually moved beyond the image of the hell-raising cowboy and opted for a headband and leather biker clothes, a more universal symbol of the outlaw character. The language of some of his recordings was graphic enough to limit their advertising to adult magazines. Even with this image of crude lawlessness, Coe still conveyed sensitivity and savvy as a singer and songwriter. His performance of the ballad "Please Come to Boston" is tender and moving, and his

Singer and songwriter Willie Nelson in 1985, pioneer of the Austin, Texas–based *outlaw country* of the 1970s. This is years after he wrote hit songs for other country artists, such as "Crazy" for Patsy Cline.

performance of Steve Goodman's "You Never Even Called Me by My Name" takes a good-natured poke at all the clichéd themes in honky tonk lyrics: trains, getting drunk, pickup trucks, prison, and Mama.

The most popular exponents of the Austin *outlaw country* crowd are Willie Nelson and Waylon Jennings. Both are Texas natives and both have experience with Nashville's music scene; but neither performer reached his commercial potential until joining the Austin scene in the 1970s.

Waylon and Willie

Waylon Jennings, born in 1937, began his career as the electric bassist for Texas rockabilly artist Buddy Holly. After paying his dues in southwestern bars, Jennings came to the attention of Chet Atkins and RCA, who signed him to a contract in 1965. Their relationship was plagued with conflict; Jennings refused to have his style either pigeonholed or tamed according to Atkins's production standard. He maintained an eclectic repertoire that was always rock-influenced, and it was this independence that eventually gained him superstardom. While he never moved his base of operations to Austin, it was there that he found the most favor. There he could nurture his dark outlaw image, particularly with the 1976 release of his album *Wanted, the Outlaws*. Jennings died in 2002.

Willie Nelson's early success was as a songwriter, not as a performer. He was born in Fort Worth, Texas, in 1933 and came to Nashville in 1960. He composed country classics such as "Night Life," "Hello Walls," "Crazy," and "Funny How Time Slips Away" (*SCCCM*, 16/7, CD 3/18), but these songs were popularized by other performers. In 1972 he made a calculated move to capture both the honky tonk crowd and the youth counterculture. His earlier fans must have been shocked at the transformation: Nelson let his hair grow, braided it into pigtails, and donned jeans, headband, T-shirt, and sneakers. Among other projects, his duet ventures with fellow Texas outlaw Waylon Jennings proved the most successful. Another highlight in his career was his 1975 album *Red-Headed Stranger*, featuring a plaintive rendition of Fred Rose's song "Blue Eyes Cryin' in the Rain" (*SCCCM*, 16/8). (Songwriter and publisher Fred Rose will be discussed in the next chapter.)

Nelson's performing style is unique and personal. In his Nashville years it proved to be a liability, but ultimately it was his greatest asset. He has a repertoire of great depth, ranging from Tin Pan Alley standards to western swing and honky tonk. His voice is delicate and nasal, colored with a narrow and quick vibrato. Nelson's vocal phrasing is defined by his free rhythmic treatment of the melody that floats over the steady beat of the band. This type of phrasing is common among jazz singers, but it is most unusual in country music and is probably Nelson's most controversial stylistic feature. While most country bands strive for a full-sounding texture, the texture of Nelson's band is characteristically sparse, and his arrangements are uncomplicated and compatible with his own guitar playing and vocal style.

Nelson has continued to move freely between mainstream celebrity status and premiere western tonker. He has done character acting in motion pictures, sponsored several Farm Aid concerts and other benefits, and helped the careers of stars as diverse as Julio Iglesius. How long stars such as Willie Nelson can manage to keep country music in the limelight of mainstream popular music is a moot point. Whereas country music seems to be fading east of the Mississippi, even in Nashville itself, the devotion of country fans in the West surely will keep the music alive and well for years to come.

Analysis of "Up Against the Wall, Redneck Mother" (*Viva Terlingua*, CD format, MCA MCAD-919)

Jerry Jeff Walker is one of the royalty of the 1970s Texas outlaw country scene. Walker, however, is actually a native of New York State (born Ronald Clyde Crosby in 1942). His biggest hit song was "Mr. Bojangles," though his own 1968 recording paled in sales to the cover by the Nitty Gritty Dirt Band in 1971. (It was also a bit hit for cabaret artist Sammy Davis, Jr.)

In the early 1970s Walker moved to the Austin, Texas, area and, in 1973, recorded *Viva Terlingua* in front of a live audience in Luckenbach, Texas, a tiny town immortalized in a Chips Moman and Buddy Emmons song recorded by Waylon Jennings and others. Only a live recording like this can capture the rowdy atmosphere of the style in its time. Walker's Lost Gonzo Band seems to go out of its way to play up the stomping, honky tonk style, twangy steel guitar, and sloppy, drunken vocal style. The song is a wonderful self-parody of the fist-fighting, beer-slinging redneck, conservative enough to beat up hippies but accountable for little else. The song also turns the traditional angelic mother image of country music on its ear, as does the last verse of David Allen Coe's "You Never Even Called Me by My Name."

The recording opens with the sound of the boisterous crowd and an acoustic rhythm guitar. Walker's vocal enters for the first verse. His sound is folksy and unadorned, almost defiantly careless in its delivery and already capturing the don't-care attitude of the outlaw country style. The electric bass and drums enter with him. After a few seconds, a harmonica begins playing around Walker's vocal. As you will hear throughout this and many country recordings, different instruments in the band take turns in this role. It is also notable that using a harmonica in the band adds to the backwoods, Woody Guthrie–type imagery to the band and its music.

As the first chorus comes around, the steel guitar gives a prominent lead-in, the instrument unrepentantly pushing out its whining sound so beloved by country music's fans and despised by its detractors. Background singers join Walker for the chorus, not so worried about precise harmony as creating the sound of a freewheeling sing-along in a honky tonk. This type of presentation, and probably this song in particular, must surely have inspired Garth Brooks's "I Got Friends in Low Places" (see Chapter 14).

Listening Guide   12.3
"Up Against the Wall, Redneck Mother" 4 beats per measure

ELAPSED TIME	FORM	EVENT DESCRIPTION
:00	Intro	Guitar strumming chords alone
:06	Verse 1	Vocal, bass, and drums enter; harmonica creeps in later (16 measures)
:34	Chorus 1	Background vocalists and steel guitar join Walker (16 measures)
1:03	Verse 2	Harmonica and piano prominent behind vocal (16 measures)
1:31	Chorus 2	Similar to previous chorus but more excited and rowdy (16 measures)
2:00	Chorus 3	First half guitar solo, second half steel guitar (16 measures)
2:29	Verse 3	Walker performs in spoken recitation
2:59	Chorus 4	(16 measures)
3:27	Chorus 5	(16 measures)
3:56	Tag	Based on the last four measures of the chorus
4:13	End	

In the second verse, honky tonk styled piano competes with the harmonica for the role of playing around Walker's vocal. Making the musical texture busier adds to the progressive intensity of the performance. The second chorus responds in kind with a more excited delivery and the sudden presence of a Hammond organ, a sound borrowed more from rock, gospel, and rhythm and blues than country.

Next, Walker turns the song over to the band to feature two instrumental solos. The band uses the chord progression of the 16-measure chorus. The electric guitar plays the first half of the chorus (eight measures), and the steel guitar plays the second half. Walker is inspired enough by the steel guitar to yell out some encouragement. For the last measure of this instrumental chorus, the band hits a short chord and remains silent for four beats, putting a big finish on the song to this point and creating anticipation for Walker's reentry with the next verse.

Walker's last verse is a spoken recitation rather than singing, spelling "M-O-T-H-E-R" and obviously poking fun at an old sentimental song that uses a similar ploy. The background singers sing "ooh" like a church choir, contributing to the false reverence of the verse. The chorus follows, done twice in succession, probably giving the crowd a chance to sing along. The band then plays a "tag," repeating the last portion of the chorus to extend the ending and to signal the end of the performance.

Chapter Summary

The "western" side of country and western started with some of the songs of Jimmie Rodgers and with the advent of the singing movie cowboy. While contrived in their presentation, these songs did manage to turn hillbilly music's focus to the western states and added to the polish of country music performances. Gene Autry brought a sophisticated crooning sound to country vocal styles, and the Sons of the Pioneers established a distinctive cowboy harmony style. Hollywood western musicals also gave female country stars some of their first significant exposure.

Meanwhile, in the 1930s, Decca Records and powerful border radio X stations helped to disseminate country artists in the Southwest. The music demonstrated a diversity and eclecticism that distinguished it from its more conservative southeastern counterpart. These distinguishing elements included the use of jazz, boogie woogie, blues, and electric instruments.

Western swing, pioneered by Bob Wills and others, was a versatile dance music reflecting a number of folk and popular music styles. Honky tonk was another style of dance hall music and one that nurtured the human foibles of its audience.

In the passing years, two regionally distinctive western styles came about: the Bakersfield sound from California, characterized by rockabilly-influenced electric sounds; and Austin, Texas's outlaw country sound, characterized by a blend of 1960s rock, urban folk, and country.

Additional Listening

Refer to citations in the footnotes and the body of the text.

Lefty Frizzell, "I Love You a Thousand Ways" (1950) (*SCCCM*, 10/3). Lefty Frizzell was second only to Hank Williams in popularity during the early 1950s. No song could be truer to the woes of honky tonk life, since Frizzell actually wrote the song in jail after a barroom fistfight.

Buck Owens, "Excuse Me (I Think I've Got a Heartache)" (1959) (*SCCCM*, 12/8). This recording is a good example of the "Bakersfield" sound discussed in this chapter. The sound is electronic, with piercing, high singing and edgy steel guitar.

Merle Haggard, "Mama Tried" (1968) (*SCCCM*, 15/9). This is a semiautobiographical song that also features the Bakersfield approach to country music.

George Jones, "The Grand Tour" (1974) (*SCCCM*, 16/4). This honky tonk song describes the anguish of divorce. Jones's subjective performance allows him to be the protagonist of the scene, not just the storyteller.

Willie Nelson and Waylon Jennings, "Mamas, Don't Let Your Babies Grow Up to Be Cowboys" (1977) (*SCCCM*, CD 4/10). Nelson and Jennings were the icons of the outlaw country scene in Austin. This song exhibits the typical sixties and seventies image of the cowboy—not as a clean-cut hero, but as a dark social outcast, a free and wandering spirit that ultimately breaks the hearts of all the women he encounters.

Review Questions

1. How did movie westerns affect country music's style and popularity? Was movie cowboy music authentic cowboy songs?
2. What was the impact of Decca Records and border radio on western music?
3. How did the development of electric guitars affect western country styles?
4. How is the ethnic diversity of Texas reflected in the origins of western swing?
5. What was the instrumentation of a typical western swing band?
6. What brought about the rise of the California scene in country music? Who were its main proponents?
7. What was the instrumentation of a typical honky tonk band?

8. What are the characteristics of honky tonk lyrics? What was the atmosphere in the bars and towns that inspired them?

9. Describe the *redneck rock* or *outlaw country* that emerged in the Austin, Texas, area.

10. What songs did Willie Nelson pen early in his career for other artists? How did he change his image in the 1970s?

Notes

1. For a sampling of authentic cowboy music, see John Lomax's anthology *Cowboy Songs and Other Frontier Ballads* (New York: Sturgis and Walton, 1910) or listen to the Library of Congress recording *Cowboy Songs, Ballads, and Cattle Calls* (AAFS L28).

2. On the second edition of *SCCCM*, "You Are My Sunshine" is performed by Jimmie Davis (CD 1/25), whereas Autry performs "South of the Border" (CD 1/17).

3. Charles Townsend, "Bob Wills," *Stars of Country Music*, eds. Bill C. Malone and Judith McCulloh (Urbana, IL: University of Illinois Press, 1975), p. 160. Also see Townsend's book-length biography of Wills, *San Antonio Rose: The Life and Music of Bob Wills* (Urbana, IL: University of Illinois Press, 1976).

Chapter 13

Nashville Becomes Music City, U.S.A.

Under the careful supervision of George Hay, WSM's Grand Ole Opry proved to be a success despite the ambivalence of many Nashvillians. Nashville of the 1920s strove for urban sophistication. It is Tennessee's state capital and sent two of its politicians, Andrew Jackson and James K. Polk, to the White House. It is the home of Vanderbilt University; Belmont College, the prestigious women's institution; and Fisk University, one of the nation's first black universities. Nashville formed its symphony orchestra in 1920, the year it built a full-size replica of the Greek Parthenon as a monument to its self-proclaimed title "Athens of the South." The folksy format of the Grand Ole Opry undermined the image and goals that Nashville had for itself. The show was an embarrassment, a feeling exacerbated by Hay's presentation of Opry artists as hicks in overalls and straw hats.

"Judge" Hay, however, was a romantic and a dreamer. His love for rural music and his desire to present it to the public would not be thwarted. Obviously, he was not alone in his enthusiasm. Rural dwellers in the broadcast area began to crowd outside the studio on Saturday night, prompting the show to change locations several times over the years. The most famous location for Opry broadcasts, beginning in 1941, was Ryman Auditorium, a converted tabernacle in downtown Nashville.

The first quantum leap in the Opry's success was due to the charismatic entertainer "Uncle Dave" Macon (1870–1952). He learned how to entertain early in his childhood, from performers that stayed at his parents' boardinghouse. After working for years in the wagon transport business, Macon began performing professionally at the age of 48. He joined the Opry in 1926, after several years of playing the vaudeville circuit and recording in New York.

Macon was a competent banjoist, a lively comedian, and a versatile singer. He possessed a vast repertoire of nineteenth-century minstrel and vaudeville songs, southern black and white folk songs, and songs lampooning local politics and society. Typical of his repertoire is "Jordan Is a Hard Road to Travel" (*SCCCM*, 1/4, CD 1/2), an old nineteenth-century minstrel song. The chorus of the song is all Macon retains; the rest is a vehicle for his own topical verses satirizing social life in the 1920s.

A typical blocks-long line waiting to get into the Grand Ole Opry at Ryman Auditorium in Nashville, Tennessee. The Opry moved to a modern theater in 1975, but this Civil War era tabernacle has remained its spiritual home.

Dave Macon appeared on the Opry for 26 years, helping to establish a consistency in the show's presentation and a familiarity that was rewarded by the public's loyalty.

The Grand Ole Opry was becoming more professional. Artists were now being paid for their performances, and their acts were more diverse. The next step was to advance from a regional success to a national one. The Opry became a booking agency as well as a radio program. The ever-expanding cast made live appearances ranging from tent shows to films to a 1947 performance at Carnegie Hall.

By the 1930s the Federal Communications Commission began licensing certain radio stations to broadcast at higher wattages, assigning them exclusive frequencies that could be received regionally or even nationally. These "clear channel" stations included WLS in Chicago and WSM in Nashville, home of the National Barn Dance and the Grand Ole Opry, respectively. WSM increased its power in 1932 from 1,000 watts to 50,000 watts, allowing them to reach from the East Coast to the Rockies. Network radio, with the help of commercial sponsorship, began carrying portions of local barn dance programs, bringing country music to a larger audience. In October 1939 Prince Albert Tobacco began sponsoring a 30-minute portion of the Grand Ole Opry on NBC.

Roy Acuff

The single act that ensured the national prominence of the Grand Ole Opry was its perennial host, beginning in 1938, Roy Acuff (1903–1992). Born in eastern Tennessee, Acuff planned for a career in professional baseball. His hopes were dashed by a series of damaging sunstrokes. He took up the fiddle and began traveling with medicine shows. Acuff and his band, the Crazy Tennesseeans, first appeared on the Grand Ole Opry in 1938; and favorable response from listeners secured his permanent membership in the cast.

Acuff sang with a powerful voice that outshone his predecessors. It lacked finesse, but its clarity was better suited to survive the primitive equipment used to broadcast the show. Acuff brought several firsts to the Opry. He was the first real singing star on the show. Prior to his arrival, the Opry had bands with members who sang but not featured vocalists. Also, Acuff and his band are credited with introducing the Dobro guitar to the Opry; its consistent and prominent use is one of Acuff's trademarks.

Roy Acuff captured the hearts of his audience with his sincere, forceful, and often emotional renditions of old-time ballads and gospel songs from his native Tennessee hills. He was an ardent preserver of traditional south-

Fred Rose (seated at the piano) and Roy Acuff formed Acuff-Rose Publications, the catalyst for the Nashville music industry and the firm that helped establish Broadcast Music, Inc.

eastern songs and string band music. Acuff welcomed southwestern honky tonk, bluegrass, and other styles to the Grand Ole Opry; but he would forever be called upon to render quaint numbers like "The Great Speckled Bird" (*SCCCM*, 4/7, CD 1/14), "Death on the Highway," "The Precious Jewel" (*SCCCM*, 4/8), and "Wabash Cannonball" (*SCCCM*, 8/1, CD 2/4).

The Nashville Music Industry Diversifies

As Roy Acuff's popularity grew, he began writing original songs; but his work was falling victim to piracy by publishers and recording companies. He needed someone familiar with the publishing business. In 1942 he formed a partnership with veteran Chicago songwriter Fred Rose (1897–1954), and they established Acuff-Rose Publications in Nashville. It was the first publishing firm devoted solely to country music, and was one of the first firms to be associated with the new licensing organization Broadcast Music Incorporated.

Acuff-Rose became one of the largest music businesses in the world. It provided publishing opportunities for new country songwriters, many of whom had been previously shunned by ASCAP affiliates. With Acuff-Rose as a catalyst, publishers, agents, and other peripheral music businesses came to Nashville.

By 1945 Decca began making records in WSM's Studio B, and by the late 1950s RCA (formerly Victor Records) and other major labels had independent studios in Nashville. Acuff-Rose's most successful venture was their acquisition of the song "The Tennessee Waltz." It was written and recorded by Pee Wee King and Redd Stewart in 1948 as a country song (*SCCCM*, 9/8, CD 2/15). In 1950 pop singer Patti Page recorded a cover version, and within a year it had sold almost five million copies. It was the greatest single event leading to the establishment of Nashville as a world music center and to the establishment of fledgling BMI as ASCAP's formidable competitor.

Hank Williams

The most legendary figure to come out of Acuff-Rose was Hank Williams (1923–1953). He was country music's most influential musician since Jimmie Rodgers and its first cult figure. Williams successfully blended the elements of blues, gospel music, traditional southeastern mountain music, and southwestern honky tonk and still managed to win more pop music devotees than any country artist up to that time.

Hiram Hank Williams was born in rural Alabama and raised by a strong-willed, overbearing mother. She was an organist in the Baptist church, exposing her son to gospel music; but the only real training the boy ever received was from a black Alabama blues musician nicknamed Tee-Tot. Williams was also affected by the dual influence of Roy Acuff's traditional sentimental songs and Ernest Tubb's southwestern honky tonk style.

Hank Williams, the first country music legend after Jimmie Rodgers. His plaintive style and masterful songwriting had made him one of the most enduring figures in country music.

In 1946 Williams went to Acuff-Rose seeking a recording contract but was initially signed as a staff writer. The combination of Hank Williams's raw talent and Fred Rose's sensitive direction led to a body of immortal country and gospel songs, including "Your Cheatin' Heart" (*SCCCM*, CD 2/18), "Cold, Cold, Heart," "I Saw the Light," "Hey, Good Lookin'," and "I'm So Lonesome I Could Cry" (*SCCCM*, 10/8). "I'm So Lonesome" is a particularly striking example of the poetic strength of Williams's lyrics as polished by Rose. Fred Rose and his son Wesley also directed Hank Williams's performing career, coaching his live appearances and recording sessions. Williams finally became enough of a name to join the Grand Ole Opry. By carefully designing his songs and his performing presentation, Williams crossed over to the world of pop music. The mutual benefit of Acuff-Rose Publications and Hank Williams to each other is incalculable; it is no wonder that Fred Rose and Williams (along with Jimmie Rodgers) were the first inductees into the Country Music Hall of Fame in 1961.

As far as Williams's performing style and stage presence are concerned, he was gangly but good-looking and always dressed in western wear. His stage manner was casual and natural. His voice was piercing and reedy and had a break, similar to a yodel, that put a "cry" in his voice. Williams described his own vocal style the best, labeling it a cross between Roy Acuff's and Ernest Tubb's, his primary musical heroes. He sang his own compositions almost exclusively; they used the plainest language and were direct in their emotion. This simplicity was the key to Williams's success, allowing the sentiments of his songs to have an immediate impact on his audience.

By 1950 Hank Williams was a wealthy superstar. His career was full of promise, but he and his career fell victim to his own self-destructive tendencies. He was an emotional wreck, scarred by his fatherless childhood. He was an alcoholic and drug addict, and his love relationships were stormy. All of these things made him a true-life tragic figure, which only added to his cult mystique. In 1952 the Grand Ole Opry banned him from its show for drunkenness and unreliability. His body could take no more. While the cause of death is uncertain, he died in his car, in his own garage, on New Year's Day, 1953.

Hank Williams became a major influence to a new generation of country performers, much as Jimmie Rodgers had the generation before. His compositions have been performed by legions of country music stars, and his plaintive honky tonk style has influenced artists such as Charley Pride, Bill Anderson, Moe Bandy, and Joe Stampley. In an effort to keep his record sales going after Williams's death in 1953, MGM kept rereleasing his recordings with overdubbed backup bands, strings, and simulated stereo in an attempt to update the sound for modern audiences. These questionable presentations continued to be issued until Williams's material was released on compact discs in the 1980s; only then was the restored original sound widely available.

Listening Guide   13.1
"Lovesick Blues" *4 beats per measure*

ELAPSED TIME	FORM	EVENT DESCRIPTION
:00	Intro	Electric guitar, Rodgers's yodel melody (4 measures)
:07	A	Vocal (32 measures: 2 + [1]* + 2 + 4 + 4 + 3 + [1] + 2 + 6 + 4 + 4)
1:07	B	Vocal (16 measures: 8 + 8)
1:37	A'	Vocal (32 measures: 2 + [1] + 2 + 4 + 4 + 3 + [1] + 2 + 6 + 4 + 4)
2:37	End	

*Brackets indicate measures with only two beats. The two measures of 2/4 included in this section of the form result in a total of 32 measures of 4/4.

Analysis of "Lovesick Blues" (*SCCCM, 10/9, CD 2/17*)

"Lovesick Blues" is not a Hank Williams composition but an old Tin Pan Alley vaudeville blues tune from the 1920s. The lengthy form of the song and the complexity of its chords make it an unusual part of Williams's repertoire. Made in 1948, this was Williams's first successful recording for the new MGM label, and it earned him his invitation to perform on the Grand Ole Opry the next year.

The backup band is a large honky tonk group that includes electric lead guitar, acoustic rhythm guitar, electric steel guitar, piano, bass, and drums.[1] "Lovesick Blues" requires several listenings to hear the role each instrument plays in the accompaniment.

The rhythm guitar, true to its name, provides the chords and a swing rhythm pattern similar to what the drummer is playing with his brushes on the snare. The piano adds further dimension to the rhythm by playing a simple "oom-pah" bass note/chord pattern. The electric lead guitar, steel guitar, and piano provide filler lines between the vocal phrases and sustaining notes to fatten up the overall texture of the background. Dividing these duties among the different instruments at different times in the song adds variety to the sound of the accompaniment and propels the arrangement forward. The skill and sensitivity of these musicians become more apparent when we realize that their interaction is, for the most part, improvised and was designed during the course of the performance. Their sensitivity to each other's playing, as well as their collective function as accompanists for Williams, comes from years of practice and experience.

Hank Williams's vocal is exuberant and exhibits a number of clever and expressive vocal techniques. The most prominent is the yodel, the technique of quickly flipping between falsetto and chest voice. Williams got the yodeling idea not from Jimmie Rodgers, as one might expect, but from an earlier version of "Lovesick Blues" recorded by fellow Alabaman Rex Griffin. Williams aptly applies the yodel to the word "cry," since the yodel has a crying effect; and its use on each syllable of "lo-o-onesome" is the high point of the entire performance. In any event, the speed and ease with which Williams flips notes within the yodel is nothing less than amazing.

Another vocal propensity in "Lovesick Blues" is sliding from one pitch to another. The slide on the word "just" in "just wouldn't stay" gives the maximum emphasis to just the right part of the phrase. In fact, Williams's use of slides generally seems to give strength to the notes rather than giving them a sagging, drawling quality.

Country Crossover and the Nashville Sound

During the 1940s country music steadily emerged as a national phenomenon. Shortly after World War II it became a formidable enough force in the music industry to merit its own category in *Billboard Magazine's* listing, graduating from the "race" category it had shared with black music. (The black music that remained was renamed "rhythm and blues.") As the popularity of country music became more widespread, its producers were more inclined to soften its sound in an attempt to reach the larger and more diverse audience. Nashville's efforts were increasingly directed at developing a crossover country music.

Crossing-over, that is, presenting a smoother and more commercial style, was not particularly new in country music. Gene Autry had done it in his movie westerns in the 1930s. Vernon Dalhart had done it in New York with his Victor recordings from the 1920s, as did New York country songwriter Bob Miller. Miller's "country" song of 1942, "There's a Star-Spangled Banner Waving Somewhere" (*SCCCM*, 7/4, CD 2/2), was one of World War II's biggest hits. However, these were isolated cases, and none of these artists worked out of Nashville.

The first Nashville artist to make a significant crossover into the pop field was Eddy Arnold, a native Tennessean born in 1918 who began recording in the 1940s. He took the nickname "the Tennessee Plowboy" and exuded a down-home, relaxed, country-boy image, but his music was only marginally country. He sang with a smooth, baritone voice that was more reminiscent of Perry Como than anything out of Nashville. Nevertheless, he proved to be a great ambassador of country music and was the first country star to regularly appear on national television variety shows both as guest and as host.

The architect of the most successful crossover formula in country music is Chet Atkins (1924–2001). Chester Burton Atkins was born in eastern Tennessee. He be-

An early photo of Chet Atkins, extraordinary guitarist and RCA record producer. He was responsible for the easy-listening *Nashville sound* of the 1950s and 1960s.

came a dedicated and proficient guitarist. He has an intricate fingerpicking guitar style, modeled closely after one of his idols, Merle Travis. The bass strings are played with the thumb of the right hand, while the other fingers pick the melody. Unlike plucking or strumming the strings with a pick, this more intricate picking technique allows a full-bodied solo style of guitar playing, with no need for a bass player or other guitarists to fill out the rhythm or chords. Atkins's playing is facile, full-textured yet uncluttered, always faithfully bringing out the melody of the song. He is one of the most admired and influential guitarists in the world.

By the late forties Atkins began to establish himself in the emerging Nashville recording scene not only as a consummate studio guitarist but also as a contractor and producer for sessions. In 1952 he became the official artist and repertory man between Nashville and RCA in New York. This new role was ensured in 1955 when he produced "Heartbreak Hotel," the first RCA record by Memphis "country" artist (as he was then considered) Elvis Presley. When RCA opened independent studios in Nashville in the late 1950s, Atkins was appointed head of that division.

Atkins made a conscious attempt to develop an easy-listening style of production for the recording of country artists. The style that evolved was eventually dubbed the *Nashville sound*. Rhythm sections were toned down, soft background voices and a vibraphone were added; all were drenched in deep reverberation. In many cases, lush string arrangements were also added.

Atkins's next goal was to find an appropriate voice to go over all this lushness. He found several artists who fit his criteria, but the most compatible was Jim Reeves (1923–1964). Originally from Texas, he was a singer and announcer who came to the attention of Chet Atkins and RCA in 1955. By the late 1950s his voice had lowered into a pleasing and mellow baritone that was perfectly suited to Atkins's production philosophy. The resulting RCA recordings proved to be the most commercially far-reaching since Patti Page's monumental success with "The Tennessee Waltz." A prime example of his "touch of velvet" sound is "He'll Have to Go" from 1959 (*SCCCM* 11/6, CD 3/5). The lyrics and melody are country enough and could have been done by any number of honky tonk artists. In the hands of Reeves and Atkins, however, it becomes "country by candlelight," with Reeves's resonant and intimate baritone, ethereal female background voices, sustaining vibraphone chords, and a sparse piano ostinato.

Patsy Cline and Women in Country Music

Not to be outdone by the crossover approach, Decca countered RCA with their biggest country/pop star, Patsy Cline. Patsy Cline represented not only a new era of popularity for country music but also a new role for women in country music.

The first 30 years of commercial country music were male-dominated. There were popular women country performers, to be sure, but they were never stars in their own right. They were invariably grouped with other women, like the Coon Creek Girls and the Girls of the Golden West, or teamed with brothers or husbands. Few things in southern culture were as guarded as womanly virtue. Women would never have been tolerated singing a hoboing song like Jimmie Rodgers or a honky tonk drinking song like Webb Pierce. Road life for a woman would have been equally frowned upon, and the thought of a single woman traveling with a band of men would have been totally reprehensible.

A major coup for women came in 1952 when Kitty Wells recorded "It Wasn't God Who Made Honky Tonk Angels," her rebuttal to Hank Thompson's honky tonk hit "The Wild Side of Life." It was the first number one hit on the *Billboard* country charts for a female singer, and Wells continued to be a superstar into the 1960s. Yet for all her fame, Kitty Wells still was not a "liberated" woman. She had a quiet, modest nature; she dressed in lacy, farm-girl calico dresses and was an emblem of propriety, hardly the image of the seedy world she sang about.

Patsy Cline, female country superstar and crossover pop artist. This photo from the 1950s shows Cline in western wear, typical for country artists of any style at that time.

Patsy Cline (1932–1963) launched the era of the modern female country singer. A native of Virginia, she first gained fame in the Washington, D.C. area, then appeared on national television in 1957. In 1960 she appeared on the Grand Ole Opry and recorded her first monumental hit, "I Fall to Pieces." She maintained superstar status in both country and pop music until she died in a plane crash.

Cline came from a country background, but she was heavily influenced by pop singers such as Patti Page, Doris Day, and Kay Starr. Her style was suitable to both country and pop audiences, which is exactly the way Decca marketed her. Cline's voice was powerful and strident and, above all, extremely expressive. Her female predecessors in country music were careful to give a wholesome, pleasant presentation, and maintained an emotional distance from their material. They also tended to use the archaic nasal Appalachian vocal style. On the other hand, Patsy Cline's voice was rich and pop-oriented. Her renditions of songs were passionate and engaging. She had a number of expressive vocal tricks at her disposal, such as crylike breaks, a versatile vibrato, growls, and a wide range of pitch and volume.

Analysis of "Faded Love" (*SCCCM, 12/7, CD 3/6*)

"Faded Love" is a classic Bob Wills song based on an older folk fiddle tune. Patsy Cline's 1963 recording was made for Decca Records in Nashville and is indicative of the pop crossover the country music industry was striving to achieve at this time. Cline is accompanied by 10 violins, background vocals by the Jordanaires, four guitars, piano, bass, and drums. Electronic reverb (or echo effect) is prominent in the audio mix, adding to the richness of the overall sound.

Most of Patsy Cline's predecessors and contemporaries in country music rendered songs with little change in dramatic level. The distinction of her renditions is the emotional range they encompass. The form of "Faded Love" in this recording is comprised of an introduction, a first verse and chorus, an instrumental interlude, and a second verse and chorus. Cline's basic dramatic plan is to sing each verse softly and each chorus loudly. However, to keep the momentum in the arrangement, the second verse/chorus must have more relative intensity than the first verse/chorus. This requires Cline's careful choice, pacing, and execution of her vocal devices to ensure that she does not reach the dramatic peak of the song too soon, leaving her nowhere to go for the remainder of the performance.

Listening Guide
13.2

"Faded Love" 4 beats per measure

ELAPSED TIME	FORM	EVENT DESCRIPTION
:00	Intro	Strings, then voices (8 measures)
:21	Verse 1	Vocal (16 measures)
1:07	Chorus 1	Vocal (16 measures)
1:43	Tag 1	Strings (4 measures)
1:53	Verse 2	Vocal (16 measures)
2:35	Chorus 2	Vocal (16 measures)
3:15	Tag 2	Vocal (4 measures), out of tempo
3:38	End	

Cline's opening verse is soft and subdued, richly sung in the bottom of her vocal register. Yet there is a restrained passion already present that begins to reveal itself within a few measures. For instance, on the word "so" in the phrase "so dear," she applies the now-familiar "cry" technique that forecasts the emotional release of the chorus. In the first chorus, as anticipated, Cline increases the intensity of her delivery, moving to a higher register and louder volume. She brings out the peaks of each phrase with an increase in volume or a stress in her vocal sound. These points of emphasis are made even more striking because Cline backs off just before the peak of the phrase, then swells into it, such as on "stars above."

After the instrumental interlude, the challenge for Cline is to do the second verse and chorus even better. While maintaining the basic plan of soft/loud, Cline does not back down as far emotionally. The passion is not as restrained and her voice is fuller. Her involvement with the song has intensified, as hopefully, has the listener's. In the second chorus, Cline gives it everything. She makes more frequent use of the cry technique and supplements it with a vocal quiver that sounds like her powerful voice may succumb to the emotion she is expressing. In fact, at the end of the song, the emotion seems to overtake her. She sounds spent, her weakened voice barely able to push out the last few notes.

By the late 1950s the reputation and earnings of Nashville's music industry became formidable enough to get the attention of city leaders. Once a blemish in the business community, country music became its crown jewel. In light of the expansiveness and diversity of the music business, the Country Music Association was formed in 1958 as a trade organization to promote country music in all its forms. It was not concerned with defining country music or preserving any particular musical or cultural tradition but was concerned almost solely with promotion. It sponsored the first all-country radio stations, built the Country Music Hall of Fame and Museum in 1967, and today sponsors an annual country music awards show on national television.

Country Music and Television

As television became a viable medium after World War II, country artists began to use it. Most shows were small local affairs, and others were syndicated to local markets throughout the country. The most significant of these was *The Porter Wagoner*

Show, a program of more traditional country music and humor. Dolly Parton started her career on the show in 1967 and went on to gain international fame.

In the 1950s and 1960s music variety shows on network television were dominated by popular crooners such as Frank Sinatra and Dean Martin. A few crossover country artists, however, did manage to invade the territory. The first was Eddy Arnold, who appeared on CBS in 1952 as a summer replacement for Perry Como. Jimmy Dean, a Texas native with an amiable personality, down-home humor, and a pleasing voice, first appeared on CBS in 1957. With a 7:00 A.M. time slot, he was up against NBC's *Today* show. He had a more successful three-year run on ABC beginning in 1964. In 1969 three network shows featured country artists: *Glen Campbell's Goodtime Hour, The Johnny Cash Show,* and *Hee-Haw.*

Hee-Haw was Nashville's first major television production. It appeared on CBS and was intended to be a hillbilly parody of NBC's popular, sophisticated comedy series *Laugh-In.* The show unabashedly presented cornball country humor but also featured fine performances by legendary country music stars. *Hee-Haw* provided crucial national exposure for country artists, especially since the Grand Ole Opry has allowed very little televising. *Hee-Haw* was canceled after a few seasons but continued successfully in syndication for years afterward.

This nurturing of Nashville's video production resulted in The Nashville Network (TNN), which debuted on cable television in 1983. Following the lead of the rock music television network MTV, TNN featured country music videos, country music variety and talk shows, nonmusic programming such as fishing and racing shows, and reruns of movie and television westerns. Soon to follow was Country Music Television, which at first focused on the emerging and more fashionable *young country* artists and was more devoted to straight music video without other programming. The company is owned by Gaylord Entertainment, an immense media company at the core of Nashville's entertainment, broadcasting, publishing, tourism, and convention business. MTV eventually bought out TNN and, in 2000, changed the network's name to The National Network, purging the country format to pursue more general entertainment and compete with cable networks such as TNT and USA. But with the loss of a country format on TNN, country music found its way onto adult contemporary pop television formats, such as VH-1 and Gaylord's own Music Country, a network the company describes as "featuring a creative blend of rock, country, rhythm and blues, and roots music from around the corner and around the world."[2]

Because of the success of country music, Nashville has become known as Music City, U.S.A. The city's entertainment industry has expanded to include television and film production, recording and publication of national jingles, pop-rock, contemporary Christian music, and a burgeoning convention and tourism business. (The acquisition of a successful NFL football team didn't hurt the city's stature, either.) In 1975 the Grand Ole Opry moved from Ryman Auditorium, its home for 34 years, to a state-of-the-art theater at Opryland, U.S.A., a theme park and hotel/convention complex. There were many teary eyes at the last Ryman performance, but the Opry's move was generally viewed as a positive symbol of country music's endurance and adaptability in an increasingly competitive and sophisticated entertainment business. In 2000 the Country Music Hall of Fame moved from Nashville's Music Row, the recording and publishing district, to a contemporary new building in the heart of downtown near the Ryman and the legendary row of honky tonk bars on Broadway.

With all this modernization and updating, controversy remains as to whether country music is losing its folksy roots and essence. The Ryman Auditorium still holds a mystique that far overshadows its modern successor at the Opryland site. Many country music pilgrims still flock to the old nineteenth-century tabernacle, and young artists still desire to perform and shoot videos there. The funky bars at the Ryman's back door still intrigue tourists and fans more than the Opryland theme park or the Hard Rock Café and other yuppie establishments on nearby 2nd Avenue. The Opryland theme park, in fact, was closed and converted into a huge outlet mall called Opryland Mills. All these venues are tangible evidence of the tradition versus innovation struggle country music will always face.

Chapter Summary

Nashville's Grand Ole Opry continued to expand in its presentation and popularity, spurred on primarily by the presence of stars Uncle Dave Macon and Roy Acuff. The advent of clear-channel radio and network radio broadcasts of the Opry were also beneficial to its success.

The diversification of Nashville's music industry beyond the Opry began when Roy Acuff and Fred Rose established Acuff-Rose Publishing, the first exclusive country music publisher. It was affiliated with the new Broadcast Music Incorporated, the licensing organization established by the broadcast industry to rival ASCAP.

The greatest product of Acuff-Rose was Hank Williams, a honky tonk singer who successfully blended the styles of Roy Acuff and Ernest Tubb and his own inimitable singing and songwriting style.

Decca began recording in Nashville in the mid-1940s, eventually leading to an explosion of country music recording activity in that city. Led by Chet Atkins and RCA Records, Nashville pursued an easy-listening Nashville sound in the 1950s, a sound that successfully won over new country music fans. One of the greatest of the country/pop singers was Patsy Cline. She not only established a new role for women performers in country music but also personified the crossover style Nashville strove for.

Nashville has kept up with the times and with the intense competition of the entertainment industry. The Grand Ole Opry moved to a modern theater, and the Nashville music industry began extensive national television and cable production, centralizing their efforts under the auspices of the Country Music Association.

Additional Listening

Refer to citations in the body of the text.

Eddy Arnold, "The Cattle Call" (1944) (*SCCCM*, 8/4, CD 2/3). This song is typical of the radio and movie cowboy songs of the thirties and demonstrates Arnold's pleasing crossover vocal sound.

Chet Atkins, "Country Gentleman" (1953) (*SCCCM*, 11/5, CD 2/23). This performance gives just a glimmer into the immense talent that Atkins possesses. Through countless recordings that feature his highly personalized and self-sufficient picking style, he set the standard for the electric guitar as a fine solo instrument in country music.

Review Questions

1. Who were the key performers that led the Grand Ole Opry to worldwide fame?
2. What is clear-channel radio? What was its effect on the Grand Ole Opry and other country radio shows?

3. What were some of the accomplishments of Acuff-Rose Publishing in the country music industry?

4. Describe Hank Williams's style and influences and his interaction with composer and publisher Fred Rose.

5. What songs in the history of country music represent efforts at crossing-over into the popular music field?

6. Describe stylistic elements of Chet Atkins's Nashville sound and some of the stars that represent crossover country.

7. What is the legacy of women stars in country music?

8. What is the function of the Country Music Association?

9. How do changes in the Nashville music and media industries illuminate the struggle between tradition and innovation in country music?

Notes

1. Mandolin and fiddle are listed in the personnel in the *SCCCM* liner notes, but they are not on this particular recording. Conversely, piano and drums can be heard on the recording but are not in the personnel listing. Personnel data in liner notes and discographies often comes from the studio's log of an entire session and may not apply to a particular recording done on that session.

2. www.gaylordentertainment.com

Chapter 14

From Bluegrass
to Young Country

The earliest recorded country string bands, from the Carolinas to Texas, were comprised of various combinations of fiddle, guitar, and banjo. Their function was primarily to accompany dancing, and emphasis was placed on instruments playing with a strong rhythm. Vocals were almost an adjunct feature, alternating space with the instrumental *breakdown* sections.

Significant among the string bands was Gid Tanner and the Skillet Lickers of Atlanta, comprised of two fiddles, banjo, and guitar. They played traditional fiddle tunes as well as ragtime and popular songs. Similar outstanding string bands included the North Carolina Ramblers, with banjoist Charlie Poole (*SCCCM*, 1/6), and Mainer's Mountaineers (*SCCCM*, 4/5). These bands provided aspects of repertoire and technique that would forecast bluegrass, a unique substyle of country music.

Bluegrass developed relatively late in country music's history, but when first heard it seems to be a throwback to the older southeastern string bands. While the string band tradition does figure heavily in the legacy of bluegrass, bluegrass is much more eclectic, both in its repertoire and in its manner of performance. Perhaps the most unique aspect of bluegrass is that its origin is indisputably attributable to one man, Bill Monroe.

Bill Monroe (1911–1996) was born in Rosine, Kentucky, the youngest of eight children. His mother played several instruments and sang traditional ballads and sentimental songs. Both of his parents were excellent dancers. Monroe absorbed the local string band music as well as the Baptist and Methodist shape-note hymns that were taught to the congregations in summer singing schools. He learned a bit of guitar and, when his older brothers began playing together, took up the mandolin.

His real instrumental training began at the age of 10 when, after the death of his father, he went to live with his Uncle "Pen." Pendleton Vandiver was a fiddler at local dances and allowed Bill to accompany him on guitar. A more significant influence was Arnold Shultz, a popular black musician in the area. Black musicians of Appalachia and the surrounding hill country were equally adept at traditional Anglo hoedown music and the blues. Playing this

Bill Monroe, the father of bluegrass music, performing with his mandolin at the Newport Folk Festival in Rhode Island, 1965.

combination of styles with Shultz, along with hearing a similar blend of black and white styles on Jimmie Rodgers records, would be a major factor in Monroe's later development of bluegrass.

Monroe performed in the Midwest with his two brothers until Birch Monroe quit the group in 1934. Bill and Charlie then formed the duo the Monroe Brothers, performed live and on radio, and recorded for Victor's subsidiary Bluebird label from 1936 to 1938. Their best-selling record from these sessions was the gospel number "What Would You Give in Exchange" (*SCCCM*, 3/9). Brother mandolin/guitar duos became a popular format in the Southeast during the 1930s. Duos such as the Delmore Brothers, the Louvin Brothers, the Callahan Brothers, and the Blue Sky Boys (Earl and Bill Bolick) most often featured old-time music, gospel numbers, and an occasional blues. The Monroe Brothers were no exception. What did make them exceptional was their manner of performance, and that was primarily due to Bill.

A general statement that could be made about the Monroe Brothers' style, and Bill's later bluegrass style, is that it was conspicuously more aggressive and technically demanding than existing string band styles. Most mandolin players employed a gentle parlor style, softly trilling sustained notes and sparsely filling between the guitar's rhythm. Monroe played a much more advanced, assertive style. The Monroe Brothers played fast numbers at blazing tempos, Bill's rapid-fire melodies underpinned by Charlie's bass runs on guitar.

Bill also set himself apart in his vocal technique. He was a tenor with a prodigiously high range and cutting tone. Whether a vocal group is a barbershop quartet, a gospel quartet, or a pop group, a common practice is to put the tenor on a high harmony part above the melody to give the overall sound a brighter quality. As a tenor, that was Bill's function in the Monroe Brothers and with his bluegrass group later on. His piercing tone, wailing style, and tremendous range (later dubbed his "high, lonesome tenor") became his trademark and the standard by which all subsequent bluegrass tenors would be judged.

The brothers broke up in 1938, and Bill eventually formed the Blue Grass Boys, named after his home state of Kentucky. They made their first appearance on the Grand Ole Opry in 1939, performing Jimmie Rodgers's "Mule Skinner Blues" (*SCCCM*, 13/1).[1] The instrumentation of the group was mandolin, guitar, fiddle, and bass. Bill often sang lead instead of tenor harmony, and on the "Mule Skinner Blues" recording he is playing guitar, not mandolin.

By 1945 Monroe's Blue Grass Boys had standardized its instrumentation, adding a banjo to the other instruments. More than the instrumentation, it was the personnel who would help Monroe define bluegrass and make the Blue Grass Boys such an inspiration to future musicians. Robert "Chubby" Wise was the fiddler, possessing dazzling technique and a style that was equal parts traditional fiddle and blues. Lester Flatt (1914–1979) was the guitarist. He contributed many of the band's original songs and lead vocals, allowing Monroe to resume his role singing high tenor harmony. The banjoist was Earl Scruggs, one of country music's most technically advanced musicians and a tremendous asset to the maturation of the bluegrass style. He and the banjo will be discussed in greater detail later.

The Blue Grass Boys' program was a balance of traditional pieces and pieces newly composed by Lester Flatt and Bill Monroe. Instrumental features were given equal exposure with vocals, and everyone was given an opportunity to solo. It is this emphasis on virtuoso instrumental display that distinguishes bluegrass from other forms of country music, and it has prompted many to compare bluegrass to jazz.

Another distinguishing characteristic of bluegrass, as Bill Monroe and the Blue Grass Boys defined it, is its use of rhythm. First of all, be aware that the group did not include drums; it was up to the string instruments to provide the rhythm. The distinctive rhythm of bluegrass is made up of two parts: a duple meter with a strong backbeat (1–**and**–2–**and**) and a constant patter of sixteenth notes (where four notes are played to each beat) that gives bluegrass its "chugga-lugga" feel—reminiscent of a speeding train's "clickety-clack" rhythm. Both of these rhythmic elements are always present, and the job of playing one or the other is passed around the group. The sixteenth note rhythm is picked with the fingers on the banjo, mandolin, or guitar and bowed on the fiddle. The backbeat is executed by playing a quick downstroke with the fingers or bow while the left hand dampens the strings so that they do not sustain. This gives a short, percussive "chop" sound that simulates a drum.

Analysis of "It's Mighty Dark to Travel" (*SCCCM*, 13/2, CD 2/9)

This recording was made in 1947 with the star-studded group that defined bluegrass: Monroe, Flatt, Scruggs, Wise, and Howard Watts on bass. The song was composed by Monroe; it was filled with the imagery of wandering and loneliness that he favored. Both verse and chorus are 16 measures long, and both use the same chord sequence. They are distinguished only by the lyric.

The arrangement equitably features alternation of vocals and instrumentals. Monroe plays an introductory verse on his mandolin. Notice that rather than merely trilling a note to keep the sound going, Monroe picks the note he wants to sustain in strict sixteenth note rhythm, contributing to the composite pulse of the band.

The vocalists enter singing the chorus. Lester Flatt is singing the lead below Bill Monroe's "high lonesome" tenor harmony. The fiddle follows with a paraphrase of the chorus melody, concluding the introductory segment of the arrangement (instrumental/vocal/instrumental).

Lester Flatt now sings the first verse. Notice that any vocal entrance following an instrumental is delayed by one measure. This was a technique developed by Flatt to add space between the conclusion of the instrumental solo and the resumption of the vocal. Since many bluegrass pieces employ very fast tempos, this

Listening Guide   14.1

"It's Mighty Dark for Me to Travel" 2 beats per measure

ELAPSED TIME	FORM	EVENT DESCRIPTION
:00	Instr. verse	Mandolin (17 measures: 16 + 1 extension)
:13	Chorus	Vocal duet (16 measures)
:27	Instr. verse 1	Fiddle (17 measures: 16 + 1 extension)
:40	Verse 1	Vocal (16 measures)
:52	Chorus	Vocal duet (16 measures)
1:06	Instr. verse 2	Banjo (17 measures: 16 + 1 extension)
1:19	Verse 2	Vocal (16 measures)
1:30	Chorus	Vocal duet (16 measures)
1:44	Instr. verse 3	Mandolin (17 measures: 16 + 1 extension)
1:57	Verse 3	Vocal (16 measures)
2:09	Chorus	Vocal duet (16 measures)
2:23	Instr. verse 4	Fiddle (17 measures: 16 + 1 extension)
2:35	Chorus	Vocal duet (16 measures)
2:50	End	

delaying technique (in this case, adding a seventeenth bar to the instrumental chorus) was used for a number of aesthetic and logistical reasons. An aesthetic reason would be to "let the smoke clear" from the instrumental display and give the listener time to make the transition back to the vocal. A logistical reason would be to give the instrumentalist time to back away from the microphone and the singer(s) time to move in. (Keep in mind that many bluegrass bands had only one microphone to work with; they developed smooth choreography and musical devices such as this delay to get in and out of the microphone area.) This technique is not necessary and is not used going from the vocal verse to the vocal chorus. Notice that the only time that Monroe sings harmony with Flatt is when the chorus is sung.

The first verse/chorus combination is followed by Earl Scruggs's banjo solo. He picks out his improvised melody on the lower strings while playing harmony and maintaining a sixteenth note patter on the upper strings. Most banjoists before Scruggs used a "frailing" or "claw hammer" technique, brushing down the strings with the backs of the fingers followed by picking a note with the thumb. Scruggs uses an energetic three-finger picking technique in his right hand, allowing him to pick faster and to play more complex melodies and rhythms. From his performance, it is easy to recognize what a crucial addition the banjo was to the bluegrass string band texture.

Flatt and Monroe follow with a second verse/chorus combination. Monroe then plays the chorus melody on the mandolin, as he did in the introduction; this acts as an interlude to the second half of the arrangement. A third verse/chorus combination is sung, followed by "Chubby" Wise's improvised fiddle solo. Wise uses rapid single-line figures and slides into blue notes, taken from blues and jazz, as well as employing double notes and more traditional fiddle devices. After the fiddle solo, Flatt and Monroe sing the chorus alone, as they did in the introduction. This concludes the piece.

Flatt and Scruggs

Bill Monroe and the Blue Grass Boys established the repertoire, the instrumentation, and the technical standard for bluegrass, as well as giving the style its name. (Actually, disc jockeys and fans named the style after the band. Note that the style, *bluegrass,* is one word and the band's name is two words, *Blue Grass.*) In 1948, at the height of the group's popularity and influence, Lester Flatt and Earl Scruggs left and formed their own band.

Flatt and Scruggs were one of country music's most popular acts in the 1950s and 1960s and probably did the most to bring bluegrass to national attention. They achieved this when they performed "The Ballad of Jed Clampett" for the popular television series *The Beverly Hillbillies* in 1962 and "Foggy Mountain Breakdown" in the 1967 film *Bonnie and Clyde.*

The group was named the Foggy Mountain Boys after a Carter Family song they often played, "Foggy Mountain Top." Their instrumentation was the same as Bill Monroe's band, though they made the significant addition of the Dobro in 1955. While not the first to include the Dobro in a bluegrass band, they did popularize its use and nurtured the development of a fast fingerpicking Dobro technique similar to what the other string instruments were playing. Lester Flatt played the guitar and did the lead singing; Earl Scruggs did a bit of harmony singing but mainly played the banjo. Scruggs went on to expand his already incredible technique, raising the standard of the banjo to unprecedented heights.

Analysis of "Earl's Breakdown" (*SCCCM*, 13/3)

One of the techniques Scruggs perfected on the banjo was tuning it as he played. He composed "Earl's Breakdown" to showcase this technique. Instead of just sliding his finger along the fretboard to raise and lower the pitch of a string, Scruggs actually turned the tuning peg on the head of the instrument to make a note slide up or down. The trick was to then quickly and accurately reset the string to its original open tuning. To this end, Scruggs developed a special tuning gear for the banjo; the peg comes out the back of the head instead of from the sides. This makes it easier for the banjoist to manipulate the gear while playing.

The form of "Earl's Breakdown" is verse/chorus, typical of many fiddle tunes and many folk songs. Scruggs demonstrates again the syncopated rhythms and intricate melodic lines that can be rendered by his three-finger right-hand technique. The other members of the Foggy Mountain Boys perform equally sterling solos.

In the verses, Scruggs used the common technique of sliding his finger along a string to raise or lower its pitch. The melody of the chorus is designed to feature Scruggs's tuning trick, a virtuoso display that has delighted audiences for years. At the beginning of the chorus melody, Scruggs picks his high D string once, then moves to the lower B string. Immediately after picking the B string, he turns its tuning peg to loosen the string and make the note slide down. Lester Flatt finishes the melody on the guitar while Scruggs tightens the string back up to its original note.

Flatt and Scruggs broke up in 1969. Lester Flatt returned to more traditional bluegrass, with his Nashville Grass, until his death in 1979. Earl Scruggs formed the Earl Scruggs Revue with his three sons. They experimented with electrifying

Listening Guide   14.2
"Earl's Breakdown" 2 beats per measure

ELAPSED TIME	FORM	EVENT DESCRIPTION
:00	Verse 1	Banjo solo (17 measures: 16 + 1 extension)
:15	Chorus 1	Banjo solo, string slides (17 measures: 16 + 1 extension)
:29	Verse 2	Fiddle solo (17 measures: 16 + 1 extension)
:43	Verse 3	Fiddle solo (16 measures: 7 + 8 + 1 extension)
:57	Verse 4	Banjo solo (17 measures: 16 + 1 extension)
1:10	Chorus 2	Banjo solo, string slides (17 measures: 16 + 1 extension)
1:25	Verse 5	Fiddle solo (17 measures: 16 + 1 extension)
1:39	Verse 6	Mandolin solo (17 measures: 16 + 1 extension)
1:54	Verse 7	Banjo solo (17 measures: 16 + 1 extension)
2:07	Chorus 3	Banjo solo, string slides (17 measures: 16 + 1 extension)
2:21	Verse 8	Fiddle solo (17 measures: 16 + 1 extension)
2:36	Verse 9	Banjo solo (17 measures: 16 + 1 extension)
2:50	Ending	Banjo solo (6 measures)
2:57	End	

bluegrass, indicative of the cross-influence bluegrass and progressive rock were having on each other at the time.

The Bluegrass Legacy Continues

Ralph and Carter Stanley were Bill Monroe's first stylistic descendants that had not been members of his band. Ralph played banjo Scruggs- and claw hammer–style and sang a high, Monroe-style tenor. Carter was the guitarist. The Stanleys held down the more traditional side of bluegrass, which was more heavily influenced by older string bands and southeastern sentimental ballads and gospel music. Their original material was consistent in character with their traditional material, such as Carter Stanley's "The Lonesome River" (*SCCCM*, 13/4), a nostalgic sentimental song glorifying rural life.

Many other bluegrass stars came on the scene in subsequent years, some veterans of Monroe's Blue Grass Boys: Jim and Jesse McReynolds, Mac Wiseman, the Osborne Brothers, to name a few. The rock milieu's fascination with acoustic folk music in the late 1950s and early 1960s led to the inclusion of bluegrass. Some young people embraced it because it seemed to be a vestige of tradition amid the commercial artificiality of both mainstream popular music and Nashville's crossover country. Others embraced the music for its own sake rather than as a symbol of a cherished cultural tradition. Many old and new bluegrass practitioners openly experimented with the music Monroe developed, adding electric guitars and keyboards, electric pedal steel, and drums, and using elements of jazz, rock, and other styles. Earl Scruggs eventually explored these resources, as did the Osborne Brothers.

The experimentation of youthful new bluegrass artists in the 1960s led to the adoption of the term *newgrass*. The Country Gentlemen were at the forefront of this expansion of style and repertoire within bluegrass, including bluegrass ren-

Béla Fleck and the Flecktones, a pioneering group that uses bluegrass as a stylistic launching pad.

ditions of songs made famous by folk-rock groups such as Crosby, Stills, and Nash, Bob Dylan, Creedence Clearwater Revival, and the Byrds. The Country Gentlemen broke up at the beginning of the seventies, and members formed separate groups that became just as famous and influential, groups such as the Second Generation and Seldom Scene.

From the 1980s on, bluegrass has continued to flourish along the continuum from traditional acoustic music to progressive. Since bluegrass has dealt with instrumental virtuosity and improvisation, it has a kindred spirit with jazz. It is not surprising that some bluegrass artists have exhibited strong jazz characteristics in their music. Béla Fleck (b. 1958) is a New York–born banjoist, influenced by banjo playing he heard on the television show *The Beverly Hillbillies* and in the movie *Deliverance*. At the same time, he intently studied the music of jazz pioneers Charlie Parker and John Coltrane. During the 1980s he was a member of New Grass Revival; he then became a member of Strength in Numbers, a remarkable group of musicians who would shape virtuoso instrumental country music, including Dobro guitarist Jerry Douglas, mandolin player Sam Bush, fiddler Mark O'Connor, and bassist Edgar Meyer. In 1989 Fleck assembled a remarkable band for a PBS television special, thereafter known as the Flecktones. Most remarkable among the members was bassist Victor Wooten, a musician with incredible technique and heavily influenced by R&B, funk, and jazz.

In 2000 bluegrass again found favor with a mainstream youth audience with Nickel Creek, comprised of father and son Scott and Chris Thile and siblings Sean and Sara Watkins. They have won numerous awards as individual instrumentalists and as a group at bluegrass festivals. With a young, fresh, alternative music-type look, virtuoso talent, and original compositions that range in influence from Bill Monroe to Ella Fitzgerald, they have made bluegrass appealing to a young audience. They released their first self-titled album in 2000 (Sugar Hill 3909), and their videos were programmed regularly on music television. In 2001 they appeared with veteran country singer/songwriter Dolly Parton on her "Shine" video.

Fiddler Mark O'Connor was born in Seattle, Washington, in 1961. He was a championship fiddler while still a boy and toured with French jazz violin legend Stephane Grappelli before moving to Nashville in 1983. He became the first-call session fiddler in town, recording for a score of country stars on more than 450 releases. On the side he recorded with such jazz luminaries as saxophonist Michael Brecker. In 1990 he assembled 54 of the top instrumentalists in Nashville to record the remarkable *The New Nashville Cats* (CD format, Warner Brothers 9 26509-2). The album shows a remarkable range of style—Cajun, Applachian, bluegrass, swing, bebop, and Celtic. O'Connor eventually left the demanding studio scene to pursue his own artistic endeavors, including the composition of a fiddle concerto (*Fiddle Concerto,* Warner Brother 45846), featuring himself with symphony orchestra, and jazz sessions paying homage to Grappelli (*Hot Swing* OMAC 2001).

Other major artists who have exhibited both traditionalism and innovation within bluegrass include Alison Krauss (b. 1971 in Champaign, Illinois), a classically trained violinist and championship fiddler whose group, Union Station, plays repertoire ranging from traditional fiddle tunes to the Beatles. Ricky Skaggs, born in Kentucky in 1954, played guitar with most of the first-generation bluegrass legends as a boy. In later years he was influenced by rock and jazz, but he never strayed far from his traditional bluegrass roots. In the late 1970s he teamed up with young traditionalists Emmylou Harris and Rodney Crowell. After reaching his commercial peak during the 1980s, he then suffered from the favored slick, crossover sound of country in the 1990s.

Bluegrass in all of its forms continues to flourish at music festivals all over the country. It has managed to capture the attention of devotees of classical, folk, jazz, country, and rock and continues to draw prodigious young talent into its ranks.

In 2001, bluegrass and old-time music in general enjoyed tremendous popularity with the release of Joel and Ethan Coen's movie and soundtrack *O, Brother Where Art Thou,* a 1930s era southern setting of Homer's *Odyssey.* The dashing portrayal of the Ulysses character by actor George Clooney and the integration of delta blues, gospel, work songs, and early country folk music into the atmosphere of the film suddenly made the Old South and its music chic. Under the direction of old-time music performer and authority T-Bone Burnett, a stellar line-up of artists was assembled for the soundtrack, including Ralph Stanley, Alison Krauss and Union Station, John Hartford, Emmylou Harris and others. Particularly successful was the rendition of "I Am a Man of Constant Sorrow," performed in the film by Clooney and his two cohorts as the fictitious Soggy Bottom Boys, but actually performed by Union Station member Dan Tyminski.

The soundtrack swept the 2001 CMA awards, taking the album and single of the year awards, and two nominations for best vocal event. At the 2001 International Bluegrass Music Association Awards, held October 4 in Louisville, Kentucky, and simulcast on radio stations across the country, the soundtrack won Album of The Year, Song of the Year, and Gospel Recorded Performance of the Year. Additionally, it was honored with a Distinguished Achievement Award for filmmakers, the Coen Brothers, and soundtrack producer, T Bone Burnett. Widely credited with propelling the popularity of bluegrass music beyond it's core audience, *O Brother Where Art Thou* sold nearly 3 million copies and held the #1 position on the Billboard Country Album Chart for an astonishing 21 weeks. The follow-up album *Down from the Mountain* sold over 300,000 copies. In the fall of 2002 there was a 25-city tour with the soundtrack artists and an accompanying D. A. Pennebaker documentary on PBS-TV. CMT had begun airing a 30-minute documentary in November 2000.

New Artists and Renewed Traditions in Country Music

As it emerged from the 1950s, country music was solidly divided into two camps: the Nashville crossover country music producers and the upholders of Texas honky tonk. Roles were reversed in the 1960s. For years the Southeast was the custodian of traditional country music, whereas Southwest styles acted as the force for eclecticism. By the sixties southwestern honky tonk became the threatened bastion of traditionalism, endangered by the emergence of rock and roll and country crossover's attempts to compete with it.

Rock and roll was a threat from within; a large portion of its ancestry is from country music, realized in the music of southerners like Elvis Presley, Jerry Lee Lewis, Buddy Holly, and Carl Perkins, just to mention a few. The country music industry made several attempts to deal with this new *rockabilly* style with offerings ranging from Tennessee Ernie Ford's "Sixteen Tons" (*SCCCM*, 11/3, CD 2/25) and Marty Robbins's "El Paso" (*SCCCM*, 12/4, CD 3/8) to the Everly Brothers. The Everlys were a continuation of the brother duets of the 1930s, evidenced by their reworking of Charlie Monroe's (comember with Bill in the Monroe Brothers) 1947 recording of the nineteenth-century murder ballad "Down in the Willow Garden" (*SCCCM*, 11/4). In subsequent years, rockabilly artists such as Charlie Rich, Johnny Cash, Conway Twitty, and Jerry Lee Lewis comfortably crossed back and forth prompting country music to electrify other instruments, even the fiddles, and to make the drums a permanent part of the band. Since Webb Pierce's recordings in the early 1950s, no instrument has been more associated with honky tonk than the electric pedal steel, its plaintive sliding adding the perfect instrumental touch to hard country vocal stylings. So-called country rock or southern rock bands have convincingly occupied both the country pop and honky tonk camps of country music. The Allman Brothers and Lynyrd Skynyrd are country rock bands that illustrate the obscuring of stylistic boundaries that has typified rock since its beginning. Artists such as Charlie Daniels and Hank Williams, Jr., represent the honky tonk end of the country rock spectrum, as do many of the bands and artists of the Austin outlaw country scene discussed earlier.

Country Peaks at the Millennium

Country music of the 1990s rose to unprecedented heights of popular success. The industry and its artists were more sophisticated than ever, as were the songs they purveyed. Female country artists were dominant figures with multidimensional personas that reflected the expressions and images of the modern woman. Country music saw its first billionaire artist in the person of Garth Brooks, the pioneer of the most convincing country/pop crossover in the history of the genre. Still, as it has always been in country music, there were battles between traditionalists and those who sought to redefine the music to reach a wider audience.

Garth Brooks, the most successful artist in country music history and one of the most successful artists in all of popular music. After a hiatus from the music scene, his *Scarecrow* album even knocked teen pop idol Britney Spears out of first place within a week of its release in November 2001.

A good point of departure for a narrative of 1990s country music is a group of male artists sometimes referred to as "the class of '89." This would include Alan Jackson, Clint Black, Travis Tritt, and Garth Brooks. (Other references to this fraternity have included Marty Stuart and a couple of others who found success at the end of the 1980s.)

Alan Jackson is an artist who has preserved a strong honky tonk tradition in his music, and his song lyrics have often commented sarcastically upon the trendy activity in the

Honky tonk traditionalist, singer, and songwriter Alan Jackson.

Nashville music scene as the commercial tide of country music rose. Jackson was born in Newman, Georgia, in 1958. After writing and playing music part-time, his wife got him a connection with country/pop legend Glen Campbell and his formidable country publishing and management company in 1985. He eventually hooked up with Arista Records' new Nashville division, becoming their first country artist in 1990. His debut album, *Here in the Real World,* went platinum, and his second album, released a year later, went double platinum. "Don't Rock the Jukebox," the title cut from the second album, accurately reflected Jackson's style and sentiment. Depicting the image of the brokenhearted cowboy at the honky tonk jukebox was a staple formula, reaching back to Hank Thompson's "The Wild Side of Life" and its rebuttal song, Kitty Wells's "It Wasn't God Who Made Honky Tonk Angels." The style of Alan Jackson's song is pure honky tonk shuffle, and the lyric admonishes the patrons not to dial up rock music on the jukebox, that only the honky tonk moans of George Jones could express the lovesickness of the protagonist listener.

Jackson also reached many listeners with his musical tributes to working-class people, struggling families, and small-town parties. "Livin' on Love" is a heartwarming song about couples young and old who have little but each other. "(It's Alright to Be) Little Bitty" glorifies small towns and common people. "Little Man" pays tribute to the hardworking underemployed. As mentioned earlier, Jackson could also offer biting commentary about the country music world itself. In "Gone Country," Jackson observes how people from every location and background, no matter how far removed from the country culture, bought a pair of boots and came to Nashville to cash in on country music, no matter how insincere the effort. "Murder on Music Row," recorded with country titan and fellow traditionalist George Strait, is a polemical view of what was passing for country music in Nashville in the late 1990s. Each artist exaggerates the sounds and styles of George Jones and Merle Haggard for all they are worth, probably to spite the slick, prevailing crossover style and cram raw honky tonk down the throats of their musical adversaries.

Historically, Clint Black served as the transitional figure between the country stars of the 1980s, such as George Strait and Randy Travis, and the new generation that reached its apex with Garth Brooks. Born in New Jersey but raised in Katy, Texas, Black began his songwriting collaboration with Hayden Nicholas in 1987 and was contracted to RCA Nashville the next year. In 1989 his single "A Better Man" became a huge hit, paving the way for his successful debut album *Killin' Time. Killin' Time* yielded a remarkable number of hit singles, including the title track and "Nobody's Home." In 1991 he married television actress Lisa Hartman and recorded a duet with her on his 1999 self-produced album *D'lectrified.* He has continued his success to the time of this writing, but Black has never matched the achievement of his first album.

To many, the main thing that distinguishes Travis Tritt from the rest of the country "class of '89" is that he is the only one who doesn't wear a western hat. He was also the only one to reflect a strong influence of southern rock along with traditional honky tonk. In 1989 he signed with Warner Brothers Nashville and debuted his album *Country Club*. The country music establishment was hesitant to promote Tritt because of his rock-style presentation and look (he continues to sport shoulder-length hair). In 1994 Tritt recovered from a slight popularity slump with arguably his most famous song, "Ten Feet Tall and Bulletproof."

Whereas Travis Tritt met resistance from the custodians of traditional country music because of his high-energy rock influence, the juggernaut of Garth Brooks created an explosion that marked a pivotal moment in the genre. His dominance of the country and pop world was a verbose fulfillment of the promise made by Patti Page's crossover rendition of "The Tennessee Waltz" in 1950.

Brooks achieved his success by creating a most successful fusion of traditional country styles and images combined with rock music. Whereas most of his immediate predecessors (George Strait, Randy Travis, Clint Black) just stood on stage and sang, Brooks brought dramatic heavy metal, stadium rock aspects into his show, replete with fireworks, guitar smashing, mosh pit jumping, flying over the audience on cables, and a cordless head-mounted microphone usually found on dancing pop acts like Madonna or the Backstreet Boys. His vocal style was true to his Oklahoma-born, post–Merle Haggard roots, and his dress was pure rodeo. Like any young man his age (he was born in Oklahoma in 1962), he was familiar with heavy rock music and stage presentation. He combined honky tonk with dramatic narrative, humor, and pop power-ballad style. While staying fairly close to country themes, his music had an edge and sense of high drama that immediately connected with a mass audience, thrusting him as far into the mainstream as any artist could hope to be.

After honing his skills in Oklahoma, Garth Brooks made an abortive attempt of landing a contract in Nashville. He returned two years later and got Capitol Records to accept his demo and sign him in 1988. He gained good initial success with four hit singles from his self-titled first album, including "If Tomorrow Never Comes" and "The Dance." With the release of his second album, *No Fences*, the Garth phenomenon was well under way. Riding on the wave of one of its singles, the class-conscious, sing-along party song "Friends in Low Places," *No Fences* topped the country charts for 23 weeks and cranked out a number of hit singles. In September 1991 Garth Brooks' third album, *Ropin' the Wind*, was released. It was the first country album to debut at the top of the pop charts.

Over the 1990s Brooks released several recordings and reissue packages with remarkable sales figures, but he peaked so strongly with *No Fences* and *Ropin' the Wind* that the later releases will always be viewed as mere aftermath. The intensity of his career led Brooks to other pursuits. Always interested in sports, he tried out unsuccessfully for the San Diego Padres baseball team. He also became interested in acting, particularly a film project about a dark figure of a rock star named Chris Gaines. Prior to the film's release in 2000, Brooks set about gradually acclimating his fans to his new image as the Chris Gaines character. He did a television special and released an album of songs portraying Gaines. His slim, gaunt, and brooding look was shocking and unconvincing to legions of fans accustomed to the affable, flamboyant, chubby Brooks in his cowboy hat. Bewildered by the huge commercial *faux pas* and suffering domestic problems at home, Brooks announced his retirement from show business.

Just when we thought we had seen the last of Garth Brooks, he released a new album in November of 2001, *Scarecrow*. It was not indicative of any radical change in Brooks's style, but it did prove how eagerly fans would grab up any new material that he would issue. Within two weeks after *Scarecrow* hit the stands, sales of the compact disc eclipsed established pop diva Britney Spears.

Female Country Artists in the 1990s

In the 1980s and early 1990s there were many pioneering female artists in country music, offering a variety of images, topics, and expressions. Some had tough feminist stances; some were more good-humored in their rebuttals to men; some offered wry, intellectual views of the world; and some offered torchy, emotional love songs. Mary Chapin Carpenter brought a cerebral folk-like quality to her music, establishing a hit with "I Feel Lucky," about a down-on-her-luck waitress who suddenly wins the lottery. Martina McBride, Suzy Bogguss, Lari White, Trisha Yearwood, and Pam Tillis featured many great songs. Perhaps the most successful woman country artist at the time was Reba McEntire. An Oklahoma ranch girl, she brought her hard western accent and tough-but-sensitive image to the forefront of country music, while also making significant impact on the pop music market. She also had several successful roles acting on television and in film.

However, in the mid-1990s women country artists were to become a commercial phenomenon that could almost rival the unheard-of success of Garth Brooks. Shania Twain is an artist who many consider outside the circle of country music; and as many have done before her, she redesigned the music and imagery of country until its roots are barely evident. Twain was born in Ontario, Canada, in 1965. She signed with Mercury Nashville and released a debut album in 1993. Shortly afterward, she met and eventually married Robert John "Mutt" Lange, a producer known for his work with hard-rock bands like AC/DC, Foreigner, and Def Leppard. He had shown an interest in moving into country music production and thought Shania just the vehicle for doing so. Together they wrote the material for her second album, *The Woman in Me.*

Canadian-born Shania Twain, collaborating with husband and rock producer Mutt Lange, became one of the most successful crossover country stars of all times.

The music had a rock production feel uncommon to other country albums at the time. In many cases only the presence of a fiddle or steel guitar gave any indication that the music was intended to be country at all. However, Shania Twain's biggest innovation, and the greatest affront to the traditional country establishment, was her image in concerts and music videos. Staggeringly beautiful and sexy, Twain bared her midriff and presented herself in a decided MTV-like way. In her high-energy and pop-styled concerts she wore Madonna-like head mike and competed for the pop diva's audience. Twain's life has been the ultimate Horatio Alger story, from raising herself and her orphaned siblings to the ultimate country/pop diva. At the end of the 1990s Twain retreated from her successful career to the isolation of her home in Geneva, Switzerland. In the fall of 2001 she gave birth to her and Lange's first child. No one in the press ever saw her trademark tummy "in a family way."

Close on Shania Twain's heels has been Faith Hill. Born in Jackson, Mississippi, in 1967, she was part of the coterie of new country females in the early 1990s, scoring a hit single with "Wild One" in 1993 and a second hit single the next year with "Piece of My Heart." In 1996 she married country star Tim McGraw and, in 1999, released the album *Breathe* and hit title song. By the end of the 1990s Hill had overtaken Shania Twain as the most beautiful female country crossover artist. She and husband Tim McGraw swept the country awards shows coming into the twenty-first century; and at the time of this writing, Hill has been marketed full steam as a pop music artist in the vein of Celine Dion.

Equally successful in country and mainstream arenas has been a female vocal group called the Dixie Chicks. The group began as a neo-western cowgirl and bluegrass group, similar to the kitschy Riders in the Sky (prominently featured in the Disney computer-animated feature *Toy Story 2*). In fact, its first album, recorded in 1992 for the independent Crystal Clear label, was entitled *Thank Heavens for Dale Evans*. Darlings of the alternative Deep Ellum club scene in Dallas, Texas, and frequent guests of eclectic programs like NPR's *A Prairie Home Companion*, the group decided to go with an edgier, more contemporary sound and youthful look. The decision meant the demise of bassist Laura Lynch and guitarist Robin Lynn Macy. The remaining members, champion fiddler Martie Seidel and banjoist sister Emily Erwin (Robison) added then 21-year-old Natalie Maines, daughter of steel-guitarist Lloyd Maines.

The Dale Evans–like movie western wardrobe was abandoned for a more pop look, and Natalie added an edgy persona and sound that was part traditional Appalachian twang and part alternative Irish reminiscent of the Cranberries' lead singer Delores O'Riordan. The Dixie Chicks left the obscurity of indie labels and made its first major label album, *Wide Open Spaces*, for Sony's Monument. No one could have ever predicted its success. Its advance single, "I Can Love You Better than That" hit the top 10 right away, followed by "There's Your Trouble." Within

The Dixie Chicks, a female country trio and one of the most successful country acts ever. Left to right: Emily Erwin Robison, Natalie Maines, and Martie Seidel holding their 2000 Grammy awards for best country album and best country performance with vocals by a duo or group.

a year *Wide Open Spaces* went quadruple-platinum, the best-selling country duo or group album in history. Like Garth Brooks and Shania Twain, the Dixie Chicks became superstars in both country and pop. While always intense and edgy, the group shows a range of style and emotion with torchy ballads like "Without You," honky tonk bar shuffles like "Tonight the Heartache's on Me," and a controversial yet lighthearted description of the justifiable homicide of an abusive mate in "Goodbye Earl." (The video featured *N.Y.P.D. Blue* star Dennis Franz as the wretched Earl.) The popularity of the country girl group format of the Dixie Chicks has inspired attempts at knockoff groups such as the Utah sister group SHeDAISY.

In 2000 the Dixie Chicks, weary of touring and concertizing, took time out of the limelight to stay home and have babies. It was symbolic of an overheated country music machine that had reached unimagined heights over the last decade. After a good run, neither the industry nor its stars could top itself and a decline followed. Recording projects and contracts were canceled, studios on Nashville's Music Row closed up, and country stations have repeated worn playlists of 1990s hits. This cycle is not unfamiliar in country music: Tradition revives the music, outsiders moves in and slicken it up, it enjoys a couple of years of crossover, then collapses once again. Like forest wildfires it is both destructive and cleansing, causing the strictly commercial venturists to disperse and the artists who cherish the heritage of the music to once again fan the flames of tradition in a young and renewed way. All the while, country music would do well to watch the career of George Strait, a loyal honky tonker with a modest persona who has endured through all kinds of stylistic trends for the last 20 years.

Ultimately, the universal appeal of country music is not that it is a southern thing or a rural country thing. In all parts of the United States and the world there is always a class-consciousness that country music has consistently addressed. It draws attention to the unglamorous world that defines most of the populous: people who aren't necessarily pretty or rich; people without position or advanced education; people who don't live in particularly interesting places; people in dead-end jobs, dead-end relationships, or conversely, people in wonderful relationships that don't look particularly remarkable to any one else. Country is one of the few styles that openly glorifies marriage and family, kids and old folks, fond and sentimental memories, and devastating heartache.

Country music's traditions have also made it distinctive in contemporary popular song. It is one of the few places you will still find a song in waltz time (3/4 meter). It is one of the few places you can find a new song based on the blues form. It is one of the last bastions of the songwriter's craft, with distinctive melodies, form, and a lyric that tells a story. It is aware of its "hick" image among much of the general population and often indulges in wonderful and conscious self-parody more to make fun of outsiders who don't know any better than to foster a stereotype. It exacts an ultimate revenge on its snooty urban detractors, such as that found in Toby Keith's award-winning song from 1999, "How Do You Like Me Now."

Chapter Summary

In the midst of southwestern honky tonk and Nashville crossover, Bill Monroe forged a distinctive style of acoustic string band music that came to be known as *bluegrass*. Characterized by a driving backbeat, a propulsive sixteenth-note pulse, and virtuosic instrumental and vocal techniques, it quickly gained a large and faithful following. Particularly notable is Earl Scruggs's development of the three-finger roll banjo technique. Bluegrass's blend of old-time repertoire and instrumentation with progressive, complex improvisation has led to future generations of eclectic practitioners who have blended elements of modern jazz, pop, and ethnic music into their repertoire.

In the early 1960s honky tonk became the more traditional country music set against Nashville's attempts at a more sophisticated crossover country style. This dichotomy of stylistic tendency has continued to this day with artists representing every point on the continuum between traditional and pop music styles. In the 1990s artists such as Alan Jackson and George Strait were immensely successful in maintaining traditional honky tonk, while Shania Twain and Faith Hill essentially redefined themselves as pop music divas. Garth Brooks found a middle ground and became, arguably, the most commercially successful artist in country music history.

Additional Listening

Refer to citations in the body of the text.

Béla Fleck and the Flecktones, *Flight of the Cosmic Hippo* (CD format, Warner Brothers 2-26562). This album shows the eclectic influences and virtuoso style of the Flecktones, replete with banjo power chords and Victor Wooten facile, funky bass.

Alan Jackson, *The Greatest Hits Collection* (CD format, Arista 18801). This collection is a useful source for all the defining Alan Jackson songs and performances of the early 1990s. It also brings together a stellar lineup of Nashville's greatest studio musicians.

Garth Brooks, *The Hits* (CD format, Liberty 29689). This album conveniently compiles all the major Brooks hits from the phenomenally successful albums *No Fences*, *Ropin' the Wind*, and others. It was only in print for a year but sold over eight million copies, so it should not be hard to find.

Shania Twain, *Come On Over* (CD format, Mercury 536003). Many of Twain's definitive hits are found on this album, and it is a good illustration of the heavily produced, big sound brought about by husband/producer "Mutt" Lange. Only subtle shadings of a country sound remain, as even the fiddles are so electronically processed as to sound like synthesizers.

The Dixie Chicks, *Wide Open Spaces* (CD format, Monument 68195). This was the Dixie Chicks' breakout album and the premiere of lead singer Natalie Maines. The album demonstrates a wide variety of moods and a convincing combination of traditional elements, such as the prominent use of banjo and fiddle, and grittier, rock/pop-oriented sensibilities.

Review Questions

1. What musical influences did Bill Monroe encounter in his upbringing that can eventually be found in bluegrass?
2. Describe the aggressive nature of bluegrass vocal and instrumental performance compared to earlier country string band styles.
3. Describe the five-string banjo techniques pioneered by Earl Scruggs.
4. What was bluegrass's relationship with the urban folk revival in the late 1950s and early 1960s?

5. How did southwestern honky tonk become the conservative faction of country music in the 1960s?

6. What instruments and lyric topics prevail in *hard country?*

7. How does Alan Jackson and George Strait's "Murder on Music Row" reflect the ongoing tradition versus crossover controversy in the country music scene?

8. What commercial strides did women country artists make in the 1980s and 1990s?

9. Describe Garth Brooks's stage and music style that made him such a commercial phenomenon in the 1990s.

Notes

1. Jimmie Rodgers can be heard singing "Mule Skinner Blues (Blue Yodel No. 8)" on the second edition of *SCCCM,* CD 1/7.

Rock and the Gathering of America's Music

Part 4

15

The Origins and Development of Early Rock

It is a source of argument as to when rock began and from whom it came. Some think it started with Jackie Brenston's "Rocket 88" from 1951 or "Sh-Boom" by the Chords in 1954. It could have been "Rock Around the Clock," recorded in 1954 by Bill Haley and His Comets or Elvis Presley's "That's Alright Mama" from 1954. The truth, of course, is that rock came from several styles and several regions at once. Rock successfully fused disparate ethnic musical traditions with the pop music industry of the dominant culture. It is a culmination, a summit of all the music that is America.

World War II drastically changed the social structure and cultural geography of America. The general pace of life accelerated, diverse cultural groups intermingled, and more Americans than ever settled into a period of unprecedented prosperity. Suddenly, America had ample time and money for leisure, and the burgeoning middle class became the hungry consumers of products like cars and entertainment. The increased prosperity and leisure time engendered a new consumer market that no one had anticipated: America's youth. The youth market of post–World War II arrived as unexpectedly as the Negro entertainment market after the postwar boom of World War I—and the effect on the music industry was infinitely more far-reaching.

ROCK BEGINS

"It seemed to me that Negroes were the only ones that had any freshness left in their music," remembered Sam Phillips of his early days in Memphis when he ran a recording studio and was looking for a unique new sound.[1] America's youth was bored with the polite music of their parents, and they were looking for a unique sound, too. What they found was the driving rhythm and raw excitement of black rhythm and blues, the urban version of southern country blues that was characterized by a heavy backbeat and an amplified sound. Rock historian Charlie Gillett notes:

> In almost every respect, the sounds of rhythm and blues contradicted those of popular music. The vocal styles were harsh, the songs explicit, the dominant instruments—saxophone, piano, guitar, drums—were played loudly and with an emphatic dance rhythm, the production of the records was crude. The prevailing emotion was excitement.[2]

We cannot be completely certain how music confined to black audiences fell into the hands of white American youth. It was probably due to a cult subculture of eclectic whites who had listened to blues on records and, starting around 1948, on black radio. From this subculture, the music spread to and found favor with the mainstream of America's young people. Doubtless, parents were outraged when they heard this antithesis to their own music blaring through their children's bedroom doors—which suited the kids just fine. If the young people had originally been drawn to rhythm and blues for its sound alone, they soon embraced it as a tool of rebellion against the conformist expectations of their parents. With the reinforcement of generation gap themes in the movies of the day, like those of James Dean and Marlon Brando, the youth became a viable cultural group within America, characterized not by race, ethnicity, or region, as in the past, but by age.

Early Influences on Rock

Rock did not suddenly appear in the mid-1950s; it evolved logically from available folk and popular music of America's history. By taking inventory of the regional and ethnic musical elements that contributed to rock, we can better appreciate what a remarkable synthesis of styles it really is while displaying a distinctiveness of its own.

The Southwest

Jazz from the Southwest was deeply indebted to the blues. A good deal of the material played by southwestern bands like Count Basie's and Jay McShann's consisted of blues sung by a singer fronting the band—singers like McShann and Basie's Jimmy Rushing. The arrangements of southwestern bands were also simpler compared to those of the swing bands in New York. The bluesy vocals, the hard-edged tenor sax solos, and the driving rhythm and brass riffs had a profound impact on early northern rock and roll.

Country music in the Southwest was the vanguard in developing the use of electric guitars and steel guitars. The same was true for southwestern blues and jazz. Oklahoman Charlie Christian developed modern jazz electric guitar, making it more of a hornlike instrument. Other pioneers of southwestern electric blues and jazz guitar were southwestern arranger, trombonist, and guitarist Eddie Durham and Texan Aaron "T-Bone" Walker. Walker took advantage of the electric guitar's ability to sustain notes, an ability that allowed him to use slow pitch bends and finger vibrato that lent the same expressiveness to the guitar that blues singers enjoyed. Combined with the sheer power and potentially raucous tone of the electric guitar, Walker helped to usher in hard-driving urban blues that were devoid of the delicacy of acoustic country blues. He also recast the role of the guitar as a strong lead instrument, able to hold its own even when backed by a large horn band.[3]

The Southwest was also the home of boogie-woogie blues, a rhythmic bass pattern idiomatic to the piano. It is a bass pattern of eighth notes one measure in length. The actual series of notes varies somewhat from player to player, but the notes are secondary to the rolling, rhythmic feel it creates. Boogie-woogie was developed by black blues pianists such as Meade Lux Lewis, Albert Ammons, Pete Johnson, and Jimmy Yancey. Boogie piano soon found its way to Chicago's South Side, as well as into the country repertoires of the western swing bands of Bob Wills and Milton Brown, the honky tonk piano of Moon Mullican, and the duets of the Delmore Brothers—all country artists who would heavily influence the young rockabilly artists of the South.

Boogie-woogie enjoyed brief popular success when entrepreneur John Hammond brought Kansas City blues singer Big Joe Turner and pianist Pete Johnson to Carnegie Hall for his Spirituals to Swing concert in 1938. The catchy boogie rhythm led to popular white imitations, such as Tommy Dorsey's "Boogie-Woogie" and the Andrews Sisters' "Boogie-Woogie Bugle Boy."

The Southeast

The center for urban blues activity was Chicago, but the Windy City had direct ties to the urban blues development in Memphis. Beale Street had been a gathering place for country blues musicians since the turn of the century, and W. C. Handy had developed a highly successful commercial version of the blues on Beale in the early part of the century. The blues tradition of Beale Street remained strong into the fifties, evolving into urban electric blues like that found in Chicago. In 1951 Sam Phillips, a white radio man from Florence, Alabama, (Handy's birthplace, coincidentally), opened a recording studio in Memphis. He recorded Memphis bluesmen and then leased the masters to labels like Chess in Chicago and Modern in Los Angeles. Now-famous bluesmen like B. B. King, Bobby Bland, and Chester Burnett (Howlin' Wolf) were recorded by Phillips. One of the most influential records from this period was "Rocket 88," performed in 1951 by Jackie Brenston and backed by Ike Turner's Kings of Rhythm of Clarksdale, Mississippi. The song had a boogie rhythm, distorted electric guitar, a gutsy sax solo, and a lyric about cars. Some feel that this hit R&B record was also the first rock record in history.

Another influential element in the Southeast was the black church, which was a strong repository for black music. The Pentecostal-Holiness movement around the turn of the century led to the establishment of many new fundamentalist sects; it also led to a new era in sacred music that would affect both whites and blacks. The Church of God in Christ, a predominantly black sect found in Memphis in 1895, greatly contributed to black music in this century, as did the existing black Baptist, Sanctified, and African Methodist Episcopal churches. One distinctive product of music in southeastern black churches was the unaccompanied male gospel quartets. By the 1920s, jazz and blues stylings and instrumentation were coming out of the bars and into the church, aided in large part by the work of Thomas A. Dorsey, the father of gospel music. (Dorsey and gospel music will be discussed further in Chapter 19.) The rollicking rhythms and group harmony of black and white Pentecostal music would prove to be strong influences on rockabilly, vocal group rock, and soul music.

As rock and roll began to appear as a distinctive entity around 1954, and until around 1956, it was comprised of five basic styles, defined by region, that developed independently of each other but depended on the rhythms of black music for their beat.

Five Styles of Rock and Roll from 1954–1956[4]

Northern Band Rock and Roll

This style can be basically described as white cover versions of certain black rhythm and blues numbers. The primary inspiration for northern band rock and roll was *jump blues,* based on a heavy boogie rhythm, a strong backbeat, and characterized by high-spirited feelings with novelty appeal rather than the lugubrious nature of other blues. One of the most influential performers of jump blues was Arkansas-born Louis Jordan, whose black band the Tympany Five made a seldom-seen appearance on the pop charts in 1946 with "Choo-Choo Ch'Boogie" on Decca Records. Jordan played good alto sax; he had a pleasing, smooth voice; he sang his words with clear enunciation; and he had an effervescent stage personality. His combination of lively boogie dance rhythms and his humorous, good-natured approach to the woeful subject matter of the blues made him a favorite throughout the forties.

Louis Jordan was the primary model for Bill Haley, a Detroit-born guitarist and singer. In the late forties Haley led a western swing band in the northeast. During that time he began to incorporate elements of Jordan-style jump blues into his style, essentially becoming a white rhythm and blues band with a country flavor. In 1951 Haley changed the name of his group from the Saddlemen to Bill Haley and His Comets, disassociating the band from country music and moving toward rock and roll. This evolution culminated in his recording of "Crazy, Man, Crazy" in 1953 and "Shake, Rattle, and Roll" in 1954 (a modified cover version of Big Joe Turner's recording from the same year). His biggest hit was "Rock Around the Clock," a 1954 cover version of an unsuccessful R&B record by Sonny Dae. However, the real popularity of the tune came about as the result of its inclusion in the teen-oriented movie *Blackboard Jungle*. The successful features that can be found on most of Haley's records are twangy guitar solos, growling saxophone solos, lively shouting-style vocals that rely more on their musical appeal than the appeal of the singer himself, and the group riff sections á la the big bands.

Bill Haley and His Comets, rehearsing at London's Dominion Theatre during their European tour on February 6, 1957.

New Orleans pianist and singer Fats Domino performing in Stockholm, Sweden on May 22, 1973.

New Orleans Dance Blues

In addition to its distinctive jazz tradition, New Orleans had a thriving tradition of rhythm and blues that is being tapped to this day. In the forties some R&B labels began recording their artists in New Orleans, as well as scouting out new talent already there. By the fifties there was a distinctive style of rock and roll that came from that city, primarily due to the efforts of producer and local big band leader Dave Bartholomew and recording engineer Cosimo Matassa.

Their greatest find among the local talent was Antoine "Fats" Domino, a rotund young pianist and singer. He was discovered in a bar in 1949 singing "Junker's Blues." His recording career began with "Fat Man" for Imperial in 1949, which was a tremendous R&B hit. Over the next five years Domino and his producers modified his style and found tremendous success in his recordings of "Ain't That a Shame" (1955) and "Blueberry Hill" (1957). Domino was not a "shouter" like Bill Haley; he sang a relaxed tenor that was mellow but had just a tinge of coarseness, and he had a charming Creole accent that delighted the American youth.

Domino's New Orleans studio band featured a thick bass sound, developed by the seminal New Orleans blues pianist Henry Roeland Byrd, known professionally as Professor Longhair.[5] The overall rhythmic feel was looser than other types of rock; it lacked the riveting drive of northern band riff-style boogie. The recordings also featured a horn section throughout and a sax solo about two-thirds of the way through, playing the same combination of warmth and grit heard in Domino's singing. In New Orleans the band played more of a subordinate role to the singer, letting his expressiveness—to whatever extreme—dominate the performance rather than featuring just the rhythmic feel and overall effect of the band as Haley's Comets did.

A dramatic contrast to the vocal style of Fats Domino was Richard "Little Richard" Penniman. He was not a shouter either; he was a screamer, performing in a frantic, even hysterical manner. He was a blues singer from Macon, Georgia, with a strong background in gospel shout-singing. After an uneventful start to his recording career, he came to Cosimo Matassa's J&M Studios in New Orleans in 1955 and recorded his first hit for Specialty Records, "Tutti Frutti," a nonsense bowdlerization of an obscene song that was sung among southern black homosexuals. Penniman continued recording this same hit formula with, among others, "Long Tall Sally" (1956) and "Lucille" (1957). Little Richard was equally outrageous in his appearance with his six-inch high hair, baggy and glimmering suits, and gaudy jewelry. Little Richard, his white counterpart Jerry Lee Lewis, and blues singer Screamin' Jay Hawkins (who did vampire/coffin routines before large audiences) set the precedent for rock singers to be aggressive extroverts, demonstrating outrageous behavior in their performances.

Memphis Rockabilly

As mentioned earlier in this chapter, Sam Phillips recorded black urban blues singers and leased the recording masters to R&B labels. The success of some, like B. B. King and Howlin' Wolf, encouraged him to form his own record label in

1952, Sun Records. It was during this time that Phillips became aware of the new interest young whites had in rhythm and blues. He thought that if he could find a young white man with the black sound, he could make a million (or perhaps a billion) dollars.

Phillips found his dream in Elvis Presley. Through one of those fateful occurrences, young Presley, a truck driver and transplant from Tupelo, Mississippi, came by the studio in 1953 and recorded a couple of Ink Spots songs, supposedly for his mother's birthday. Phillips was not in the studio that day; but after hearing the tape he called Presley back, along with some of Phillips's favorite instrumentalists, to find the winning formula he was looking for. It did not happen overnight. Phillips, Presley, and the musicians turned the studio into a laboratory and experimented with every possible combination of styles. Finally, on the night of July 5, 1954, they discovered the hit formula while clowning around between takes, just as Little Richard had come up with "Tutti Frutti." That night, Phillips taped Presley's cover version of Arthur Crudup's "That's Alright Mama." Rockabilly, a style that had been quietly evolving since the beginning of the fifties, came of age. The single was backed by a version of bluegrass founder Bill Monroe's "Blue Moon of Kentucky."

Presley was young and good-looking, with a sexy and defiant James Dean look. He wore outrageous clothes that could only be found at a shop on Beale Street. He had equally outrageous body movements on stage, and he could convincingly sing country, gospel, and blues with a breathless, impatient, high voice. His vocals had a rhythmic fluidity and inventiveness uncommon for white singers of black material. He became a regional hit as a country artist among southern youngsters who had grown up on country music. His Sun singles during this time invariably had a blues number backed by a country number, showing the two prominent styles found in Memphis rockabilly.

Elvis Presley, circa 1975, wearing a white-studded jump suit, his signature outfit in the latter part of his career.

In order to get needed capital to promote his other artists, Phillips sold Presley's recording contract to RCA and his managerial contract to Colonel Tom Parker, who had successfully managed country stars Eddy Arnold and Hank Snow. He signed Presley exclusively to RCA Records in Nashville, where producers Steve Sholes and Chet Atkins immediately set about glamorizing and smoothing out Presley's sound.

They employed the same techniques of sophisticated arrangements and instrumentation that they used for Jim Reeves and the Nashville "smoothies."

Presley's first Nashville releases were "Heartbreak Hotel" and "Hound Dog" in 1956. "Heartbreak Hotel" was an urban bluesy torch song more typical of Peggy Lee than Presley, and "Hound Dog" was a bubblier cover version of a song recorded in 1954 by R&B singer Willie Mae "Big Mama" Thornton. Presley continued with a string of hits throughout the fifties. Then he entered military service, after which he vanished into Hollywood for an extended motion picture contract. From the beginning of his Nashville days, Presley became more self-conscious and artificial in the excitement he generated in his songs. Though he remained popular all his life, he never recaptured the unfettered spontaneity and natural exuberance of his original Sun recordings.

Although Elvis Presley was certainly the most successful exponent of the Sam Phillips Sun stable, there were other young, southern, white singers who shared his culture and musical development; many recorded at Sun. Warren Smith and Malcolm Yelvington were from the Memphis area; Johnny Cash and Charlie Rich were from Arkansas; Jerry Lee Lewis was from Ferriday, Louisiana (near Meridian, Mississippi); and Carl Perkins was from nearby Jackson, Tennessee. These rockabilly artists' recorded performances share certain traits: They were spontaneous and unbridled; production was minimal; they featured a solo male singer, without the benefit of group harmony anywhere in the song; they possessed equal portions of country and blues influence; and, above all, they were *very* southern. Rockabilly was sung by kids who grew up listening to Hank Williams, Lefty Frizzell, and the Delmore Brothers, but who also worked and sang alongside blacks of the southern region.

Carl Perkins probably had the greatest potential for rivaling the success of Elvis Presley. He came to Memphis a year after Sun sold Presley's contract to RCA. His style was similar to Presley's but had developed independently of him. In 1956 he recorded "Blue Suede Shoes," his own composition about vehemently protecting a pair of gaudy shoes, whatever personal sufferings he might endure in the process.[6] It became a national hit and climbed to number two on the charts. Perkins seemed destined for stardom; he even made a national television appearance on *The Perry Como Show*. Unfortunately, his career was cut short by a near-fatal auto accident that left him in the hospital for months and stifled his career permanently.

The other Sun sensation was Jerry Lee Lewis, who had been playing professionally since the age of 15. His piano style was a blend of boogie blues and Pentecostal church piano, and he knew a wide range of songs, from rhythm and blues to country songs like Ray Price's "Crazy Arms." In 1957 Sun released "Whole Lotta Shakin' Goin' On," a number one hit that, from the outset, was quintessential Jerry Lee. Lewis plays a relentless boogie bass with the left hand and torrential glissandi and high hammered chords in the right hand. His voice is bold and commanding, but it also quivers softly with barely restrained lust implied in the lyric. With calculated pacing Lewis brings the hard-driving band down to a whisper before the final exciting push to the end of the song. His stage appearance proved equally outrageous; he pounded the piano with his feet, kicked the bench across the floor, and slouched over the microphone with a wild lock of blond hair hanging over his eyes. His wild-man extroversion was reminiscent of Little Richard, another influence on the style of Lewis. Like Perkins, however, his meteoric rise to fame was prematurely cut short—in this case, by a scandalous marriage to his 13-year-old cousin.

Chicago Rhythm and Blues

As blacks steadily migrated to the North during and between the two world wars, many found homes in Chicago, hoping to find work in that city's factories. The South Side, Chicago's black district, was also home to jazz musicians of the

Chuck Berry in performance around 1955.

twenties like King Oliver, Louis Armstrong, and Jelly Roll Morton. Country blues musicians like Blind Lemon Jefferson could be found there, as well as blues and boogie-woogie pianists like Little Brother Montgomery, Pine Top Smith, and Roosevelt Sykes.

From about the mid-thirties, country blues changed to reflect its new urban environment and the loud bars where blacks came to hear the music and to dance. Like the music of the white honky tonks of the Southwest, the country blues became heavily amplified, and drums added a prominent dance beat. As certain blues artists became local celebrities among the patrons of the South Side bars, they began to be recorded on race record labels for the black market (see Chapter 5).

The most famous labels for rhythm and blues were Chess Records, which began in 1947 as Aristocrat Records and changed its name in 1950, and its subsidiary Checker. Both were founded by white bar owners Leonard and Phil Chess in 1947 and 1953, respectively. The most famous artists on their roster included Muddy Waters, Howlin' Wolf, Little Walter, and Sonny Boy Williamson. While these musicians were influential in the development of rock and roll, they themselves would not be able to make the transition from the black R&B market to the youth pop market until the 1960s. Their blues were a bit too crude and sullen; they sang with deep, growling, *adult* voices and did not enunciate their words very clearly.

In 1955 Chess broke into the pop market with Chuck Berry, a guitarist/singer who aimed his music at the burgeoning youth market. Berry was originally from St. Louis and combined a rockabilly-style twangy guitar with a lively backbeat rhythm. He also had a high, youthful, clear tenor voice, with which he sang clearly enunciated lyrics about subjects that were the preoccupation of America's youth, like fast cars and school problems. His first hit was "Maybellene," originally conceived as a country song and modified to appeal to the car-worshiping teens of the fifties. His next four hits, including "Roll Over, Beethoven" and "Too Much Monkey Business," were bluesier and more cynical about American life and were not as successful as "Maybellene" was in the youth market.

Aside from Chuck Berry and guitar stylist Bo Diddley, the influence of black Chicago R&B is less direct. The bulk of the songs on Chess and Checker records would be accepted by young rock audiences from 1964 on through the interpretations presented by British rock artists, who based their own styles on the recorded performances of the original blues artists.

Vocal Groups (Doo-Wop)

Black vocal harmony goes back quite a way in America's history. Earlier in this chapter, we discussed the tradition of black male gospel quartets that dates back to the jubilee quartets of the 1870s. Their background probably had its sacred roots in the homemade harmony black singers made up by ear that approximated the choral harmony of published hymnals. There were secular influences as well, such as group work songs, barbershop quartets, and black minstrel shows. Some black vocal quartets in the twenties, like the Monarch Jubilee Quartet, would record sacred material on race records on one occasion and at another time would record a cappella quartet versions of blues material under the name Monarch Jazz Quartet.[7] Further north, some black male vocal groups developed a smoother, croonier pop sound. Dressed in tuxedos, they sang sophisticated vocal arrangements designed to appeal primarily to white audiences. The most influential group was the Ink Spots, who inspired many younger black vocal groups and entertained the broader public with silky performances of songs like "Java Jive" and "If I Didn't Care."

Some of the up-and-coming black quartets that would become part of early rock were modest groups, untrained singers that started out on the streets of northern cities, without instrumental accompaniment. Their usual method of group singing was a common format used over the years in male vocal quartets: A high tenor sang the melody; the two middle voices sang notes of the harmony in a much more subordinate role; and the bass singer sang far below the others and had a prominent, independent part that worked against the other three voices and was second only to the melody in importance. Because they had no instrumental backup in their rehearsals, the singing groups not only had to provide their own harmony but also had to provide their own rhythm. Therefore, the group members who sang background for the singer of the melody would use nonsense syllables to create a rhythmic pattern, such as repeating the syllables *doo-wop* for a riff of paired eighth notes. That syllabic phrase also became the name used by fans and historians for this style of rock and roll, just as *bebop*, another syllabic phrase for two eighth notes, came to be the name for jazz in the forties.

In the early fifties, records of these vocal groups on independent labels, now with bare instrumental backup, began to be found on the phonographs of white teenagers. The most successful doo-wop records were either torchy slow ballads, accompanied by a triplet rhythm pattern in the high register of the piano, or novelty fast tunes featuring the booming bass singer on rhythm breaks and chicken-cluck (or yakety-yak) tenor sax solos. Sometimes their very crudity and quaintness were sources of charm to listeners; on other occasions they gave genuinely stirring performances and became the anthems of lovesick teens across America.

There were many groups that flourished during the fifties, and rock trivialists love outdoing each other by naming the most obscure songs, groups, and labels they can think of. However, a mention of some exemplary and influential groups will have to suffice within the scope of this book.

The beginning of doo-wop in the context of rock and roll really begins with "Sh-Boom," recorded in 1954 on the Cat label by a black vocal group called the Chords. It was a rhythm and blues song that became popular enough to get onto *Billboard*'s top 10 list in the pop category; a later cover version by a white vocal group, the Crew Cuts, did even better. "Sh-Boom" was not the first doo-wop song to cross into the pop category; the Crows' recording of "Gee" had done so a few months earlier. But "Sh-Boom" was far and away more popular—popular enough to establish a trend and a standard in the pop music field that would be imitated by countless groups for years to come. This was such a turning point in the development of rock that Carl Belz emphatically declares the Chords' "Sh-Boom" as *the first* rock record.[8]

One of the most successful of the doo-wop groups was the Platters, a Los Angeles–based group produced by Buck Ram for Mercury Records. The star

The Coasters, masters of novelty doo-wop in the 1950s.

of the group was lead singer Tony Williams, who was especially adept at heart-wrenching ballads such as "Only You" and "The Great Pretender," both composed by Ram. Williams had a high, soaring voice, modeled after Bill Kenny of the Ink Spots, whom Buck Ram produced before the Platters. Williams also had a distinctive "hiccup" effect that he used in his vocals, as if his voice was cracking under the emotion he poured into the song. "The Great Pretender" was the first doo-wop record to be number one on the *Billboard* pop listing in 1955, eclipsing the entry of the Chords' "Sh-Boom" into the top 10 a year earlier.

The doo-wop group that was closest in popularity to the Platters—and the most diametrically opposed to them in the character of their repertoire—was the Coasters, another Los Angeles group. They were formed from an earlier group, the Robins, and produced by two young songwriting prodigies, Jerry Lieber and Mike Stoller (more on them in Chapter 16), for Atco Records, a subsidiary of Atlantic. Unlike the Platters, with their serious ballads, the Coasters' success lay in their novelty numbers. These were an original concept of Leiber and Stoller and had no precedent in the tradition of doo-wop. The Coasters' biggest hits were "Yakety Yak" and "Charlie Brown" from 1958 and "Along Came Jones" from 1959. These songs typically featured comical, deadpan utterances by bass singer Bobby Nunn and the growling, staccato "yakety sax" solos of King Curtis. Usually, the songs were social commentaries from a teen point of view, but it was good-natured complaining as in the jump blues of Louis Jordan. "Yakety Yak," for example, is a fast tune with a heavy backbeat and an almost country flavor. The lyric whines about a teenager being put upon by his mother to do an insurmountable list of chores if he wants to go out and have fun with his friends. It was an entertaining statement about rebellion that kids could relate to but certainly did not take seriously; it gave teens a few laughs and gave parents another reason to hate rock and roll.

A brief mention should be given to Frankie Lymon and the Teenagers, who were just that. They were a group of black youngsters fronted by a pudgy and diminutive Frankie Lymon, singing with a prepubescent boys choir soprano and portraying a model of wholesomeness with songs like "I'm Not a Juvenile Delinquent." Their biggest hit was "Why Do Fools Fall in Love," which appeared on the Gee label in 1955 and featured an assortment of nonsense syllables in the background, bass breaks, and Lymon's lamenting lyric. They were basically a novelty group and soon faded into obscurity, but their age appealed to the young while their clean-cut appearance gave little offense to elders.

These were the styles of rock music in the beginning, and various combinations of these formats were the basis of rock for the next three decades. The next generation of rock musicians would do much better in terms of money and fame, thanks to cover versions, the introduction of new artists by the major labels, and the role of technology in the late fifties.

Buddy Holly

Buddy Holly (1936–1959) is akin to the artists mentioned in the previous pages in that he is one of the early major influences on rock and roll and a pioneer of its musical character. While his early music is related somewhat to rockabilly found in Memphis and the mid-South, his home turf was the panhandle of West Texas and his style is really uniquely his own.

As a high-schooler in Lubbock, Texas, in the early 1950s, Holly and his friends were avid listeners to country and bluegrass artists such as Hank Williams, Bill Monroe, and Jim and Jesse and country radio broadcasts such as the Louisiana Hayride and the Grand Ole Opry. He also heard black rhythm and blues on radio stations from Memphis and other cities. He eventually formed a country band with childhood friend Bob Montgomery, playing for all sorts of local events in Lubbock. In 1955 Holly's band witnessed Elvis Presley performing in Lubbock, astounded by his stage presence and his hybrid country/R&B style.

Buddy and Bob secured a recording contract with Decca in Nashville and recorded a dozen tracks with Nashville session players under the direction of famed producer Owen Bradley. Bradley had developed a successful, formulaic country sound that had worked for some artists, such as Patsy Cline, but it didn't work with Buddy Holly. Nashville and Holly parted ways. He returned to Texas to begin intense practice and songwriting. He teamed up with Norman Petty, a musician, producer, and owner of a recording studio in Clovis, New Mexico. With his band, the Crickets, Holly recorded his first hit, "That'll Be the Day."

Holly's voice had a light, tense exuberance with an occasional cry-like hiccup that added to the excitement of his performances. The members of the Crickets were all an important part of the Holly sound. Niki Sullivan's open-chord guitar strumming and Jerry Allison's busy drumming contributed power to the small group's sound.

In March 1958 Holly and the Crickets embarked on a 25-day tour of England. The British were already big fans of American rock and roll, and many young British musicians were watching their favorite artists at live concerts and television appearances. Among them were some young men in Liverpool who eventually named themselves the Beatles as a parody of the Crickets. An early hit for the Rolling Stones was a cover of Buddy Holly's "Not Fade Away."

Texas rock and roll pioneer Buddy Holly in the 1950s.

By 1958 Holly had married a New York girl, moved to that city, and broke up the Crickets. He continued songwriting, recording, and producing. Unfortunately, his career would be cut tragically short. He took a three-week tour of the Midwest in January 1959. A small plane attempted to transport Holly, Ritchie Valens, and J. P. Richardson (the Big Bopper) from Clear Lake, Iowa, to Fargo,

North Dakota, in bad weather. The plane crashed within five minutes after take-off, killing all aboard.

The style, sound, and instrumentation of Buddy Holly and the Crickets were reflected in many bands for years to come. Along with Chuck Berry, Holly was one of the first rock and roll acts to prominently feature original compositions. As a producer, Holly's recording ingenuity was legendary. He was one of the first rock and roll artists to employ overdubbing, using different tracks on the recording tape to replicate the same voice or instrument to sound like a larger group. He added orchestral strings and celeste to his recordings. In his short life and career, Holly set a high standard for early rock and roll.

Chapter Summary

Rock cannot be attributed to any one artist, style, or locale. It was a natural blend of American music styles dominated by white country music and black rhythm and blues. This unique blend was encouraged by a burgeoning new record-buying market, the postwar American youth. When rock and roll began to emerge as a distinctive musical entity, between 1954 and 1956, it could be linked to five distinctive styles: northern bands like Bill Haley and His Comets; New Orleans' dance blues, epitomized by Fats Domino and Little Richard; Chicago rhythm and blues that led to Chuck Berry and Bo Diddley; Memphis rockabilly, dominated by Elvis Presley and Jerry Lee Lewis; and vocal group rock and roll (or doo-wop) from the Northeast. This last style can be divided into the subcategories of torch ballads, exemplified by the Platters, and novelty doo-wop, dominated by the Coasters.

As a second generation of rock and rollers came on the scene in the late fifties, they generally drew upon these five initial styles. These styles, in turn, were derived from prewar folk and popular music traditions: electric rhythm and blues from Chicago and Memphis, shouting black church music styles from the Southeast, and boogie-woogie, jump blues, riff arrangements, and western swing from the Southwest.

Additional Listening

Bill Haley and His Comets, "Rock Around the Clock" (1954) (*Star Power: Bill Haley and the Comets*, CD format, Direct Source Special Products). Notice the fusion of a western swing shuffle with rhythm and blues that made the Comets a distinctive band for their day. The highlight of the recording is the ensemble riff in the middle.

Elvis Presley, "That's Alright" (1954) (*The Best of Elvis Presley*, CD format, RCA 69384). This recording is from Presley's days at the Sun studios in Memphis. Listen to how high and young his voice is and to the restless passion in his style. The accompaniment is dominated by Scotty Moore's country style electric guitar picking.

Little Richard, "Tutti Frutti" (1956) (*The Georgia Peach*, CD format, Specialty SPCD-7012-2). Even though Little Richard's style stands in frantic contrast to the more subdued style of other R&B artists recording in New Orleans, the dark, greasy sound of the backup arrangement and instrumentation still prevails.

Jerry Lee Lewis, "Great Balls of Fire" (1957) (*All Killer, No Filler*, CD format, Rhino R2-71216). It is easy to hear that Lewis was the Little Richard of Sun Records. His performance is wild and forceful, but he also carefully controls the pacing of the performance, knowing when to back off momentarily before again attacking the listener with a barrage of vocal yelps and piano-pounding.

The Chords, "Sh-Boom" (1954) (*Doo Wop: Sh-Boom,* CD format, Rhino Flashback 72716). This recording is of the definitive performances by black R&B vocal groups in the early fifties. It is deliberately smooth in its delivery but still robust and exciting, especially when compared with the more successful cover version by the white vocal group the Crew Cuts.

Fats Domino, "Ain't That a Shame" (1955) (*My Blue Heaven: The Best of Fats Domino,* CD format, EMI America E2-92808). This recording demonstrates the relaxed and pleasing sound of Domino's vocal style and the loping sound of the New Orleans backup bands. The band plays a slow boogie bass pattern, and the horn section of tenor and baritone saxes gives the group a dark timbre.

Aaron "T-Bone" Walker, "Stormy Monday" (1947) (*Straighten Up and Fly Right,* LP format, New World Records NW 261). This recording demonstrates Walker's pioneering efforts in the development of electric blues guitar that influenced so many early rock artists. The entire album *Straighten Up and Fly Right* has many wonderful and enlightening recordings documenting the rhythm and blues roots of rock and roll.

Louis Jordan, "Choo Choo Ch'Boogie" (1946) (*The Best of Louis Jordan,* CD format, MCA MCAD-4079). This is an example of jump blues, with a shuffle/boogie rhythm, horn riffs, and lighthearted vocals that influenced early rockers such as Bill Haley and His Comets. Jordan enjoyed somewhat of a comeback during the retro-swing movement of the late 1990s (see Chapter 23).

The Coasters, "What About Us" (1957) (*Shake, Rattle, and Roll,* LP format, New World Records NW 249). This is an example of novelty doo-wop, recorded by the foremost group in that style. The song is by the formidable songwriting team of Jerry Lieber and Mike Stoller. Notice that it has a calypso rhythm, like some other novelty doo-wop tunes. This album is another in a fine series of early rock anthologies from New World Records.

"Big" Joe Turner and Pete Johnson, "Roll 'Em Pete" (1938) (*Straighten Up and Fly Right,* LP format, New World Records NW 261). This is the song and the performers that set off a fire of boogie-woogie popularity in the late 1930s.

Buddy Holly and the Crickets, "That'll Be the Day" (1957) (*The Chirping Crickets,* CD format, MCA MCAD-31182). This was Holly's first big hit. Written and recorded soon after his failure in Nashville, the song has an enticing toughness in the lyric and in the band that accompanies it.

Video Source

History of Rock and Roll (VHS format, 10-volume set, Warner Studios, 1995). This series has aired at various times and various places on the television cable landscape. It is well done, particularly notable for letting the musicians themselves speak for their music.

VH1: Behind the Music (VHS format, Uni/Beyond). This is an ongoing series running on the music cable channel VH1. There are a number of documentaries on different artists, and are mostly human interest in nature rather than a lot of focus on the music. One would need to browse a current list of titles on tape for availability status.

Review Questions

1. Why were white youths in the late 1940s and early 1950s fascinated by black rhythm and blues?
2. What influences on early rock came from the Southwest? What influences came from the Southeast?
3. What are the five styles of rock and roll that developed between 1954 and 1956?
4. Who are representative artists from each of these five styles?
5. Describe the combination of instrumentation and repertoire that made Bill Haley and His Comets a hybrid of rhythm and blues and western swing.
6. What elements in New Orleans rock accounts for its more laid-back character?
7. What are the similarities in style between Little Richard and Jerry Lee Lewis?
8. What were the qualities of style and appearance that made Elvis Presley the most successful of the Sun Records stable?
9. How did Chet Atkins and RCA records change Presley's style?
10. How was Chuck Berry's style different from other R&B artists at Chess Records? How was his style well suited to the burgeoning teenage rock market?
11. What was the role of each singer in a doo-wop group?
12. What were the two substyles of doo-wop? What vocal groups were exponents of these two styles?
13. What were the musical characteristics of Buddy Holly and the Crickets? What studio techniques did Holly pioneer?

Notes

1. Cited in Greil Marcus, *Mystery Train; Images of America in Rock 'n Roll Music* (New York: E. P. Dutton & Co., 1976), p. 18.
2. Charlie Gillett, *The Sound of the City,* rev. & exp. (New York: Pantheon Books, 1983), p. 10.
3. Mosaic Records has compiled the complete recordings of "T-Bone" Walker, including their typically excellent liner notes (Mosaic MD6-130). Unfortunately, it is now out of print.
4. See Gillett, Chapter 2, pp. 23–35.
5. Critic Langdon Winner writes, "If Sun Records [Memphis] created rock's excited treble, New Orleans provided its solid bass foundations." Langdon Winner, "The Sound of New Orleans," *The Rolling Stone Illustrated History of Rock & Roll,* ed. Jim Miller, rev. and exp. (New York: Random House, 1980), p. 36.
6. Bright, garish clothes, such as "blue suede shoes," were a trademark for young country boys who had just come to town in the fifties. See Ed Ward, *Rock of Ages: The Rolling Stone History of Rock and Roll* (New York: Summit Books, 1986), p. 118.
7. Listen to "What Is the Matter Now?" from *Let's Get Loose* (New World Records, NW).
8. Carl Belz, *The Story of Rock* (New York: Oxford University Press, 1969), p. 25.

Chapter 16

Fifties Pop and Folk Rock

In 1954 *Billboard* magazine had three stylistic categories for their ratings: pop, rhythm and blues, and country music. The latter two earned their own listings in 1948, when *Billboard* eliminated their "race" record category. As the demands of the youth culture began to gain power, the walls that divided these categories in the marketplace began to crumble. By the mid-fifties, youthful white performers from the North occupied positions on both the pop and the rhythm and blues listings; young white performers from the South were simultaneously on the country and R&B lists; and blacks were on the pop and R&B lists.

Until the emergence of rock, the music business was dominated by the publishing houses of Tin Pan Alley, their allies at the major record labels and Hollywood movie studies, and by the fifties, the fledgling medium of television. The product of these entities was aimed at the tastes and conservative cultural values of the white, middle-aged, middle-class urbanite. The music and its artists, like its target audience, became predictable, complacent, and polite, seeking to adhere to reliable stylistic formulas without giving offense.

Black music artists were rarely allowed to flourish as star performers in this pop music milieu. The few black performers that were accepted into the pop mainstream were successful only because they either maintained the comic black image dating back to minstrelsy, like Fats Waller or Louis Jordan, or squelched much of the African-American characteristics from their repertoire and performing style, like the Ink Spots, the Mills Brothers, and Nat "King" Cole.

Country music fared better than black music, primarily because it was performed by whites—with all its inherent accessibilities. It had also made some inroads in the pop market through the years due to the movie cowboys, some Bing Crosby cover versions in the war years, and Patti Page's recording of "The Tennessee Waltz." All these smooth urban products were deliberately designed to appeal to the pop market. In the fifties, mainstream country music was just as conservative, inoffensive, and in the doldrums as mainstream pop.

With the emergence of rock, the pop music industry experienced an unprecedented infiltration by blacks and young whites performing black material. Industry leaders fought, with all their considerable strength, against this threat to their comfortable formula of music making and marketing; but eventually they accepted the new trend. Even though the pop industry submitted to what became known as *rock and roll*, they did so on their own terms. They eventually succeeded in chasing the original, earthier styles out of the popular music arena and back into their own cultural milieu.

Rock and roll threatened Tin Pan Alley on several levels, and the industry devised an effective counterattack for each of these threats. The first major threat was that rock was solely the property of small, independent record labels. Almost every new rock artist had an independent studio issuing his record, and that record also found entry to the pop marketplace. None of these "indies" were as powerful as the major labels, but they far outnumbered them. Having initially rejected rock and roll artists as substandard, the major labels such as Columbia, RCA, Decca, Capitol, and others suffered a severe blow as the independent labels increased their market share by 50 percent.

The second major threat to Tin Pan Alley was that many of the rock artists wrote their own songs. Like the major record labels, ASCAP, representing the closed fraternity of professional Tin Pan Alley songwriters, suffered from its arrogance, having shunned rock and rhythm and blues songwriters. ASCAP, therefore, missed out on the rock and roll bonanza of the fifties, while its rival, BMI, which prided itself on taking in the downtrodden songwriters of the world, flourished. Rock also established a precedent in the music industry: The performance of a song, recorded or otherwise, was more important than the song itself. Many of the rock musicians were untrained, and their songs existed only in their heads and in their performances, effectively breaking Tin Pan Alley's long-standing definition as a sheet music industry.

A final major threat to the established music industry had to have been considered a violation of the accepted aesthetics of artist image and performance style. To the establishment, rock songs and performances were crude, amateurish, and tediously repetitive. The artists exhibited no restraint in vocal technique, onstage gestures, or personal grooming and attire. After 10 years of Perry Como, for example, the initial impact of Elvis's hips, Little Richard's hair, or Jerry Lee Lewis's piano technique (which included playing with his feet) must have been quite a shock to the pop music moguls.

The counterattack was swift and sure. The first strategic effort by the major labels was to produce cover versions of songs originally recorded by black rhythm and blues artists. The covers featured neat, restrained, and wholesome white artists, who invariably outsold the original. The most successful of these cover artists was Pat Boone, who built a career on polite renditions of songs originally recorded by Fats Domino, Little Richard, Ivory Joe Hunter, and others. History usually condemns such exploitative practices, but these white cover artists may have done rock and roll a service by providing accessible, watered-down presentations to the uninitiated of the day, eventually winning them over to more authentic fare.

Crusading radio disc jockeys such as Alan Freed vehemently refused to air cover versions of rock and roll songs, but the marketing and distribution powers of the industry majors won out. The majors created markets that independent labels could not reach, such as selling records through suburban supermarkets and mail-order record clubs. Another strategy by the majors was the seven-inch vinyl 45 rpm record, developed by RCA Victor. These disks were lighter and more durable than the prevailing 78 rpm type; they were quicker and easier to manufacture and to ship; and the small diameter of the record and the larger spindle hole made it easier for the consumer to store and to mount on their phonographs. Weaker independent labels could not compete financially with the manufacturing transition to the newer type records or the resultant retail price reduction per unit.

Finally, Tin Pan Alley set about its usual task of cleaning up rock music—to the point that it was no longer recognizable as a distinctive style—and making it presentable to the American masses. In addition to white cover artists, the major labels supplanted the first generation of rock artists and their songs with carefully groomed stables of entertainers and songs. These so-called teen idols were drawn primarily from Philadelphia; and the national exposure of the one-time local television program *American Bandstand* contributed to this. Handsome, wholesome, and almost identical teenage boys, such as Fabian, Tommy Sands, Paul Anka, and Frankie Avalon, sang inoffensive Tin Pan Alley versions of rock music with great success in the late 1950s. Female artists, such as Brenda Lee and Connie Francis, were fewer in number and even more chaste in their presentations.

Rock and Radio

Rock and radio became mutually dependent in the 1950s. When television became a viable medium after World War II, the networks essentially abandoned radio. Radio then returned to community programming, often specializing in music of local interest such as country or rhythm and blues. Local radio became the most effective and accessible way for independent labels to promote new rock talent, first in the local community, then nationally. Conversely, the immense popularity of rock and roll saved radio.

Disc jockeys had heretofore been benign figures on the radio, spinning records and making a few announcements. With radio's new role in the 1950s, DJs also became stars in their own right, linking themselves with the music and musicians they featured. Their power increased significantly with the implementation of the top 40 radio concept. Created by the owner of a chain of radio stations, the concept involved the constant rotation of only the 40 top-rated recordings as determined by *Billboard* magazine. This ensured that whenever listeners tuned in, they would hear something they liked. This practice made access by record companies to the airwaves extremely competitive; it increased the power of DJs and station program managers to influence the next big hit; and it further diminished the concept of popular music as a sheet music industry.

Such circumstances led to the bribing of disc jockeys and station managers by agents and record companies in order to get their product on the air. In 1959 and 1960 the Federal Trade Commission launched an investigation into the practice of *payola*, the covert buying of airplay privileges. No doubt this attack on the practices of rock music promotion was egged on by the conservative factions of both society and the music establishment. Rock and radio survived, of course, and remained deeply indebted to each other for that survival.

The Road to High-Production Rock

In the early days, rock records sounded like they were recorded in someone's garage, which often was actually the case. Between the gradual maturing of grassroots rock and the attempts by Tin Pan Alley to raise rock's songwriting

Mike Stoller (seated at the piano) and Jerry Lieber, the prolific songwriting team whose work was featured by many early rock artists.

and production standards, the sound of rock recordings advanced. Increasingly, professional songwriter/producers exerted their influence on the production of rock records and created new acts for the sole purpose of displaying their wares.

The earliest and greatest of these songwriter/producer teams was Jerry Lieber and Mike Stoller. They were teenage prodigies, too young to even sign their own contracts when they moved from the East to Los Angeles in 1950. A mutual interest in rhythm and blues brought them to a songwriting partnership, their initial efforts culminating with the recording of Houston blues vocalist Willie Mae "Big Mama" Thornton singing their song "Hound Dog" in 1953. Lieber and Stoller were signed as songwriters/producers for the Atlantic label in 1956, an R&B specialty label founded in 1946 by Ahmet Ertegun, the son of a Turkish diplomat to the United States, and Herb Abramson. Using the Los Angeles–based Coasters as their vehicle, Lieber and Stoller designed novelty doo-wop intended to reach the teen market for Atlantic. They also wrote the music for the movies *Jailhouse Rock* and *King Creole,* which featured Elvis Presley. Elvis also covered their "Hound Dog" in his first RCA session in Nashville. The list of Lieber and Stoller hits in the 1950s and early 1960s is astounding.

This songwriting team's songs and productions helped to ensure the early popularity of rock and roll. In their earliest R&B sessions they were able to create well-crafted songs and professional recordings without depriving the artists of their vitality. They set the standard for an entire subgenre of rock, novelty doo-wop, through their work with the Coasters and others. They tailored rock to suit a new generation of performers; and they pioneered expanded orchestration and recording techniques for rock and roll, well illustrated by the 1959 recording of the Drifters performing their song "There Goes My Baby."

The advent of Phil Spector marked a new plateau in rock songwriting and producing. He apprenticed with Lieber and Stoller and, like them, had been a teenage whiz kid. Under their auspices, he produced a couple of early hits for Atlantic, then formed his own label, Philles. Between 1961 and 1964 Phil Spector produced a series of number-one hits, including the Crystals' "He's a Rebel" and "Da Doo Ron Ron" and the Righteous Brothers' "You've Lost That Lovin' Feelin' " and "Unchained Melody."

One of Spector's innovations was the *girl group.* Female vocal groups had been around for a long time (the Boswell Sisters or the Andrews Sisters, for instance) but not in the area of rock and roll. Spector freshened up the concept of doo-wop for the 1960s by replacing male quartets with girl groups. The Shirelles, the Crystals, and the Ronettes were nurtured by Phil Spector and would become models for others—like the Marvelettes or the Supremes at Motown Records.

Spector was conspicuous in the music industry in that he sought to control every aspect of his product, from creative conception to distribution. Rock historian Ed Ward lists one of Spector's "Four Commandments" (for the music business) as "Create a sound on record that no one else can copy or cover."[1] To that end, Spector developed what has been popularly dubbed the Spector "wall of sound." He filled Gold Star Studios in Los Angeles with an army of musicians; whole sections of guitarists, pianists, bassists, and drummers, horns, and an assortment of percussion instruments and hand-clapping. As if these weren't enough, he made liberal use of *overdubbing,* or *stacking,* the instruments on tape. This is the technique whereby the musicians are recorded a number of times on different tracks of the tape to be played back simultaneously. The result was a cavernous, loud, almost cluttered sound that was miles away from the spartan garage sound mentioned earlier.

While his songs were often trite and commercial, in order to reach the broadest teenage market, Spector clothed them in a luxurious production that gave rock a sound that had been reserved for the likes of Frank Sinatra. His work showed the level of production sophistication that was possible in rock, and it must have influenced later progressive rock and high-production rock in the 1970s.

The culmination of this high-production lineage was the Beach Boys, particularly the work of Brian Wilson, one of its members. The group was formed in Hawthorne, California, and was comprised of the three Wilson Brothers, Brian, Carl, and Dennis; a cousin, Mike Love; and friend Al Jardine. The Beach Boys tapped into California's distinctive version of the endless teenage summer, surfing and the beach, with their song "Surfin' " in 1961 and worked their way up to national success on the Capitol label. They were not the first or only group to draw upon West Coast beach imagery. Dick Dale, Jan and Dean, and instrumental guitar bands such as the Ventures and the Surfaris are among the

The Beach Boys on November 17, 1964 (Left to right: Mike Love, Al Jardine, Brian Wilson, Dennis Wilson, Carl Wilson)

prominent names, but the Beach Boys have been the farthest reaching and the most enduring.

Beneath the sophomoric subject matter of the Beach Boys' songs was a high level of arranging and producing that maintains its sophistication even today. Beginning in 1963 with the album *Surfer Girl,* Brian Wilson took over as producer. Wilson was strongly influenced by Phil Spector. This was reflected in his use of deep echo, large bands, exotic instruments, and effective multitrack recording. The vocal arranging was the most sophisticated yet in rock music, utilizing overdubbing to give the effect of double choirs weaving in and out in intricate counterpoint. Wilson used his own high, piercing falsetto voice over tight vocal harmony, techniques derived from jazz male vocal groups like the Hi-Los and the Four Freshmen. The songs and tracks also drew heavily upon the guitar and songwriting style of Chuck Berry; the Beach Boys' "Surfin' U.S.A." was a rip-off of Berry's "Sweet Little Sixteen."

Analysis of "California Girls" (*Classic Rock 1965: The Beat Goes On*, Time-Life Music 2CLR-08, Track 4)

"California Girls" was recorded in 1965 and marks the fully developed songwriting and production style of Beach Boys member Brian Wilson. It contains all the familiar elements of mature Beach Boys records: cavernous echo, exotic instrumentation, unusual chord changes, and precision vocal work.

The song begins gently with guitars playing a riff in octaves, saturated with heavy studio reverberation. The electric bass joins in the riff the second time, punctuated by occasional taps on the suspended cymbal. The third time through the riff, the horns enter softly with sustained chords. The intensity of the introductory riff builds when the horns accent the fourth beat of the measure and add more notes to the chords they are playing. The band finally slows the cadence of the introduction and the tune proper begins.

The tempo of the song is set by the bass and a portable electric organ with two keyboards. One keyboard of the organ plays a bouncing repeated chord, using a bright, percussive timbre. The other keyboard on the organ and the electric bass play a four-note riff, reminiscent of a boogie-woogie bass line. After two measures of the new tempo, the drums and vocals enter. The strong backbeat does not sound like a single drummer playing on a single snare drum, but an army of drummers. The melody of the verse is sung in unison by the first vocal choir. Their sound is midrange and down-to-earth, giving the impression of any group of guys at the beach singing about girls.

The sparkle is added on the chorus when the second male choir enters. This group sings in full harmony, topped by Wilson's high, piercing falsetto. Just as this group reaches the word "girls," the first vocal group dovetails over them, repeating the same line. This counterpoint process occurs once more for the third line of this chorus. The vocal overlapping technique is strongly enhanced by Wilson's harmonic scheme, where each entry of the melodic line is in a different key. Also notice that, in both choirs, the bass singer's melodic line moves quite independently of the other voices, adding to the rich overall texture of the choral sound.

When the second verse is sung, the unison vocal group (melody) is supported by the falsetto-lead vocal group, singing backup chords on the vowel sound

Listening Guide   16.1
"California Girls" 4 beats per measure

ELAPSED TIME	FORM	EVENT DESCRIPTION
:00	Intro	Light guitars, then bass, cymbal, horns (10 measures)
:23	Tempo in	Repeated organ chord and bass/organ riff (2 measures)
:27	Verse 1	1st vocal group in unison (16 measures)
1:01	Chorus 1	1st and 2nd vocal groups alternate line (8 measures)
1:19	Verse 2	1st group melody with 2nd group "oohs" (16 measures)
1:23	Chorus 2	1st and 2nd vocal groups alternate line (8 measures)
2:10	Interlude	Bells and doo-wop bass lead-in (2 measures)
2:15	Chorus 3	Both vocal groups vamp to fade-out
2:48	End	

"ooh." On the second line of the melody, the second group adds motion and timbral contrast to the texture by alternating between the vowel sounds "ooh" and "aah." The same procedure is used for the second half of the verse, followed by the second chorus.

After the second chorus there is a brief interlude that begins with bells and a light, high organ sound playing a slight variation of the boogie bass riff that set the tempo earlier in the song. The bass singer then sings a doo-wop style lead-in to the chorus. The chorus is now modified to create an endless vamp on the melodic line. The harmonic scheme has been altered so that the chorus remains in the same key, facilitating the extended repetition leading to the fade-out. The two groups are now singing at the same time; their lines are much busier but still do not sound cluttered.

The composition and arrangement by Brian Wilson and the precision performance by the Beach Boys are a fine example of a production that is better than it had to be to put across a song about one's geographic preference for girls. It is a testament to Wilson and the group's artistry that so much intricacy took place without spoiling the surface character of a light, fun-loving song.

Rock and Television

With the reluctant adoption of rock by Tin Pan Alley, some of the industry's sophistication, which came from years of experience, was injected into the new music. But rock was becoming cautious, formulated, and insincere, not to mention so slick that teenagers could no longer relate to it. This was evident in Tin Pan Alley's failed attempts at network television rock variety shows in the early sixties. In shows such as *Shindig* and *Hullabaloo*, which only lasted a couple of years, teen audiences saw professional dancers, orchestras, and lighting that seemed to place rock music into their parents' world of Las Vegas floor shows. Only *American Bandstand* managed to find the formula that other national music moguls had overlooked—keep it simple. Hosted by the unassuming Dick Clark, all attention was focused on the teen audience participating in a high school sock hop, with eavesdropping television cameras. The surrogate Beatles group the Monkees enjoyed a brief success with preteens in the late sixties; but television and rock would not coalesce until the 1980s, when the MTV music television network came to cable subscribers.

The Urban Folk Revival

As rock and its audience matured in the late fifties, another musical movement proved that Tin Pan Alley glitter wasn't the only way to go. When teens graduated from high school, their concerns moved beyond their car and the prom. Working their way through college, some young people turned their attention to social causes, intellectualism, and the arts. Their increasing awareness and changing tastes instilled in them an aversion to the artificiality and adolescence of Tin Pan Alley rock. Rather than screaming through rock concerts, these music fans preferred the more intimate and sober atmosphere of coffee shops and bars featuring cool jazz, poetry, and acoustic American folk music. For the first time, the age range of the youth market expanded.

The *urban folk revival* was related to rock music only insofar as it was a youth movement that occurred at about the same time as the rise of rock and roll. It was a "revival" in that it brought to national popularity a body of American folk songs and ballads that had previously been of interest only to folklore, music, and history scholars. It also brought about a new generation of youthful songwriters in the rustic folk-song mold and was the basis of other rock styles, such as San Francisco rock in the 1960s.

Though the history of folk music dates back further than anyone can determine, the real beginnings of the American folk movement must begin with two giant figures of American folk music from the 1930s and 1940s, Huddie Ledbetter ("Leadbelly") and Woody Guthrie.[2] Both were discovered by John Lomax and his son Alan, folklorists doing field research for the Library of Congress in the 1930s. Leadbelly was a blues singer and folksinger, born in 1889 in Caddo Parish, Louisiana. He was serving time in prison when the Lomaxes discovered him and sought a pardon so he could record and tour. Woody Guthrie was born in Okemah, Oklahoma, in 1912 and came to the Lomaxes' attention with his songs of social reform, particularly the plight of his fellow Okies who were victims of the Depression and the dust bowl of the 1930s.

In 1950 the folk songs of these men became fashionable among the middle-class college crowd when a quartet called the Weavers, led by Pete Seeger, a folklorist protégé of Leadbelly and Guthrie, recorded Leadbelly's "Goodnight Irene." Released shortly after Leadbelly's death, the Weavers' record was a number-one hit for 13 weeks. This brought folk music into a phase of popularity, but the left-wing politics it expounded caused it to be forced underground by the McCarthy-esque communist paranoia of the day.

Folk and blues artist Huddie Ledbetter ("Leadbelly") and his wife around 1920.

The next advance for the folk revival was the Kingston Trio's 1958 Capitol recording of "Tom Dooley," a North Carolina murder ballad with no political overtones. The

American folk revivalist Bob Dylan performing at the Newport Folk Festival in 1965.

Kingston Trio was a wholesome, clean-cut group of college lads better suited for the campus than the coffee shop. The apex of this more mainstream folk music was Peter, Paul, and Mary, a polished group from New York's Greenwich Village. They recorded a number of hits for Warner Records, including Pete Seeger's "If I Had a Hammer" (1962) and "Blowin' in the Wind" (1963)—both protest songs but acceptable. "Blowin' in the Wind" was composed by Bob Dylan.

Bob Dylan was born Robert Zimmerman in 1941. Around 1959 he became a passionate devotee of folk music, particularly the music of Woody Guthrie. He moved from his native Duluth, Minnesota, to Greenwich Village in 1961, trying out his performing and songwriting talents, and tutoring with Woody Guthrie, who was suffering from a debilitating and ultimately fatal neurological disease. He was discovered by jazz entrepreneur John Hammond and recorded his first album for Columbia in 1962. It was a simple presentation, with Dylan's scratchy, mumbling voice accompanied by his own acoustic guitar and harmonica. At this point his songwriting and performing mannerisms were very close to Guthrie's.

By 1963 Dylan was the darling of the folk scene, fraternizing at concerts with Joan Baez, Peter, Paul, and Mary, and others. His protest songs were relevant to 1960s concerns such as civil rights, just as Woody Guthrie's songs had been relevant to labor unions and the plight of the common man in the 1940s. Dylan eventually rebelled against his own stardom, first by turning from sociopolitical topics to more intimate topics of inner strife, then shocking his orthodox folk fans by going with an electric rock presentation at the 1965 Newport Folk Festival.

As harsh as the initial reception to electric folk was, Dylan persevered, as did later groups forged from the same mold. From the West Coast came the Byrds, a

Oklahoma folk music legend Woody Guthrie.

folk-rock group that featured enigmatic lyrics, rolling electric-guitar picking, and smooth folksy vocal harmonies. "Mr. Tambourine Man" became a hit in 1965, followed by "Turn, Turn, Turn," a Pete Seeger song based on a passage from the Bible. One of the Byrds' members was David Crosby, who eventually teamed up with Stephen Stills and Neil Young, members of the folk-rock group Buffalo Springfield, and Graham Nash, formerly of the Hollies, to form one of the most popular folk-rock groups of the late sixties.

Listening Guide   16.2
"Teach Your Children" 2 beats per measure

ELAPSED TIME	FORM	EVENT DESCRIPTION
:00	Intro	Steel guitar accompanied by acoustic guitars (8 measures)
:13	Verse 1	Two-part harmony, melody on bottom (16 measures)
:38	Chorus 1	Fuller 4-part harmony + tambourine (28 measures)
1:21	Interlude	Steel guitar solo (6 measures)
1:31	Verse 2	Melody with harmonized countermelody (16 measures)
1:57	Chorus 2	Four-part harmony, steel guitar more active (28 measures)
2:42	Coda	Steel guitar solo (6 measures)

Analysis of "Teach Your Children" (*Deja Vu*, Atlantic 7200)

This popular song by Crosby, Stills, Nash, and Young was recorded on their 1970 album *Deja Vu* for the Atlantic label. While the group was generally known for their soft rock and acoustic folk sound, "Teach Your Children" has a distinctive country flavor because of the prominent role of the steel guitar. This instrument would also be used in other folk rock bands such as Poco.

The most distinctive feature of CSN&Y is their soft vocal blend, carefully honed from hours in the studio. The melody was usually the bottom note of the harmony; the upper voices provided a light, pleasing timbre to the overall sound of acoustic rhythm guitar and gentle drums.

The song is about relationships between the generations. It asks parents to teach their children as best they can but to let them find their own way in the world. In the second verse, children are admonished to respond to their parents, to help them seek the truth in their advancing years so that they may find inner peace before they die.

Chapter Summary

When rock and roll emerged as a distinct entity in the mid-1950s, it reshaped the entire music industry. It broke down categorical barriers that had been set up by the *Billboard* listings; it gave small, independent record labels the opportunity to challenge the major labels; and it dismantled Tin Pan Alley as a sheet music industry. Tin Pan Alley was eventually forced by public demand to produce its own brand of rock and roll, characterized by formulated, innocent tunes sung by wholesome teen idols and cover versions of black artists' songs by white artists.

In terms of media impact, radio and rock were interdependent. The emergence of rock coincided with the development of the top 40 radio concept, making disc jockeys powerful and influential celebrities. The 45 rpm record became the new format for rock and roll music. With the exception of *American Bandstand* initial attempts to televise proved unsuccessful.

The late fifties and early sixties witnessed a rise in the sophistication of producing rock records, beginning with Lieber and Stoller and continuing through Phil Spector, with his "wall of sound" concept, and Brian Wilson of the Beach Boys. Their use of elaborate studio effects, expanded instrumentation, and well-thought-out arrangements helped bring rock into the realm of production previously reserved for Tin Pan Alley pop stars.

In the meantime, a grassroots folk music movement rose among bohemian college students in America's cities, particularly the music of Leadbelly and Woody Guthrie. One of the greatest exponents of the movement was Bob Dylan, a protégé of Woody Guthrie. Dylan stirred up controversy when he and his band "went electric," but it paved the way for other folk-rock groups like the Byrds.

Additional Listening

The Righteous Brothers, "You've Lost That Lovin' Feelin' " (1965) (*Classic Rock 1965*, CD format, Time-Life Music 2CLR-01, Track 6). This may be the most celebrated example of Phil Spector's songwriting and production work. The production has an enormous, expansive sound to it; and no two voices could be more dramatic, yet more different, than Bill Medley's gutsy baritone and Bobby Hatfield's driving tenor.

The Byrds, "Turn, Turn, Turn" (1965) (*Classic Rock 1965: The Beat Goes On*, Time-Life Music 2CLR-8, Track 12).

The Monkees, "I'm a Believer" (1966) (*Classic Rock 1966*, Time-Life Music 2CLR-02, Track 20). This track is an example not only of the Monkees performing but also of the songwriting craft that was contributed by the writers at Aldon Music—in this case, Neil Diamond.

Review Questions

1. What were the three style categories listed in *Billboard* in 1954?
2. In what ways did rock and roll threaten the established practices of Tin Pan Alley?
3. In what ways did Tin Pan Alley try to undermine rock and roll?
4. How did the Top 40 change the sheet music market? How did it empower local disc jockeys?
5. Describe Lieber and Stoller's songwriting and production approach, and list artists who have performed their music.
6. What was Phil Spector's "wall of sound"? What other production innovations did Spector conceive?
7. What aspects of Brian Wilson's productions reflect the influence of Phil Spector? What other influences are evident in Wilson's songs and productions?
8. Why did *American Bandstand* succeed when other television shows like *Shindig* and *Hullabaloo* failed?
9. What and who were the roots of the urban folk revival of the late fifties and early sixties?

Notes

1. Ed Ward, *Rock of Ages: The Rolling Stone History of Rock and Roll* (New York: Rolling Stone Press/Summit Books, 1986), p. 226.
2. A highly recommended video documentary is *A Vision Shared: A Tribute to Woody Guthrie and Leadbelly,* hosted by a former member of the Band, Robbie Robertson, and featuring a number of prominent folk and rock artists.

Chapter 17

The British Invasion

By 1964 American rock was ruled by the major record labels. It fragmented into styles as diverse as calypso and pseudo-Japanese folk songs. Vocalist Chubby Checker had everyone doing the twist, and Frankie Avalon and Annette Funicello cavorted in beach films shown in drive-in movies across the country. The folk music scene continued in relative obscurity. It was time for rock and roll to be revitalized, a service ultimately rendered, not by an American group, but by youthful bands from England. These bands did not offer a peculiar British breed of rock (at least at first) but brought American rock music home, and young Americans embraced it as if they were hearing it for the first time.

England had followed African-American music for decades, particularly traditional New Orleans jazz. There were also groups interested in American folk songs and folk blues; a postwar fascination with the likes of Leadbelly and Woody Guthrie existed in England much as it did with American youth. All these musical developments combined with the first wave of imported American rock and roll records to create a youth music movement in Britain.[1]

The road to British rock began with a Pan-English craze called *skiffle* (American and English folk songs played on rustic acoustic instruments such as acoustic guitars, a washboard, and a washtub bass), with songs simple enough to be duplicated by young amateur musicians. The popularity of skiffle began in 1956 with the record release of British jazzman Lonnie Donnegan performing "Rock Island Line" and "John Henry," both American folk songs popularized in the United States by Leadbelly.

As the skiffle fad passed away, British youth music developed along regional lines. In the city of Liverpool, 200 miles north of London, former skiffle groups continued to follow American rock and roll, particularly rockabilly, as performed by Carl Perkins, Elvis Presley, Buddy Holly, and others. The Liverpool bands were made up of tough, less-educated working-class boys who identified with the insistent beat of rock and roll better than with the polite popular music their parents favored. From this setting came the first of the significant British rock bands, the Beatles. In London, meanwhile, upper-class college students skipped over rock and roll and gravitated toward earthier American rhythm and blues by artists such as Muddy Waters, John Lee Hooker, and Howlin' Wolf. From this musical setting came the second of the significant British rock bands, the Rolling Stones.

THE BEATLES

The Beatles as a group had its beginning around 1956 when 15-year-old Liverpoolian John Lennon (1941–1980) formed the Blackjacks, soon renamed the Quarry Men. The group was a skiffle band that also played American rock and roll. In 1957 Paul McCartney (b. 1942) was added to the group, followed by George Harrison, (1943–2001). Stu Sutcliffe, a fellow student with Lennon at the Liverpool Art College, was added as bassist. He was musically inept but, more than any of the other members, possessed the rebellious James Dean image the group was trying to put across.[2] An initial tour of Scotland prompted a name change to the Silver Beetles, in deference to Buddy Holly's Crickets, then finally to the Beatles.

Drummer Pete Best was added to the Beatles when the group was booked to play in the rough club district of Hamburg, Germany, in 1960. In Hamburg, the strenuous hours of the Beatles' engagements quickly tightened the group. With the exception of Best, they abandoned the rocker look and adopted their famous hair style of a shorter cut with long bangs. The group returned to Liverpool to play in the Cavern Club, a basement bar and former jazz club that had yielded to the local youth's infatuation with rock and roll.

The group made a second trip to Hamburg, where Sutcliffe left the band, and a series of fruitless recordings were made with singer Tony Sheridan for the German Polydor label. Back at the Cavern Club in Liverpool, the Beatles came to the attention of local record store owner Brian Epstein, who became their manager. Epstein groomed their music and stage presentation and attempted to get the group a recording contract, eventually signing them with EMI/Parlophone. Parlophone was run by George Martin, a well-trained musician and producer who would prove to be an invaluable contributor to the young Beatles' musical growth.

The Beatles at the airport in London on February 8, 1964.

Martin's first move was to replace drummer Pete Best with an EMI session drummer, Ringo Starr (born Richard Starkey in Liverpool, 1940). In September 1962, the Beatles' personnel and management were established, and they entered Parlophone's studio in London to record a single record, "Love Me Do" and "P.S. I Love You." Local success in recordings, television, and live appearances led to an album release that included covers of existing songs and original songs by Lennon and McCartney. By 1963 the Beatles was the top pop band in England.

George Martin and the Beatles now attempted to break into the American rock scene, a feat previous European rock bands had not accomplished. EMI, with great difficulty, finally convinced its American subsidiary, Capitol Records, to release a Beatles single, "I Want to Hold Your Hand." This was followed by a February 1964 appearance on *The Ed Sullivan Show,* an established CBS television variety program. By the time the Beatles landed at Kennedy Airport in New York, "I Want to Hold Your Hand" had become a number-one hit. Five thousand people met them at the airport; 70 million watched them on *The Ed Sullivan Show;* and by mid-April 1964, Beatles' singles occupied an unprecedented 14 spots in *Billboard*'s top 100. They released a successful movie and soundtrack album, *A Hard Day's Night* (Capitol 5222), in the summer of 1964. Their second film, *Help!,* was released the next year.

In both their image and their music, the Beatles provided 1964 America with just the right formula, just when it was needed. The country was still reeling from the assassination of President John F. Kennedy, and the Beatles helped America out of the doldrums with their charm and wit, their unusual but adorable looks, and the sheer exoticism of their Britishness. Their music, rich in the tradition of classic fifties rockers, put America back in touch with the grassroots sound that had been undermined by the majors. It also proved that, despite what the urban folk revival tried to suggest, America was not through screaming and jumping up and down at rock concerts.

The music of the Beatles in the group's first year of American popularity covered the gamut of American rock styles: rockabilly, rhythm and blues, and sentimental ballads. The recording productions were modest, easily translated to live performances. The songs were generally high-spirited, adolescent, and danceable. The group was nothing revolutionary, but it was remarkable on a couple of counts. First of all, the Beatles did not present a quaint European parody of American rock, as would have been the case on British television in the late fifties. It was a solid rock and roll band, as valid and as convincing as any American rock band could be. Even the members' thick Liverpool accents disappeared when they sang.

The second remarkable feature of the Beatles was the prolific songwriting talents of John Lennon and Paul McCartney. In personality, business, performance, and songwriting, Lennon and McCartney were opposites. Lennon was rebellious and dark, more willing to be experimental and idealistic. He served as the rock shouter of the group and was the better wordsmith of the songwriting team. McCartney was more conservative and amiable, willing to conform to the norms of the music business and profit therefrom. He served as the sweet-voiced balladeer and was the better musician of the two. Yet these differences resulted in great songs that exhibited a variety of styles and moods; they kept the group successful yet progressive but, ultimately, also led to the demise of the band.

By 1965 the group was commercially secure enough and musically mature enough to begin experimenting with their repertoire. That spring Paul McCartney wrote "Yesterday" (Capitol 5498), a well-crafted ballad that did not fit into a rock band context; the chord progression was too sophisticated and the general character was too delicate. McCartney intended to record the song as a solo, accompanied by his own acoustic guitar. Producer George Martin suggested the additional accompaniment of a string quartet, more suggestive of classical chamber music than the lush string section accompaniment of a pop album. "Yesterday" was released as a single in the United States and shot to number one on the charts.

"Yesterday" marked the Beatles' move away from the formula of light, flippant dance songs to a new formula: "Don't have a formula." The group increased its experimentation and demonstrated disparate contributions by each member of the group and their producer. In late 1965 the album *Rubber Soul* (Capitol SW-02442) was released. The cover displayed an askewed portrait of four slightly pensive and more thoughtful Beatles. In addition to another McCartney ballad, "Michelle," unique in rock in that it was bilingual, other new elements were introduced into the Beatles sound. George Harrison used the Indian sitar on "Norwegian Wood." John Lennon's lyrics moved from adolescent romanticism to subjects of social consciousness and universal love, inspired by Bob Dylan and other 1960s folk rockers. With the aid of George Martin, the Beatles also experimented with recording effects that were unobtainable in live performances, such as multitracking and varying the speed of the tape, as on "In My Life."

Experimentation continued through two more Beatles albums, *Yesterday and Today* and *Revolver* (Capitol 5810). In late 1966 came the release of "Penny Lane" and "Strawberry Fields Forever," a double-sided single that exemplified the increasing dichotomy between Lennon and McCartney. Both songs were reminiscences of Liverpool. "Penny Lane" is charming and bouncy and features a baroque piccolo trumpet solo, inspired by Bach's second Brandenburg Concerto. It is typical of McCartney's songwriting style. "Strawberry Fields Forever" demonstrates John Lennon's fascination with surrealistic lyrics and musical depiction of his increasingly drug-laden lifestyle. Two contrasting versions were cut, which George Martin combined by careful tape manipulation techniques, creating an eerie sonic landscape.

In 1967 the Beatles recorded what many feel is the group's crowning achievement, the album *Sgt. Pepper's Lonely Hearts Club Band* (Capitol SMAS-02653). There were song contributions by Lennon, McCartney, and George Harrison. The songs, not originally intended to complement each other, were compiled in a programmatic package that resembled a musical play on record. The title song begins the album and is reprised toward the end, giving all of the songs the effect of a single multimovement work. The cover art, worthy of a whole chapter unto itself, shows the costumed Beatles assuming the characters of Sgt. Pepper's Lonely Hearts Club Band.

There are techniques of multitracking, tapes running backward, the splicing together of tape fragments, and the use of synthesizers. There are brass bands, a string orchestra, a clarinet choir, kazoos, a calliope, and Indian folk instruments. Compositionally, the record contains a variety of styles: old English music hall ("When I'm 64"), Indian folk music ("Within You Without You"), and straight rock and roll ("Sgt. Pepper"). "Lucy in the Sky with Diamonds" alternates between a gentle triple-meter feel on the verse to a rocking duple feel on the chorus, indicating that the album is intended to be listened to, not danced to. Lyrically, Lennon continued his penchant for surrealism and drug allusion. "Being for the Benefit of Mr. Kite" was taken almost word-for-word from an old theater poster. "When I'm 64" was McCartney's tribute to his father. History has dubbed *Sgt. Pepper* rock's first *concept album,* where a central theme is imposed on an album. This concept would be imitated by countless future rock bands in Britain and in the United States.

Listening Guide   17.1
"A Day in the Life" 4 beats per measure

ELAPSED TIME	FORM	EVENT DESCRIPTION
:00	Intro	Acoustic guitar, piano
:15	Verse A-1	Lennon vocal (10 measures)
:45	Verse A-2	Vocal (9 measures)
1:10	Verse A-3	Vocal (11 measures)
1:45	Transition	Orchestra (10 measures)
2:15	Verse B-P1	McCartney vocal (12 measures: 2 + 5 + 5)
2:50	Verse B-P2	Wordless vocal and unison orchestra (10 measures)
3:20	Verse A-3	Lennon vocal (12+ measures)
3:55	Coda P1	Orchestra climb and pause (10+ measures)
4:20	Coda P2	Loud chord and long fade-out
5:05	End	

Analysis of "A Day in the Life"

"A Day in the Life" is the finale of the *Sgt. Pepper* album. Actually, it is more of an encore, since it follows the reprise of the "Sgt. Pepper" theme near the end of the album. It is a prime example of the ambitious creativity that the Beatles and their producer, George Martin, were exercising at this time. The piece—one can hardly call it a mere song—incorporates different rhythmic feels, surrealistic lyrics that arouse suspicion of reference to drugs, studio overdubbing techniques, and unusual use of orchestra and other instrumental colors.

The song opens with acoustic guitar, followed shortly by piano. The tempo for the verse of the song is set with rhythm provided only by maracas. John Lennon sings the vocal; his lyric uses his avid newspaper reading as a point of departure. In the second verse his lyric becomes more surreal and disjointed, its growing strangeness made more dramatic by sporadic and aggressive rhythmic figures on the drum set. By the halfway point in the verse the drums settle into an easy rock beat. The accompaniment for the third verse is virtually the same. It is interesting to note that each of the three successive verses varies in length by one measure; the first verse is 10 measures long, the second verse is 9 measures long, and the third verse is 11 measures long. The extension of the third verse is created by the drawn-out line "I'd love to turn you on" (a drug allusion if there ever was one).

A 40-piece orchestra now fades in, beginning with a two-note oscillating pattern that the "turn you on" vocal line just completed. Over the next 10 measures, each instrument of the orchestra begins climbing up in range, the note choices of the ascent left to the spontaneous discretion of each musician. The total effect is a slow, rising cluster of pitches with no key or chord center.

The building tension of the rising orchestra figure is suddenly interrupted and "A Day in the Life" enters a new song section. The peppy, steady new rhythmic feel is provided primarily by the piano and drums. An alarm clock sound effect is heard, and Paul McCartney sings about waking up and hurrying to the bus. After singing "I went into a dream," there is an ethereal wordless vocal in deep echo, creating a dreamlike environment. The vocal is eventually overpowered by an ominous unison line played by the orchestra. The orchestra is abruptly cut off once again as Lennon returns with the first melody (verse melody). After the strangest lyric yet heard in the song, the line "I'd love to turn you on" leads into a second orchestra climb. This time the orchestra reaches its goal, a predetermined high note. There is a brief pause, followed by a powerful chord. The chord is allowed to slowly fade away over a period of some 45 seconds, a rather open-ended finish for an adventurous song and an adventurous rock album.

Brian Epstein died on August 27, 1967, from a drug overdose. Left without a manager, the Beatles fell victim to their own ineptitude in business and increasing friction between personalities in the group. McCartney's film concept *Magical Mystery Tour* proved to be a flop, though the subsequent album fared better. Their 1968 album, entitled simply *The Beatles* (Capitol SWBO-00101) but popularly known as the *White Album*, shows a fragmented but still successful rock group. The package was an ambitious two-record set containing 30 songs; it demonstrated the highest degree of eclecticism and individual expression yet. The Beatles pay tribute to earlier musical influences ("Back in the U.S.S.R.," "Rocky Raccoon") as well as forging new experimental paths (Lennon's "Revolution 9").

The release of *The Beatles* marked the first venture of the Beatles' new label, Apple Records, as part of their Apple Corps, Ltd., which dealt with film, management, and other aspects of the arts and entertainment business. In 1968 a Beatles cartoon movie, *Yellow Submarine,* was released. "Hey Jude" and "Get Back," from 1968 and 1969, respectively, were released as singles and were number-one hits. The stellar achievement of Apple Records, and the Beatles' biggest seller, was *Abbey Road,* released in 1969. Among other things, *Abbey Road* (Capitol SO-00383) certified George Harrison as a significant songwriter for the Beatles, with his "Something" and "Here Comes the Sun."

In 1970 the film *Let It Be* was released with an accompanying album. The stock of songs for the album had been recorded a year earlier, with song selection and postproduction work still to be done; but the Beatles broke up, and Phil Spector was brought in to finish the project.

In the succeeding years, Paul McCartney had the greatest musical success with his group, Wings, in the 1970s. Ringo Starr tried his hand at acting, even appearing on a public television children's show, and touring with all-star rock bands on occasion. John Lennon continued his experimental music projects, then retired to his New York apartment to devote more time to his family. He was murdered by a deranged fan in 1980, making him the first Beatle to die and dashing hopes of any reunion of the "Fab Four." However, in the 1990s the surviving Beatles did collaborate on an unprecedented series of biographical documentary projects released on CD, video, and television. Their 368-page *Beatles Anthology* book was released in October 2000 and a retrospective 27-track CD, *Beatles 1,* was released the next month; both were best-sellers. George Harrison, always known as the "quiet" Beatle, became increasingly reclusive, performing occasionally with various bands, most notably the Traveling Wilburys, which included the talents of Roy Orbison, Bob Dylan, and Tom Petty. After John Lennon's murder, Harrison feared his own demise at the hands of a lunatic. Indeed, another demented fan broke into his home in England in 1999 and stabbed him in the chest several times, but Harrison survived the attack. He wasn't as fortunate in his battle against his longtime smoking habit. After a long intermittent bout with lung and throat cancer, George Harrison succumbed on November 29, 2001.

THE ROLLING STONES

The Beatles were by far the most popular of the British rock bands of the 1960s and the group most responsible for whetting the American audience's appetite for all things British. The Beatles created a tidal wave that many other English groups rode across the Atlantic. Some of these groups attempted to imitate the Beatles' earlier style, looking cute and inoffensive and playing peppy rock-and-roll songs. Others offered a different bill of fare, an attitude and a music that contrasted sharply to the lovable moptops from Liverpool. The most significant of these bands was the Rolling Stones.

Founded by singer Mick Jagger (b. 1943) the group was part of the burgeoning rhythm and blues scene among London youth in the late fifties and early sixties. The center of the R&B activity was club owner Alexis Korner's band, Blues Incorporated, and the Stones were assembled from musicians who occasionally sat in with Korner's group. The band's name was taken from a song by Chicago R&B star Muddy Waters.

The Rolling Stones outside St. George's Church, Hanover Square in London, January 17, 1964.

By 1963 the personnel of the Rolling Stones solidified to include Mick Jagger, guitarists Keith Richard and Brian Jones, bassist Bill Wyman, and drummer Charlie Watts. The shadow of the Beatles' popularity was looming over all English bands, including the Stones, but the Beatles' prominence actually offered the Stones their first break. Andrew Oldham, a former agent for Brian Epstein, became the Rolling Stones' manager, and an endorsement from Beatle George Harrison got them their first recording contract with Decca Records. Their first significant hit was a cover of a Lennon/McCartney song, "I Want to Be Your Man."[3]

By 1964 it became obvious to the Rolling Stones that the only way to compete with the Beatles was to develop a counterimage to the Fab Four. They wore casual street clothes and ill-kept long hair and presented themselves to the press as rebellious and aloof. Their stage presentation and song content was more sexually explicit. Mick Jagger eventually incorporated footwork used by soul singer James Brown in his concerts. Their music was markedly different from the Beatles as well; it was derivative of black Chicago rhythm and blues singers from the 1940s and 1950s rather than the succeeding rockabilly that so influenced the Beatles. Jagger and Keith Richard began a Lennon/McCartney-type songwriting partnership, which would not bear significant fruit until the release of the song "Satisfaction" in 1965.

Meantime, in mid-1964 the Rolling Stones decided to try their hand at invading the United States, with disappointing results. A second U.S. tour later that year proved more successful. In 1965 "Time is on My Side," from their second album *12 X 5*, reached number six in the United States. Later that year Jagger and Richard wrote, recorded, and released "Satisfaction" in the United States, and it shot to number one in the summer of 1965. By December another album was released, containing the hit "Get off My Cloud."

The Stones continued with a string of hit singles through 1967, when the Beatles released *Sgt. Pepper's Lonely Hearts Club Band*. It was a significant event, and the Beatles once again posed a serious threat to the Rolling Stones' career, a situation they tried to remedy with a similar album project, *Their Satanic Majesties Request*. It proved a dismal failure. They returned to their more successful R&B format with the song "Jumpin' Jack Flash." In the late 1960s they demonstrated a preoccupation with the occult in "Sympathy for the Devil."

The decadent lifestyle of the Rolling Stones, both real and portrayed, was catching up with them. Guitarist Brian Jones became so incapacitated by drugs that he was fired from the band; he died in a drug-related accident in 1969. In December 1969 the group gave an ill-planned and disastrous concert at Altamont Speedway near San Francisco. The facility was overcrowded and Jagger had invited Hell's Angels motorcycle gang members to serve as security. There were riots, beatings, stabbings, and other mishaps that resulted in the death of four people.[4]

The Altamont incident established a tradition of destruction and violence at the Stones' concerts. Going into the 1970s their albums continued to be outrageous. *Sticky Fingers* contained sex- and drug-related material; its cover art personified sexual innuendo. The Stones' collective drug abuse had an adverse effect on their careers in the mid-1970s, but they managed a comeback in 1978. In 1983 they left the Atlantic label for CBS. Mick Jagger, Keith Richards (he added the "s" back to his name), and Charlie Watts have done solo projects, and the group has occasionally seemed on the verge of a breakup; but they have confounded the industry experts with extremely successful, if infrequent, concert tours. As they have aged, they have mellowed in their lifestyle—but not in their concert presentations. They continue to live up to the expectations of two or three generations of Rolling Stones fans.

Listening Guide   17.2
"Satisfaction" 4 beats per measure

ELAPSED TIME	FORM	EVENT DESCRIPTION
:00	Intro	Guitar riff and bass, add drums and tambourine (8 measures)
:15	Verse 1	Vocal with guitar answers (12 measures)
:35	Chorus 1	Vocal group, solo, group (20 measures: 4 + 10 + 8)
1:16	Verse 2	Vocal with guitar answers (12 measures)
1:37	Chorus 2	Vocal group, solo, group (20 measures: 4 + 10 + 8)
2:18	Verse 3	Vocal with guitar answers (12 measures)
2:39	Chorus 3	Vocal group, solo, group (20 measures: 4 + 10 + 8)
3:19	Coda	Vamp and fade on "I can't get no" (16 measures +)
3:49	End	

Analysis of "Satisfaction" (*Hot Rocks, 1964–1971*, Abkco 6667-1)

"Satisfaction," the Rolling Stones' first smash hit, was born from a riff Keith Richard conjured up while fooling around with a fuzz box (a device that distorts the sound of the electric guitar). He played the riff for Jagger, who set about composing a lyric for it. The new song was recorded in May 1965 and released that summer.

The inspired guitar riff begins the song. The electric guitar's sound has a grating, brassy quality. The riff is played in the lower register of the instrument, giving it the character of a bass line. The rhythm of the riff strongly emphasizes successive downbeats; this gives it a strong, emphatic quality. Almost immediately, the bass guitar enters with its own line. Whereas the distorted guitar riff emphasizes downbeat quarter notes, the bass emphasizes lighter upbeat eighth notes, creating an interesting counterpoint between the two low-register instruments. The drums enter with a solid rock beat. The tambourine also enters with a distinctive rhythm of three consecutive eighth notes beginning on the third beat of each measure.

After the eight-measure introduction, Jagger enters with a soft but menacing vocal. The phrasing of the line "I can't get no satisfaction" is fragmented; each syllable of the line is separated by three eighth notes, giving the rhythm of the melody the effect of a triple meter over the duple meter of the underlying rhythm section. This rhythmic duality somehow gives the simultaneous effect of floating and forward momentum—a forward spiraling effect, if you will. The vocal then builds to the shouting sound of the chorus.

The words of the chorus are as repetitive as the verse, but they are set rhythmically in such a way as to perfectly complement the signature guitar riff of the song. It is, in fact, the interplay of rhythms between the voice and guitar riff, rather than the lyric itself, that ultimately accounts for the success of this song. We can be certain that this was Jagger's strategy when composing his melody line and lyric.

Other British Bands in the 1960s

Between the initial British invasion by the Beatles in 1964 and approximately 1966, many English groups came and went. Some were light novelty groups, cute, inoffensive, and best forgotten. Others proved more musically significant but lacked the staying power of the Beatles or the Rolling Stones. Noteworthy among the lighter groups was Gerry and the Pacemakers, a Liverpool group that rivaled the popularity of the Beatles in England prior to the latter's American debut. Also managed by Brian Epstein, their "Ferry across the Mersey" (the river running through Liverpool) rose to number six in the United States in 1965. From the R&B Rolling Stones camp came the Animals, a group from Newcastle upon Tyne. Led by sultry lead vocalist Eric Burdon, they rose to number one in the United States in 1964 with an old New Orleans folk song, "House of the Rising Sun." The Kinks were from London and initially attempted a smooth, Liverpool "Merseybeat" sound. Meeting with little success, they began writing their own songs, hardening their sound and beat. Two hits emerged that were similar in style, and both reached number seven in 1964 and 1965, respectively: "You Really Got Me" and "All Day and All of the Night." One sound they pioneered was *power-chord* guitar, a strong, open chord voicing played by distorted guitar.

The British R&B scene spawned a second wave of bands that included the Yardbirds, Them, the Who, and the Spencer Davis Group. The trendiest band was the Who, representing the mod sector of youthful British fashion. Comprised of guitarist Pete Townshend, vocalist Roger Daltrey, bassist John Entwistle, and drummer Keith Moon, the Who began as an R&B band called the High Numbers. Their manager, Peter Meaden, honed their mod image and helped launch their premiere single "I'm the Face" and "Zoot Suit." Their music was laden with mod slang, making it hard to sell outside their own milieu.

The hallmark that saved the group's popularity proved to be not a musical feature but a theatrical one. In a concert mishap, Townshend found that he got more reaction from the audience smashing his guitar than playing it. Soon afterward, instrument destruction became an integral part of the act, with all members of the band participating. These antics enhanced the rebellious English mod nature of the Who's music, written in large part by Townshend. Its intensity still made marketability elusive, particularly in the United States, where girls were squealing over the cherubic British band Herman's Hermits. Recognition finally came in 1969 with the release of the concept album *Tommy*, a rock opera about a blind pinball wizard.

The Who, like the Rolling Stones, represented a rebellious side of rock music; however, if the Stones were smug and hedonistic, the Who were downright angry. Townshend commented that their music "threatens a lot of crap which is around at the moment in the middle class

British rock group the Who on January 1, 1978. (Left to right: Keith Moon, Pete Townshend, Roger Daltrey, John Entwistle)

and in the middle-aged politics of philosophy." The Who's music better matched the emotional tone of American youth in the last half of the 1960s, when the escalating Vietnam conflict threatened their very lives. At the same time, the Who was thoroughly British in its presentation, a vivid icon of English mod fashion. They represented a maturity in the development of the British rock invasion, where British fashion and music asserted its own originality and no longer had to pay homage to American culture.

By the 1970s British music became an integral part of the rock mainstream. The stream of heavy metal, punk, art rock, and pop rock styles flowed with equal force from both sides of the Atlantic. British rock was an exotic novelty in the early sixties, but its power as an influence in popular music would ultimately be undeniable.

Chapter Summary

In the late 1950s and early 1960s American rock and roll made the transition from self-assured grassroots music to polished commercialism. In England, meanwhile, British youth were still digesting American folk and jazz music from the 1930s and 1940s and rock and roll from the early and mid-1950s. Skiffle, a rustic style based on American folk music, was the first significant step toward a British brand of rock. This gave way to two distinct regional styles: Merseybeat, the favored style of working-class Liverpool that was based on rockabilly; and a rock style from London that university students based on black, electric rhythm and blues. The former style yielded the Beatles, the latter style the Rolling Stones.

The Beatles took the United States by storm with their first live American appearance in 1964. Their initial style was based on light, danceable rock styles of the fifties. After several successful years, the prodigious songwriting team of John Lennon and Paul McCartney began experimenting with music in a studio setting, culminating in 1967 with the concept album *Sgt. Pepper's Lonely Hearts Club Band*.

The Beatles' biggest British rival was the Rolling Stones, in many ways the antithesis of the Beatles' image and music. The Stones were solidly based in Chicago rhythm and blues and exhibited a rude and rebellious image. Their style was established with their first big hit, "Satisfaction," in 1965. Other British bands followed, ranging in style from raunchy blues to bubblegum, but none achieved the stature of the Beatles and the Rolling Stones. The most significant of the other British bands was the Who, a band that brought a distinctively British style of music and fashion to the fore.

Additional Listening

Refer to citations in the body of the text (all are LP format).

The Animals, *The Most of the Animals* (LP format, Music for Pleasure MFP-5218).

The Who, *The Best of the Last 10 Years* (LP format, Polydor 2664 323).

Review Questions

1. What were the American music influences evident in England just prior to the emergence of British rock?
2. What were the regional differences in British rock after the skiffle craze?
3. Compare the Beatles' pre–*Sgt. Pepper* music with their later material.
4. Compare John Lennon and Paul McCartney in terms of their personal and musical inclinations.

5. What types of studio effects are utilized in *Sgt. Pepper* and later Beatles recordings?

6. How did the Rolling Stones contrast with the Beatles, both in image and in musical approach?

7. What was another British band that more closely resembled the Beatles? What was another British band that more closely resembled the Rolling Stones?

8. What cultural and musical segment of British rock did the Who represent? How did they represent it?

Notes

1. An excellent video accompaniment to this chapter is *British Rock: The First Wave*, produced by Patrick Montgomery and Pamela Page, available from RCA/Columbia Home Video.

2. Sutcliffe's image brings up the whole issue of British youth's style in looks and attitudes in the 1950s. Young people were usually separated into two groups: *rockers* or *mods*. Rockers (or "teddy bears") wore black leather jackets and wore their hair in greased-back pompadours. The mods wore shorter hair and were smarter in their dress. The pre-Beatles Quarry Men fit into the rocker style. For more details on British youth fashion, see David P. Szatmary, *Rockin' in Time: A Social History of Rock and Roll* (Englewood Cliffs, NJ: Prentice Hall, 1987), pp. 82–88.

3. In his marvelous rock text, Joe Stuessy points out that the Rolling Stones continued in the shadow of the Beatles' success, that the highest position they ever attained was that of the Beatles' greatest rival but never their equal. See Joe Stuessy, *Rock and Roll: Its History and Stylistic Development* (Englewood Cliffs, NJ: Prentice Hall, 1990), pp. 170–172.

4. The incident at Altamont was recorded in a film documentary, *Gimme Shelter*, available at most video rental stores.

Chapter 18

Psychedelic Rock and Roots Revivalists

The Beatles' *Sgt. Pepper's Lonely Hearts Club Band* is a strong symbol of rock's musical experimentation in the last half of the 1960s. It did not, however, initiate *progressive rock*, nor did it claim the idea solely for the British bands that followed. America had its own alternative rock styles running parallel to the British; in fact, the American and British scenes fed off each other. The two main centers for this American activity were Los Angeles and San Francisco, California.

The social tone of the late 1960s that the music undergirded was one of youthful rebellion to materialism and political policies of the adult establishment. This youth movement was evident in cities around the world, particularly in university communities. A big issue in this *generation gap*, as it came to be called, was the American involvement in the conflict in Vietnam. As America's involvement in Southeast Asia escalated, university students throughout the nation became outraged that the old establishment was sending scores of young people into a war that had never been declared. Rebellion took the form of a lifestyle that ran completely contrary to the morals and ethics of the previous generation, and San Francisco became a focal point for this lifestyle and attitude.

San Francisco is a beautiful city, just across the bay from the University of California's Berkeley campus and not far from Stanford University. Like New York's Greenwich Village on the East Coast (adjacent to New York University), San Francisco had a thriving bohemian community in the 1950s and 1960s, with a fine literary tradition and a freethinking social code. In the Haight-Ashbury district of San Francisco a communal tribalism arose, incorporating elements of Eastern culture and religion. Hippies, the people of this youth culture, preached "love, not war" and openly experimented with sex and drugs, the former aided by the development of the birth control pill in the late 1950s, the latter by the development of hallucinogenic drugs, particularly LSD. Concerts in San Francisco clubs attempted to simulate, or enhance, the drug experience with entrancing repetitive rhythmic music and disorienting light shows.

Jazz and folk music found a home in San Francisco, playing to coffee house beatniks and their 1960s incarnation, hippies. This was fertile ground for a new and experimental brand of rock, immune to the high pressure and corporate conservatism of the New York and Los Angeles music industry. The music reached unprecedented levels of loudness that could be felt like a hand against the body, and the numbing effect of such intense volume likely added to the drug effect. What could have been three-minute songs were opened up for extended instrumental improvisations, sometimes a half hour in length. There were also changes of tempo and mood throughout the course of a song. This was commonplace in jazz and European art music but quite rare in the vocal-oriented, three-minute hit concept of popular music. The music was also unabashedly drug-related, uninterested in the subtle techniques of covert drug messages used by other rock bands (the Beatles' "Lucy in the Sky with Diamonds," for instance). All these musical features indicate that the music was maturing and deemphasizing rock as dance music. This more ambitious music may also represent the only significant contribution middle-class, college-educated, white American culture made to popular music in the twentieth century.

While vehemently trying to remain anticommercial, the music, fashion, and lifestyle of the San Francisco counterculture soon caught on around the country. Two vehicles helped to solidify and disseminate the counterculture. The first consisted of concert hall events and outdoor music festivals. Bill Graham's Fillmore West was the most famous of the concert halls that, despite the antimaterialistic motives of the hippies, proved a huge moneymaker for Graham. The other important vehicle for San Francisco psychedelic rock was FM radio. In these early years of FM radio programming, the Federal Communications Commission mandated that a radio station could not duplicate programming on its AM and FM frequencies. This led to hours of unused airtime on FM that the lengthier, more experimental music could benefit from. FM was already broadcasting classical and easy-listening music, considered by some as the only genres worthy of FM's better-sounding quality. Then in 1967 a former San Francisco AM disc jockey, Tom Donahue, took a job at KMPX–FM and began playing the longer, experimental music of the San Francisco bands. Since most of the music never would have appeared on AM radio, with its three- to four-minute restrictions, conservative content, and hyperactive disc jockeys, Donahue and FM provided an important outlet for the local music scene.

Grace Slick, lead singer for Jefferson Airplane in the 1960s.

Jefferson Airplane

In 1965 Jefferson Airplane became the first San Francisco band to sign with a major label, RCA. The band was founded by folk musician Marty Balin, who was assembling a house band for his club in San Francisco. He recruited another folkie, Paul Kantner, blues guitarist Jorma Kaukonen, and folksinger Signe Anderson. Later, bass and drums were added. As a result of the members' disparate musical backgrounds, a distinctive folk and R&B hybrid developed in their music.

After the release of their first album, *Jefferson Airplane Takes Off* (RCA LPM-3584) in 1966, Anderson was replaced by Grace Slick. A charismatic addition to the group, Slick was a former model whose stage presence was striking. Musi-

Listening Guide   18.1
"White Rabbit" 4 beats per measure

ELAPSED TIME	FORM	EVENT DESCRIPTION
:00	Intro	Bass, snare drum, electric guitar fill (12 measures)
:28	Verse 1	Vocal with Spanish march feel (12 measures)
:57	Verse 2	Vocal (12 measures)
1:28	Chorus P1	Vocal with folk-rock feel (8 measures)
1:44	Chorus P2	Vocal with Spanish march feel (12 measures)
2:12	Coda	Vocal with eighth-note figure (9 measures)
2:35	End	

cally, she was a powerful vocalist and a scathingly sarcastic songwriter. She became the first tough-image female rock star, a departure from the wholesome image maintained by personalities like Annette Funicello and Connie Francis. She premiered on the Airplane's second album, *Surrealistic Pillow*. Released in 1967, it is the group's most popular and representative work and yielded two hits, "Somebody to Love" and "White Rabbit."

Analysis of "White Rabbit" (*The Worst of Jefferson Airplane*, RCA LSP-4459)

"White Rabbit" is from Jefferson Airplane's 1967 album *Surrealistic Pillow*, the first recording from the San Francisco scene to gain national attention. On this album the group's sound had matured around Grace Slick's penetrating vocal style. Their song topics addressed intimate romantic love and broader universal love; but true to the culture of the times, they also addressed the drug experience.

Reference to drugs was not unprecedented in literature and the arts. In the nineteenth century, opium and opium-based pharmaceuticals were the prominent drugs. Sir Arthur Conan Doyle's famous fictional detective Sherlock Holmes was an opium user. The famous French composer Hector Berlioz based his *Symphonie Fantastique* on an opium drug experience. Lewis Carroll's story *Alice's Adventures in Wonderland* was a metaphor for a drug experience, though its popularity as a children's story has played this down. Jefferson Airplane, on the other hand, played the drug reference to the hilt in "White Rabbit."

The electric bass begins this song with a two-note pattern; it seems to imitate timpani drums in an orchestra. In the third measure the snare drum enters with a military style rhythmic pattern, and the bass notes move up a half step. This half-step bass motion (1 to flat-2) is common in Spanish folk music, and "White Rabbit" does take on the character of a Spanish march. The electric guitar enters with a brief melody to finish out the introduction.

Grace Slick enters with the first verse; it is easy to hear the strength and assertiveness in her voice, although, at this point, she is singing in a soft and spellbinding manner. Her voice becomes more commanding over the course of the two verses, as she points out Alice's constantly altered state after ingesting one thing or another and questions what is in the caterpillar's water pipe. As the song's chorus begins, the band breaks away from the Spanish march feel and goes into a folk-rock beat. When Slick sings the recurring line "go ask Alice," the march beat is resumed. The group's intensity builds over the next 12 measures as Slick vividly describes Alice's strange world. The final push of the song is signaled by an electric guitar chord played in persistent eighth notes, supported by a similar rhythmic pattern in the drums. A crashing chord concludes the performance, a dramatic climax to a song of fearsome majesty.

The Grateful Dead

The Grateful Dead was the psychedelic era's most beloved band and its most enduring. The band's faithful fans, Deadheads, reach across generations. The Dead became enduring stars outside the mainstream of the music business, creating a world unto itself. Like many of the San Francisco bands, the band had strong ties to folk music roots, presented a message of utopian love and hope, and was also inextricably linked to the drug culture.

The Grateful Dead began with Jerry Garcia (1942–1995), an enthusiast of bluegrass and folk music. Garcia met lyricist Robert Hunter, who helped him pen many of his songs. In 1964 he formed Mother McCree's Uptown Jug Champions with guitarist Bob Weir (b. 1947) and keyboardist Ron "Pigpen" McKernan (1946–1973). The next year the band changed its name to the Warlocks. Added to the lineup was Phil Lesh (b. 1940), a bassist and computer music specialist, and Bill Kreutzmann (b. 1946) on drums. Later in 1965 the band once again renamed itself, this time the Grateful Dead, the name taken from an Egyptian prayer discovered by Garcia. It was the house band for early LSD gatherings and became a prominent part of the San Francisco music scene.

The Grateful Dead's music was quite eclectic, including elements of country, bluegrass, folk, and the blues. Its music is more a process than a product, utilizing a lot of experimentation and improvisation that also flourishes most in live

Bob Weir (left) and Jerry Garcia of the Grateful Dead in concert.

performance situations. It also employed electronic effects of the day: distortion, feedback, and audio signal processors.

Commercial success eluded the Grateful Dead. The band signed with MGM Records in 1966 but was soon dropped. It later signed with Warner Records. After a couple of false starts with studio albums, the Dead recorded *Live/Dead* in 1969, its first live album and capturing its best context. It features a version of Jerry Garcia's "Dark Star" that clocks in at over 23 minutes on the recording. In 1970 two successful studio albums were produced, *Workingman's Dead* and *American Beauty*. These albums generated the band's most enduring repertoire, including "Truckin'," "Uncle John's Band," and "Sugar Magnolia."

The Grateful Dead remained primarily a live touring act, creating a world of hippie fashion and heavy drug use that continued for 25 years. Deadheads were a cult, following the band everywhere it toured and recording thousands of hours of homemade bootleg recordings with the band's blessing. Personnel changes occurred along the line (second drummer Mickey Hart in 1967, keyboardist Keith Godchaux to replace McKernan in 1973, Brent Mydland to replace Godchaux in 1979), but Garcia was the foundation, both musically and spiritually. Plagued with physical problems stemming from substance abuse, Garcia finally succumbed in 1995. A few months later the band broke up.

Janis Joplin

Janis Joplin was born in Port Arthur, Texas, in 1943. After attending the University of Texas at Austin for a year, she moved to San Francisco to be lead singer in the band Big Brother and the Holding Company. The band got its big break, as so many West Coast bands did, at the 1967 Monterey International Pop Festival and came to the attention of Bob Dylan's manager. This led to a recording contract with Columbia records and the release of the 1968 album *Cheap Thrills* (Columbia PC-9700).

Rock and blues singer Janis Joplin.

Joplin's vocal style came from the tradition of black gospel and blues shouters. Her voice was coarse and screaming, well suited for cutting through the incredible volume of the band, and forecasted the heavy-metal screamers of the 1970s. One of her major influences was Houston blues singer Willie Mae "Big Mama" Thornton, who originally recorded Jerry Lieber and Mike Stoller's "Hound Dog" in 1953. In fact, the highlight of *Cheap Thrills* is Joplin's rendition of Thornton's "Ball and Chain." Joplin, more than any other white singer, accurately captured the raw sound of black blues singers.

Joplin's image also epitomized the new female rock star. Grace Slick of Jefferson Airplane had broken ground for the new image, leading audience expectations away from the wholesome girl-next-door look, but she was subtle in comparison with Janis Joplin. Joplin, unlike Slick, was not physically attractive; but she was still sensual. She wore garish clothes, stomped around the stage, and screamed her vocals with a gusto that would be the envy of every macho male. As writer Ellen Willis states, "[Joplin] could not only invent her own beauty . . . , but have that beauty appreciated. Not that Janis merely took advantage of changes in our notions of attractiveness; she herself changed them."[1]

Joplin went solo in 1969, with the album *I Got Dem Ol' Kosmic Blues Again* being released mid-year. In 1970 she formed a polished backup band, Full-Tilt Boogie, whose work can be heard on her last album *Pearl* (Columbia PC-30322). She died of a drug overdose before the album's release but left a monument to her uniqueness in rock music. The album displays her penchant for flat-out rock and roll, as on "Move Over"; but it also demonstrates her versatility, as on Kris Kristofferson's "Me and Bobby McGee," a country rock song that became her only top 40 single, holding number one for two weeks.

Jimi Hendrix

The artistic height of the West Coast rock scene was achieved by Jimi Hendrix. Rock historian Joe Stuessy makes a significant point: What Bob Dylan did for the advancement of lyric writing in rock, Jimi Hendrix did for technique in electric rock guitar. In the thirties and forties, Southwest jazz and blues guitarists, such as Eddie Durham, Charlie Christian, and Aaron "T-Bone" Walker, explored the possibilities of the amplified guitar: its ability to sustain and to project over the band and to emulate the expressive nuances of blues vocalists. Some 20 years later Jimi Hendrix harnessed newer techniques of distortion and feedback, added radical new techniques of his own, and elevated rock guitar and improvisational creativity to an unprecedented artistic plane.

Jimi Hendrix was born in Seattle, Washington, in 1942. His music career began as a sideman for R&B acts that included the Isley Brothers, Little Richard, King Curtis, and Ike and Tina Turner. In 1965 he formed his own band, Jimmy James and the Blue Flames. This required him to venture into singing, an activity at which he was painfully self-conscious; but he figured that if Bob Dylan could call himself a singer, then so could he. The band played in New York's Greenwich Village, where it came to the attention of "Chas" Chandler, the bassist for the British R&B band the Animals.

Rock guitar virtuoso Jimi Hendrix at a live performance in 1970.

Chandler talked Hendrix into moving to England in 1966, where the R&B scene was flourishing. Hendrix formed a trio with English musicians, bassist Noel Redding and drummer Mitch Mitchell, calling it the Jimi Hendrix Experience. They adopted the bright-colored fashions of British psychedelia and recorded an album, *Are You Experienced?*, that yielded Hendrix's most enduring songs, among them "Purple Haze" and "Hey Joe."

In 1967 the Jimi Hendrix Experience debuted in the United States as part of the continuing wave of British bands. The band followed an electrifying set by the Who at the Monterey Pop Festival, but Hendrix was prepared to do them one better. He played amazing guitar, played it behind his back, with his teeth and with the microphone stand, then put the instrument on the floor, dowsed it with lighter fluid, and burned it (take that, Pete Townshend!).

Hendrix played a right-handed Fender Stratocaster guitar left-handed, with the strings arranged backward on the instrument so the low strings would still be positioned on top. While this did not necessarily give Hendrix any particular technical advantage, it did mean that the volume and tone knobs and the tremolo (or "whammy") bar were in a different position. Hendrix did not invent amplifier distortion or feedback, by-products of playing extremely loud. But he did harness the effects and use them in well-paced and meaningful ways, making them an integral part of the performance's dramatic shape rather than a gimmick. He also used external effects devices: a fuzz tone box for distortion, a Uni-Vibe box that simulates the swirling sound of the rotating speakers found in a Leslie speaker cabinet, and a wah-wah pedal that alters the timbre of the guitar. In the studio Hendrix utilized special tape effects as well. On his 1968 album *Electric Ladyland*, he manipulated the speed of the tape to create unique instrumental effects on the song "And the Gods Made Love."

For all his genius, Jimi Hendrix was an anomaly. He was a black American rhythm and blues guitarist who did not fit in, neither in music, fashion, or social viewpoint, with the soul music scene that most black musicians were involved in at the time. Musically, he was far more advanced than his fellow rock musicians; certainly he was light years beyond his audience. The audience, as sophisticated as it may have thought it was, preferred Hendrix's on-stage theatrics to his involved music; he came to resent the audience's superficial view of him.

To fulfill his artistic needs, in the summer of 1969 Hendrix gathered a close circle of musicians in upstate New York for intense musical experimentation. He also disbanded the Experience and formed an all-black trio, the Band of Gypsys. He opened his own Electric Ladyland studio in New York City for album projects and intimate jam sessions. His artistic progress came to an end in London on September 18, 1970, when he died from inhalation of vomit, intoxicated on barbiturates.

The impact of Jimi Hendrix on music history was tremendous. He, along with British guitar wizards like Eric Clapton, influenced many future guitarists, setting a new performance standard for the instrument as well as contributing new techniques idiomatic to the electric guitar. He has had many imitators but few with his subtlety and depth. He was a master improviser, certainly the most qualified of the West Coast rockers to indulge in the long instrumental stretches indigenous to the style. His improvisational skills even caught the attention of the jazz community, particularly trumpeter Miles Davis and his longtime arranger Gil Evans. In 1975 Evans arranged and produced an album of Hendrix material, and one number, "Little Wing," reappeared on Sting's album *Nothing Like the Sun* (A&M SP6402).

Listening Guide   18.2
"I Don't Live Today" 4 beats per measure

ELAPSED TIME	FORM	EVENT DESCRIPTION
:00	Intro	Drums, "choked" guitar riff (4 measures: 2 + 2)
:08	Verse 1	Vocal and descending blues riff (24 measures)
1:00	Chorus 1	Vocal and quarter note hit riff (8 measures)
1:16	Instr. 1	Chantlike guitar solo (16 measures)
1:50	Chorus 2	Vocal and guitar note hit riff (8 measures)
2:07	Instr. 2 P1	Guitar solo, no accompaniment (out of tempo)
2:21	Instr. 2 P2	Verse riff, guitar solo over drums, studio fades
3:46	End	

Analysis of "I Don't Live Today" (*Are You Experienced?* Reprise RS-6261)

Other songs from Jimi Hendrix's *Are You Experienced?* album are more famous, but "I Don't Live Today" is a fine single example of Hendrix's songwriting, guitar playing, and use of studio techniques. Solo drums begin the song, soon joined by a rhythmic pattern from Hendrix's guitar. The structure of the verse is a long call-and-response pattern between a bluesy, descending guitar riff and Hendrix's vocal. The lyric is an expression of personal hopelessness and uncertainty of the future. The chorus is a similar call-and-response form. This time the riff is two consecutive quarter notes at the beginning of each measure answered by the vocal.

The first chorus is followed by the first guitar improvisation. With the underpinning of a driving rock beat, Hendrix plays an expansive chantlike, almost meditative solo. The disparity of character between his solo and the hard drive of the band is mesmerizing; Hendrix is obviously saving something for another solo later in the song, a true sign of his artistry and immaculate sense of pacing. The vocal chorus returns, acting as a bridge or interlude to the next instrumental section.

The second solo begins with an effect electric guitarists sometimes termed a *dive bomber*. With the tone of the guitar heavily distorted, Hendrix slowly slides down and up a low string. He then manipulates the tone of the guitar by flipping a switch that turns each of the guitar's pickups on and off. The rest of the band has dropped out at this point, adding to the floating sensation of this part of the song. The spell is suddenly broken when the first guitar riff (from the verse) returns, played over and over in rapid succession. The momentum builds, the instrumentalists gradually drift away from the riff and create an engulfing wall of sound. Using a studio "board fade," the track is brought down in volume and Hendrix fades in with the line "Oh, there ain't no life nowhere." This effect is repeated two more times before the final fade-out. Programmatically, Hendrix is at his deepest point of despair, his senseless mutterings on the fade-outs and the pounding effect of the band suggest a raging storm of emotional or drug-induced insanity.

The Doors

Four hundred miles south of San Francisco, Los Angeles developed its own brand of psychedelic rock. The San Francisco bands such as Jefferson Airplane and the Grateful Dead had a more utopian view of the world, singing about free love and leaning on a gentler, folksy side to their music. The Los Angeles style was darker, more cynical, introspective, and brooding. A couple of the major bands from Los Angeles were Iron Butterfly, whose 17-minute "In a Gadda Da Vida" sold over four million copies, and Steppenwolf, who recorded the biker anthem "Born to Be Wild." The song used the phrase "heavy metal thunder," a term that would be assigned to the music that emerged in the early 1970s.

The most legendary of the southern California bands, however, was the Doors. Jim Morrison, the band's vocalist, was born in Florida in 1943 and came to Los Angeles to attend film school at U.C.L.A. There he met another film student, Chicago native and classically trained organist Ray Manzarek. They teamed up with guitarist Robby Krieger and drummer John Densmore to form the Doors.

From the outset the group's sound was distinct from any other band of the time. It was dominated by Manzarek's dense and technically challenging electric organ work. The group did not have an electric bass guitar. They borrowed stylings from West Coast surf guitar, jazz, blues, European classical music, British and San Francisco psychedelia, and Middle Eastern music. Morrison's vocal sound was deep, rich, and often saturated with studio reverberation. His lyrics were often thoughtful, dark, and poetic, inspired by the writings of Frederick Nietzche and other classic figures of literature and poetry.

After playing in local clubs, the Doors signed with Elektra Records in 1966 and released their first album, *The Doors*, the next year. It was one of the most successful albums of the psychedelic genre, reaching number two on the album charts. The single from the album, "Light My Fire," reached number one on the singles charts.

Morrison's lyrics, dealing with death and the dark side of human life, possibly reflected his own manic outlook on life. He was an alcoholic and a drug addict and was occasionally dysfunctional at concerts, as evidenced at a 1969 Miami concert where he exposed himself to the audience.

Subsequent albums did well on the charts, even when the group flirted with a softer rock sound. Morrison's final album with the Doors was *L.A. Woman*, which yielded the hit "Riders on the Storm." Jim Morrison died of a heart failure in July 1971, at the age of 27.

The Doors in Germany (left to right: Ray Manzarek, John Densmore, Jim Morrison, Robby Krieger)

Listening Guide   18.3
"Light My Fire" 4 beats per measure

ELAPSED TIME	FORM	EVENT DESCRIPTION
:00	Intro	Heavy drum clap; electric organ solo á la Bach
:09	Verse 1	Morrison's vocal enters
:25	Chorus 1	Melody at end descends to a low note
:38	Verse 2	Morrison begins to play with the melody more
:53	Chorus 2	Morrison ends with a hesitation, a high note, and a "Yeah" to build up a send-off to the solos
1:07	Organ solo	Improvisation based on the two chords of the verse (70 measures)
3:18	Guitar solo	Improvisation based on the two chords of the verse (70 measures)
5:31	Intro	Intro returns to lead back into the vocals
5:41	Verse 2	Repeated from before the solos
5:56	Chorus 3	Similar to treatment of chorus 2
6:10	Verse 1	Repeated from before the solos, but sung in a higher range and with more intensity
6:25	Chorus 4	Sung in the same intense manner as the preceding verse; last line is repeated several times; band stops the rhythm, hesitates
6:49	Intro	Abbreviated version of the introduction; chord held out at the end
7:03	End	

His mystique and his image as the self-destructive rock star have actually gotten more attention than his music. He has been the subject of many tabloid biographies and a 1991 film by Oliver Stone, starring Val Kilmer as Morrison.

Analysis of "Light My Fire" (*The Doors*, CD format, Elektra 74007)[2]

The root of "Light My Fire," the Doors' biggest hit, was organist Ray Manzarek's and guitarist Robby Krieger's love of modern jazz, particularly that of pioneering saxophonist John Coltrane (see Chapter 9). The two were determined to figure out how they could bring the improvisational freedom and expansiveness of jazz, as exemplified by Coltrane, into rock music. But as mentioned above, influence from blues, surf music, beat poetry, and many other elements came into play as well.

"Light My Fire" was Krieger's first compositional contribution to the band, but it was in a very embryonic state when first presented to the rest of the band. Starting out with a folksy flavor, Manzarek added an electric organ solo reminiscent of Johann Sebastian Bach. With Krieger stuck for words by the second verse Morrison began playing around with rhyme combinations to flesh it out, such as "wallow in the mire" with "our love is a funeral pyre."

After the first two verses Manzarek and Krieger get to indulge their passion for open jazz improvisation over a two-chord vamp, inspired directly by John Coltrane's 1960 treatment of the Rodgers and Hammerstein song from *The Sound of Music*, "My Favorite Things" (*My Favorite Things*, Atlantic SD-1361-2). Both

Manzarek and Krieger had witnessed Coltrane in live settings in Los Angeles where he improvised for over a half-hour on the two-chord vamp he created on his version of "My Favorite Things." In turn, the Doors would improvise for 15 minutes or more over their two-chord vamp on "Light My Fire." For the studio recording their improvisations extend the song to just over seven minutes, inappropriate for AM airplay at the time. After the album's release, the Doors produced a whittled-down three-minute version hoping for the AM hit, but fans who owned the album demanded that radio stations play the full album version.

Both the organ and guitar solos build to a climax with driving triplet rhythms. It is also interesting to note that, toward the end of the guitar solo, the organ returns to a more soloistic role, interweaving improvised melodic lines with the guitar. The Bach-like intro reintroduces the vocal at the end of the solo section.

Morrison does the verses in reverse order (second, then first), giving the overall format of the song an arch form or mirror image from the first half of the recording to the last half. This arch form is also enhanced by the use of the organ introduction at the beginning, middle, and end of the performance.

"Light My Fire" became a number-one hit in 1967 and was a turning point for hit songs. Its extended length, ambitious instrumental solos, and brooding view of love made it a watershed in the history of rock.

BLUES AND FOLK-ROCK ARTISTS IN THE LATE 1960S AND 70S

As mentioned earlier in this chapter, much of West Coast psychedelic rock derived from urban blues, country, and the urban folk revival. Outside the San Francisco milieu there were other significant manifestations of these traditions that occurred in the late 1960s and early 1970s. Young white rockers across the country began exploring purer forms of black rhythm and blues. Southern rockers came up with a new, post-rockabilly hybrid of country and R&B. Inspired by earlier folk artists, a new wave of gentle, introspective folksingers/songwriters emerged. On the West Coast rock bands sought distinctive new blends of folk and country music.

The Band

During its heyday, from about 1968 until 1975, The Band was one of the most influential folk-rock bands in the world. The group began in 1958 with two Arkansas-born musicians, Ronnie Hawkins and Levon Helm. The two toured Canada and eventually added Canadian musicians to The Band. The eventual lineup included Robbie Robertson on guitar, Rick Danko on bass, Richard Manuel on piano, and Garth Hudson on organ. After some time playing and touring together, they came to the attention of John Hammond, Jr., and, through him, hooked up with folk-rock singer Bob Dylan.

Dylan transformed The Band from a blues-based rock band to one that did electric adaptations of folk music. They toured with Dylan in 1966, then procured their own recording contract, changing their name from the Hawks to The Band. Their 1968 album, *Music from Big Pink,* became one of the most talked about and influential albums of the day, its style running counter to the counterculture of Britain, San Francisco, and Los Angeles. The Band had a unique collective sound, lacking a blended or categorizable style, blending elements of folk, rhythm and blues, classical, gospel, and rock and roll.

The Band's legend and record sales grew quickly with their follow-up album, simply titled *The Band,* and included the memorable "The Night They Drove Ol' Dixie Down," with its folksy images of Americana. They grew beyond their association with Bob Dylan to stand as folk-rock stars in their own right and became a major catalyst for the folk-rock movement of the 1970s.

Various tragic circumstances impacted The Band, leading to their ultimate demise. Their did a farewell tour in 1976 that became the subject of a Martin Scorcese film, *The Last Waltz.*

The Paul Butterfield Blues Band

British rockers had a head start on Americans as far as the urban blues revival was concerned. In the late 1950s London had a large contingent of electric blues devotees, centered around Alexis Korner's club. The Rolling Stones, John Mayall's Bluesbreakers, and the Yardbirds sprang from this movement. In America, however, the enthusiasm for Muddy Waters, Howlin' Wolf, John Lee Hooker, and others was slower to catch on. Historian Ed Ward blames this hesitation on the pervasive influence of the urban folk movement, which preferred the folksier, acoustic country blues of the twenties and thirties.[3]

Michael Bloomfield was one of the first young American musicians to embrace electric blues with the orthodox fervor of the British. He came from a well-to-do family in Chicago and began a fascination with the black blues tradition in his city. (This is reminiscent of young, white Chicagoans' fascination with black jazz in the 1920s.) While still a teenager Bloomfield began playing with older R&B musicians. He soon met blues harmonica player Paul Butterfield, another young, white, middle-class blues enthusiast. Bloomfield and Butterfield formed the Paul Butterfield Blues Band, becoming the most influential blues revival band in America. Their first album was recorded for Elektra in 1965. Their second album, *East-West* (1966), helped to establish their second guitarist, Elvin Bishop, as a top-notch bluesman.

Southern Rock

Rhythm and blues rock took on a country flavor also, due to the efforts of some white rock groups in the South. Country music was a significant factor in the birth of rock and roll, reflected in the rockabilly music of the Sun Records stable, Bill Haley and the Comets, Buddy Holly, and the Everly Brothers. By the mid-sixties, however, country-flavored rock fell from favor, and recording in southern studios was dominated by black soul artists. Eventually, a resurgence of southern rock came about with the Allman Brothers Band.

Guitarist Duane Allman was already well regarded in the studios of Muscle Shoals, Alabama, backing soul singers such as Wilson Pickett and Aretha Franklin. He recorded a memorable guitar duet with Eric Clapton in Miami on a Derek and the Dominoes cut, "Layla." Allman formed his own band, which included his brother, organist and vocalist Gregg Allman. Duane and second guitarist Dickey Betts developed a distinctive, tight twin guitar sound similar to what Allman and Clapton had achieved on "Layla." Their first album, simply entitled *The Allman Brothers Band* (1969), was an admirable regional success and introduced the southern rock concept to popular music. Their most successful recording came two years later with the live double album *At Fillmore East.* The sound of the intricate twin guitar work and driving rhythm section captivated the

The Allman Brothers Band around 1973 (back row from left: Gregg Allman, Jaimoe Jai Johanny, Butch Trucks; front row from left: Chuck Leavell, Dickey Betts, Lamar Williams)

national rock audience; and the lyrics, laden with southern pride, elevated a new generation of southern working-class fans. The meteoric rise of the Allman Brothers Band was cut short when Duane was killed in a motorcycle accident in 1971. The band continued for a few more years and managed one more significant hit, "Ramblin' Man," capably written and sung by Dickey Betts.

The southern rock band that most closely matched the style and stature of the Allman Brothers was Lynyrd Skynyrd. The group was from Jacksonville, Florida, and was led by singer Ronnie Van Zant. The group was more hard-rock oriented than the Allmans, but they held firm to the image of southern working-class pride and the redneck stereotype of hell-raising. They also tried to best the Allmans with *triple* guitar passages in their songs. Their biggest single hit came in 1974 with "Sweet Home Alabama," a prideful rebuttal to Neil Young's brooding song "Southern Man." Unfortunately, Lynyrd Skynyrd's parallel to the Allman Brothers carried over to their tragic end. Three members of the group, including Van Zant, were killed when their private plane crashed in 1977.

Even further to the country side of southern rock are the Charlie Daniels Band and the Marshall Tucker Band. Daniels was born in Wilmington, North Carolina, in 1936 and is a virtuoso on fiddle, guitar, and banjo. His session work included several albums with Bob Dylan. He formed his own band in the early 1970s and was able to cross easily between rock and country audiences. He commonly uses two drummers in his band and often utilizes a strong rock boogie beat. Lyrics typically deal with strong southern stereotypes. His biggest hit, however, was a storytelling country ballad, "The Devil Went Down to Georgia," found on the 1979 album *Million Mile Reflections.* The song is about a Georgia boy who must save his own soul by winning a fiddling contest with the devil. The song displays a dazzling fiddle performance by Daniels and the driving beat of his band.

The Marshall Tucker band was from Spartanburg, South Carolina, and shared Charlie Daniels' leaning toward the country side of southern rock. Their sound was eventually softened by the use of flute and saxophone, played by Jerry Eubanks. They were more successful as a concert group than as recording artists, but they did manage a couple of top 40 hits with "Fire on the Mountain" (1975) and "Heard It in a Love Song" (1977).

In Texas, southern rock and its audience took on a distinct character. As mentioned in Chapter 12, the clubs and outdoor concerts around the University of Texas at Austin gave rise to a southern brand of rock often called *redneck rock* or *outlaw country.* Country stars such as Waylon Jennings, Willie Nelson, and David Allan Coe became part of this scene. The power trio Z. Z. Top did as much as anyone in establishing the Austin scene and virtually defined the southwestern style of southern rock. The group was extremely loud, employed a shuffling boogie beat, and added distinctively southwestern paraphernalia, such as cactus and cattle, to their stage props. In more recent years they have changed their image, resembling the Blues Brothers with long beards.

West Coast Country and Folk Rock

On the West Coast folk and country influences readily combined in a number of rock bands. Members of these various bands mixed and matched over the years to create a stellar roster of folk/country rock bands. A central figure to this development was Gram Parsons. In Chapter 16 we discussed the Los Angeles folk-rock group the Byrds. Parsons was a key member of that band, joining in 1968. Their album from that year, *Sweetheart of the Rodeo,* demonstrates Parson's attempt at incorporating country music styles into the group's sound. He left the group later that year to form the Flying Burrito Brothers, delving further into country stylings by adding steel guitar and country-style group harmony. In 1970 he teamed with Emmylou Harris for two albums, *GP* (1972) and *Grievous Angel* (1973). These successful recordings elevated Harris's celebrity status and established her as one of the premier folk and country music revivalists in the world. Parsons died of drug and alcohol complications in 1973, but he left a legacy that inspired many other West Coast country rockers.

Among those inspired by Parsons was the Nitty Gritty Dirt Band, who gained an early hit with a cover version of Jerry Jeff Walker's "Mr. Bojangles." In 1972 the band went to Nashville and recorded the three-album set *Will the Circle Be Unbroken.* The session was a significant event in American popular music history. It matched this group from the world of West Coast rock with the legends of mainstream country music, including Roy Acuff, Mother Maybelle Carter, Earl Scruggs, and Merle Travis.

The West Coast country rock group that had the greatest popular appeal was the Eagles. The group was formed soon after the individual members were backups for Linda Ronstadt's 1972 country album *Linda Ronstadt.* Their music easily moved along the continuum between, rock, folk, and country, utilizing acoustic guitars, banjo, and soft vocal harmony, all to a gentle rock beat. "Lyin' Eyes," recorded in 1975, uses a down-home rhythm sound that includes acoustic guitar, steel guitar, and gospel-style piano. The bassist emphasizes the first and third beat in the manner of a country-style bassist, but his bass pattern is slightly modified to add a rock flavor to the rhythm.

Throughout the sixties and seventies, numerous other artists explored a grassroots style of rock and roll, including Creedence Clearwater Revival (later yielding solo artist John Fogerty), the New Riders of the Purple Sage (which included Jerry Garcia of the Grateful Dead), Poco (an offshoot of Buffalo Springfield), and .38 Special (with Donnie Van Zant, brother of Lynyrd Skynyrd's Ronnie Van Zant). All explored lyrics that told stories, waved the banner of southern pride, used triple meter, and incorporated instrumentation usually associated with country bands.

Woodstock: The Accidental Utopia

The Woodstock Music and Arts Festival was held on Max Yasgur's farm near Bethel, New York, from August 15 to August 17, 1969, about a month after Neil Armstrong became the first human being to set foot on the moon. Organized by a few wealthy entrepreneurs, it followed the trend of other successful music festivals being held around the country at the time, a notable example being the Monterey Pop Festival in California.

In one sense, things went terribly wrong. There was food, medical facilities, water, and toilets for 150,000 people; 400,000 showed up. The musical offerings included some of the finest acts of the late 1960s, but the real star of the festival was the vibe created by the throngs of young people. The peace, love, and order that came out of such an overrun, disorganized mess could never have been achieved by design, as proven by the disastrous festival at the Altamont Speedway that December and the price-gouging sequel *Woodstock '99* held on the thirtieth anniversary of the original event. The universal love of the "Woodstock Nation" epitomized the tribal ideal so longed for by the antiwar generation. The phenomenon of Woodstock could never be repeated; the same can be said for the remarkable decade that it so appropriately brought to a close.

Chapter Summary

The social experimentation of the 1960s also was reflected in experimentation in popular music and art. Shaped largely by drug experiences, the music developed both in San Francisco and in Britain. It was part of a revolutionary counterculture, a tribal communalism based on free love and hedonism that defied the hypocritical conformity and workaholism of the previous generation.

San Francisco rock was at once radically experimental and based on older grassroots music such as rhythm and blues, country, and folk. Lengthy, often rambling, instrumental improvisations expanded songs well beyond the limits of AM airplay. This practice helped give rise to the concept of *album rock* and FM album rock radio programming.

Groups such as Jefferson Airplane, the Grateful Dead, and Big Brother and the Holding Company blended folk, R&B, and country with the idea of extremely high volume and new timbral possibilities offered by current electronic sound technology. Jimi Hendrix used this new technology to advance not only guitar technique and style but also the entire standard of creativity within the realm of psychedelic rock. Meanwhile, in Los Angeles, the Doors were creating their own brand of psychedelia, combining Jim Morrison's dark vocal quality and mysterious persona with Ray Manzarek's inventive organ work.

Blending grassroots music with rock became a preoccupation with many rock groups in the sixties and seventies. The Paul Butterfield Blues Band, along with artists such as Robert Cray and George Thorogood (whom we have not mentioned before), sought to create urban R&B in the purer form that British rockers such as Eric Clapton had done for years. In the Southeast, rock bands such as the Allman Brothers and Lynyrd Skynyrd added country themes and instrumentation to R&B to create a new generation of rockabilly. In Texas, ZZ Top conjured up a Texas version of redneck rock; and back on the West Coast the Eagles designed a soft rock equivalent of country rock that proved to be one of the most successful popular music formulas of the 1970s.

Additional Listening

Refer to citations in the body of the text.

Sly and the Family Stone, "Everyday People" (1968) (*Classified Rock 1968*, Time-Life Music 2CLR-04, Track 8). This song reflects the sense of community portrayed by Sly and the Family Stone, a racially and sexually integrated group that effectively blended soul and psychedelia.

The Grateful Dead, "Uncle John's Band" (1970) (*Sound of the Seventies: 1970*, CD format, Time-Life Music SOD-01, Track 6). The Dead reaffirms its acoustic country roots in this song from their album *Workingman's Dead* (Warner Bros. 1869). The well-rehearsed group harmony is reminiscent of Crosby, Stills, Nash, and Young.

The Grateful Dead, "Truckin' " (1971) (*Sound of the Seventies: 1971,* Time-Life Music SOD-02, Track 18). This song demonstrates a shuffling boogie beat and a blues flavor, though the vocal harmony is more a country/folk style.

Review Questions

1. What was the cultural and musical background for San Francisco's rock scene?
2. What did the Vietnam conflict and the drug culture have to do with the content of San Francisco's brand of rock music?
3. What was different about the new FM radio rock format? How did it help San Francisco rock?
4. How were Grace Slick and Janis Joplin unique in rock at that time?
5. What Houston R&B singer influenced Janis Joplin's vocal style?
6. What stylistic and technical innovations did Jimi Hendrix pioneer on electric guitar?
7. Why was Hendrix a musical and cultural anomaly in his time?
8. Describe the elements that created the unique sound of the Doors.
9. Describe the instrumentation and lyric content that distinguishes southern rock from other forms of American rhythm and blues–influenced rock.
10. Who were proponents of country/folk rock on the West Coast? How did their sound contrast with those rock bands from the Southeast?

Notes

1. Ellen Willis, "Janis Joplin," *The Rolling Stone Illustrated History of Rock and Roll,* ed. Jim Miller (New York: Random House/Rolling Stone Press, 1980), p. 276.
2. Much of the anecdotal information for this analysis came from interviews with the surviving members of the Doors (Manzarek, Krieger, and Densmore) conducted by National Public Radio for their series *The NPR 100,* NPR's selection of the most significant musical pieces of the twentieth century. The series was broadcast on NPR's *All Things Considered* over the course of the year 2000 and is archived on NPR's website, www.npr.org. A superb feature on Manzarek appears in *Keyboard* magazine, February 1991, including his observations on the Doors' unique sound and transcriptions of his famous solos on "Light My Fire" and "Riders on the Storm." The issue even highlights Manzarek's signature keyboards from the 1960s, the Vox Continental organ and the Fender Rhodes Piano Bass.
3. Ed Ward, "The Blues Revival," *The Rolling Stone Illustrated History of Rock and Roll,* p. 359.

Chapter 19

Gospel, Soul, and Motown

Soul music is another one of those terms that rock historians find difficult to define. None of the stylistic elements of soul were new in the 1960s, but their unrestrained application to rock music was new. Also new was the record industry's ability to sell it. The raw vitality of soul represented, perhaps for the first time in American popular music history, a no-compromise presentation of black music for the masses, comparatively free of being commercially watered-down.

Blues and gospel are the parents of soul—and most other popular forms of black music. Until the 1960s, however, small independent labels trying to sell blues- or gospel-derived music were inclined to squelch the hard-driving beat, the shouting vocal style, and the impassioned emotionalism to some extent in order to broaden its market to white teenagers. Doo-wop, while raw and exciting by Tin Pan Alley's standards, still reflected the softening influence of smooth, black vocal performers like the Mills Brothers, the Ink Spots, and Nat "King" Cole. Some R&B artists changed their song content from oppression, poverty, unrequited love, and general misery to cars, puppy love, and nagging parents.

Once in a while amid the stylistic compromises of the 1950s, some artists like Little Richard slipped through the cracks, with their raw, screaming, church-derived style intact. Before the term *soul* came to be commonly applied to their style, Ray Charles, James Brown, Sam Cooke, Solomon Burke, and Aretha Franklin were pulling out the stops and turning their concerts and recorded performances into revival meetings. By the mid-1960s the fervent expression of these "proto-soul" artists became the rule rather than the exception. This general stylistic assertiveness neatly coincided with the rise of civil rights activism in America, a time of peaking black pride and optimism. Soul dispensed to the public at large the unfettered passion of R&B from the honky tonks and gospel music from the Pentecostal churches, boldly proclaiming "Take it all or none."

Atlantic Records

Before discussing soul music and its artists, it is important to recognize the one record company that made the music commercially possible, Atlantic Records. The company was founded in 1946 by Ahmet Ertegun, son of a Turkish ambassador to

This photograph shows some of the major figures of rhythm and blues and soul including (kneeling from left) Atlantic producer Jerry Wexler, disc jockey and rock promoter Alan Freed, and Atlantic Records founder Ahmet Ertegun. The tallest man in the back row is Kansas City blues singer "Big" Joe Turner.

the United States, and Herb Abramson. It began as a small independent label specializing in R&B and gradually gained success featuring crossovers like the Coasters (with songs and production by Jerry Lieber and Mike Stoller) and Ray Charles. Atlantic also signed Bobby Darin, a popular white singer, with its Atco subsidiary. In the 1960s the label specialized in the new gospel-based form of black rock—called soul—and graduated from a small, independent label to a major label on a par with RCA and Columbia.

Atlantic's nurturing of soul music was the work of its vice president and top producer, Jerry Wexler. Wexler, like John Hammond at Columbia, had a knack for finding good raw talent and matching it with the right musicians in the right studio. (As we shall see, Aretha Franklin passed between the two producers.) Wexler utilized independent studios all over the country; but in the 1960s he concentrated on a handful of studios in the South, including Cosimo Matassa's studio in New Orleans, Stax studios in Memphis, and Fame studios in Muscle Shoals, Alabama. Wexler's sensitive producing fully exploited the compatibility of raw soul singers and the ability of southern musicians to provide the proper accompaniment for them.

Gospel Music

The term *soul* reveals the most fundamental aspect of its style; it is the secular offspring of music from the black church. Most soul artists learned their style from singing in church, so it is necessary to look at the development of black church music, both as a significant music in its own right and as a stylistic companion of soul. The most important development in black church music in the twentieth century was the coming of *gospel music* and its creator, Thomas A. Dorsey.[1]

"Georgia Tom" Dorsey, born in Georgia in 1899, was a popular vaudeville blues composer, singer, and pianist in the 1920s. He was famous for his sugges-

Blues composer and American gospel music pioneer Thomas A. Dorsey.

tive blues songs such as "It's Tight Like That," and his Georgia Jazz Band backed one of the most famous vaudeville blues divas, Gertrude "Ma" Rainey. In his heart, however, this minister's son had never left the church; and, beginning in 1929, he devoted the remainder of his life to composing and performing religious music. His first great hymn was "Precious Lord, Take My Hand." A fervent plea for the Lord's comfort, it was written upon the death of his wife and newborn child in 1932. It marked the beginning of Dorsey's music as a major force upon the religious expression of many black and white Christians. A prolific writer, his songs have taken their place in the canon of hymns written by Isaac Watts, Lowell Mason, and others. His songs have also enjoyed popular music success; the recorded performances of Dorsey's "Peace in the Valley" by country singer Red Foley and Elvis Presley have sold in the millions.

Dorsey's way of performing was as important as the songs themselves. When he left the dance hall for the church, he brought the rollicking rhythm and instrumentation of ragtime and the blues with them. Tony Heilbut, in his pioneering study *The Gospel Sound,* said that Dorsey "consciously decided to combine the Baptist lyrics and Sanctified beat with the stylized delivery of blues and jazz."[2] Beginning in 1932 at Ebenezer Baptist Church in Chicago, Dorsey and singer/business manager Sara Martin redefined the manner in which hymns and devotional songs were rendered, eventually incorporating guitar, drums, electric organ, and boogie-woogie or blues-style piano. Initially, this approach met with much resistance. For a long time, black religious music had involved a shouting, fervent style and a driving rhythm, but the style of Dorsey's music was too close to the sound of the blues, considered by the faithful to be the devil's music. But through the persistence of Dorsey and singers such as Sallie Martin, Roberta Martin, Mahalia Jackson, Sister Rosetta Tharpe, and Willie Mae Ford Smith, the new church music, which came to be known as *gospel* music, caught on. Dorsey founded an annual Gospel Singers Convention in Chicago to train generations of choirs and soloists in performing the music and the style he helped to create.

This is the legacy of soul. Dorsey brought the blues style into the church as gospel music, then soul brought the gospel style back into the world of rhythm and blues. The passion, the hope, and the pain of a people was imposed on the popular scene, and that music was adapted to serve as a new branch of rock. Through the pioneering efforts of artists like Ray Charles, James Brown, and Aretha Franklin, and record companies like Atlantic, soul became the new black musical expression for the sixties.

James Brown

James Brown was born in Augusta, Georgia, in 1933. In the 1950s he formed his band the Famous Flames and landed a record deal with the Federal label, a subsidiary of King Records in Cincinnati. His first hit was "Please, Please, Please," released in 1956. The song was fairly close to conventional doo-wop torch songs, with a perpetual triplet pulse in the piano and smooth background vocals to Brown's passionate lead vocal. When "Think" was released in 1960, a new style began to

Soul singer James Brown (at the piano) with the Famous Flames around 1965.

emerge. The song demonstrated a crisp drumbeat and horn section that functioned as background vocalists, responding to Brown's screaming, percussive vocal. His style was further defined when he won a legal battle with King to gain complete artistic control of his career. The first fruit of his new creative freedom was "Papa's Got a Brand New Bag," released in 1965 and his first top 10 hit.

"Papa's Got a Brand New Bag" was closely followed by "I Feel Good (I Got You)," both based on a 12-bar blues form. The open/close hi-hat (a pair of cymbals mounted on a stand and brought together with a foot pedal) pattern led to the strong snare drum backbeat. All other instruments played punctuated, broken riff patterns, carefully worked out so that the rhythm of each part led naturally to the rhythm of another—simple components that led to a highly active but curiously uncluttered composite. Even Brown's vocals, for all their extemporaneous grunts and shrieks, function as a contributing percussion instrument, finding its place in the overall texture.

James Brown also developed a unique style of live performance, its energy unequaled by anyone. The music and the stage antics were calculated and precise; the performance was loud and unrelenting. Brown modeled his appearance after the likeness of Little Richard, sporting a tall pompadour hairstyle and a flashy wardrobe that included shiny suits and skintight pants. He worked out precise and spectacular dance steps that became the inspiration of countless soul acts to come, most notably Michael Jackson. His most famous routine was to collapse on the stage, seemingly exhausted by emotion and exertion. Band members reverently attend him, draping a cape over his shoulders and helping the broken man offstage. Suddenly, he is miraculously revived, shrugging off the cape and returning to center stage for more. His stage acrobatics earned James Brown the title of "the hardest working man in show business."

In the late sixties Brown's music experienced another change. His songs abandoned the blues form and most other popular song forms for a single chord riff. The songs were in two parts, each part made up of a distinctive riff faithfully maintained by the band. After the first riff simmers for a length of time determined by Brown, he cues the second riff with a line like "Go to the bridge!" The band changes key (often up a fourth) and continues the second riff to a fade-out.[3] The rhythm of each individual part is a crisp, percussive, and complex pattern of sixteenth notes, groundwork for the staccato rhythms of funk in the 1970s.

Ray Charles

Another pioneer of soul in the 1950s was Ray Charles Robinson, born in 1930 in Albany, Georgia. At age six, he lost his sight to glaucoma and was sent to the St. Augustine School for the Deaf and the Blind in Florida. It was there that he was trained in music, played a number of instruments and learned to read and write

Soul singer Ray Charles (at the piano) performing in London on May 21, 1963.

music in braille. He began his career as a traveling musician at the age of 15, eventually settling in Seattle, Washington.

His earliest influences were the great jazz pianists of the 1930s and 1940s, particularly the smooth crooner/pianist Nat "King" Cole. Charles began his recording career for Swingtime Records in Los Angeles and moved to Atlantic Records in 1952. He worked for the next year as a session pianist and arranger, encountering a number of influential R&B artists. Absorbing their influence, Charles's style began to adopt the raw, emotional, church-derived flavor of the music. By the time he recorded "I've Got a Woman" in Atlanta in 1953, he had fully developed his strident gospel vocal style and applied it to rhythm and blues. Soul historian Peter Guralnick states, "There was an unrestrained exuberance to the new Ray Charles, a fierce earthiness which, while it would have been unfamiliar to any follower of gospel music, was almost revolutionary in the world of pop."[4]

Charles's gospel tendencies led to the inclusion of a female backup vocal group, the Raelettes, who acted as congregational respondents to his R&B "preaching." While his sanctified singing style remained a constant, Charles demonstrated his uncanny versatility; his performing repertoire included jazz, country and western, Tin Pan Alley standards, and rhythm and blues. He even brought black gospel songs out of the churches and made them into popular hits. He also wrote original material, arranged the music, and produced and mixed the recording dates. He has performed in a variety of contexts, from small rhythm sections to jazz big bands and string orchestras.

The first high point of his musical success came in 1959 with the release of "What'd I Say." Recorded as "Part I" and "Part II," the song was unusually long for AM airplay (about six and a half minutes). It was blues with a funky Latin beat, a gospel shout, and a lusty love song. The climax of the performance is a nonsense syllable exchange, a gimmick that historian Katharine Charlton attributes to the influence of jazz singer Cab Calloway.

In 1959 Ray Charles signed with ABC records, allowing him even greater creative and production freedom. He has survived the whims of fashion over the years and continues to impact new generations of musicians with his distinctive gospel/R&B stylistic fusion and his versatility.

Stax Records

By the 1960s Memphis, Tennessee, already had a formidable musical legacy. Beale Street was a bastion of blues stylists ranging from W. C. Handy to B. B. King. The music of black Baptist and Sanctified churches flourished in Memphis and the mid-South. Black kids raised on blues and white kids raised on

Memphis instrumental soul group Booker T. and the MGs around 1965 (left to right: Donald "Duck" Dunn, Booker T. Jones, Steve Cropper, and Al Jackson).

country comfortably and unconsciously mixed and matched their musical upbringings to create a hybrid called *rockabilly*, epitomized by Elvis Presley. As the fifties came to an end, many of the blues singers had moved on to Chicago, Elvis Presley and Sam Phillips had gone to Nashville, and the "country-fried blues" sound began to shift to a new recording studio housed in an old movie theater in a predominantly black section of Memphis.

Studio owners Jim Stewart and Estelle Axton renamed their studio Stax in 1961. It had been a casually run affair where a blend of white and black kids gathered after school to jam and experiment with their music. R&B veteran Rufus Thomas and his daughter Carla recorded a couple of numbers at Stax and helped bring it to the attention of Jerry Wexler at Atlantic Records. Atlantic became the exclusive distributor of Stax's recordings, inaugurating the most fruitful period for soul music.

The first big hits for Stax were instrumentals, performed by the house rhythm section—Booker T. Jones on organ, Steve Cropper on guitar, Donald "Duck" Dunn on bass, and Al Jackson on drums—and by a horn section called the Mar-Keys. Soon Wexler began to send singers from Detroit and Miami to Memphis to have them backed by the cohesive and distinctive sound of these Stax staff musicians.

Stax Vocalists

Wilson Pickett was a gospel-rooted singer from Detroit and one of the Stax studio's greatest stars. "In the Midnight Hour," written by guitarist and staff writer Steve Cropper, became a huge hit for Atlantic and defined the Stax style. Pickett went on to record "Funky Broadway" and "Mustang Sally," exhibiting the same menacing, shouting style.

Otis Redding, Stax's greatest artist, came from Little Richard's home town of Macon, Georgia, and had groomed himself to be a Little Richard imitator. He eventually developed his own intimate style and became the crown jewel of Memphis soul. He began recording sentimental songs for Stax as early as 1962, but he worked toward a more successful formula by 1965 with his own composition "Respect." Though this song became a bigger hit when covered later by Aretha Franklin, it established Redding as both a singer of hard-driving soul songs and a romantic balladeer. He died in a plane crash at the height of his career in 1967. "(Sittin' on) The Dock of the Bay," written with Steve Cropper, was released in early 1968; it was his only number-one hit.

Sam Moore and Dave Prater signed with Atlantic in Miami and were sent to Memphis for their sessions. They scored a major hit with "Soul Man," written and produced by the staff team of Isaac Hayes and David Porter. The foursome continued with a number of hits, including "Hold On, I'm Comin' " and "I Take What I Want."

In 1968 Stax entered its next phase. It ended its distribution partnership with Atlantic. Isaac Hayes stepped out of the production and songwriting background to become the studio's most successful star. The dry recording mix and basic instrumentation were replaced by lush strings and thick mixes. This new sound was solidified with the release of the Isaac Hayes album *Hot Buttered Soul* and culminated with the soundtrack to the motion picture *Shaft* in 1971. The studio left its original formula to compete with the slick sound enveloped by Motown in Detroit and Gamble and Huff's productions in Philadelphia, an attempt at which Stax ultimately failed. The studio went bankrupt in 1975.

Analysis of "Memphis Soul Stew" (*Atlantic Rhythm & Blues Vol. 6: 1966–1969*, Atlantic 81298-1)

"Memphis Soul Stew" is a novelty number featuring legendary rock tenor saxophonist King Curtis. Curtis played what has been commonly titled "tough Texas tenor," a sound and style of saxophone descended from jazz great Coleman Hawkins and continuing through artists like Arnett Cobb and Illinois Jacquet. Curtis played the raucous saxophone solos on many legendary rock recordings in the fifties and sixties and also recorded an occasional instrumental feature number. "Memphis Soul Stew" is one of those features. This recording was chosen over more famous Stax vocal numbers because, while it is essentially a novelty number, it is a from-the-ground-up demonstration of the Stax sound.

Having said that, it must now be revealed that this recording was made on July 4, 1967, at American Studio in Memphis, not Stax, and that the Stax stable rhythm section (guitarist Steve Cropper, bassist Duck Dunn, organist Booker T. Jones, and drummer Al Jackson) are not the instrumentalists on this date. However, this illustration is still valid, because the musicians on this session— Reggie Taylor or R. F. Jackson on guitar, Tommy Cogbill on bass, Bobby Emmons on organ, and Gene Chrisman on drums–sound remarkably like the Stax rhythm section, indicating perhaps there was as much a Memphis sound as a Stax sound.

The number opens with a busy, funk bass line. Curtis begins reciting the recipe for the ultimate soul groove. The drums are the next instrument to join in, laying down a strong snare backbeat and constant eighth notes on a closed hi-hat. The guitarist is next, playing a distinctive line that is equal parts blues and country. The organ adds a bluesy trill, followed by King Curtis himself on tenor sax. Like the guitar, his sound is as country as it is blues.

The line "beat well" launches the band into a rollicking series of blues choruses, with Curtis soloing over the top. In the first chorus, listen particularly to the stabbing riff played by the organ and the masterful fills played in between the riff by the guitar. In the second chorus the horn section is added to the organ riff. At this point they are playing in their middle register. In the third chorus the horns continue the riff but in a higher register, constantly building the excitement of the solo. Leading into the fourth chorus the drummer plays a climaxing fill that is technically simple but unmatched in its effectiveness. At this point Curtis's saxophone is screaming. Over the span of the fourth chorus

Listening Guide   19.1
"Memphis Soul Stew" 4 beats per measure

ELAPSED TIME	FORM	EVENT DESCRIPTION
:00	Intro P1	Electric bass (13 measures)
:27	Intro P2	Add drums (5 measures)
:39	Intro P3	Add electric guitar (5 measures)
:51	Intro P4	Add organ (6 measures)
1:03	Intro P5	Add tenor sax, monologue (13 measures: 4 + 9)
1:32	Chorus 1	Sax solo with organ riff (12 measures)
1:58	Chorus 2	Sax solo with mid-range horns riff (12 measures)
2:25	Chorus	Sax solo with high-range horns riff (12 measures)
2:51	Instr. Verse 3	Sax solo with high-range horns riff (12 measures +)
3:02	End	

the recording slowly fades, the whole band still wailing away underneath Curtis's solo.

Aretha Franklin

Aretha Franklin was born in Memphis, Tennessee, in 1942. Her father was a prominent Baptist minister who moved the family to Detroit when she was still quite young. Her childhood was spent in the musical ministry of her father's church, and her early influences were gospel stars Mahalia Jackson and James Cleveland. In the late fifties Franklin decided to cross over into pop music and came to the attention of swing era jazz producer John Hammond. He saw her as another Billie Holiday and signed her with Columbia Records. Unfortunately, Columbia's A&R (Artist and Repertoire) head, Mitch Miller, was more interested in making her into a Nat "King" Cole–style black crooner, a contrivance that pleased neither the white easy-listening audience nor the R&B set.

Aretha Franklin, circa 1975.

When Franklin's Columbia contract expired in 1967, Jerry Wexler and Atlantic grabbed her. Using his experience producing soul sessions with Ray Charles and Stax artists, Wexler knew how to tap into the gospel roots that were so prominent in Aretha's style. He began by sending her to Rick Hall's Fame Studios in Muscle Shoals, Alabama, where the house band achieved a similar sound to Stax musicians in Memphis. He also gave her control over the songs and the arrangements; but more important, he encouraged her to sing in an unbridled, fierce, shouting gospel style. Her first album for Atlantic, *I Never Loved a Man the Way I Love You*, was an immediate success, reaching number two on the album charts. It contained her biggest hit single, "Respect," recorded earlier at Stax by its composer Otis Redding. Over the years Aretha Franklin has, like Ray Charles, recorded songs and arrangements from a variety of styles while retaining the tough, unfettered gospel approach in her singing.

Motown

The most successful soul factory of the 1960s was Motown Records in Detroit, Michigan. It was founded by Berry Gordy, Jr., an ex-boxer and jazz record store owner. In 1960 he started Tammie Records, soon renamed Tamla, and teamed up with Smokey Robinson, a talented songwriter, singer, and leader of the Miracles. Robinson's "Shop Around" became the label's first big hit, reaching number two on the charts. Gordy explored the clubs of Detroit for other talent, discovering Mary Wells, the Marvelettes, and Marvin Gaye.

The staff at Motown included its most important songwriting team, brothers Eddie and Brian Holland and Lamont Dozier. Known collectively as H-D-H, this trio composed and produced 28 top 20 Motown hits between the years 1963 and 1967. Their successes include "Heat Wave" by Martha and the Vandellas, "Where Did Our Love Go?" by the Supremes, and "Baby I Need Your Loving" by the Temptations.

This trio developed not only a songwriting and production strategy that ensured hit after hit but also the distinctive "Motown sound." Lyrics were disposable, especially on the verses, but the *hook line* (the part of the chorus where the song title is uttered) was rendered so effectively and so often that it stuck in the listener's mind immediately. The studio was small (formerly a photography portrait studio), and overdubbing was necessary to record a large group for a big sound. Whatever sweetening was added to the tracks, the most important component to an H-D-H production was the percussion track, assaulting the backbeat with a wide assortment of noisemakers, from tambourines to ballpoint pens. It provided a relentless drive to Motown songs and made the urge to dance irresistible.

While the Motown product was consistently successful, it had as much of an assembly line as the automobile plants Berry Gordy had worked in. A song was generic, passed around among different Motown acts until it was decided who would record it. The artists were well groomed and poised, even when doing their distinctive dance steps. Lyrics were romantic and inoffensive, the beat was danceable, and the recording stayed well within the time constraints of AM airplay. The music had a wholesomeness and elegance that was quite unlike the raw aggression of Stax artists or James Brown, but the payoff was that Motown was much more successful with white audiences. The last word was Gordy, the patriarch of the company. From the nurturing of new talent to the sound of the final audio mix, everything bore his stamp. This paternalistic policy eventually proved too much for some of the more creative members of the Motown stable; they either left the label or recontracted to gain more creative and production control. Thus, in the 1970s the Jacksons, Marvin Gaye, and Stevie Wonder brought forth

The Motown songwriting team of (from left) Eddie Holland, Lamont Dozier, and Brian Holland.

adventurous and highly personal recordings, no longer bound by the conservative Motown formulas.

Motown Vocalists

Marvin Gaye began at Motown as a session drummer. He began recording as a vocal soloist in 1962 and scored a significant hit with H-D-H's "How Sweet It Is (to Be Loved by You)" in 1964. He recorded a notable series of duets with Tammi Terrell in 1967, heavily orchestrated, dramatic love songs such as "Ain't No Mountain High Enough." His biggest hit came in 1968 with "I Heard It through the Grapevine," which had been recorded a year earlier for Motown by Gladys Knight and the Pips. Gaye was a talented songwriter and producer and, by the end of the sixties, demanded more artistic control over his product. The earliest product of this new business arrangement was the song "What's Going On," a lengthy, epic social commentary far removed from Gordy's sweetness-and-light production philosophy. Succeeding recordings offered a more erotic style of love song, epitomized by "Sexual Healing," a 1983 hit that made it to the top five. This recording was made after he moved to Columbia Records. The next year Gaye was shot and killed by his own father. He was conspicuous among Motown artists in that he was usually a solo act, not the frontman of a vocal group. He was the romantic lead of the Motown cast, enigmatic and troubled.

Motown featured a number of male vocal groups in the tradition of gospel quartets and doo-wop groups. The two most remarkable groups were the Four Tops and the Temptations. The Four Tops were organized in the fifties and sang a mixed bag of R&B and smooth crooning numbers. Gordy signed them to Motown and teamed them up with Holland, Dozier, and Holland, resulting in their 1964 hit "Baby I Need Your Loving." The Four Tops/H-D-H combination continued with hit after hit, peaking with "Reach Out and I'll Be There" in 1966. Conversely, the group died when H-D-H left Motown over a royalties dispute in 1967.

The Temptations were the finest singers of all the Motown vocal groups and made the most effective use of dance steps. Their primary song suppliers

Motown's most sensational girl group, the Supremes, around 1965 (left to right: Diana Ross, Mary Wilson, and Florence Ballard)

were Smokey Robinson and Norman Whitfield, producing such classics as "The Way You Do the Things You Do" from 1964 and "My Girl" in 1965. The group and their writers displayed great versatility of style, ranging from hard-driving R&B to lush romantic ballads.

Berry Gordy also had a fair stock of girl groups, the musical institution most identified with Phil Spector. Martha and the Vandellas and the Marvelettes were highly successful acts for Motown, but nothing like the Supremes. The trio of ladies—Diana Ross, Mary

Listening Guide   19.2
"Where Did Our Love Go?" 4 beats per measure

ELAPSED TIME	FORM	EVENT DESCRIPTION
:00	Intro	Foot stomps (2 measures)
:03	Verse 1	Vocal, piano, and rhythm section (8 measures)
:19	Verse 2	Vocal (8 measures)
:33	Verse 3	Vocal and background vocal riff (8 measures)
:48	Verse 4	Vocal and background vocal riff (8 measures)
1:03	Verse 5	Vocal and background vocal riff (8 measures)
1:18	Verse 6	Baritone sax solo (8 measures)
1:32	Verse 7	Vocal and background vocal riff (8 measures)
1:47	Verse 8	Vocal and background vocal riff (8 measures)
2:01	Verse 9	Vocal and vocal riff, foot stomp break (8 measures: 6 + 2)
2:16	Verse 10	Vocal and vocal riff, foot stomp break (8 measures: 6 + 2)
2:30	Verse 11	Vocal and vocal riff with fadeout (8 measures +)
2:35	End	

Wilson, and Florence Ballard—was signed with Motown in 1962 but did not achieve success until they were matched up with H-D-H songs. The first super-hit was "Where Did Our Love Go" in 1964, followed by 10 number-one hits over three years, including "Stop! In the Name of Love," "I Hear a Symphony," and "You Can't Hurry Love." While the catchy hooks and relentless backbeat of the H-D-H songs were the Supremes' only initial asset, the captivating presence of Diana Ross eventually moved her to the forefront of the act. Her slinky elegance epitomized the finishing school ideal Berry Gordy had for all his artists, helping to get the Supremes into the nation's finest venues of white entertainment. Ross's voice was soft but provocative, aloof yet pleading. By 1969 the Supremes had amassed an impressive list of hit recordings, but Diana Ross left the group to pursue her inevitable solo career as a singer and film actress.

Analysis of "Where Did Our Love Go?" (*Classic Rock 1964: The Beat Goes On*, Time-Life Music 2CLR-09, Track 2)

"Where Did Our Love Go?" was a watershed for the success of the Supremes, H-D-H, and Motown. The story of its creation, from concept to final recording, is typical of many Motown songs. The song is extremely repetitious but with an unforgettable and often reiterated hook line. It was originally planned for the Motown girl group the Marvelettes, and the track had already been cut in their key. It was then decided to give the song to the struggling new group the Supremes. The key was too low for Diana Ross, but it is by this circumstance that Motown producers found the most compelling quality of her voice.

The track itself exemplifies the winning H-D-H percussion track. In this case the backbeat is heavy enough, but the real characteristic rhythm of "Where Did Our Love Go?" is the constant beating of quarter notes. For this recording a number of Motown staff members actually marched in place on a raised platform in the studio. When Ross enters with the vocal, the piano joins in the quarter-note rhythm, playing chords in the upper register of the keyboard. The backbeat becomes stronger as the song progresses, played by the snare drum and the guitar. By the time the two other women's voices enter, there is also the prominent sound of the vibraphone striking an occasion chord to fill out the texture of the band. The groove remains unchanged through the baritone sax solo to the fade ending.

Stevie Wonder

As mentioned earlier, some of the more creative Motown artists resisted being the pawns of either Berry Gordy or his songwriters/producers. Michael Jackson and Marvin Gaye stayed with Motown until the 1980s, then moved to Columbia. Stevie Wonder has remained loyal to the label and has been a consistent hit maker, while remaining free of the assembly line formula that burned out the rest of the Motown stable by the early 1970s.

Like Michael Jackson, "Little Stevie Wonder" represented the cute-kid-act segment of the Motown cast. He was born Steveland Morris in 1950 in Saginaw, Michigan, not far from Detroit. In 1960 he auditioned for Berry Gordy, who was immediately impressed by the 10-year-old lad's ability as a multi-instrumentalist and singer. He became a cog in the Motown song wheel, marketed as a young Ray Charles (Wonder was blind since birth). His trademark instrument was his harmonica, the first instrument he learned to play. His first big hit was "Fingertips," the single from his album *Little Stevie Wonder, 12 Year Old Genius.* That was just before his voice changed. During the rest of his teenage years, Wonder recorded a variety of material, from the R&B hit "Uptight (Everything's Alright)" to the Sinatra-styled "For Once in My Life."

In 1970 Wonder recorded his first self-produced album, *Signed, Sealed, and Delivered,* and was on his way as an autonomous artist doing most of the writing, playing, and producing. He renegotiated his Motown contact at age 21 for a considerable portion of royalties. The remainder of the seventies were highly creative, productive, artistic, and commercially and critically successful. Wonder's albums demonstrated a wide variety of influences: gospel, blues, jazz, easy-listening, soul, funk, reggae, and African music. He began to use synthesizers extensively and to overdub himself on most of the rhythm tracks. His spirit of experimentation has been one of the most consistent aspects of his nature; each new album utilizes the latest in instrument and studio technology.

Chapter Summary

The 1960s was a period of redefinement in black culture and music. American teen idols and the first British invasion threatened to drive black music into the underground, but Atlantic and Motown led the way to a reinvigoration and recharacterization of black rock. Soul music was a more fervent, shouting style of black rock, a secular version of a style used in the black church. It began to surface in the late fifties with the music of Ray Charles, James Brown, Sam Cooke, and a few others; but in the 1960s, gospel-styled soul would be the rule instead of the exception.

The black church of the twentieth century, in turn, borrowed from ragtime, blues, and jazz, elements brought into church use by Thomas A. Dorsey, the father of gospel music. Gospel was music of praise; but it was also music of pain, the music of a poor and oppressed people. Black kids who grew up singing the gospel songs of Dorsey and others brought their experience into popular music, reflecting the pride and optimism of blacks in the early 1960s when the Civil Rights Bill was passed by Congress.

Jerry Wexler of Atlantic Records tapped into the pool of gospel-bred black singers and backed them up with compatible house musicians from studios in the South, most notable Stax Studios in Memphis. Wilson Pickett, Eddie Floyd, Otis Redding, and many others sang raw, shouting vocals, accompanied by a racially mixed and similarly raw band. Meanwhile, in Detroit, Berry Gordy developed a more elegant style of soul that managed to appeal to black and white audiences alike. Motown created a consistent hit formula with writers like Smokey Robinson and Holland, Dozier, and Holland. Soloists and groups were groomed by Gordy and his songwriters/producers to break out of the "chittlin circuit" and into the mainstream of popular music. Some Motown successes, like the Temptations and the Supremes, were totally dependent on this paternalism; others, like Stevie Wonder, were creative enough to demand artistic independence. These were the artists that took soul into the 1970s and beyond.

Additional Listening

Thomas A. Dorsey, *Gospel Songs of Thomas A. Dorsey* (LP format, Columbia KG 32151). This is a 1973 compilation of various gospel artists, including Dorsey himself, featuring his legacy of gospel song compositions.

The Temptations, "The Way You Do the Things You Do" (1964) (*Classic Rock 1964: The Beat Goes On*, Time-Life Music 2CLR-03, Track 18). This Smokey Robinson composition displays the light lead vocal sound of David Ruffin, the shuffling rhythm section, and the perfunctory hand claps on the backbeat.

The Four Tops, "Baby, I Need Your Loving" (1964) (*Classic Rock 1964: The Beat Goes On*, Time-Life Music 2CLR-04, Track 16). By contrast with the Temptations, the Four Tops (particularly the lead singer Levi Stubbs) have a much more dramatic delivery, well displayed in this recording. The extra voices and the 40 strings that were packed into the small studio give this production a symphonic orchestra-and-chorus effect.

Marvin Gaye, "How Sweet It Is" (1964) (*Classic Rock 1964: The Beat Goes On*, Time-Life Music 2CLR-09, Track 14). This track combines the sexy intimacy of Marvin Gaye's vocal style with the happy-go-lucky backbeat lope that identified so many Motown hits (such as "The Way You Do . . ." cited above).

Wilson Pickett, "In the Midnight Hour" (1965) (*Classic Rock 1965*, Time-Life Music 2CLR-01, Track 3). This production demonstrates the Stax studio musicians' concept of the horns as backup singers. We also hear the crisp, staccato drum patterns of Al Jackson. The insistent bass riff underpins Pickett's gravelly, screaming gospel style.

Sam and Dave, "Soul Man" (1967) (*Classic Rock 1967: The Beat Goes On*, Time-Life Music 2CLR-10, Track 4). This track places the Stax sound in a vocal-duet setting. Listen for the country flavor Steve Cropper's opening guitar riff gives to this soul sound.

Aretha Franklin, "A Natural Woman" (1967) (*Classic Rock 1967: The Beat Goes On*, Time-Life Music 2CLR-10, Track 11). This song stands in stark contrast to the simpler and more driving material that Franklin did in Muscle Shoals. The song is a Carole King (of Aldon Music) composition in triple meter and is thickly orchestrated with strings and French horns. Listen to how the exciting rawness of Franklin's vocal style perseveres over this slicker production.

Otis Redding, "(Sittin' on) The Dock of the Bay" (1968) (*Classic Rock 1968*, Time-Life Music 2CLR-04, Track 6). This is undoubtedly Redding's most famous performance. Notice that it is much more intimate and introspective than most Stax productions. Steve Cropper (the co-composer) still adds the twangy country flavor to the tune with his guitar style, and Al Jackson maintains the tight drumbeat that is the signature of Stax songs.

Marvin Gaye, "What's Goin' On" (1971) (*Sound of the Seventies: 1971*, Time-Life Music SOD-02, Track 1). This recording is reflective of the transition of Marvin Gaye's music when he broke away from the production dictates of Berry Gordy and Motown. The song is more serious and topical in the lyric and lush in the production.

The O'Jays, "Back Stabbers" (1972) (*Sound of the Seventies: 1972*, Time-Life Music SOD-03, Track 9). This topical song is perhaps the best product of the (Kenny) Gamble and (Leon) Huff sound that emerged out of Philadelphia in the late 1960s. The thick orchestral accompaniment of Gamble and Huff productions defined soul and disco in the 1970s, even influencing Issac Hayes and Stax Records.

Review Questions

1. What was the difference between the style and presentation of black doo-wop in the 1950s and soul music in the 1960s?
2. What was the significance of the Atlantic record label in the development of soul? Who were the primary people responsible for that significance?
3. What were Thomas A. Dorsey's innovations in the presentation of black religious music?
4. What were the characteristics of James Brown's style in terms of song forms, role of the instruments, and the way in which he used his own voice in the band?
5. How did Brown's stage act influence other black rock artists?
6. Explain the definitive style of Ray Charles and the many contexts to which he successfully applied it.
7. What was the ethnic and stylistic blend of Stax studio musicians that accounts for this unique Memphis sound?
8. What was the role of the horn section in Stax recordings? What were Stax recordings like after 1968?
9. What was the Holland-Dozier-Holland songwriting and production strategy that accounts for so many Motown hits?
10. What was Berry Gordy's role in the Motown product? Why was it unsuitable to some Motown artists?

Notes

1. An excellent video documentary on the legacy of Dorsey and gospel music is *Say Amen Somebody*, by George T. Nierenberg (GTN Productions, 1982).
2. Anthony Heilbut, *The Gospel Sound: Good New and Bad Times*, rev. and updated (New York: Limelight Editions, 1985), p. xxvi.

3. Some scholars have noted how similar this performance practice is to African music. An African master drummer typically sets the drum line into a pattern and, after a period of time determined by him, cues a change of pattern. It is notable that James Brown enjoyed remarkable popular success in Africa, due in no small part to his music's similarities to African music.

4. Peter Guralnick, "Ray Charles," *The Rolling Stone Illustrated History of Rock and Roll*, ed. Jim Miller (New York: Random House/Rolling Stone Press, 1980), p. 111.

20

From Progressive Rock to Reggae in the Seventies

In the midst of the rock experimentation in the sixties, there were a number of high-minded artists and groups who were fascinated with the possibility of fusing rock stylings with the broader instrumentation and forms of European art (or classical) music. By this time rock had established itself as a powerful idiom within the larger picture of musical culture, defining a serious musical language for a new generation of musicians. Songwriters and producers from the early sixties, such as Phil Spector and Brian Wilson, had brought rock out of the garage and into a more ambitious context of orchestras and multitrack studio effects, but the music itself was still of a light, trivial nature. Later works, such as the Beatles' *Sgt. Pepper* album and the lengthy psychedelic music of Jimi Hendrix, and formats such as concept LPs and the FM stations that played them, proved that rock had matured enough to attempt more ambitious compositional and improvisational experiments. Rock artists felt compelled to prove to the adult world that their music was serious enough to transcend its reputation as "greasy kid stuff."

This new serious tendency in rock historically has been labeled *progressive rock*. The movement was primarily British, representing the work of a second wave of British rockers that were active from the late sixties to the end of the seventies. The reason for progressive rock's dominance in England was not that its musicians were more conversant with classical music than their American counterparts; it was that they were more conscious of the European art music tradition and the distinctions of social class that went along with it. Historian John Rockwell contends that, because of these unique social circumstances, British rockers "seem far more eager to 'dignify' their work, to make it acceptable for upper-class approbation, by freighting it with the trappings of classical music."[1]

One can gather from the tone of Rockwell's comment that the ambitious efforts of progressive rockers were not widely applauded. Many critics from the classical and the rock sides of the fence have condemned progressive rock as affected, pretentious, and naive. Many attempts at progressive rock are certainly deserving of these labels, but many other attempts should be acknowledged for their daring sense of exploration and occasional success. Critics from both musical camps should realize that progressive rockers were not necessarily dealing in comparatives; in most cases they considered their music neither better nor worse than extant rock or classical works. They were merely seeking a fresh form of expression drawn from the totality of their musical experiences and realities. To many rock musicians and fans who had been raised on love songs that rarely exceeded three chords, progressive rock was a refreshing and ambitious development that offered the awe and seriousness of a classical setting within the familiar context of a rock concert. The headiness of the music, no doubt, also fit in with the psychedelic counterculture of the time, as did the subject matter, ranging from the utopian imagery of the band Yes and the apocalyptic fears expressed by King Crimson.

PROGRESSIVE ROCK EMERGES

The band Procol Harum created one of the first, most accessible, and most successful recordings categorizable as progressive rock with their 1967 release of the song "A Whiter Shade of Pale." The song is based on "Air on a G String" from the *Suite No. 3 in D Major* by baroque composer Johann Sebastian Bach (1685–1750). It eventually sold six million copies worldwide. At this point the group existed only in the recording studio and had transient personnel, a couple of different names, and no live act to speak of. It was literally a one-hit wonder. After the success of "A Whiter Shade of Pale," a second album, *Shine on Brightly*, was released, featuring an 18-minute piece, "In Held 'Twas I." Procol Harum's third album, *A Salty Dog*, was released in America on A&M Records in 1969 and is considered by many its finest album. As with many of the early progressive rock bands, it combined energetic rhythm and blues with grand-scale classical music influences, evident in the compositions and in the sound and style of individuals in the band. Matthew Fisher played organ in a stately churchlike manner, whereas Robin Trower offered an earthy R&B style of guitar. In 1972 the band released an album of a live performance with the Edmonton (Alberta, Canada) Symphony Orchestra. Unfortunately, the album had to compete with the rerelease of its first album "A Whiter Shade of Pale," but it did muster a hit single, "Conquistador."

Another British band, the Moody Blues, shared a similar style as Procol Harum; in fact, the groups shared the same producer and label in England (Denny Cordell of Deram Records, a subsidiary of English Decca), and the Moody Blues had their first hit shortly after the release of Procol Harum's "A Whiter Shade of Pale." After an early career as an R&B band, the Moody Blues joined forces with the London Festival Orchestra in 1968 and produced the concept album *Days of Future Passed.* This initial attempt at classical-rock fusion was rather superficial, resulting in a pastiche of pleasant mood music with little cohesive interaction between the rock band and the orchestra. However, one piece from the album, "Nights in White Satin," rose to number two on the U.S. charts when it was reissued in 1972.

Another group that combined the rock combo with orchestra was Deep Purple. Their basic sound was harder than the Moody Blues; their 1973 hit "Smoke on the Water" fit well into the heavy metal style that developed in the early seventies. In 1969 Deep Purple joined forces with the Royal Philharmonic Orchestra to record "Concerto for Group and Orchestra," composed by the group's keyboardist Jon Lord. The piece is in three movements, with the rock group maintaining a hard rocking sound throughout. The next year Lord composed *Gemini Suite*, a six-movement rock band and orchestral work commissioned by the British Broadcasting Corporation. Each movement features a different soloist in the band, and Lord is quite successful in blending the band and the orchestra into a convincing fusion.

King Crimson was led by guitarist and Mellotron[2] player Robert Fripp, and while the group's personnel was often in flux, it included some of the major figures of British progressive rock, including Greg Lake and Adrian Belew. The band derived its name from the lyrics to Peter Sinfield's song "Court of the Crimson King." In 1969 they appeared before 650,000 people in London's Hyde Park, sharing a bill with the Rolling Stones. Later that month the band released its first album *In the Court of the Crimson King*. It combined challenging instrumental work, powerful rock guitar, orchestral Mellotron textures, and doom-laden lyrics. It was such a powerful statement that King Crimson could never really top itself. At the height of the album's success, members of the band began leaving. While the band continued to record and tour, never again did it have the impact it did with *In the Court of the Crimson King*.

Of the first generation of progressive rock bands, none has been more celebrated than Pink Floyd. Typically, it began in the mid-1960s as a psychedelic blues band, named after bluesmen Pink Anderson and Floyd Council. The band was led by guitarist Syd Barrett, accompanied by bassist Roger Waters, keyboardist Rick Wright, and drummer Nick Mason. Pink Floyd began experimenting with long improvisations, electronic effects, and light shows, with Barrett providing most of the compositions.

Pink Floyd in July 1967. Left to right: Roger Waters, Nick Mason, Syd Barrett, and Rick Wright.

The band signed with EMI in 1967 and soon produced its first album, *The Piper at the Gates of Dawn. The Piper* contained images of childhood, strange characters, and space travel, and it featured lengthy instrumental stretches. Unfortunately, it would be the only Pink Floyd album under Syd Barrett's leadership. Increasing mental problems made it difficult for him to continue working with the band, so he was replaced by guitarist Dave Gilmour, and Roger Waters took over as the primary composer for the group. Now following Waters's vision, Pink Floyd became even more experimental and classically formal. It abandoned record singles in favor of concept albums, but it still maintained an essence of bluesy pop that would endear it to its audience.

After producing a few albums, Pink Floyd, and progressive rock, reached their peak in 1973 with *Dark Side of the Moon.* The album featured well-crafted and brooding songs, breathtaking sound effects, female backup vocals, long instrumental stretches, and generally top-notch production. The album made number one in the United States and spent an astonishing 741 weeks on *Billboard*'s album chart.

With the enormous success of *Dark Side of the Moon*, it is to Pink Floyd's credit that it could ever produce an album that could match its significance. In 1979 *The Wall* was released, a double-album concept project addressing the walls humans build around themselves. The music was more approachable than *Dark Side of the Moon,* and electronic effects were deemphasized. The live touring production of *The Wall* demonstrated the increasingly elaborate nature of Pink Floyd's stage show, which included the actual construction of a wall during its performance.

From the 1980s on, Pink Floyd fragmented, fitfully reconvening to record an album or to do re-creation performance tours of *Dark Side of the Moon* or *The Wall.* Nevertheless, the band has ensured its place in history as the ultimate progressive rock cosmic band, holding on to legions of followers, many who were born long after the production of its signature albums.

Rick Wakeman and Yes

The recorded works of the Moody Blues and Deep Purple are examples of one approach to progressive rock: plugging a rock band, with little or no classical training, into an orchestral setting, which results in two disparate styles occurring either alternately or simultaneously. The two, however, rarely mixed. Another approach to progressive rock was to confine the instrumentation to a rock band but to utilize rock musicians with extensive classical training. This approach was typical of the group Yes, formed in 1968 by singer/percussionist Jon Anderson. Yes's approach was to compose and to perform music with expansive classically derived forms and to feature virtuosic displays of technique by each instrumentalist.

Keyboardist Rick Wakeman joined Yes in 1971. Born in West London in 1949, he entered the Royal Academy of Music at the age of 16 and studied piano and clarinet. He was a session pianist for artists like David Bowie and Cat Stevens before joining Yes, who had already released three albums. Wakeman added an orchestral texture to the band with the use of multiple keyboard instruments, including acoustic and electric pianos, synthesizers, electric organ, and the indigenous progressive rock instrument, the Mellotron. The sight of Wakeman nested among these monolithic columns of keyboard instruments was almost as impressive as the sound he got from them.

Progressive rock keyboardist Rick Wakeman in the 1970s.

Influenced by Wakeman, Yes produced a series of albums that balanced vocals with long, ambitious instrumental cuts. This venture began with the 1971 album *Fragile* (Atlantic 7211), which yielded the group's only mainstream hit "Roundabout." Future albums were even more ambitious. *Closer to the Edge* (1973) had only three cuts, one taking up an entire side of the album. Wakeman's period with Yes culminated with the 1974 album *Tales from Topographic Oceans* (Atlantic 908), with lyrics based on Hindu scripture. He was succeeded by Patrick Moraz.

Since 1972 Wakeman had been working on his own album projects, starting with *The Six Wives of Henry VIII.* The album was an instrumental setting, featuring his multiple keyboard work. In 1974 he combined his rock band and a narrator with the London Symphony Orchestra and the English Chamber Choir. The resulting album, *Journey to the Center of the Earth,* was recorded live at London's Royal Festival Hall and was based on Jules Verne's classic science fiction tale. In a setting similar to Aaron Copland's "Lincoln Portrait" or Serge Prokofiev's "Peter and the Wolf," the music of *Journey* either underscores the narration or offers instrumental depictions of the narrative portions; a soft rock character pervades the entire work.

Emerson, Lake, and Palmer

The British progressive rock keyboardist that matched, if not surpassed, Rick Wakeman in stature was Keith Emerson. Emerson (b. 1944) first came to prominence performing with the progressive rock group Nice. One of their products was an adaptation for rock band and orchestra of an "Intermezzo" from the *Karelia Suite* by Finnish classical composer Jean Sibelius. The last album Emerson made with Nice, *Elegy* (1971), included an extended version of "America" from Leonard Bernstein's musical *West Side Story.*

While performing with the Nice at the Fillmore West, Emerson met guitarist Greg Lake, who was performing with the progressive rock group King Crimson. A year later the two recruited drummer Carl Palmer to form Emerson, Lake, and Palmer, or ELP. Their first album, *Emerson, Lake, and Palmer* (1971), featured "The Three Fates," a three-movement work based on Greek mythology. The first movement, "Clotho," features Emerson on pipe organ. The second movement, "Lachesis," features Emerson as a piano soloist, and the third movement, "Atropos," features the trio. Stylistically, the work of ELP is a seamless blend of influences, indicative of Emerson's command of jazz, classical, and rock elements as well as his proficiency with multiple keyboards and keyboard technique in general. *Tarkus,* the group's second album from

Progressive rock group Emerson, Lake, and Palmer, in the studio recording their Trilogy album on November 18, 1971 (left to right: Carl Palmer, Greg Lake, and Keith Emerson).

1971, was a seven-part programmatic work depicting a world inhabited by mechanical animals.

ELP's work included not only extended original compositions based on classical models but also rock adaptations of existing classical works. Their most ambitious effort was their third album, *Pictures at an Exhibition* (1972), a setting of Russian composer Modest Mussorgsky's 1874 multi-movement work. ELP's version uses a good portion of the original work and adds newly composed material inspired by Mussorgsky's piece. Their next album, *Trilogy* (1972), features an adaptation of "Hoedown" from American composer Aaron Copland's ballet *Rodeo.* Following that album was *Brain Salad Surgery* (1973), with an adaptation of the fourth movement of the *First Piano Concerto* by Argentine classical composer Alberto Ginastera. Finally, the fourth side of ELP's *Works, Volume I* (1977) features an extended arrangement of Copland's popular "Fanfare for the Common Man."

All the while, the members of the group composed and recorded ambitious and extended pieces of their own. Perhaps the most impressive is Emerson's "Karn Evil 9" from *Brain Salad Surgery.* The group managed to re-create this massive three-movement work in a 1974 American tour that required 36 tons of equipment. In addition to a remarkable live musical performance, the accompanying visual effects were stunning.[3] The tour probably marked the high point of ELP's career.

Analysis of "Karn Evil 9: 1st Impression, Part 2" (*Brain Salad Surgery*, Manticore MC-66669)[4]

"Karn Evil 9" is a three-movement work recorded by ELP in 1973. Each movement is called an *impression,* and the first impression has two parts. We will speak generally of the entire work, then concentrate on part 2 of the first impression. The work features a balance of vocal and instrumental sections, the latter usually demonstrating the dazzling virtuosity of the players. The lyric of the first impression portrays a dreary other world inhabited by joyless people. The second impression is purely instrumental. In the third impression the singer/hero promises to liberate the land of its mysterious oppressor, which is finally revealed as a computer. The battle is ultimately lost as the computer says, "I'm perfect! Are you?"

Part 2 of the first impression describes the wasteland as a carnival sideshow. The opening line is a sinister circus barker welcoming us back to the show that never ends. There are visions of freaks, bishops' heads in jars, ragtime bands, Jesus, and a blade of grass. The section opens with a repeated synthesizer note

Listening Guide   20.1

"Karn Evil 9, 1st Impression, Part 2" 4 beats per measure

ELAPSED TIME	FORM	EVENT DESCRIPTION
:00	Intro	Repeated synthesizer note and tambourine (8 measures +)
:06	Vocal 1	A Voice with synthesizer and tambourine (8 measures)
:14	Vocal 1	A Vocal with organ riff (8 measures)
:21	Vocal 1	B Vocal and organ on same melody (8 measures)
:29	Vocal 1	B Vocal in different key, drums enter (8 measures)
:37	Vocal 1	C Vocal (8 measures)
:45	Vocal 2	A Vocal (8 measures)
:53	Vocal 2	B Vocal (8 measures)
1:00	Vocal 2	C Guitars with vocal responses (9 measures: 3 + 2 + 4)
1:08	Instr. open	Bluesy organ solo over vamp (47 measures)
2:03	Instr. sec. 2	Classical guitar solo (8 measures: 4 + 4)
3:00	Instr. close	Drums solo (8 measures)
3:07	Vocal 3	A Vocal, drums only (8 measures)
3:13	Vocal 3	A Vocal, with band (8 measures)
3:21	Riff 1	Synthesizer solo, "Roll up" vocal riff (18 measures)
3:37	Vocal 4	A Vocal (8 measures)
3:44	Vocal 4	A Vocal (8 measures +2)
3:52	Riff 2	"Come and see the show" riff with band (14 measures)
4:03	Ending P1	Synthesizer solo (20 measures)
4:21	Ending P2	Organ-dominated riff (12 measures)
4:34	Ending P3	Classical ending (7 measures +)
4:50	End	

and tambourine. After 8 measures of vocal the organ begins a riff, and 16 measures later the drums enter. On this section of the piece, Emerson is playing bass on one of the keyboard instruments and Greg Lake is playing guitar.

The verses are of different lengths throughout the piece, but the vocal portions draw from three basic melodies, which we will label A, B, and C. The first vocal portion is an AABBC grouping; the second is a shorter ABC grouping. This is followed by an instrumental section with two subsections: a vamp under a bluesy organ solo and a semiclassical guitar solo with several changes of rhythmic feel underneath. An ensemble riff leads into the instrumental section, and a drum solo leads out of it. Lake reenters with two A melody lines, the first with drums only and the second with the whole band. This is followed by a short synthesizer solo and a riff on the words "Roll up!" The two A melodies are sung once again, followed by a second riff on "Come and see the show." An extended instrumental ending follows. The first part is a synthesizer solo; the second part is a riff dominated by the organ; and the third part is a pompous classical ending.

American Progressive Rock: Frank Zappa

The primary exponent of American progressive rock was Frank Zappa, although his manner of presentation would hardly bring progressive rock to mind. On the surface Zappa's music seems satirical, obscene, and, above all, strange. His subject

American progressive rock artist and satirist Frank Zappa in 1974.

matter lampoons almost every facet of politics, religion, and society, and is flavored with a dark and cynical brand of humor seemingly based on lofty intellectualism or a perception distorted by drugs. Zappa did not even attempt the serious pretention of the British progressive rockers. Yet underneath all the satire and strangeness, Zappa was a serious and structured composer whose music was some of the most challenging and creative in the history of rock or any other musical genre.

Frank Zappa was born in Baltimore, Maryland, in 1940. His family moved to California when he was 10 years old, and it was there his musical development began. A guitarist, singer, and composer, Zappa had an equal affinity for rhythm and blues and the contemporary works of classical composers Karlheinz Stockhausen, Igor Stravinsky, and Edgard Varèse. These latter two composers were renowned for their complex experimentation with different rhythms, a trait that would identify Zappa's music. Moving to Los Angeles in 1964, Zappa formed a group, the Soul Giants, that eventually was renamed the Mothers of Invention.

The Mothers' strange music and stage antics made them a favorite in the Los Angeles drug culture, though Zappa himself was a teetotaler. Their first album, *Freak Out!* (Verve 5005), was released in 1965 on the MGM/Verve label. It was very creative for its day, a concept album that not only preceded the Beatles' *Sgt Pepper* by a year but also, according to Paul McCartney, inspired it. The honor was not returned, however; Zappa's 1967 album *We're Only in It for the Money* (Verve 5045) attacked the Beatles and their fans.

To the casual listener, Zappa's music sounds like a spontaneous and unrelated series of repetitive melodic and rhythmic figures, vocal and electronic effects, and studio techniques. But Frank Zappa was a calculating and very structured composer; the formal integrity of his music is revealed only after careful listening and analysis. One reason listeners have a hard time following Zappa's music is that it is grounded in twentieth-century classical music techniques that do not make use of tuneful melodies or regular metrical pulses. The classical borrowings of British progressive rockers, on the other hand, were based more on nineteenth-century models, using melodic and rhythmic practices more familiar to the general audience. Zappa expressed regret that many people did not realize or appreciate the careful craftsmanship he put into his music.

Fortunately, many in the music community did recognize his talent. Frank Zappa's classical prowess could be seen in his works for orchestra, such as suite of seven dances entitled *The Perfect Stranger* (1984), commissioned by renowned twentieth-century composer and conductor Pierre Boulez. Zappa organized and hosted a concert of his idol Edgard Varèse's music in New York. Zappa also wrote film music; *Uncle Meat* (1969) was music for a film never completed, utilizing a number of musical styles and effects, and studio techniques that included up to 40 overdubbed tracks. He also utilized the techniques and talents of jazz artists like violinist Jean Luc-Ponty and keyboardist George Duke; his work was as respected in the jazz world as the rock world.

Zappa was a highly visible spokesman for free expression in the arts. Much of the language in his music is quite explicit, a manifestation of the freedom he exercises; it has effectively kept him off radio and television and eventually strained his partnership with record companies. He attacked proponents of musical censorship both in his music and in testimony before government subcommittees. He also expressed his disdain toward the mercenary attitude of professional studio musicians, compelling him to restrict his composing and performing to computer sequencing and the use of synthesizers. (See Chapter 22 for a more in-depth explanation of synthesis.) Zappa died of prostate cancer in 1993.

REGGAE

The United States and Great Britain have been the primary producers of rock, but rock has also become a world music phenomenon. Other countries and cultures have been influenced by rock music and have assimilated it into their own native musics to create many distinctive hybrids. These hybrids and, occasionally, the pure folk musics of other countries have come into mainstream rock. One hybrid that developed close to the United States was *reggae.*

Reggae is a musical product of the lower-class blacks of Jamaica, a Caribbean island near Cuba. Jamaica was settled by the Spanish, then taken over by the British in the seventeenth century. African slaves were brought in to work the land and, over the centuries, grew to be the dominant culture on the island. The country gained its independence from Britain in 1962, harboring a conglomeration of cultural influences that would be reflected in reggae.

The grandfather of reggae was a rural, local music called *mento.* Mento rhythm was influenced by many African-American and African-Caribbean styles, such as calypso from Trinidad and merengue from the Dominican Republic. Its melodies were often derived from Anglo-American folk songs. The music was played on rustic instruments such as bamboo trumpets, glass bottles, and metal scrapers. In later years it was considered quaint by the young urban Jamaicans and was reserved for entertaining tourists.

During the 1950s Jamaican music came under the spell of American rhythm and blues. Because of Jamaica's close proximity to the southern United States its people were able to pick up AM radio broadcasts from cities like New Orleans and Miami and to hear the music of Louis Jordan, Fats Domino, and doo-wop vocal groups. From their attempts at playing rhythm and blues, Jamaican musicians developed a style known as *ska.* Familiar elements of R&B can be found in ska: the 12-bar blues form, chord patterns from doo-wop torch ballads, and the shuffle rhythm and strong backbeat. The guitar and piano often played a constant upbeat rhythm, giving the simultaneous effects of a slow, walking 4/4 pulse and a trotting 2/4 oom-pah pulse. Unlike American R&B, little emphasis was given to the bass, resulting in ska's smooth rhythmic texture. Vocalists preferred the crooning style of doo-wop balladeers, and male-female duos were a common vocal format. These are general characteristics, but it is important to understand that ska was comprised of so many disparate musical elements that each group had its own distinctive stylistic characteristics, so no real standard can be defined.

Instrumental ska groups were as popular as vocal groups. The most popular of these instrumental groups was the Skatalites, formed in 1963. The band included four trumpets, two trombones, two alto saxophones, two tenor saxes, and a rhythm section of bass, two guitars, three keyboards, and three percussionists. The concept of the horn section was derived from influences as wide as Mexican mariachi bands and the horn sections at Stax studios in Memphis. No single instrument dominates the style; the horns contribute as much to the rhythm as to the melody or harmony of ska.

The next step in the progression of Jamaican music was *rock steady*. The name indicates a heavier bass line and a slower tempo. Rock steady reflected the dominance of soul music in the mid-1960s, with more gospel-flavored vocal styles and the format of a soloist and backup singers playing off each other in a churchy call-and-response style. The rock steady style was epitomized by Desmond Dekker and Alton Ellis.

In 1968 the ska group the Maytals recorded "Do the Reggay," a term that eventually evolved into *reggae*. Reggae uses slower tempos (a trait it took from rock steady). It uses a lighter bass line that does not emphasize the downbeat of each measure (typical of ska). It uses a guitar rhythm of two eighth notes played on the second and fourth beats of each measure (a modification of the constant upbeat of ska). And it uses interlocking rhythms descended from an older Jamaican drumming style called *burru*.

Reggae centers around the religious practice of Rastafarianism that raised Ras Tafari, a deposed emperor of Ethiopia, to messianic status. Rastafarians were vegetarians, made sacramental use of marijuana (which they called *ganja*), and wore their hair in braided tails they called *dreadlocks*. Many reggae songs were Rastafarian praise songs and contained religious imagery from American gospel music. The prevailing subject matter of reggae and most earlier Jamaican styles was political protest demanding justice for the downtrodden lower class and threatening rebellion against the authorities.

Reggae was a product of the poor blacks of Kingston, Jamaica's capital. Since the oppressive ruling powers of the island did not allow reggae to be played on the local, government-controlled radio stations, the music was disseminated by "sound systems," portable disc jockey systems set up on the streets that played favorite records for the crowds. A local reggae record industry emerged, but it was Chris Blackwell who ventured to take the music out of Jamaica and show it to the world. Blackwell was born in London in 1937 of Jamaican descent, the son of a wealthy businessman. Moving to Jamaica when he was 18, he became enamored with reggae music and established Island Records to record it. He had his first hit with Millie Small's "My Boy Lollipop" in 1964 and continued to record reggae artists throughout the decade. Because of his ties with England, Blackwell's reggae recordings were exerting great influence on the English rock musicians, notably artists and groups

Reggae legend Bob Marley in performance on January 1, 1974.

like Eric Clapton, the Police, and the Specials, the latter two emerging from the British punk and new wave scene. By the same token, Blackwell's records increasingly moved toward American and British rock groups like Jethro Tull, Traffic, and Emerson, Lake, and Palmer, narrowing his stable of reggae artists considerably.

In 1972 Island's reggae star was Jimmy Cliff. Cliff had a soft, sensual vocal style that contrasted with the defiant or childish styles of earlier reggae singers. He starred in a popular underground reggae film, *The Harder They Come* in 1972, shot in the black ghettos of Kingston. The film featured the music of Cliff and

Listening Guide   20.2
"Get Up Stand Up" 4 beats per measure

ELAPSED TIME	FORM	EVENT DESCRIPTION
:00	Intro	Guitar/bass riff, "changa" guitar
:08	Chorus 1	Group vocal (16 measures)
:33	Verse 1	Solo voice (16 measures)
:58	Chorus 2	Group vocal (16 measures)
1:22	Verse 2	Solo vocal (16 measures)
1:47	Chorus 3	Group vocal, solo interjections (16 measures)
2:11	Verse 3	Solo vocal (16 measures)
2:35	Chorus 4	Group vocal to fade (16 + measures)
3:16	End	

other prominent reggae bands, offering an effective vehicle for getting the music out of Jamaica. But it was also in 1972 that Chris Blackwell began to devote his attention to the reggae band the Wailers, led by Bob Marley. The group was formed in 1963; its members often sang with the instrumental ska band the Skatalites. Their music was popular but was confined to Jamaica until Blackwell began recording them. In 1973 the Wailers' albums *Catch a Fire* and *Burnin'* became hits in England. British guitar legend Eric Clapton soon recorded a highly successful cover version of Marley's "I Shot the Sheriff" on his *461 Ocean Boulevard* album, helping to bring the reggae star further into the international limelight.

About this same time Peter Tosh left the Wailers and went on his own as a solo artist. He wrote, produced, and released most of his own material. True to his Rastafarian beliefs, he promoted the use of marijuana, epitomized in his hit "Legalize It" from 1976. His espousal of the illegal substance kept him in trouble with the law but endeared him to young people. It seemed fitting that he would team up with the Rolling Stones, another controversial act, on the 1978 album *Bush Doctor*.

Reggae enjoyed greater popularity in England than it did in the United States. American audiences had a hard time figuring out how to dance to the disjointed rhythms of reggae. Americans had also become accustomed to slick, lavish stage shows; and since reggae was primarily a studio music, it often proved rather disappointing in concert. Nevertheless, the influence of reggae found its way into the music of American artists like Paul Simon and Stevie Wonder.

Analysis of "Get Up Stand Up" (*Burnin'*, CD format, Tuff Gong 422-846200-2)

"Get Up Stand Up" is one of the early and strongest statements of social protest from Bob Marley and the Wailers. Another influential track from this album (*Burnin'*) was "I Shot the Sheriff," later covered by Eric Clapton. The song is largely a declaration of Rastafarian doctrine and an appeal to self-help.

The song is a basic verse/chorus alternation, with Marley singing the verses alone and the vocal group joining in on the repetitive choruses. Notice the upbeat "changa" rhythm in one of the guitars. The other plays an off-beat riff figure in unison with the bass. Blended in are percussion instruments, all set over a slow-feeling, loping speed, though the actual tempo may be twice as fast as it sounds. (This so-called cut-time is the reference used in the preceding measure count.)

Chapter Summary

Progressive rock strove to blend rock with European classical music. The movement was centered in England, closer to the pervasive influence of the classical music tradition. Progressive rock was fashioned in several ways. Procol Harum and the Moody Blues brought R&B roots to a classical setting, even performing with classical symphony orchestras. A signature instrument of the time was the Mellotron, a keyboard instrument capable of re-creating the sound of orchestral instruments with loops of recording tape.

Progressive rock was furthered by two great keyboardists of the day, Rick Wakeman and Keith Emerson. Wakeman was a multiple keyboardist with the group Yes; he brought extensive classical training to the rock band format. He collaborated on extended multimovement works with Yes and also performed as a solo artist, both with rock bands and orchestras. Keith Emerson likewise composed and performed a number of original extended works inspired by classical models. His trio, Emerson, Lake, and Palmer, also arranged rock adaptations of classical works by American and European composers such as Stravinsky, Mussorgsky, and Copland. Pink Floyd combined live visual spectacle, technology, and extended compositions to create a unique and influential style, epitomized in its incredibly successful album *Dark Side of the Moon*.

American progressive rock was epitomized in the work of Frank Zappa and the Mothers of Invention. Unlike the nineteenth-century styles of classical music preferred by British progressive rockers, Zappa's music was based on the more atonal and rhythmically complex twentieth-century art music composers. His music came off as freaky, haphazard, and humorous, but it was actually highly structured and carefully composed.

Rock in the late sixties and the seventies demonstrated the equal weight America and Britain had in influencing up-and-coming styles. Meanwhile, other cultures around the world were assimilating rock from America and Britain into their own musical traditions; some would return to influence mainstream rock. Jamaican reggae was such a music, a blend of Afro-Caribbean traditional music and African-American rhythm and blues. This music of the downtrodden blacks of Kingston had a particularly large impact on England, the former ruling country of Jamaica. This was due in part to the formation of Chris Blackwell's Island Records, which brought reggae artists Jimmy Cliff and Bob Marley to prominence. Blackwell went on to record nonreggae English bands as well.

Additional Listening

Procol Harum, *A Salty Dog* (CD format, JVC Japan 61311).

Pink Floyd, *Dark Side of the Moon* (CD format, EMI 679180).

Deep Purple, "Hush" (1968) (*Classic Rock 1968: The Beat Goes On*, Time-Life Music 2CLR-11, Track 22). This is a cover of a Joe South R&B tune with an arty twist, due mostly to the classical influence of organist Jon Lord. Deep Purple is the harder side of art rock and went on to become one of the premiere heavy metal bands.

The Moody Blues, "Nights in White Satin" (1972) (*Sound of the Seventies: 1972*, Time-Life Music SOD-03, Track 15). This song was mined from a larger 1968 album project. Most of the orchestra sounds are generated from the group's signature keyboard instrument, the Mellotron.

Frank Zappa, *Overnite Sensation* (CD format, Rykodisc 10518). This 1973 album is arguably the culmination of Zappa's late 1960s formulations. It combines juvenile crassness with extraordinary musicianship. The musical personnel is loaded with stellar jazz and rock artists of the day. Particularly enjoyable is the fun, silly, and nonsensical "Montana," about a Montana owner of a dental floss ranch. Zappa is assisted by Tina Turner and the Ikettes.

Various Artists, *Harder They Come* **(soundtrack)** (CD format, Island 586158).

Various Artists, *This Is Reggae Music* **(5 volumes)** (CD format, Mango 539251, 9327, 162-539391-2, 9850, CCD9851).

Review Questions

1. What country produced most of the progressive rock and why?
2. Describe the mechanics of the Mellotron, the instrument that was so important to many progressive rock bands.
3. What are the different contexts for a rock/classical fusion, exemplified respectively by the Moody Blues and Yes?
4. What classical works got a rock adaptation from Emerson, Lake, and Palmer? What were ELP's own compositions like?
5. Frank Zappa's music seemed humorous and strange to many of his listeners. What is a more realistic view of his music?
6. What are the individual characteristics of and influences on mento, ska, and rock steady, the predecessors of reggae?
7. What is the cultural background of reggae? How was the music primarily disseminated?
8. What media events helped to spread reggae beyond Jamaica? What other country was most receptive to reggae and why?

Notes

1. John Rockwell, "Art Rock," *The Rolling Stone Illustrated History of Rock and Roll,* ed; Jim Miller (New York: Random House/Rolling Stone Press, 1980), p. 348.
2. The signature instrument of the Moody Blues—and the most important instrumental innovation in the development of art rock—was the Mellotron. The Mellotron is a keyboard instrument with a six-foot-long loop of prerecorded tape for each key. The tape loops are actual recordings of orchestral string sections, choirs, and other acoustical musical sounds. Years before the development of synthesizers that could accurately re-create this natural sound, the Mellotron allowed rock groups in the sixties to capture a semblance of orchestral texture without taking a large orchestra on the road. Even though more viable replacements have been developed in recent years, the Moody Blues still uses the Mellotron in its concerts. A detailed look at the history and mechanics of the Mellotron and an interview with Moody Blues keyboardist Patrick Moraz can be found in *Keyboard* (May 1991).
3. At the tour performance this author attended in Memphis, Tennessee, ELP presented as its encore the entire *Pictures at an Exhibition.*
4. This portion can also be found on *The Best of Emerson, Lake & Palmer* (CD format, Rhino 72233).

Chapter 21

Hard and Soft Rock in the Seventies

As the decade of the 1960s waned, so did much of its cultural and musical experimentation. The disillusionment and demise of the counterculture was due in part to the deaths of its central political and entertainment figures between 1968 and 1971, including Martin Luther King, Robert Kennedy, Janis Joplin, Jimi Hendrix, and Jim Morrison. The movement also lost momentum as a result of the Rolling Stones concert at Altamont, which ended in violent disaster, as did the antiwar protests at Kent State University in Ohio, where the National Guard fatally shot four students. Naive middle-class youth who had abandoned themselves to drugs and nonmaterialistic communal living soon realized the harsh consequences of their lifestyles. As the 1970s dawned, the Vietnam conflict was winding down and everyone was getting back to reality. College students returned to school and took their place in the corporate world. The "us" generation became the "me" generation.[1]

Historian Joe Stuessy vividly describes how increasing "me-ism" in the 1970s resulted in the fragmentation of society into many distinctive groups. Business sought to provide a wide range of products, including styles of music, to cater to the varied tastes of these groups.[2] With all this fragmentation, the only thing that seemed to coalesce in the 1970s was the dominance of the music industry by a very few record labels. These labels, which included CBS, RCA, Atlantic, and Warner, sought to identify and feed the disparate musical tastes of the country. The music business reached unprecedented heights of profitability in the seventies, creating a conservative institution that left little room for experimentation; therefore, no bold new directions were forged, merely more polished continuations of the styles carried over from the sixties. And with the existence of so many substyles of rock, ranging from the velvety soft rock of the Carpenters to the savage heavy metal sound of AC/DC, no one style or artist dominated the decade. It is also notable that in the seventies British and American rock groups were equal contributors to popular music. Whether it was pop rock, heavy metal, or punk, both countries developed along parallel lines.

HEAVY METAL

Before discussing the origins and development of hard rock and heavy metal, we must pause to consider terminology. Existing studies of these two rock styles have made little headway in sorting out clear-cut distinctions between them. The most valiant attempt has been made by Katherine Charlton in her book *Rock Music Styles: A History*.[3] Among fans of the music, however, the criteria for labeling a band *hard rock* or *heavy metal* are much more vague and inconsistent, and the designation is ultimately a personal matter. It has been this author's experience that students have a clearer idea of what heavy metal is than what hard rock is. The terms are often used qualitatively; *hard rock* is an amorphous catchall for any kind of loud, aggressive rock that isn't heavy metal.

To understand heavy metal, it is first important to understand its audience, dominated by white male teenagers with tastes leaning toward aggressiveness and strength. Hard rock and heavy metal presentations include flamethrowers, smoke machines, and guitars that shoot fireballs. The artists are often clad in black leather and menacing makeup. They fly around the stage on cables and perform acrobatic feats on stage. Lyrics and stage presentations sometimes draw on themes of horror. American metal bands have tended to tap into horror movie references, emphasizing violence and gore. British metal bands have often drawn from the tradition of English and Celtic lore, a more Gothic style of horror (dark castles, trolls, and the occult).

Musically, the key to heavy metal is power. It is extremely loud and its evolution parallels that of amplification technology. The style does not emphasize danceability; it is more of a concert music and often involves changes of tempo and long, instrumental stretches that would not be conducive to dancing. Songs are harmonically simple for the most part and are often based on a powerful recurring riff in the bass. The center of attention and the most fundamental criterion for a quality heavy metal band is the guitarist, who is expected to offer spectacular displays of technical virtuosity. The guitarist's performance actually outweighs that of the lead vocalist, and metal fans are more likely to recall guitar solos from their favorite albums than a song's lyrics (another fact that may calm parental fears about the music).

Origins of Heavy Metal

Heavy metal had its beginnings in the blues-based rock bands of Britain and the more aggressive rock bands in the United States. The British roots can be traced back to the Rolling Stones and the Animals, as much for their rebellious image as for their hard-driving, blues-derived music. The Who would also be included as a forebear, particularly their song "My Generation" from 1965. Pete Townshend pioneered spectacular feedback and distortion techniques as well as on-stage instrument demolition. The idiomatic electric guitar artistry of Jimi Hendrix played a major role in the development of heavy metal, especially its penchant for high-profile guitar playing, though few metal guitarists have displayed a tenth of his ability or creativity.

A major American precursor of heavy metal was the group Steppenwolf, whose 1968 biker anthem "Born to Be Wild" actually used the term *heavy metal* (referring to a motorcycle). A more accurate American forecast of heavy metal came from the group Iron Butterfly, whose 1968 song "In-A-Gadda-Da-Vida" presented a catchy bass riff rivaled only by Cream's "Sunshine of Your Love."

The band that birthed the pioneering guitarists of heavy metal was the British group the Yardbirds. Founded in 1963 during the English blues craze, the Yardbirds' personnel included Eric Clapton, the first true rock guitar star. In its first year the group did cover versions of Chicago rhythm and blues songs. After their American premiere they moved to a more commercial style, prompting blues purist Clapton to leave the band. He was succeeded by another guitar star, Jeff Beck, and later by Jimmy Page, the founder of what many consider the first metal band, Led Zeppelin. The Yardbirds 1966 recording of "Shapes of Things" demonstrates an early use of feedback guitar and forecasts heavy metal.

Meanwhile, in 1966 Eric Clapton formed the power trio Cream with bassist Jack Bruce and drummer Ginger Baker. Intended to be another R&B cover band, Cream eventually adopted high volume, feedback, and distortion techniques, and extended improvisations, traits they shared with the Jimi Hendrix Experience. The group only lasted two years, but it deeply influenced heavy metal of the 1970s, particularly the song "Sunshine of Your Love" from their 1967 album *Disraeli Gears*. It is a blues-based song held together by a strong descending riff. The melody and lyrics are quite disposable; but it is the bass riff and the flashy guitar work that determine the worth of the song, the same criteria that most heavy metal bands would use.

Led Zeppelin

Led Zeppelin was formed in 1968 by ex-Yardbird guitarist Jimmy Page, and it was this group that turned the corner from the blues-based British rock bands of the late sixties to the heavy metal bands of the seventies. The group began as a continuation of the British blues band tradition; in fact, they recorded a never-released Yardbirds blues cover, "Dazed and Confused," on their premiere album *Led Zeppelin* in 1969. They soon moved toward more experimental guitar solos, using effects like drawing a violin bow across the strings of the guitar. Vocalist Robert Plant defined a high, shrieking heavy metal style of singing.

In the early seventies Led Zeppelin's music and lyrics began to lean toward Celtic folk traditions, a passion of Jimmy Page. The group also began to show great diversity in their presentation, best demonstrated in their most popu-

British heavy metal pioneer band Led Zeppelin.

lar album, *Led Zeppelin IV* (also called *ZoSo*), released in 1971. Topics included sex, rock music, and mysticism; and the instrumental presentation expanded to include acoustic folk instruments. This diversity culminated in "Stairway to Heaven," the song that became the rock anthem of the early seventies but, curiously, was never released as a single.

Listening Guide   21.1
"Stairway to Heaven" 4 beats per measure

ELAPSED TIME	FORM	EVENT DESCRIPTION
:00	Sect. 1 VI	Solo acoustic guitar, recorders (8 measures: 4 + 4)
:28	Sect. 1 C1	Recorders (8 measures: 4 + 4)
:56	Sect. 1 V2	Vocal (8 measures: 4 + 4)
1:24	Sect. 1 C2	Vocal (4 measures: 1/2 chorus)
1:38	Sect. 1 V3	Vocal (8 measures: 4 + 4)
2:06	Sect. 1 V4	Recorders (4 measures 1/2 chorus)
2:20	Sect. 2 Int. 1	Guitars and electric piano (8 measures)
2:46	Sect. 2 V1	Vocal (8 measures: 4 + 4)
3:12	Sect. 2 Int. 2	Guitars with vocal responses (9 measures: 3 + 2 + 4)
3:39	Sect. 2 V2	Vocal (8 measures: 4 + 4)
4:04	Sect. 2 Int. 3	Guitars with vocal responses (9 measures: 3 + 2 + 4)
4:31	Sect. 3 V1	Vocal (8 measures: 4 + 4)
4:55	Sect. 3 Int. 1	Guitars with vocal responses (9 measures: 3 + 2 + 4)
5:21	Sect. 3 V2	Vocal (8 measures: 4 + 4)
5:45	Sect. 3	Transition—guitar fanfare (10 measures: 2 + 4 + 4)
6:11	Sect. 4	Electric guitar solo (20 measures: 2 meas. × 10)
7:02	Sect. 5	Scream vocal (26 measures: 8 + 10 + 8)
8:06	Coda	Soft vocal alone (2 measures+)
8:19	End	

Analysis of "Stairway to Heaven" (*Led Zeppelin IV*, Atlantic 7208)

"Stairway to Heaven" remains a classic in the history of rock. It is a model of the multisection heavy metal concert epic, traversing from gentle acoustic music to raging electric rock in eight minutes. Jimmy Page's fascination with old English lore is apparent from the beginning. He opens "Stairway to Heaven" with a supple acoustic guitar solo passage. It is repeated, accompanied by an ensemble of recorders (vertical wooden flutes prominent in the Renaissance, roughly thirteenth to sixteenth centuries). In the chorus, the recorders play a more dominant, melodic role. This section of "Stairway" consists of a minor-key verse and a major-key chorus.

Robert Plant enters with a subdued but pain-filled vocal. The story line of the song is disjunctive, its meaning as elusive as many a John Lennon psychedelic lyric. But a pained, lonely feeling remains a constant throughout. The form of the vocal in this section is somewhat different from the introduction's form: a verse, a half-chorus, then a closing vocal verse and an instrumental verse similar to the introduction. This concludes the first section of the song.

An interlude begins and the acoustic guitar changes from a light picking style to a stronger strumming pattern. A Wurlitzer electric piano and an electric guitar join in. The second section of the song has a verse similar to the first section, except the chord progression has been altered a bit. The interlude now acts as a chorus. The form for this section is interlude, verse, interlude, verse, interlude.

The drums enter for the third section. The form is based on repetition of the interlude from the second section. A new vocal melody is now heard over that interlude. There is a fanfare-like guitar transition to the fourth section, a guitar solo. The form is a two-measure, three-chord figure over which Page plays a screaming, blues-based prototypical heavy metal guitar solo. The song has been making a gradual buildup all along, and Page's solo brings us to the climax of the song, the fifth section.

The fifth section features Robert Plant singing in the upper-most register of his voice, a characteristic of the heavy metal style of singing that has influenced singers to this day. Plant's verse is based on material heard earlier in the piece, but it is superimposed over the chord progression used in the previous section for Page's guitar solo. The band suddenly slows to a halt and Plant finishes the song alone, bringing back the earlier mood of loneliness and melancholy.

Black Sabbath and Other Heavy Metal Bands

Another early heavy metal band was Black Sabbath. Formed in 1969, their first album was released in 1970 and exhibited a full-blown heavy metal style. Like Led Zeppelin, they projected images of mysticism and the occult. The inside of the album shows an upside-down cross containing an eerie bit of verse reminiscent of Edgar Allan Poe. Black Sabbath's music relied heavily on repetitious bass riffs and the screaming vocal style of Ozzy Osbourne, who went on to a successful solo career in 1978. After 1973 Black Sabbath began to stretch beyond its demonic format, losing its image and, subsequently, its popularity.

America's strongest early contribution to heavy metal was Blue Öyster Cult, organized in 1967 at the Stony Brook College campus on Long Island by two rock critics. After an unsuccessful stint with Elektra Records, the band signed with Columbia in 1971. Their third album, *Secret Treaties,* was released in April 1974 and became their first to break into the top 100 bestsellers. They maintained a close tie with literary figures in science fiction and horror. In fact, the band's 1976 hit single, "(Don't Fear) the Reaper," was featured in John Carpenter's classic horror film *Halloween,* and some of their music was used in a television miniseries version of horror writer Stephen King's *The Stand.* (King is a huge heavy metal fan.)

As the 1970s progressed, hard rock and heavy metal evolved into a more appealing, high-production genre commonly labeled *stadium rock* or *arena rock* because of its grand design to accommodate huge crowds in huge spaces. The style also marked the inclusion of the *power ballads,* slow but powerful, dramatic songs that were anything but intimate expressions of love. The musicians' hair got bigger and costumes more garish, leading to a substyle called *glamour rock.* One of the early bands to represent this trend was Aerosmith, formed in Boston in 1970. Aerosmith, with its lead singer Steven Tyler, modeled itself after the Rolling Stones, heavily blues-based and danceable. After a time the group blended the macho power of hard rock with a perverse extroversion more associated with glam rockers like the New York Dolls. Aerosmith's third album for Columbia, *Toys in the Attic,* was its breakthrough. In that recording, the band perfected a combination of songwriting craft, heavy and catchy riffing, and lighthearted sexual innuendo in the lyrics and in Tyler's stage presentation.

In the early 1980s Aerosmith was in a popular slump, and two of its members, Steven Tyler and Joe Perry, were increasingly debilitated by substance abuse. Then in 1986 Aerosmith recorded a single from *Toys in the Attic,* "Walk This Way," with the popular rap group Run D.M.C. (see Chapter 23). The recording and the companion video got heavy airplay on MTV and marked the beginning of Aerosmith's comeback. From that point they collaborated with professional songwriters for material and, after a number of years with Geffen Records, signed a lucrative contract with Columbia in the 1990s and have made numerous appearances live and on television.

Van Halen set a new standard for heavy metal with its premiere in 1978. Eddie and Alex Van Halen moved with their family from Amsterdam to California in 1968 and formed the band Van Halen in 1974. Their first album was produced by Gene Simmons of Kiss, a band popular for its theatrics but less significant musically. The Van Halen brothers had received formal training on piano, and the classical music influence and a blazing technique became Eddie Van Halen's trademark. Aside from fast-moving fingers, Van Halen also used *harmonics*, high, bell-like notes created by lightly touching a string at one-third, one-fourth, or one-half of its length instead of pressing the string down to the fingerboard. Van Halen also employed combinations of picking, pulling, and hammering the strings with either hand, creating innovative new effects on the electric guitar.

Van Halen stretched the concept of heavy metal, successfully broadening its appeal while still retaining hard-core metal fans. On its *1984* album (Warner 23985), the group legitimized the use of the keyboard on the song "Jump." It features a synthesizer riff that has become as cherished as any bass riff heavy metal has seen. Vocalist David Lee Roth could scream with the best of metal singers, but he also demonstrated a light, good-natured, naughty style that was a distinctive change of pace from the dark, angry persona of most metal singers. Roth eventually left the group to pursue a solo career, and his subsequent recordings and videos demonstrate his brand of lighthearted sexiness and his fondness for popular music and singers dating back as far as Al Jolson. His first big hits as a solo artist, in fact, were a cover of the Beach Boys' "California Girls" and a medley of "Just a Gigolo" and "I Ain't Got Nobody," the latter two Tin Pan Alley songs from the twenties and thirties.

Stadium rock continued through the 1980s with bands such as Styx, Rush, Boston, Kansas, and Heart. The music of these bands was inherently formulaic and corporate and would lead to major underground rebellions along the way with musical styles such as disco, punk, and grunge.

FUNK

Soul music was a powerful black expression, first emerging in the late 1950s with Sam Cooke, Ray Charles, Aretha Franklin, and James Brown. Through the first half of the 1960s soul music held strong against the onslaught of the first British invasion. By the last half of the decade, however, it began to follow safer pop sensibilities and a growing black middle class. But soon a new music came forth with renewed boldness—funk. The founders of this style were James Brown and Sly and the Family Stone. Late 1960s songs by James Brown, such as "Sex Machine," "Get It Up or Turn It Loose," and "Cold Sweat," were seamless vamp tunes with intricate, pounding bass lines and crisp, staccato guitar and horn section lines. The music of Sly and the Family Stone also had intricate grooves driven by Larry Graham's thumping bass guitar, but it also incorporated elements of West Coast psychedelic rock and a utopian message of universal love.

The terms *funk* and *funky* were not in common use in the 1960s. Jazz pianist Horace Silver and other jazz artists at Blue Note Records had established a down-home gospel-flavored bebop style that they called *funky* jazz, but the term was not widely applied in pop music until the popularity of Dyke and the Blazers' "Funky Broadway" thrust it into the mainstream in 1967. At about the same time Kool and the Gang emerged with songs like "Funky Man." True to the definition of funk, it is about a nasty man with smelly armpits. Kool and the Gang peaked in 1974 with "Jungle Boogie" and "Funky Stuff."

Though there were clear antecedents, the looming "father of funk" is George Clinton (b. 1940). He had begun his career in the 1950s with a doo-wop group, the Parliaments. In 1968 he renamed his band Funkadelic and changed his format to a free-form psychedelic style band inspired by Sly and the Family Stone, Jimi Hendrix, and Frank Zappa. The band adopted bizarre costumes and developed a theme of black science fiction. Further honing his funk style, he recorded the band under two names: Funkadelic and Parliament, dropping the "s" as a result of a legal battle. During the 1970s he had 40 R&B hits, 3 of them going to number one. By the mid-1980s Clinton's career was ebbing, but he enjoyed renewed fame when many of the emerging rap artists began using snippets of his recorded funky grooves in their rap songs.

On the more mainstream side of funk was Earth, Wind, and Fire, a group led by former Chess Records drummer Maurice White (b. 1941 in Memphis, Tennessee). Earth, Wind, and Fire had the same Sly and James Brown roots as many funk bands, but they moved more in the direction of jazz, African music, and soft soul music. They combined a cosmic religiosity and space-age African dress with a smooth, high male vocal harmony, ably led by the voice of Philip Bailey. The horn section, separately known as the Phoenix Horns, became an in-demand unit, recording for many artists, including former Genesis drummer Phil Collins. (The Memphis Horns, the horn section from Stax Records, also hired out as a unit.

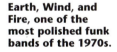

Earth, Wind, and Fire, one of the most polished funk bands of the 1970s.

Listening Guide   21.2
"Shining Star" 4 beats per measure

TIME	FORM	EVENT DESCRIPTION
:00	Intro	Choked guitars; add bass, add drums; horn section blast, vocal calls (16 measures)
:20	Verse 1	Uses one chord, solo voice (12 measures)
:48	Chorus 1	Hushed vocals in octaves; uses more chords (4 measures)
:57	Interlude 1	Electric piano (2 measures) followed by guitar solo with strong horn section background (5 measures)
1:14	Verse 2	Melody is freer and in a higher range; more group vocal interaction; verse is twice as long (24 measures)
2:10	Chorus 2	Repeated three times (12 measures)
2:28	Ending	Two-bar riff in vocals repeated three times, instruments gradually drop out, last time without reverberation
2:50	End	

They can be found on recordings such as Steve Winwood's Stax-like "Roll with It.") Earth, Wind, and Fire hit its peak with the 1975 Columbia album *That's the Way of the World* (Columbia/Legacy 65920), the soundtrack to an extinct movie they briefly appeared in. It is a masterpiece of production and songwriting.

Funk also had a high impact on the jazz world of the 1970s. Many jazz-rock fusion bands adopted the precise, interlocking grooves of funk, including Tower of Power, the Brecker Brothers, the Jeff Lorber Fusion, and Herbie Hancock's Headhunters. By the end of the 1980s funk was undermined by hip hop and rap, but it gained new life as cannibalized groove samples in rap recordings and performances.

Analysis of "Shining Star" (*That's the Way of the World*, CD format, Columbia/Legacy 65920)

Earth, Wind, and Fire's 1975 soundtrack album *That's the Way of the World* was the group's finest and best-selling album. Every track is a winner and the production is excellent. The 1999 CD release listed above includes some outtakes, or sketches.

"Shining Star" is the opening track. There are intricate solo and group vocals, well-harmonized, tight unisons with extremely high falsetto male voices. The guitar lines are short and clipped, bass lines are very active, and the horn section plays tight, staccato, intricate lines. Particularly striking is the studio reverberation effect at the end of the track. On the third time through the vocal vamp, the reverb is suddenly taken out and it sounds like the members of Earth, Wind, and Fire have jumped out of the stereo and into your lap.

The form of the song is a straightforward verse/chorus form. After the first cycle, there is an odd-length (seven measure) instrumental interlude of electric piano and guitar. In the second verse/chorus cycle, the length of each part is significantly extended and elaborated upon. The ending discussed above follows.

There is tremendous precision in every aspect of the performance—the interlocking parts of the rhythm section to create an infectious groove, the vocal acrobatics of the lead vocal, the blend, rhythmic accuracy, and intonation of the group vocals—all hallmarks of one of the best funk bands in popular music.

DISCO

There had been discotheques before the 1970s, but the environment and the culture of the *disco,* along with the spotlight on the disc jockey, took on new significance in the 1970s. The concept grew out of a need for dance music in the late 1960s and early 1970s when psychedelic, progressive rock, and heavy metal reigned supreme, music geared for listening rather than dancing. Disco was also born from an emerging gay culture in New York. Gay men were coming out of the closet but still remained socially segregated, and live acts were often unwilling to perform in gay venues, forcing them to resort to disc jockey entertainment. These discos leaned toward smooth black, urban dance music, represented by the Philadelphia sound of Gamble and Huff productions, Love Unlimited Orchestra, Barry White, and latter-day Stax recordings by artists such as Isaac Hayes.

Soon music was fashioned to suit the format of the discos. Rather than having terse, structured verse/chorus songs no longer than five minutes in length, extended remixes of songs were made, *disco singles* issued only to professional DJs on 12-inch vinyl records. As the fad caught on, there were disco versions made of everything from Tin Pan Alley pop songs to classical music and big band swing. There was unvarying bass drum on every beat, moving at an optimal 132 beats per minute. There was a heavy emphasis on instrumental textures rather than elaborate vocals.

Disco was also decidedly European in influence. There was a substantial Eurodisco movement across the Atlantic, and many popular disco hits in America were produced in Europe. A case in point is the rise of Donna Summer as the queen of disco. Born Donna Gaines in Boston in 1948, Summer was touring Europe with a stage production of the hippie musical *Hair.* She met Italian electro-pop arranger Giorgio Moroder, and in 1975 they recorded "Love to Love You Baby" in Munich, Germany. It was a sixteen-minute, riff-driven production over which Summer sang vamps and moaned and panted.

Disco diva Donna Summer performing in New Orleans, Louisiana.

The event that most thrust disco style and culture into pop dominance was the 1978 movie *Saturday Night Fever,* starring John Travolta, and its companion compilation soundtrack dominated by the Australian brother vocal group the Bee Gees but also featuring the Trammps' classic "Disco Inferno." Now everyone was on the disco bandwagon; radio stations not only featured disco but adopted all-disco formats.

While the *Saturday Night Fever* film and soundtrack gave a realistic look into New York disco culture, it was not complete. The significant gay aspect was ignored. Then French disco producer Jacques Morali decided to push that gay subculture more to the front with the Village People. The six men were costumed as distinct characters: a Native American in head-dress, a cowboy, a biker, a soldier, a policeman, and a construction worker complete with hard hat, male images juxtaposed with a homosexual image. Songs with gay underpinnings were written for the group, including "Macho Man," "Y.M.C.A.," and "In the Navy." Using silly campiness, the Village People managed to bring gayness into the mainstream. Their individual characterizations, general musical ineptness, producer-dominated artifice, and good-humored sleaziness no doubt provided a model for groups like the Spice Girls in the 1990s.

To many, disco was a painfully superficial music that had no intention of seeking anything meaningful in its message or its music, and by the end of the 1970s it had pretty much run its course. Over the next 20 years it has had fitful revivals, but always with the campy attitude of bringing back tacky period pieces, like tie-dyed shirts and leisure suits.

Analysis of "Disco Inferno" (*Saturday Night Fever*, CD format, Polydor 800068)

The 1978 movie *Saturday Night Fever* and its soundtrack were the undisputed catalysts for the disco fad of the late 1970s. The soundtrack is dominated by a number of excellent hit songs performed by the Australian brother band, the Bee Gees, but the Trammps' "Disco Inferno" is selected for this analysis because it is an example of an extended length dance mix as typically played in a disco. The Bee Gee songs conform more to the four-minute hit format.

"Disco Inferno" has a common verse/chorus format with a bridge, or contrasting section. As a typical pop hit, the song proper would only be three and a half minutes long. As a disco dance mix, however, the band vamps for a long stretch, with intermittent instrumental solos, solo and group vocal utterances, and punctuations by a brass section. The entire verse/chorus song never returns.

The recording is highly produced. The orchestra and vocals sound like an army, with a chorus of voices, an orchestral string section, and a large brass section of trumpets and trombones. The rhythm section features a busy and unfaltering four-measure figure that is labeled here as a *groove,* a lilting rhythmic vamp that is used for the song's verses, featuring a solo singer, and for the long instrumental dance passages. It is in a minor key. The chorus, by contrast, is half the length of the verse and is in a sunnier major key and features a vocal group. After two verse/chorus combinations, the song introduces a *bridge,* a completely new section of the song that sidetracks us for a moment before returning to a final verse/chorus combination. This is the end of the song for all intents and purposes.

From this point, the recording goes into a long stretch of the verse groove. For the next seven minutes or so, there is a series of unassuming events over that groove—a guitar solo, chants by the vocal group, a half-spoken, half-sung recitation by the solo singer, and a solo by an electric piano. The end of the recording is signaled by a long-awaited return of the chorus. For the first time around, only the instrumental backgrounds are heard, then the vocals reenter. The music is electronically faded out.

Listening Guide   21.3
"Disco Inferno" 4 beats per measure

TIME	FORM	EVENT DESCRIPTION
:00	Intro	Descending melody by guitar and bass; sweeping runs by the violins
:05	Groove	Low guitar, bass, keyboards; occasional punctuation by the horn section (4-measure vamp played 4 times)
:33	Chorus 1	Group chant of "Burn, Baby Burn" (8 measures)
:48	Verse 1	Based on 4-measure groove; solo singer (16 measures)
1:18	Chorus 2	Group chant but with solo over top (8 measures)
1:32	Verse 2	Solo singer; more active background vocals (16 measures)
2:02	Chorus 3	Same as Chorus 2
2:17	Bridge	Harmonized group vocals (9 measures)
2:34	Verse 3	Solo singer (16 measures)
3:03	Chorus 4	Same as Chorus 4 but done twice (16 measures)
3:33	Groove	4-measure vamp played 18 times
5:38	Groove	Spoken monologue by solo singer (70 measures)
7:45	Groove	Fender Rhodes electric piano solo (76 measures)
10:07	Chorus 5	Instruments only; vocals are not heard (8 measures)
10:22	Chorus 6	Vocals enter (chorus repeats twice into fade-out)
10:47	End	

SOFT-SOUNDING SINGER/SONGWRITERS

The preceding tongue-twisting subtitle describes another major movement in the 1970s, *soft rock*. Light love songs have always been the most successful form of popular music, even during the turbulent sixties. Soft rock is also the preferred style of adolescent females, who constitute the largest segment of the market. By the seventies the rock generation was also old enough to demand its own brand of easy-listening, so the music industry and a number of singer/songwriters delivered songs and performance styles that mirrored the encroaching calm of American society.

Some of the prominent soft rock stars of the seventies had been successful but unknown songwriters in the fifties and sixties. Carole King, Neil Diamond, and Neil Sedaka had been staff writers for Aldon Music in New York, a pop rock song factory that supplied music for the teen idols of the late fifties and early sixties, and for the fabricated television band the Monkees. Carole King wrote "I'm Into Something Good" for Herman's Hermits and "Will You Still Love Me Tomorrow" for the Shirelles. Neil Diamond wrote "I'm a Believer" for the Monkees.

By the 1970s these writers came on the music scene as solo artists, often performing their own material. Carole King's second solo album *Tapestry* was released in 1971 and, with over 13 million copies sold by the end of the decade, became one of the largest selling albums in history. Neil Diamond began successfully recording as early as 1966, but the seventies were his peak period of popularity. His well-crafted songs appealed to a broad range of listeners, from rockabilly to soft rock fans. His concert productions were lavish; he was often accompanied by a large orchestra, and his costume and hairstyle were reminiscent of Elvis Presley or Tom Jones. Neil Sedaka appealed to soft rock fans with a ballad rendition of his sixties hit "Breaking Up Is Hard to Do" and "Laughter in the Rain." His high, light tenor voice was perfectly suited for the polite pop style of his songs and productions.

James Taylor and Carly Simon were married during the height of their popularity but achieved fame individually. James Taylor, a Boston native, was a former folkie who, beginning in 1970, found success with a series of introspective soft rock songs, many written while undergoing treatment for heroin addiction. The most popular of these songs was the autobiographical "Fire and Rain." In addition to his own compositions, Taylor successfully sang cover versions of other songs, such as Carole King's "You've Got a Friend" and Holland, Dozier, and Holland's "How Sweet It Is." Carly Simon, Taylor's stylistic counterpart, released her first album in 1971, but it was her third album, *No Secrets*, that yielded her biggest hit, "You're So Vain." Her nearest female stylistic equivalent was Tucson, Arizona, native Linda Ronstadt. Coincidentally, in the 1980s both Simon and Ronstadt did recording projects of Tin Pan Alley standards with orchestral accompaniment.

One of the more eclectic singer/songwriters is Joni Mitchell, born in Canada. She came through the folksinger ranks, and her songwriting skills grew with her popularity through the late sixties. The 1970 song "Big Yellow Taxi" marked the real turning point in her development and popularity, which peaked with the 1974 album *Court and Spark* (Asylum 7E-1001), featuring her song "Help Me." "Help Me" had an unusually broad and rhythmically free melodic line, occasional meter changes, and a sophisticated chord sequence that gained the respect of musicians and fans alike. Another popular song on the *Court and Spark* album was "Twisted," recorded years earlier by jazz singer Annie Ross. The bulk of the song's melody is derived from an improvised tenor saxophone solo by bebop jazzman Wardell Gray, with words added by Jon Hendricks. The music should have been way over the heads of the popular audience, but Hendricks's humorous account of a visit to the psychiatrist's office, combined with Mitchell's wispy rendition, made the song a hit. In the late seventies Mitchell moved increasingly toward a jazz format, recording with prominent jazz musicians, peaking with the album *Mingus* in 1979 (Asylum SE-505).

Singer/songwriters abounded in the 1970s, offering various brands of soft rock. Cat Stevens offered soft rock with an English flavor, until he gave up entertainment to become a devout Muslim in 1981. John Denver offered country-flavored songs with nature-loving themes, and Jim Croce, a former truck driver, alternately offered tender love songs such as "Time in a Bottle" and shuffling ballads of rough characters like "Bad, Bad, Leroy Brown" and "You Don't Mess Around With Jim."

Billy Joel and Bruce Springsteen rose to fame in the mid-seventies and, unlike many of the singer/songwriters previously mentioned, became even more successful in the eighties. Joel, a native of Long Island, New York, had early success with his song "Piano Man" from the 1974 album of the same name. The song was a waltz-time ballad about the characters in the bars where he played. Beginning in 1977 he moved into mainstream pop-rock and released three successful albums. In his many top 40 hits, Joel's songwriting and performances demonstrate his mastery of a wide variety of styles, from doo-wop to contemporary pop-rock, confounding some critics but delighting audiences everywhere.

Singer and songwriter Bruce Springsteen, the bard of the Northeast working class, around 1985.

Rock traditions run deep in Bruce Springsteen's music, reflecting the influence of Chuck Berry, Bob Dylan, rockabilly, and many other sources. The end result, though, is what most describe as just plain old rock and roll. After working for years in the New York area as a folk rocker, Springsteen came to the attention of John Hammond, the Swing Era entrepreneur who had discovered Bob Dylan over 10 years earlier. Like Dylan, Springsteen's voice, and the sound of his band, was raw and rough. His first album for Columbia, *Greetings From Asbury Park, N.J.,* was released in 1973, but fame eluded him until the 1975 release of his album *Born to Run.* Springsteen's popularity peaked in 1984 with the album *Born in the U.S.A.* (Columbia QC-38653) and a 1986 retrospective album set of his music from 1975 to 1985. His appeal lay in his folklike social commentary on behalf of the American blue-collar worker and the unpretentious hard drive of his E Street Band.

GLITTER ROCK AND GENDER BENDERS

The increasingly theatrical nature of 1970s rock manifested itself in a number of substyles ranging from classical-influenced music to untrained, rebellious, and obnoxious racket. Heavy metal was theatrical to some extent, but the image of some

Glam rocker David Bowie as Ziggy Stardust, performing at the Hammersmith Odeon in London, July 4, 1973.

artists took a radical turn, leaning toward bizarre space-age costumes and men dressing in drag and makeup. This substyle has been dubbed *glamour rock* or *glitter rock,* and Britain was primarily responsible for its development.

David Bowie (born David Jones in London in 1947) was the primary stylist of the glitter rock brand of theatrical presentation. More actor than musician, Bowie chose the shock tactic to rise to fame, creating the character Ziggy Stardust and dressing in garish space clothes that clung tightly to his thin body. His face was made up to emphasize his gender-bender persona, unabashedly flaunting his avowed bisexuality. Musically, Bowie used a myriad of musical influences, from electronic space music to Rolling Stones–style rhythm and blues, but it was his theatrical presentation that really defined his act.

Elton John, another Englishman, also used outrageous costumes as part of his act, including bejeweled glasses, platform shoes, and enormous hats. His first American album release, *Elton John* (1970), featured song collaborations by him and lyricist Bernie Taupin. In the early years John's albums used heavy sweetening with strings and pseudopoetic and sensitive lyrics of Taupin, as on the songs "Your Song" and "Levon." Over a five-year period John and Taupin cranked out nine albums, all extremely successful and earning Elton John a place in history as the 1970s most popular artist. Other songs, such as "Honky Cat," "Crocodile Rock," and "Rocket Man," abandoned the maudlin, string-drenched, ballad format for a more traditional rocking style, defined by John's Jerry Lee Lewis–flavored piano playing.

Other glitter and gender-bender acts from American and British bands included Kiss, Alice Cooper, the New York Dolls, Mott the Hoople, Roxy Music, and Lou Reed. All incorporated transvestite costuming and bizarre theatrical stunts. Their music ranged from soft rock to heavy metal. The androgynous male rock performer survived well into the 1980s and beyond, with artists such as Boy George, Twisted Sister, and Michael Jackson.

PUNK ROCK AND NEW WAVE

Punk rock was intended to be antieverything, including antimusic. It was part of the new counterculture of the 1970s, rejecting society and the fat-cat corporate monstrosity that rock music had become. Though it claims to have roots in nothing, punk was at least partially derivative of heavy metal, gender-bender rock, and, in some cases, progressive rock. It was developed in the social underground of New York and London by those who had, in their view, been scarred by a class-conscious, homophobic, racist, and hypocritical society. Yet like the hippie culture, a softened commercialized version of punk, *new wave*, eventually deflated the original spirit of the movement.

The punk movement had its greatest impact in Britain, but it began in the United States in the 1960s. Lou Reed was a classical pianist and a poet who wrote about the world of sex, drugs, and prostitution in New York. He teamed up with avant-garde composer and instrumentalist John Cale and formed the band the Velvet Underground. The band moved beyond any rock tradition to experiment with new sounds, instruments, and styles of expression. Reed recited poetry in a stoic half-spoken, half-sung voice, accompanied by everything from electrified viola to trash can lids. The group's second album, *White Light/White Heat* (Verve 825-119-1-Y1, 1968), was their most experimental. The Underground never reached a high degree of popularity, and their music was inappropriate for airplay; they disbanded in 1972.

Coming into the seventies another significant American punk group was formed, the New York Dolls. Like Lou Reed, the group added heavy female makeup and stacked heels to their offerings of songs about sex and drugs, but they were much more lighthearted in character. They only produced two albums, in 1973 and 1974. After the New York Dolls' demise, member David Johansen went on to become a popular rhythm and blues singer as Buster Poindexter. The New York Dolls was also historically significant in that they, along with the proto-punk band the Ramones, brought punk rock to Britain, where the genre really found its home.

The British pioneer punk rock group The Sex Pistols in February 1976. Left to right: Glen Matlock, Johnny Rotten, Steve Jones, and Paul Cook.

English society was hopelessly delineated by class, with lower-class teens having little hope for a better future. They were further angered by the lavish performances of wealthy rock stars and welcomed the raw, shocking, and anarchistic style of the New York Dolls and the Ramones. Britain's first notable attempt at the punk style was the Sex Pistols. Featuring singer Johnny Rotten and bassist Sid Vicious, they were musically inept (Rotten had never sung before the group was formed) and took the rebellion part of their act a lot more seriously than their American counterparts. Their music was uncomfortably (and deliberately) pounding, sloppy, and repetitive; and their stage antics, which included sticking pins and broken glass in themselves and slapping members of the audience, were disgusting enough to have most of their American concert appearances canceled.

Punk rock's immediate underground successor was new wave music. Unlike punk, new wave did not mind being intellectual or artsy, and it borrowed from styles and techniques of twentieth-century art music composition and world music styles, similar to progressive rock. New wave liberally incorporated advanced electronic keyboard technology and exotic percussion instruments. On stage and in videos, some bands, such as Devo, appeared robotic and emotionless. Yet it is important to understand that new wave bands were quite diverse in both musical content and presentation. Some bands embraced postpunk rebellion and repudiation of technical prowess and polish. Some, like the Police and the Specials, embraced Jamaican ska and reggae. Singer/songwriter Elvis Costello matches his literate, Bob Dylanesque lyrics with an electric range of musical styles (Tin Pan alley pop, country, reggae). Most of the new wave bands that made it into the 1980s benefited from the fledgling MTV music television channel, hungry for music video material and prominently featuring new wave acts from Britain and the United States (see Chapter 22).

Devo was formed at Kent State University in Akron, Ohio, in 1972. The band's name came from the notion of "de-evolution," that mankind had regressed into a society marked by rigidity, repression, and mechanization. The visual component of the band reflected this view with robotic movements, space-age costumes, and an obsession with mechanized music realized with synthesizers (see the explanation of synthesizers in Chapter 22). Devo's biggest brush with commercial success came with its single and companion music video "Whip It," from the 1980 album *Freedom of Choice.* Four years before the band made a short film, *The Truth about De-Evolution,* which was seen by David Bowie and Iggy Pop, who helped secure Devo a recording contract with Warner Brothers and an association with producer Brian Eno. By the 1990s members of the band parted ways to pursue individual projects. Mark Mothersbaugh started a successful production company and has been a prolific composer of television soundtracks, most notably quirky kids' shows like Nickelodeon's *Rug Rats* and the inventive yet subversive *Pee Wee's Playhouse* on CBS.

Another important new wave band was Talking Heads, which tapped into geeky intellectualism as did Devo. Its recordings were also masterminded by producer Brian Eno. Talking Heads specialized in blending acoustic and electronic elements, driving funk, elements of world music styles, and singer David Byrne's sometimes overly intellectual, artsy lyrics. This experimentation is epitomized on the 1978 album *More Songs about Buildings and Food.*

Blondie was both the individual (lead singer Deborah Harry) and her band. It was a reflection of the new wave scene of lower Manhattan and a stylistic pivot point of disco and postpunk. The stunningly beautiful Harry created a parody of a Marilyn Monroe–like blonde siren, singing a sweet soprano over rocking accompaniment. Blondie's 1978 hit "Heart of Glass" was a disco-styled song that took the band to number one in the United States and in Britain. Well established in the lower Manhattan new wave and midtown disco milieus, Harry also latched on to the emerging hip hop scene in the Bronx and Queens and helped bring early rap artists to the mainstream scenes in Manhattan (see Chapter 23).

Chapter Summary

Both America and Britain modified ideas carried over from the 1960s and ventured to target a very fragmented market. Heavy metal appealed to a new generation of adolescent boys, while soft rock appealed to adolescent girls and the growing population of middle-aged rockers. Ultrasimple songs and productions coexisted with well-crafted and lavishly produced material. Lyric content and artist image explored the shocking and the unconventional, ranging from sexually ambiguous to robotic to destructive. In many cases theatrical presentation was more important than the music, and audiences came to identify with groups visually rather than musically.

Along the way, arena rock, progressive rock, and other postpsychedelic styles seemed to forsake the concept of dance music. It returned in the forms of funk and disco. George Clinton married glamour rock, psychedelia, and the music of James Brown and Sly and the Family Stone to become the unofficial "father of funk." Groups like Earth, Wind, and Fire had an even more polished version. However, the ultimate dance music of the 1970s was disco, born in the predominantly gay discotheque underground of New York and exploding into the mainstream with the popularity of the film and soundtrack to *Saturday Night Fever* in 1978.

Additional Listening

Refer to citations in the body of the text (all LP format).

The Yardbirds, "Shapes of Things" (1966) (*Classic Rock 1966,* Time-Life Music 2CLR-02, Track 15). Guitarist Jeff Beck's use of feedback and distortion in this song is one of the earliest prototypes of the heavy metal style of the 1970s.

Steppenwolf, "Born to Be Wild" (1968) (*Classic Rock 1966,* Time-life Music 2CLR-04, Track 1). The harder sound of this song was another example of proto-metal. The line "heavy metal thunder" even gave the new style its name.

Black Sabbath, *Black Sabbath* (1970) (CD format, Warner Bros. 2-1871).

Elton John, "Your Song" (1971) (*Sound of the Seventies: 1971,* Time-Life Music SOD-02, Track 10). This track is an example of the more torchy types of songs that Elton John did in his early career while collaborating with Bernie Taupin.

James Taylor, "You've Got a Friend" (1971) (*Sound of the Seventies: 1971*, Time-Life Music SOD-02, Track 13). This is a cover version of the song made famous on Carole King's *Tapestry* album the same year. Notice that Taylor's vocal style is mellower and the accompaniment is more flowing than King's version.

Carole King, *Tapestry* (1971) (CD format, Epic/Legacy 65850). One of the most successful pop-rock albums of all time, this was Carole King's unveiling as a performer and also as a songwriter.

David Bowie, *The Rise and Fall of Ziggy Stardust and the Spiders from Mars* (1972) (CD format, Virgin 21900).

Sex Pistols, *Never Mind the Bullocks, Here's the Sex Pistols* (1977) (CD format, Warner Bros. 2-3147).

Talking Heads, *Talking Heads '77* (1977) (CD format, Sire 2-6036).

Review Questions

1. What was different about the rock record business in the 1970s?
2. In what ways, theatrically or musically, do heavy metal bands satisfy the psyche of the male teen?
3. What is the difference between the stage routines and musical imagery of American heavy metal bands and British heavy metal bands?
4. What are the instrumental and formal characteristics of heavy metal bands? Why isn't heavy metal dance music?
5. What metal and hard rock stars began with the British band the Yardbirds? What prototypical pieces did they record?
6. Who was the primary audience for soft rock? Who were some of the soft rock stars of the 1970s that began as songwriters?
7. What were aspects of Joni Mitchell's music that made her such an eclectic rock star in the 1970s?
8. What was the key to Bruce Springsteen's appeal in the seventies and eighties? How could his musical style best be described?
9. Define *glitter rock.*
10. What type of musical experimentation did the Velvet Underground pursue? What other new wave bands had this same musical eclecticism?

Notes

1. An excellent sociopolitical retrospective of the counterculture is presented by the third episode of the television series *Making Sense of the Sixties,* shown occasionally on many public television stations.
2. Joe Stuessy, *Rock and Roll: Its History and Stylistic Development* (Englewood Cliffs, NJ: Prentice Hall, 1990), pp. 301–4.
3. Katherine Charlton, *Rock Music Styles: A History* (Dubuque, IA: Wm. C. Brown Publishers, 1990), pp. 175, 191.

Chapter 22

New Heights and High Tech in the Eighties

The popular music events of the 1980s reflected the diversity of a music that had been around for 40 years and had touched generations of people. Rock music was old enough to have a heritage, a sense of tradition; neo-rockabilly bands enjoyed success alongside rap groups. There was even a renaissance of crooning Tin Pan Alley tunes, spearheaded by Linda Ronstadt, Carly Simon, and Harry Connick, Jr. Some artists, like the Beatles and Led Zeppelin, never seem to be outdated. Other artists had spent the seventies honing their personal style and finally found their way to superstardom in the eighties.

Rock was also mature enough to have a conscience. The 1980s was a decade without a military war; but it was a decade of other wars, wars against the dreaded disease AIDS (Acquired Immune Deficiency Syndrome), the equally degenerative urban disease of homelessness, the failing family farm, famine in Africa, and other plights of the human condition. Live Aid, Farm Aid, the production of "We Are the World," to fund hunger relief in Africa, and "That's What Friends Are For," to fund AIDS research, were benefits that made significant charitable contributions to these causes. With the entertainment industry accounting for a significant portion of America's gross national product, it was inspiring to see its most successful artists give their time, efforts, and considerable popular influence to raise the social consciousness of the public.

A big new star in the 1980s was technology. The 1980s was the decade that saw the birth of MTV and music videos, digital and sampling synthesizers, drum machines, personal computers, and CD players. Technology changed how music was created, recorded, performed, and enjoyed. Music technology changed almost on a daily basis, and music trade magazines now look more like engineering manuals than music journals. Since technology has affected the work of almost every artist or group discussed in this chapter, it is appropriate that we look at some of these technological advances in some detail.

SYNTHESIZERS

A synthesizer is a musical instrument, traditionally a keyboard instrument, that creates sounds electronically. It can accurately re-create the sound of acoustical instruments (ones based on vibration and resonance of wood, strings, and other materials), or it can generate new and unusual tone colors. The synthesizer has been around for decades but has only been practical for live performances since the 1960s. Synthesis in the 1950s, like computing, required a room full of components just to perform the simplest of tasks. In the 1960s Robert Moog and Don Buchla independently invented the modular synthesizer, a "voltage-controlled" unit that did not require binary computer programming to create electronic music sounds. The instruments were large, resembling a telephone switchboard with a piano keyboard. They were not practical for live performance, due to their size and the fact that they usually played only one note at a time and required a multitrack recorder to be used effectively. At first these synthesizers were used for little more than broadcast music and sound effects, but Wendy Carlos's 1968 best-seller *Switched-On Bach* proved that the synthesizer (in this case, the Moog) could be an expressive musical instrument.

In the 1970s Moog, Arp, Emu, and a few other companies began to manufacture more portable instruments that can be easily taken to "gigs" and used for live performances. They were still severely limited; most could still play only one note at a time, the pitch of the instrument drifted, and there was no way to store the sound parameters that the programmer had carefully fashioned. By the end of the 1970s polyphonic synthesizers (ones able to play several notes simultaneously) became more readily available; and one synthesizer, Sequential Circuits' Prophet 5, came with a memory bank to store and instantly recall programmed sounds.

Around 1982 the gates of music technology blew wide open. Roger Linn created the Linn Drum, a machine that used computer microchips to digitally replicate the sounds of a drum set. The instrument also had a digital clock and a memory bank that allowed a programmer to create drum patterns and play them back automatically. It was also around 1982 that synthesizer manufacturers established the concept of MIDI, Musical Instrument Digital Interface. MIDI is a communication's protocol whereby different types and brands of synthesizers can be interconnected and controlled by a single source using a common digital language. Coinciding the MIDI technology was the advent of the affordable personal computer. Software was soon developed to make the computer a command station connected to several MIDI-equipped synthesizers, controlling each instrument in real time like a player piano. The computer/synthesizer connection gave musicians unprecedented musical power, the ability to program complex pieces of music and perform them with little or no ability to play keyboard or drums. The computer is able to execute rhythms and groups of notes that would be humanly impossible to play. MIDI can also be used to automate sound-mixing and lighting in a performance setting. It is, to say the least, a radical advance in music technology that has just begun to reveal its possibilities.

A more recent technological advance in music production is the *sampling synthesizer*. This instrument digitally records, or samples, real world sounds and reproduces them. A sampling synthesizer can accurately re-create almost any sound, or it can digitally alter the sound to create special audio effects. The first digital sampling units were so costly they were owned only by a few studios and universities.

Now powerful sampling units are available for less than $5,000. Because of their ability to record and play back almost anything, including other recordings, the parameters of their legal use have been questioned extensively. Rap groups and disc jockeys have often sampled excerpts from familiar recordings in their own recordings, testing the protection coverage of the country's copyright laws.

TECHNOLOGICAL ADVANCES AND THE MUSIC CONSUMER

Since the beginning of the twentieth century, flat phonograph discs were the standard format for consumer audio playback. Long-playing microgroove and 45 rpm developments supplanted the older 78 rpm technology, but the format remained basically the same. A phonograph stylus drags across the etchings in the groove of the disc. The sound is amplified and sent to an audio speaker. The problem with this format is that vinyl discs collect dirt and dust, they get scratched, and they are worn down by repeated playing, all of which adversely affects their playback quality. The only alternative for many years was magnetic audiotape spooled on open reels.

In the early 1970s the smaller and more manageable tape cassette became a practical recording and playback format, but the sound quality left much to be desired and only became worse with age and wear. As the decade went on, successful efforts were made to improve the quality of cassette sound. New particle compositions were developed in the manufacturing of the tape, and noise reduction techniques were created to minimize its inherent hissing sound. The cassette tape became a convenient way to record and listen to music. It also, unfortunately, became a prime motivation for audio piracy, making unauthorized recordings of albums an alternative to purchasing them. The biggest boon to the cassette format came in the 1980s, when Japan's Sony Corporation introduced the Walkman, a small, portable radio/cassette player with headphones. The unit clipped on the listener's clothing and was intended for personal listening when away from the car or home stereo. A similar but much bulkier concept for cassette playback was the portable stereo system with built-in speakers. They were particularly popular in the streets of urban neighborhoods, where their powerful blaring became a status symbol, hence their nicknames "boom box" and "ghetto blaster." Another impetus for the use of cassette tapes was their ability to be played on in-dash car stereo units. In 1984 cassette sales topped LP sales for the first time.

Digital technology revitalized the recording industry in the mid-1980s and revolutionized consumer-level media. Digital recording had been around since the 1970s as a means of reducing sound quality loss when recording or mastering music, but it was only available in the early stages of the production process. The consumer media, the final, mass-produced step in the production, was still an analog product, either an LP or a cassette tape. Phillips Corporation, a European electronics company, developed the first viable digital medium at the consumer level with the compact disc. The CD is a sealed optical format read by a laser beam. The digital information is converted by a computer microprocessor into pure audio sound, unblemished by inherent noises created by an analog medium. At first, the playback units and the CDs themselves were quite expensive and hard to find, appealing only to high-end stereo buffs. In the last half of the 1980s the format caught on, quickly hurling the vinyl LPs into obsolescence. They also proved advantageous to recording manufacturers because the CDs, at least at first, could not be reproduced on tape by the consumer without the loss of the desired sound purity. Japan soon invented digital audio tape units, or DAT machines; these offer the consumer a means of dubbing CDs onto tape without loss of digital sound quality. The American recording industry fought hard to keep these DAT machines out of the United States, but to no avail. DAT machines are now available but have not caught on as well as expected. This was due early on to prohibitive cost of the machines, lack of availability of blank tapes, and the subsequent development of more desirable means of recording digital sound that developed in the 1990s. These will be discussed in the next chapter.

MUSIC TELEVISION

Until the 1980s television had proven to be a surprisingly ineffective source for presenting rock music. *American Bandstand* lasted for 30 years, but it was an anomaly in the industry. There were rock television specials and syndicated programs like *Soul Train*, but radio and records remained the most viable media for rock music. Throughout the 1970s, however, cable television became increasingly prevalent, offering hundreds of channels that catered to many special interest groups. It was in this broadcast setting that ex-radio program director Robert Pittman conceived MTV (Music Television), a cable network devoted exclusively to video performances of songs by pop or rock groups.

MTV went on the air in August 1981, alternating music videos with chatter from hosts, a format similar to pop radio programming. Desperate for video material to air, the network turned to British pop groups; they had long used music videos in their country. Getting the first stab at MTV exposure, British new wave band the Buggles premiered "Video Killed the Radio Star," a seemingly custommade statement for MTV to hail the dawn of the rock video age. The Buggles were a one-hit wonder, but the group will go down in history as the first performers on MTV. Other new wave synthesizer bands followed—Duran Duran, A Flock of Seagulls, Culture Club, Devo, Talking Heads, and Men at Work (an Australian band). The content of the videos was geared to teenagers and young adults and was more concerned with stylish presentation of the artists than with creating a drama that was true to the lyric of the song.

By the end of 1983 MTV was in the black financially and on its way to making history. Music videos became a must for promoting a group's sound recordings, proving once again that record sales were still the dominant force in the music industry. There is no doubt that some artists, who may not have risen to fame on the strength of their audio performances alone, became stars by their ability to define a strong visual image in music video performances. The concept of top video countdown shows soon spread to other networks as well as the major broadcast networks. VH1 catered to

British band Duran Duran, one of the darlings of early MTV.

adult contemporary listeners, the baby boomers who preferred Barbra Streisand and Neil Diamond. Over the years VH1 would expand programming to include other adult rock acts such as U2 and John Mellencamp, contemporary crossover country artists, and a heavy emphasis on pop history documentaries, particularly its *VH1: Behind the Music* biographical series that seems to be the pop music version of the A&E cable network's successful *Biography* series.

After a time detractors from several camps began to slam MTV's programming policies. The videos were judged to be high in sex and violence content, and particularly denigrating in the portrayal of women. Another major criticism of MTV was its obvious lack of black artists. MTV's marketing research had compelled the network to program videos that catered to the white teenager's idea of rock and roll. MTV considered the exclusion of black pop artists not a racial issue but a stylistic one. In MTV's mind, blacks performed rhythm and blues, soul, or disco but not rock. That mentality was shattered when the unquestionable popularity of Michael Jackson and his music and music video concept forced the network to program not only his videos but also those of other black artists (see the section on Jackson below). By 1987 MTV was a strong showcase for rap music with a show entitled *Yo! MTV Raps.*

Michael Jackson

When Michael Jackson's *Thriller* album hit the stores in 1982 he was already a 20-plus-year veteran of show business. He was five years old when Motown discovered him and his brothers, the Jackson Five, creating what historian Geoffrey Stokes labeled *soul bubblegum.* Michael was clearly the centerpiece of the act, a darling little imp with an incredible voice and a way with a dance. Motown songwriters and producers taught the group much, leaving little room for individual interpretation but stressing precision. Their collective efforts paid off with a number of hits.

In the 1970s the Jackson Five's fame began to fade. They left Motown and changed their name to the Jacksons, since their old boss owned the original name. They tried to hang on to the disco craze with their new label Epic, a subsidiary of Columbia, but the public just was not buying. Michael had an equally

Singer Michael Jackson, whose long career peaked in the 1980s with the release of the album *Thriller.*

inauspicious movie debut as the scarecrow in the film version of *The Wiz,* but it was during that project that he met veteran composer/arranger Quincy Jones. In 1979 Jones and Jackson collaborated on Michael's first big solo album *Off the Wall,* an album that would set the stage for his superstardom in the 1980s. Michael was becoming an increasingly compelling and enigmatic pop personality. As he grew to adulthood he maintained his high, boyish voice and appearance, causing some to question his sexuality. He altered his face with makeup and plastic surgery, becoming not only a gender bender but also a race bender *and* an age bender.

One of the most significant years in rock history and in the career of Michael Jackson was 1982. That year marked the release of his second solo album with Quincy Jones,

Thriller. It had a favorable premiere, but the event that really triggered its success was the Jacksons' appearance on Motown's twenty-fifth anniversary television special. After performing a medley of nostalgic Jackson Five hits, Michael stole the show with a riveting performance of "Billie Jean," a single from *Thriller*. Sales of the album soared. Several hit singles were extracted, as were innovative videos on "Beat It" and "Billie Jean." For the video of the song "Thriller" Jackson chose John Landis as director, inspired by his film *An American Werewolf in London*. It was actually a film of adequate length to qualify as a film short subject and to vie for an Academy Award in that category. The pioneering *Thriller* videos were the catalyst for black artists gaining access to MTV, and the *Thriller* album eventually broke all existing album sales records.

Five years passed before Jackson released his next album. The public was anxious to see if he could match, much less top, *Thriller*. In 1987 *Bad* was released. It did not match the sales of its predecessor, but it was extremely popular, yielding several hit singles. Jackson also produced lengthy videos and cowrote "We Are the World" with Lionel Ritchie, but by the end of the eighties Michael Jackson was on his way out. Given the fickle tastes of the public—the preteen public at that—Jackson did remarkably well. Some apparently still see potential for him in the future. In 1991 CBS/Sony signed him to a one billion dollar contract. Time will tell.

Michael Jackson has continued the tradition of the song-and-dance man, reminiscent of his idols Gene Kelly and Fred Astaire, combined with the distinctive moves of James Brown and Jackson's fellow Motown artists. His unusual costuming is designed to keep the audience's attention on his every move: the high-water pants that expose glittering white socks, the broad-brimmed hat cocked over one eye, or the white tape around his fingers that brings attention to his expressive hands. Whether in solo or ensemble settings, his dancing is precise and exciting and accounts for the majority of his appeal with fans. His 1980s vocal style differs quite a bit from his boyhood days at Motown. In the sixties Jackson had a shouting boy-soprano voice adorned by a smooth, natural vibrato. In the eighties his voice had a nervous energy, punctuated by a quivering vibrato and Buddy Holly–type hiccups.

Michael Jackson's appeal was primarily to teens and preteens, a responsibility he apparently took very seriously. Though a curious and private man, he strove to serve as an inspiring moral model for his young fans, a Peter Pan type of figure who would not grow up. But soon his love for children and his having them at his home day and night aroused suspicion. Then in 1993 a teenage friend accused him of child molestation, a charge Jackson adamantly refuted. The case was settled out of court a year later, but serious damage had been done to Jackson's reputation. Nevertheless, his 1995 *HIStory* album sold reasonably well. Another big moment in Jackson's career was the reunion of the Jackson Five at Madison Square Garden in March 2001, though it too found controversy when Michael's brother Jermaine publicly criticized him for the high ticket prices for the show.

Jackson was a pop music pioneer, crossing all kinds of barriers and, for a time, rightly deserving of the title the "king of pop."

Analysis of "Billie Jean" (*Thriller*, Epic QE 38112)

The subject matter of "Billie Jean" was rather unusual for Michael Jackson. Where most of his songs deal with innocent romantic love, in "Billie Jean" a woman accuses the singer of siring an illegitimate son, an accusation he continues to deny.

Listening Guide   22.1
"Billie Jean" 4 beats per measure

ELAPSED TIME	FORM	EVENT DESCRIPTION
:00	Intro P1	Drums (4 1/2 beats)
:02	Intro P2	Two bass patterns (8 measures)
:19	Intro P3	Synthesizer riff with second bass pattern (4 measures)
:27	Verse 1	Vocal (28 measures: 12 + 8 + 8)
1:27	Chorus 1	Vocal (12 measures)
1:52	Verse 2	Vocal with synth voice, violins (28 measures: 12 + 8 + 8)
2:52	Chorus 2	Vocal with violins and choppy guitar (20 measures)
3:34	Chorus 3–1	Guitar solo (8 measures)
3:59	Vamp	Vocals to fade-out (28+ measures)
5:00	End	

Jackson obviously wrote the song as a vehicle for showing a tougher, more dramatic side of his stage character. His voice sounds angry and defiant throughout the song.

The infectious rhythmic feel of "Billie Jean" is as responsible for its success as its subject matter. Jackson conceived the basic drum pattern on a drum machine. It was supplemented by a live drummer on the recording. Two bass patterns were added next. The first is a constant patter of eighth notes, propelling the groove ever forward. The second bass pattern is a series of two accented notes, soon joined by a synthesizer chord riff.

Jackson begins the verse in the lower register of his voice. His vocal is laden with the shuddering vibrato and emotional hiccup fills that characterized his style from 1980 on. After four measures he is doubled by his own overdubbed voice an octave higher. In the chorus, the "Michael Jackson" choir blossoms into full harmony; the blend is sparkling and extremely precise.

In the second verse a synthesized vocal sound plays a counter line to Jackson's vocal. There are also a number of "Michaels" responding to the main vocal with echoed phrases from the verse. On the climbing portion at the end of the verse, a violin line replaces the synthesized vocal line. In the seventh and fifteenth measures of the chorus, the violins play a sweeping descending line between the vocal phrases.

A choppy electric guitar rhythm also begins to assert itself in the last portion of the second chorus. The guitar then plays an eight-bar solo based on that choppy rhythmic pattern. The vocals reenter at the halfway point in the chorus and continue with a vamp based on the chorus until the fade-out of the recording.

Madonna

Michael Jackson's female counterpart for superstar status in the 1980s was Madonna. Her persona seems ever changing, a confluence of different images, often contradictory. At first it seemed she would be another postdisco dance queen. Born Madonna Louise Veronica Ciccone in Rochester, Michigan, in 1958, she aspired to be a ballet dancer. She moved to New York in 1977 to study with

Pop diva phenomenon Madonna during her "Material Girl" era in the mid-1980s.

famed choreographer Alvin Ailey but soon got caught up in the disco scene. She teamed up with drummer Stephen Bray to write some dance-oriented material and got signed to Sire Records in 1982. "Borderline" was released in 1984 and was the beginning of a 17 top 10 hit streak.

At the end of 1984 *Like a Virgin* was released, produced by Niles Rodgers. The album sold millions on the strength of its two huge hit singles, the title track and "Material Girl." The infectious dance grooves were a big part of her success, but so was the image Madonna created. Arriving on the scene just as MTV was coming to power, she could sell a look and a character along with the music. She bared her famously flat tummy, an idea that was later imitated by music divas like Britney Spears, Christina Aguilera, and Shania Twain. She combined adolescent innocence with seething sexuality, earthy glamour with religious symbolism. With crucifixes hanging from her ears, she wore a belt buckle with the words "Boy Toy." These juxtapositions of imagery outraged and confused some audiences, particularly older observers. The Parents' Music Resource Center was alarmed at the influence Madonna had on her legions of young female fans. Italy, Madonna's ancestral home, bitterly protested her "Blonde Ambition" tour because of the show's objectionable religious allusions. Even though some felt that Madonna's show was exploitative and gratuitous, she and her fans understood the message of "sex as power" and using the power of sexuality as an aspect of women's liberation and empowerment.

Madonna also tried her hand at acting in motion pictures. She had a supporting but high-profile role in the 1985 film *Desperately Seeking Susan*. Her free-spirited and romanticized character amplified Madonna's music performance character and significantly propelled her to pop music stardom, and it landed her future film roles. Her two subsequent movies were not as successful, namely *Shanghai Surprise* and *Who's That Girl*. But with the 1990 *Dick Tracy* she truly began to garner Hollywood's respect. Playing the classic cop movie vamp, Breathless Mahoney, opposite Warren Beatty's Dick Tracy, Madonna portrayed her well-established ditsy blonde and savvy glamour girl combination. In 1992 she played a feisty baseball player along with a fine ensemble cast in *A League of Their Own*.

The 1991 documentary of her "Blonde Ambition" tour, *Truth or Dare*, and the 1993 thriller *Body of Evidence* demonstrated Madonna's continuing delving into the erotic, soon followed by an expensive, steel-bound soft pornography book, *Sex*, and an accompanying album, *Erotica*. By 1995, however, Madonna began transforming herself into a more mature, subdued actress and musical performer. She tirelessly campaigned for the leading role in the film version of Andrew Lloyd Webber's musical *Evita*, based on the life of Argentinian first lady Eva Peron. Met with favorable reviews, she sought the coveted Academy Award but won a Golden Globe instead. Yet even in this dramatic, almost operatic setting, there was still a consistency to Madonna's persona. Her Evita character was still

Listening Guide   22.2
"Like a Prayer" 4 beats per measure

TIME	FORM	EVENT DESCRIPTION
:00	Intro P1	A cappella choir (4 measures, out of tempo)
:22	Recitation	Solo voice and organ (4 measures)
:40	Groove	Synthesizer bass (4 measures)
:50	Chorus	(8 measures)
1:06	Verse	(16 measures)
1:40	Chorus	(8 measures)
1:57	Verse 2	(16 measures)
2:31	Chorus	(8 measures)
2:48	Chorus	(8 measures)
3:06	Groove	Based on recitation (4 measures)
3:14	Recitation	(8 measures)
3:31	Recitation	Extension (8 measures)
3:49	Coda	Choir (16 measures)
4:23	Groove	(16 measures)
4:58	Rec. ext.	(8 measures)
5:14	Coda	Choir and fade
5:32	End	

both glamorous and of suspect virtue, demonstrating how Madonna comfortably manipulated these conflicting characters as commodities.

Over her career Madonna has proven that she is far from an incompetent sexpot that her detractors might dismiss her to be. She has had a hand in the songwriting and production for a number of her albums. She has encompassed a number of stylistic genres, from techno-pop to power ballads, musical theater, 1960s girl group, to Latin-flavored music. She has survived every affront to the public, whether intentional or unintentional (the latter involving unearthed nude photo poses from her struggling modeling days). In 1992 she signed a multimillion dollar deal with Time Warner covering both movies and music. She also continues to present a multiplicity of images. Her early career was marked by *Truth or Dare* and a tumultuous marriage to the volatile actor Sean Penn. By the late 1990s, particularly with the release of *Evita* and the simultaneous birth of her daughter, Lourdes, Madonna had become the mom next door, married to filmmaker Guy Ritchie and appearing in homemaking magazine interviews touting the virtues of home life, marriage, and motherhood.

Analysis of "Like a Prayer" (*Like a Prayer*, CD format, Sire 2-25844)

Madonna's 1989 album *Like a Prayer* was her most ambitious album to date. She intended it to be a more serious, probing album, blending many disparate elements of rock and pop. The title track maintains a strong dance groove but also retains the religious imagery that was a part of her persona, in this case relating her sense of love to angels, a prayer, and the like. Enhancing the religious effect is the use of famous gospel composer and choir leader Andrae Crouch and a chorus of singers. There is also the use of churchlike organ at the beginning of the track. Underlying it all is a solid dance groove, created by synthesizers, guitars, and drum machines.

The construction of the song has four main parts. There is the typical verse and chorus, of course. At the beginning of the track is a section in a somber, minor key. This opens the song, first with the choir singing wordless harmony; then Madonna presents the melody. Since there is no tempo or groove stated at this point, it serves as sort of a prologue to the song proper. In the tradition of opera, a singer would often sing a portion out of tempo, a recitation, or *recitative,* followed by the main song, or *aria.* In that same spirit, this portion of "Like a Prayer" is labeled *recitation.* There are the usual verse/chorus alternations, then the recitation section returns in tempo. Madonna then extends the ideas with a rapid-fire melodic sequence. Finally, there is what is labeled here a *coda,* a musical term describing a new section that ends the piece; here it features the choir. The recitation extension is inserted before a repeat of the coda. The track fades during this second presentation of the coda.

Prince

Somewhere between the style and image of Michael Jackson and Madonna came Prince. Born to musical parents in Minneapolis in 1960, the workaholic boy genius was sort of a black Phil Spector. He came on the scene with *For You* in 1978 when he was only 18 years old. In the next few years Prince developed an image and musical leaning that was extremely eclectic. On the visual side he had the diminutive boyishness and sexual androgyny of Michael Jackson. His hair and clothing combined Little Richard, Sly Stone, Jimi Hendrix, and Louis XIV. Like Madonna, he combined religious imagery and fervor with explicit sexual expression. His band, the Revolution, was equally represented by men and women, blacks and whites. On the musical side Prince has proven to be a master of many varied styles, from dance-pop, techno, funk, guitar rock, power ballads, and soul. This eclecticism has made the character of his albums inconsistent, but he is probably one of the few producers who could get away with it.

Prince's first real success came with the double-album *1999,* released in 1983. Combining funk and dance pop with new wave synthesizer sounds, *1999* proved a more winning formula than his work to date. "Little Red Corvette" was a huge single hit from the album, as was the title track, which portrayed the end of the millennium as both apocalyptic and a time to party, in the spirit of "Eat, drink, and be merry, for tomorrow we die." The song resurged to become the virtual anthem of every New Year's Eve party in the year 1999.

1984, however, saw the peak of Prince's career. He released the film and the album *Purple Rain.* The film was essentially a long-form music video with Prince himself as star, and the album yielded an astonishing number of hit singles, with wide-ranging styles and production strategies. "Lets Go Crazy" combines funk with metal guitars. "When Doves Cry" is a minimalist throwback to psychedelia and does not use bass. "Computer Blue" uses robotic synth pop sounds. Prince intended the project to make him a superstar, a goal he apparently reached. *Purple Rain* eventually sold over 10 million copies in the United States and spent 24 weeks at number one.

Listening Guide   22.3
"Purple Rain" 4 beats per measure (occasional 2-beat measures)

ELAPSED TIME	FORM	EVENT DESCRIPTION
:00	Intro	Solo guitar
:18	Verse 1	Solo voice and drums enter (8.5 measures)
:53	Chorus 1	Violinlike guitar (8.5 measures)
1:29	Verse 2	More passionate solo voice; prominent violin/guitar (8.5 measures)
2:04	Chorus 2	Voices in harmony (8.5 measures)
2:40	Verse 3	Hysterical solo vocal (8.5 measures)
3:16	Chorus 3	Voices in harmony; piano more prominent (8.5 measures)
3:50	Solo	Guitar solo based on verse (16 measures)
4:59	Solo	Guitar solo with falsetto vocal (16 measures)
6:07	Coda	Floating, spacey held note, gradually winding down; strings and high piano
8:41	End	

The next year Prince produced the weighty concept album *Around the World in a Day* and continued with a number of successful projects. He became an in-demand producer and songwriter for other artists and projects as well, ranging from Madonna, to jazz legend Miles Davis, to providing music for the 1989 *Batman* movie. In 1986 he released an album with a cryptic symbol for its title. In 1993, after a long dispute with the Warner Bros. label, he legally changed his name to that symbol, and referred to himself as "The Artist Formerly Known as Prince." In 1994 he independently released the single "The Most Beautiful Girl in the World," his biggest hit in years and a promise of what he could do on his own. After fulfilling his Warner contract, he set up his own NPG label and released a sizable body of material, though he was plagued with distribution problems from his fledgling record company.

Analysis of "Purple Rain" (*Purple Rain*, CD format, Warner Bros. 7599 251102)

Purple Rain is Prince's most successful album; the film and movie made him a superstar in the mid-1980s. It demonstrates his command of a number of stylistic and production approaches to music.

The title cut, "Purple Rain," is a power ballad, heavily leaning toward the ballads of pop metal bands of the day. Prince's solo voice, the drums, and the guitars are heavily processed, giving the music a lonely, distant, and cavernous sound. On the verses Prince's vocal style is half spoken, half sung, reminiscent of Jimi Hendrix at times. He logically builds the intensity of his vocal delivery with each verse/chorus combination until, by the third verse, he is almost sobbing and hysterical with passion. On the second and third choruses, the vocal harmony is rich and strong. After three verse/chorus combinations, there is a metal ballad-style guitar solo that goes for a generous 32 measures at a very slow tempo. Halfway through, Prince's voice answers the guitar with high falsetto singing.

Rather than returning for a final verse and chorus, Prince chooses to have four more measures of a guitar solo, followed by powerful held notes from the guitars with no tempo. Over a two-minute long process, the held notes begin to die away and a tinkling, high piano riff is heard. It is almost like a soundtrack to a star exploding in space, its fragments gradually dissipating into the void.

Also notice in this piece that Prince does not use a conventional steady grouping of eight four-beat measures. Each verse and chorus has an extra two beats at the end of the eight-measure grouping. These 2/4 measures, as opposed to the more plentiful 4/4 measures, are indicated in the Listening Guide as *half measures* (hence 8.5 measures).

THE CONTINUANCE OF HEAVY METAL IN THE EIGHTIES

Along with the pop dominance of Michael Jackson, Madonna, and Prince, metal bands continued to thrive in the 1980s. At this point in the music's evolution two rather distinct schools of metal emerged. The first has been known as *pop metal* or, more derisively, *hair metal* because of the signature big teased hair of many of its artists. The genre was heavily centered in Los Angeles. The music had the trappings of aggressive, guitar-riff-based music, but it was carefully produced to keep it acceptable to a more mainstream public and to accommodate radio. Pop metal is probably more famous for its look than its music, but it was probably an apt focus since it emerged at the dawn of the MTV video age.

Pop metal had its roots in the glam rock of the 1970s (hence the hair and wild costumes) and was born from pioneering 1970s rock acts such as Alice Cooper and the New York Dolls. However, the granddaddy of all the 1970s acts would have to be Kiss. The group wore spacey black costumes, had big hair, and was clad in heavy makeup. Kiss had elaborate theatrics, utilizing pyrotechnics, moving stage sets, and even featuring Gene Simmons's prodigiously long tongue.

In the 1980s, one of the first big bands to continue and expand this tradition was Mötley Crüe. The band early on formed an infamous reputation, having frequent and highly publicized run-ins with the law and making controversial videos. One member, Tommy Lee, has also been famous for his relationships with actress Heather Locklear and *Baywatch* babe Pamela Anderson.

Twisted Sister was the band that most closely followed the lead of the New York Dolls. Led by lead singer Dee Snider, the band was a disconcerting blend of feminine makeup and hair combined with "wrestlemania" male aggression.

Metal band Def Leppard.

Other "makeup and hair" metal groups were Poison, Whitesnake, Ratt, and Judas Priest. Arguably, the biggest pop metal band was Def Leppard, hailing from Sheffield, England. The band toned down its sound from its Led Zeppelin roots and used good looks and video ingenuity to capitalize on the medium of MTV. The 1981 album *High and Dry* became the group's first platinum album in the United States, thanks to MTV's strong rotation of "Bringin' on the Heartbreak." The follow-up album, *Pyromania*, was produced by Mutt Lange, who would later marry and produce crossover country star Shania Twain (see Chapter 14). Once again Def Leppard had a blockbuster due to MTV's frequent airing of "Photograph" and "Rock of Ages." *Pyromania* eventually sold 10 million copies, establishing Def Leppard as one of the most popular bands in the world. One of the more inspiring aspects of the band was drummer Rick Allen, who lost his arm in a car accident but overcame his injury with a custom drum kit that allowed him to play with only one arm.

The other school of 1980s metal to emerge was *thrash* and *speed metal*. It is remarkable how this branch grew in popularity despite the dearth of radio airplay, a testament to the tenacity and loyalty of metal fans. This style grew out of the intense, pounding sound of punk. In the early days thrash and speed metal were the same thing. The music required virtuosic speed and used a percussive guitar technique done with the picking hand called *palm muting*. The most significant of the early bands of fuse punk with metal was the British band Motörhead, formed in 1975. They blended elements of British new wave with American influences, such as guitarist Ted Nugent and proto-grunge band the Ramones. As more bands grew from the root of Motörhead, the speed, technical facility, and unrelenting intensity required of speed metal proved too much for some bands, and they opted for more medium tempos and less dense solos.

The most influential heavy metal band of the 1980s was Metallica. This band had the pounding intensity of thrash and the technical facility of speed metal, but the musicians used all their resources thoughtfully in carefully crafted compositions. Metallica's 1986 *Master of Puppets* (CD format, Elektra 60439-2) is considered by critics to be the band's masterpiece and, by many, the greatest heavy metal recording ever made. The recording has great unity thematically and musically. Each track is lengthy and ambitious. Topics cover the hypocrisy of religious and political leaders, mental illness and drug use, and monsters. Lead guitarist Kirk Hammett was one of the most influential metal guitarists around, and drummer Lars Ulrich, in true speed metal fashion, could make the drums roar while offering intricate musical figures. In 2000 Metallica led the legal assault on the music-sharing computer software Napster (see Chapter 23), claiming that computer users were downloading thousands of the band's songs illegally.

Dave Mustaine, a veteran of Metallica, formed his own quartet in 1983. Megadeth had sharper instrumental skills, moved more toward the speed metal side, and leaned more toward themes of disillusion and nihilism with album titles such as *Killing Is My Business . . . and Business Is Good*; *Peace Sells, but Who's Buying*; and *So Far, So Good, So What*. In the early 1990s, with the onset of the popularity of grunge, Megadeth proved it could hold its own with its energetic, technically precise approach. Its 1992 album *Countdown to Extinction* entered the charts at number two and went double platinum.

THE CONTINUANCE OF "GOOD OLD ROCK AND ROLL"

In the midst of punk aggression and pop slickness there were rock artists who tapped into an old-school idealism, where the artists presented themselves unpretentiously and played an earthy, folksy style and presented messages of social commentary and change.

Perhaps Bruce Springsteen led the way (discussed in the previous chapter). Not possessing a spectacular voice and looking like a factory worker who just got off the night shift, Springsteen was a mirror and voice of the American urban, middle-aged working class. It seemed that superstardom was anathema to his values as an artist, and he would occasionally back off when his star was burning too brightly. A case in point: His 1980 album *The River* (CD format, Columbia C2K-36854) topped the charts and gave him his first top 10 hit, "Hungry Heart." Rather than seeking a formulaic follow-up, he retreated from his rising success and released the lower-keyed *Nebraska* in 1982. It was modestly produced, and Springsteen did not tour to promote it. Then 1984 saw the explosion of *Born in the U.S.A.*, which sold over 10 million copies, led to a two-year international tour, and lifted Springsteen to a stature of commercial success rivaling Michael Jackson and Madonna. His unprecedented success at this time prompted a desire for a live album and a retrospective collection of his performances to date. The result was a five-LP (three-CD) musical diary, *Bruce Springsteen and the E Street Band/Live 1975–85* (Columbia 65328), released in 1986. Typically, he followed up with a more introverted album, *Tunnel of Love*, in 1987.

There were other artists who connected with "just plain folks" in America. *All Music Guide* writer Stephen Thomas Erlewine aptly cites Huey Lewis and the News as "a bar band that made good."[1] Missing is the angst-ridden anthems of disillusionment found in youth-oriented bands. Instead we find unpretentious rocking out under themes of the workaday world ("Workin' for a Livin'," "Couple Days Off"), sports, and getting older ("Hip to Be Square"). To heck with heavy messages; the News was a good old "getting off work on Friday" party band with lighthearted, clever lyrics, great melodic hooks, and funny videos for music television. Even the most subversive song, "I Want a New Drug," is not what it seems. It is a humorous song in which Lewis states that he wants a drug that makes him feel "like I feel when I'm with you." The song did bring about some intrigue, however. In 1984 Huey Lewis sued Ray Parker, Jr., who wrote the theme for the popular movie comedy *Ghostbusters*, whose hook sounded suspiciously like the one in "I Want a New Drug." The suit was settled out of court.

Meanwhile across the Atlantic, the Irish band U2 became one of the most successful bands in rock history with characteristics that ran contrary to the success formulas of the time. The band was unpretentious and not glamorous. It was glib, passionately conveying messages of social justice and their Christian faith. Rather than centering on charismatic lead vocals or spectacular guitar solos, U2 relied more on an ensemble sound, with the heavily processed guitar providing more texture than lead.

Dublin pop group U2: Adam Clayton, Bono, The Edge, and Larry Mullen, Jr.

Formed in Dublin in 1976, U2 includes Bono (Paul Hewson), The Edge (David Evans), Adam Clayton, and Larry Mullen, Jr. They honed their skills and gained their success slowly through a relentless string of live gigs. After logically progressing through a series of increasingly popular albums, two monumental events launched U2 into super-stardom. The first was a spectacular live performance at the 1985 Live Aid concert at London's Wembley Stadium. The second was the 1987 release of the album *The Joshua Tree* (CD format, Island 90581-2). It was produced by Daniel Lanois, a French Canadian with a leaning toward an earthly, folk music approach, and Brian Eno, new wave producer who was more of an experimenter favoring atmospheric textures. Thematically, the album is dark, brooding, and somewhat fearful. It tapped more into American musical influences and images than U2's previous ventures and distilled wordy messages into more easily absorbed and memorable hook lines.

EIGHTIES SOFT ROCK AND NEW AGE

Soft rock continued to flourish in the 1980s. Barry Manilow and Barbra Streisand had run their course, but a variety of artists came to take their place. Central among these was Lionel Ritchie. He was part of the Motown soul-funk group the Commodores in the 1970s and embarked on a solo career in the eighties. He became a specialist in the rock love ballad, beginning with the theme for the puppy-love movie *Endless Love*. In 1982 he released his first solo album, *Lionel Ritchie*, containing three top five singles. In 1985 he co-wrote "We Are the World" with Michael Jackson. Produced by Quincy Jones, "We Are the World" was an ambitious single recording and music video bringing together an array of pop and rock stars that included Ray Charles, Bob Dylan, Stevie Wonder, and Bruce Springsteen. All sales proceeds went for famine relief in Ethiopia.

The unique soft rock phenomenon of the 1980s was *new age* music. New age is a confluence of many styles; the only overriding characteristic is its lightness. Dubbed "yuppie elevator music" by its detractors, new age became the easy-listening style for the baby-boomer generation. It emphasizes both synthesizers and acoustic folk instruments. The electronic side came from the repetitious minimalist compositions of Phillip Glass and new wave rockers like Brian Eno. The acoustic side features elements of world music styles using authentic folk instruments that are as repetitious and nonassertive as their electronic counterparts.

The primary merchant for new age music in the 1980s was Windham Hill Records, based in California and distributed by A&M Records. Their product was static and soothing, its value more therapeutic than musical. Their recordings of wind, surf, and forest noises achieved about the same effect. The music was so unassuming that its artists became as transparent as their product. Many of them became famous in name only, without anyone ever seeing their faces.

Charity Rock

The 1980s proved that many rock stars were willing to share their good fortune with those who had less. Government repression and lingering drought left thousands of people starving in Ethiopia. In South Africa blacks were victims of the dominant white culture's policy of apartheid. AIDS was spreading throughout the country, a situation treated with relative ambivalence by the government. Attention turned to the plight of the small family farm, which had fallen victim to big business and land development.

The catalyst for charity rock concerts was a series of concerts protesting the use of nuclear power in the late 1970s, most notably a concert at Madison Square

Garden in 1979. British rock musicians organized Band Aid in 1984 to support food relief in Ethiopia. The American counterpart was USA for Africa, the organization that implemented the funds raised by "We Are the World." The British and American rock communities were then combined in an ambitious 17-hour concert held simultaneously in Philadelphia and London, which were linked by satellite and broadcast to television audiences around the world.

Supporting concerns closer to home, country singer Willie Nelson and folk rocker John Cougar Mellencamp organized a 12-hour concert dubbed Farm Aid, intended to save family farms that were in danger of foreclosure. Though the concert did not attract the large audience that other causes mustered, it was reasonably successful in providing temporary relief to a few farmers.

Chapter Summary

With each passing decade of rock's history there is a broader audience for it, all faithful to a certain time in its history. The eighties proved to be a decade where dramatic innovation in style and technology coincided with a respect for the history and legacy of rock styles and their artists. Rock artists also matured enough in their public life to lend a hand to significant social causes around the world, causes such as Farm Aid and funds for AIDS research, relief for the homeless in America and starving people around the world.

The eighties were a time of dramatic technical advancements in music, particularly the development of drum machines; various analog, digital, and sampling synthesizers; the digital communications protocol MIDI that tied them all together with each other; and personal computers that could play them automatically. In the eighties the compact disc became the new standard in consumer media, though analog cassette tapes have remained popular, due in part to their widespread use in personal stereo systems.

Cable television spread to more homes in the eighties, offering a wide variety of programming. In this setting MTV got its start, proving to be the most significant entity rock television had ever seen.

There were rock superstars in the eighties. Some, like Madonna and Prince, were new faces on the scene, but Michael Jackson had been around for years. With a new look, a new sound, a new producer, and without his brothers, Jackson became an unprecedented success; his *Thriller* album becoming the all-time bestseller. Lionel Ritchie was the adult soft rock counterpart to Jackson; the two of them co-wrote the fund-raising song "We Are the World."

Heavy metal music continued to thrive in the 1980s, separating into two camps. Pop metal hair bands drew on the androgynous look of glam rock and offered lavish stage shows. They also got more radio airplay. Alternatively, thrash and speed metal bands drew more from the powerful pounding of punk but with more emphasis on fast, technical playing. Though they did not get as much airplay, bands like Metallica and Megadeth still had huge, faithful followings.

As baby boomers grew older, they needed their own brand of rock and roll, ranging from a more easy-listening sound offered by balladeers like Lionel Ritchie and from new age music, to bands that maintained a down-to-earth, unpretentious old-school rock sound. Bruce Springsteen hit his height of popularity in the 1980s with his working-class style of rock, as did the lighter messages and bar-band rock of Huey Lewis and the News. U2 brought folksy music with a message from Ireland.

Popular music was an important part for social causes in the 1980s. The "We Are the World" project and Live Aid concerts helped provide relief for famine and war-stricken countries, while other musical events helped with research for AIDS, the new disease of the eighties.

Additional Listening

Refer to discographical citations in the body of the chapter.

Wendy Carlos, *Switched-On Bach* (1968) (CD format, Columbia 63501). This album demonstrated the viability of synthesized music and the degree of expressiveness it could achieve. Carlos made follow-up albums of synthesized classical music and worked with filmmaker Stanley Kubrick, providing the soundtracks for his movies *A Clockwork Orange* and *The Shining*.

Review Questions

1. What is a synthesizer?
2. What is MIDI? How can the MIDI concept be applied to music as well as to other aspects of performance?
3. What does a synthesizer do when it samples a sound?
4. What were two advances in consumer product technology that rejuvenated the recording industry in the 1980s?
5. What was the musical reason given by MTV for not programming black artists in its early years? Why did British stars dominate the early music videos?
6. What were Michael Jackson's strategies in both his music and his appearance that led him to superstardom in the eighties?
7. How did Madonna vary and often combine disparate elements of musical style and image over her long and successful career?
8. What is the stylistic range of Prince's songwriting and production technique?
9. What were the two schools of heavy metal in the 1980s, and how could they be described?
10. What musical offerings in the 1980s appealed more to the aging baby boomers?
11. What musical products and events contributed to charitable causes in the 1980s?

Notes

1. Stephen Thomas Erlewine, "Huey Lewis," allmusic.com.

Chapter 23

Many Sounds from Many Places in the Nineties

It seems a strange coincidence that the beginning of the 1990s and the beginning of the new millennium were defined by American wars in the Middle East, and the country being led in the 1990s by President George Bush and some 10 years later by his son. On both occasions the United States was awash with patriotism. On both occasions country singer Lee Greenwood's flag-waver "God Bless the U.S.A." enjoyed a tremendous comeback. The first Middle East conflict was relatively brief, and the country returned more or less to normal; the second is still playing out as of this writing.

In popular music, light pop stars and metal *hair bands* dominated the business. As mentioned throughout this book, whenever music gets a little too slick, there is always some *garage band* movement, often from the hinterlands, to bring it back down to the earth. In the early 1990s the first major attack on glitzy pop came from America's Northwest.

GRUNGE

The Pacific Northwest, tucked away in the corner of the contiguous 48 states, seldom entered the collective consciousness of American popular culture. For many years the most notable entity in Seattle, Washington, was the Boeing airplane plant. In the last 20 years of the twentieth century, companies like Microsoft, Starbucks, and Amazon.com achieved equal or greater status in defining the Northwest corporate landscape. Beginning in the 1980s Seattle and Portland, Oregon, became a mecca for the yuppie generation and the dot-com boom, establishing a stereotype of young, latté-sipping, high-tech millionaires dwelling in a beautiful, rain-soaked environment.

In popular music the Northwest has made fitful but significant contributions. Crooner Bing Crosby was a native of Tacoma, Washington. Jazz and pop composer, arranger, and producer Quincy Jones was raised in Seattle. Ray Charles lived and worked there for a time. The Ventures, also from Tacoma, reached number two on the *Billboard* charts in 1960 with "Walk, Don't Run," a cover version of a song originally appearing on a Chet Atkins album. An instrumental *guitar band*, the group was usually heaped into the musical category of West Coast *surf music,* an image only strengthened when they performed the theme song for the 1960s television cop show *Hawaii Five-O.* Its influence was considerable, particularly in Japan, where it sold over 40 million records. Jimi Hendrix was a native of Seattle, but he achieved so little artistically or commercially during his childhood there, it would be incorrect to state that he created or reflected a local Northwest style of music. The pop group Heart (with singer-sisters Ann and Nancy Wilson) was from the Seattle suburb of Bellevue, though it deliberately marketed itself as being a band from Vancouver, British Columbia. (The Wilsons thought it sounded more exotic.)

However, the Northwest's greatest collective impact on the world of popular music came in the early 1990s. Lurking beneath the affluent, corporate, laid-back image was a disenfranchised, angry, and rebellious youth movement. The Northwest *grunge* style was not consciously honed in either music or fashion, but nevertheless it made a distinctive insurgence against the corporate pop music juggernaut and Reagan/Bush sociopolitical climate that reigned at the end of the 1980s. This grassroots music became a voice for youth angst everywhere.

The spirit and style influence on 1990s Northwest rock can be traced to punk and new wave rock of the late 1970s, with a distinction given to the Ramones, the group critic Stephen Thomas Erlewine declares as the first punk rock band. The antiart, anticorporation, anticonformist spirit of these bands was as much an influence on the culture as the music. Underground bands blossomed throughout the region, nurtured by campus radio stations featuring *independent* or *alternative* music (KAOS out of Evergreen State College in Olympia; KCMU out of the University of Washington in Seattle); indie-friendly music newspapers and magazines such as *The Rocket;* local record labels, particularly Sub Pop (short for Subterranean Pop), an extension of a homemade local music magazine; and a group of dilapidated clubs in the Puget Sound region.

The first band to make Sub Pop a significant underground label was Green River. According to member Jeff Ament, its influences included metal bands, punk, and the Ramones. It ventured to merge heavy metal with a deliberately crude, ugly sound and offensive presentation. This merger was significant since many of the punks in the Northwest condemned metal bands as slick, commercial, and cliché. Ganglike fights broke out in urban clubs when metal and post-punk fans clashed. Green River only lasted four years (1984–1988), but it established the grunge, punk/metal aesthetic, and veteran members went on to form other significant Northwest bands such as Mudhoney and Mother Love Bone, the latter eventually becoming Pearl Jam.

The breakout band was Soundgarden. It formed in 1984, recorded its first EP for Sub Pop in 1987, and then became the first Northwest band to record for a major label (A&M) when *Louder than Love* was released in 1990. Soundgarden had a characteristic blend of Led Zeppelin/Black Sabbath metal style and experimental, grinding Sub Pop elements. It was hawked by the marketing forces as a metal band and was teamed up with Guns 'N Roses on a 1991 tour. The category stuck when they won Grammys in the hard rock and heavy metal categories for their album *Superunknown,* released in 1994. The album presents songs of deep depression, sophomoric humor, and, above all, assaulting sound. *Superunknown* represented the peak of Soundgarden's success. The group amicably disbanded in 1997 to pursue other interests.

The next great Northwest band to equal the stature of Soundgarden, plus give the movement its first mythic hero, was Nirvana. Kurt Cobain and Chris (also known as Krist) Novoselic grew up in Aberdeen, Washington, but nurtured their music in the vibrant underground music scene of Olympia, the state capital about 60 miles to the east. Cobain had a traumatic upbringing. His parents divorced when he was eight and he lived with different relatives throughout his life; coupled with manic depression, chronic physical problems, and drug addiction, these devastating experiences worked their way into many of Cobain's songs. Growing up, he listened to the Beatles, metal, and punk. In Olympia he was influenced by a local band, the Melvins.

Nirvana recorded its first album, *Bleach*, for Sub Pop. It was recorded for a budget of 600 dollars and was released in 1989. It sold a respectable 30,000 copies and was a local hit on college radio. Its success led to the signing with DGC, a major label, and the release of *Nevermind* in 1991, finally locking in Dave Grohl as the group's drummer. Compared to *Bleach*, the sound was polished and sparkling, but the group's stylistic values were still deeply embedded in indie rock and an aversion for cliché, corporate pop metal. In fact, Cobain complained to the *Los Angeles Times* that "It [*Nevermind*] ended up too commercial and slick," and members were quoted as saying they wanted to follow it up with a "real punk record," the result being *In Utero* from 1993.

Being totally detached from the music industry, both geographically and philosophically, the Northwest music collective suddenly found itself unwittingly drawn into a tide of national fame. The youthful pain, sarcasm, and raw musical crudeness became the voice of a generation. Kurt Cobain was emblematic of the ironic circumstances in which the music and musicians found themselves and how they struggled with it. He could not reconcile that he was becoming rich and famous by rebelling against wealth and fame. In 1993 he took his own life (for reasons only partly musical), adding him to the long list of rock martyrs who died too young.

The dark star of the Northwest grunge group Nirvana, Kurt Cobain.

As mentioned earlier, Pearl Jam was formed from Mother Love Bone upon the death of lead singer Andrew Wood. Stone Gossard and Jeff Ament imported San Diego vocalist Eddie Vedder. It became the most successful of all the Northwest bands and spawned many imitators, most notably Stone Temple Pilots. Vedder's distinctive vocal and enunciation style is found among many rock singers of the nineties. Pearl Jam had postpunk grunge elements but clearly leaned toward early metal bands like Led Zeppelin and Black Sabbath. It had a bigger sound than groups like Nirvana (there were, after all, more people in the band), and Vedder's big voice was closer to the macho style of metal vocalists. The group displayed values of other Northwest bands, particularly the battle against the corporate music world and the aversion to their inevitable success. When the band released its 1993 album, *Vs.,* it would not put the title on any of the packaging and refused to issue singles or videos related to the album. In 1994 Pearl Jam refused to play arena-sized venues and canceled a tour to protest the high ticket prices Ticketmaster imposed upon fans. It waged an unsuccessful court battle against the ticket broker. Without compromising its business practices, the group still went multiplatinum with the 1994 album *Vitalogy.* (Nonetheless, accusations of selling out occasionally surfaced, particularly from Nirvana's Kurt Cobain, who maintained a long-running feud with Pearl Jam.) In 1995 the band collaborated with veteran rocker Neil Young, categorized by some rock historians as a protopunk artist, on the album *Mirror Ball.* Pearl Jam toured Europe and the United States extensively in 2000 and, in order to discourage bootleg recordings, issued an astounding 72-volume series of live concert recordings.

Analysis of "Smells Like Teen Spirit" (*Nevermind*, CD format, DGC 24425)

"Smells Like Teen Spirit" is arguably the most influential early recording in the Northwest style popularly known as grunge. Combined with Nirvana's music video, the imagery of the outsider and his dark, cynical view of the world connected with the youth of that generation. Cobain's lyric has no particular story line or theme, but the disparate phrases of text are unified by their brooding imagery of alienation, self-loathing, and disdain for those who love attention and popularity.

The presentation is raw, simple, and direct by design, reflecting the desire of Nirvana and like-minded groups to present a music long on power and short on high production. Nevertheless, Cobain complained that he thought the album, in the hands of the major-label producers, was too commercial.

Even with just a trio of instruments and a solo singer, the band achieves a wide range of volume and textures. The opening guitar riff sets the mood of isolation and intensity. Cobain's voice on the verses has an airy, meditative quality, very lonely in character. In the second half of each verse the band builds methodically to the chorus. On the chorus the group explodes into a rage, with Cobain kicking into a virtual scream.

The second verse/chorus cycle is virtually identical to the first. A guitar solo is then played over a half-length version of the verse. When Cobain comes back for the third verse, he has rightly intensified the softer vocal style of the first two verses to help the overall performance grow and evolve. After the third chorus, Cobain keeps repeating his last phrase in an emotional climax that is ended by a power chord in the guitar.

Listening Guide   23.1
"Smells Like Teen Spirit" 4 beats per measure

ELAPSED TIME	FORM	EVENT DESCRIPTION
:00	Intro	Electric guitar alone (4 measures)
:08	Intro	Drums and distorted electric guitar enter (4 measures)
:18	Intro	Band gets softer, bass plays intro riff with sporadic guitar (4 measures)
:26	Verse 1	Cobain enters with soft, airy, but intense, vocal (8 measures)
:42	Verse 1	Vocals sing a two-note riff; band begins driving rhythm harder toward the chorus (8 measures)
:59	Chorus 1	Cobain's voice becomes more screamlike, loud, distorted guitar reenters on main riff heard on intro and verse; the two-bar melody repeated six times (12 measures)
1:23	Chorus 1	A short figure played by distorted guitar, bass, and drums, answered with a bent note by solo nondistorted guitar (4 measures)
1:31	Interlude	Band gets softer leading into second verse, similar to :08 time line above (4 measures)
1:39	Verse 2	See :26 time-line description (8 measures)
1:55	Verse 2	See :42 time-line description (8 measures)
2:12	Chorus 2	See :59 time-line description (12 measures)
2:36	Chorus 2	See 1:23 time-line description (4 measures)
2:44	Verse	Guitar solo based on both parts of verse melody, modified to half the length (8 measures)
3:00	Interlude	Solo guitar holds out his last note while the band gets softer (4 measures)
3:09	Verse 3	Cobain's voice is more strained (8 measures)
3:25	Verse 3	See :42 time-line description (8 measures)
3:41	Chorus 3	See :59 time-line description (12 measures)
4:05	Chorus 3	Last of chorus melody is repeated 8 times; on the ninth time a final note is held out (9 measures)
4:33	End	

POSTPUNK OUTSIDE THE NORTHWEST

In the postpunk period of the 1980s Minneapolis proved to be an important center for American alternative music, yielding the Replacements and Hüsker Dü. The latter was the first significant postpunk American band. They maintained the primary punk aesthetic of loud, raw rock and biting lyrics. They also included lengthy, probing instrumentals that last as long as 20 minutes. They created a huge local following, influencing almost all local punk bands. With relentless touring they expanded their influence throughout the college-radio alternative underground. They became the first of these postpunk bands to sign a contract with a major label, releasing *Candy Apple Grey* on Warner Brothers in 1986. Substance abuse, internal friction, and suicide ultimately brought about the band's demise in 1988.

Meanwhile, in Athens, Georgia, the band R.E.M. married the southern rock tradition with a postpunk sensibility. Initiating a style known by some as jangle-pop, characterized by a strummed, chiming guitar style reminiscent of folk-rock

R.E.M.'s lead singer Michael Stipe performing at the Rock in Rio 3 Music Festival in Rio de Janeiro, January 13, 2001.

of the 1960s, R.E.M. showed roots in the Beatles, the Byrds, and Creedence Clearwater Revival. The group's 1982 EP *Chronic Town* established the folk and garage rock blend that became its signature sound. Lead singer Michael Stipe had a low, droning voice that blended into the instrumental texture, often obscuring the lyrics. When the lyrics to later albums became more sociopolitical in nature, Stipe pushed the vocals farther out to make their important messages more understandable. R.E.M. signed with the Warner Brothers label and released the album *Green* in 1988. The 1991 album *Out of Time* demonstrated and expanded instrumentation, including strings, horns, a female vocal group, and various country strings. It also marked a return to more personal and less political topics, resulting in the masterpiece "Losing My Religion." With 1994's *Monster*, R.E.M. went back to a more traditional rock band format. R.E.M. was on the ground floor with Hüsker Dü in establishing American postpunk, but whereas Hüsker Dü was relatively short-lived and financially unsuccessful, R.E.M. has proven to be one of the most popular bands for 20 years.

Where postpunk often combines humorous silliness with darkness and self-loathing, the subgenre known as *industrial rock* is even more intense. Katherine Charlton states that the style grew out of the industrial working class in England and the United States.[1] The *All-Music Guide* states that industrial rock grew out of the electronic experiments of the mid-1970s bands such as Throbbing Gristle and that the term was coined from the latter's label, Industrial Records. Chicago's Big Black was exemplary of the extremes of the style. The group used a drum machine to achieve a mechanical character devoid of emotion. Instruments and other sound sources were chosen primarily for the amount of noise they could make. Steve Albini's guitar was thin, metallic, and grinding. The vocals were distorted and the lyrics were relentless and grotesque. It could easily be the most nihilistic band of the mid-eighties. Ministry was another important Chicago industrial band. In Cleveland, Nine Inch Nails, a band of one (vocalist Trent Reznor), blended industrial punk with 1970s mainstream progressive rock. N.I.N.'s 1994 album *The Downward Spiral* included former King Crimson guitarist Adrian Belew. One of Trent Reznor's discoveries was Marilyn Manson, a group that opened for N.I.N.'s 1994 spring tour. With elaborate makeup and a gothic rock presentation, Marilyn Manson's nihilistic, satanic presentation made it one of the most controversial rock acts of the 1990s.

Analysis of "Terrible Lie" (*Pretty Hate Machine*, CD format, TVT 2610–2)

The album *Pretty Hate Machine* was frugally produced in a Cleveland studio, almost entirely done by Trent Reznor, with Richard Patrick on guitar. Due in part to the industrial style of the music, and probably for reasons of limited finances as well, the music is generated mostly by synthesizers and drum machines. The

Listening Guide   23.2
"Terrible Lie" *4 beats per measure*

ELAPSED TIME	FORM	EVENT DESCRIPTION
:00	Intro	Electronic "gunshots" echo; drums lead into verse (4 measures)
:11	Verse 1	Vocal alternates with two-note guitar riff; vocal is restrained, getting louder just before the chorus (8 measures)
:32	Chorus 1	Vocal has screaming, group sound; soaring long notes layered over ostinato (8 measures)
:54	Verse 2	Similar to Verse 1 but with added repeated note on right channel; intermittent whisperlike sounds in the background (8 measures)
1:16	Chorus 2	See :11 time-line description (8 measures)
1:38	Interlude	Begins with drum riffs and whispering voice; builds to screams with added synthesizer textures (16 measures)
2:21	Verse 3	Similar sound to first two verses; Reznor alters the melody quite a bit (8 measures)
2:43	Chorus 3	See :11 time-line description (8 measures)
3:06	Chorus 4	Another vocal layer added over the regular vocal riff (8 measures)
3:27	Chorus 5	Distorted synthesizer riff played over chorus riff; whispered vocal in background (8 measures)
3:48	Chorus 6	Synthesizer riff continues, vocal in conversational voice layered over whispered voice (8 measures)
4:10	Chorus 7	Continuation of Chorus 6 sounds (8 measures)
4:31	Ending	Beat suddenly stops, leaving a synthesizer hanging over; sound fades out
4:37	End	

guitar is used sparingly and mostly for texture rather than as a rhythmic tool or dominant solo instrument. This album was virtually ignored upon its release in 1989 and met with hostile critical response. However, it garnished a cult following among fans because of its unique presentation of industrial-style rock. Instead of relentless mechanical repetition, Reznor's music used memorable riffs and verse/chorus song structures, even softer balladlike songs. Reznor also tapped into the Generation X aesthetic in his lyrics and vocal style. His songs are filled with angst and betrayal, obsession and disillusionment, expressing mistrust of lovers, religion, and society.

"Terrible Lie" uses a lot of *gated* sounds, an electronic effect whereby the sound of a natural instrument in a natural space—for instance, a snare drum in a large room with a long reverberation time—is chopped off artificially before it has a chance to fully decay to silence. The song opens with electronic drum sounds, sharp snare drum–based sounds processed to sound like gunshots or pile drivers. They bounce back and forth stereophonically, adding to the artificial, mechanized sound of the music.

For the verses Reznor uses a vocal sound of constrained rage, which is always unleashed just before going into the chorus. It is as if with each verse/chorus cycle he makes himself mad all over again. The verse has a sparse background, defined mostly by the distorted guitar and drums playing a sharp two-note figure alternating with the vocal.

The choruses are fuller in texture, with a constant drum groove, long, rich notes from the synthesizers both in the low and high range, and with Reznor using his more screaming vocal style.

After the first two verse/chorus cycles Reznor's interlude creates a long, methodical buildup, beginning with just the drums, adding whispers, then moderately intoned vocals, and more synthesizer sounds. These additions come in four-measure intervals.

Like in any good song, the third verse is more intense than the first two, made possible by Reznor's twisting of the verse's melody. The third verse is followed by a succession of four choruses, each one adding layers of vocal and synthesizer textures. At the song's end a sharp chord is struck, leaving a soft, sustaining synthesizer chord to linger and die away.

RAP AND HIP HOP FROM THE TOP

At first, hip hop was a music culturally bound and isolated to the black inner city. Because it was characterized by rhythmic speech and repetitive underlying riffs, many observers did not even consider it music. But in the last 20 years of the twentieth century, rap and hip hop became the most powerful popular music force of all, crossing every cultural and geographic boundary and conveying every kind of message. It eventually earned its own category for the Grammy awards and came to practically dominate MTV. Though it reached its greatest strength to date in the 1990s, it is important to look back at the beginnings of this American music phenomenon.

Hip hop began with Jamaican-born Kool Herc (Clive Campbell), who moved to New York in 1967. He aspired to be a disc jockey but, in this highly competitive field, wanted to distinguish himself from the pack. He did so by choosing to play the most obscure dance music records he could find. Rather than emphasizing the vocal portion of the song, he focused on the instrumental vamp portion of the records. Through virtuoso manipulation of multiple turntables, he extended and blended *breaks* from different recordings. *Breakdancing,* an equally virtuosic dance style, evolved around the music. These breaks were similar to *dub plates,* or *versions,* used by Jamaican DJs. Another Jamaican similarity was the neighborhood street performance setting by DJs, tapping into electrical power from light poles to power their sound systems. At this point the proto–hip hop music was primarily a combination of funk, soul, and R&B music.

In the 1970s part of the hip hop agenda was to reclaim black youth music from the star musicians of disco and return it to the street level. This grassroots movement against the star system and the corporate music machine put hip hop in a similar sociomusical class with punk and its successors, alternative and grunge. A fashion statement also grew around the aesthetic, with ghetto kids wearing expensive sneakers and sportswear far beyond their economic means. In this way ghetto kids mocked affluent suburbanites.

Two other important early hip hop DJs were Afrika Bambaataa and Grandmaster Flash. Bambaataa was founder of the New York–based Zulu Nation, a community service and arts organization that combated gang culture by turning urban youth to more creative things like music and dance. It is indicative of the fact that early hip hop was conceived to have a positive effect on the black urban community, offering youth another way to compete than through gang violence. Grand-

**Rap pioneer
Grandmaster Flash
(center).**

master Flash and his student Grandwizard Theodore developed the hip hop technique of *scratching*, manually working the turntable platter back and forth with the stylus on a vinyl record to create a rhythmic noise.

Technically, *rapping* is a rhythmic recitation done over hip hop music; rap is not a style in and of itself, though *rap* and *hip hop* are commonly used interchangeably to name the music. Similar practices to rapping are found throughout African-American music history. In Africa *griots* (priest poets) recited the history of their people in speech-song. In the United States, there were colorful rhythmic poems known as *toasts*. Antecedents of rapping can even be found in the boastful renderings by prizefighter Mohammed Ali in the 1960s. Though similar to these traditions, rapping was ultimately self-developed and was yet another virtuoso element of the urban DJ's performance arsenal. It developed from the practice of *MCing*, talking to the audience between or during the playing of records at dance events. MCing could be done either by the DJ or someone else brought onto the performance expressly for that purpose. From announcements, to improvised rhythmic introductions to songs, to rhythmic recitations over the breaks, MCing became an art form in itself, eventually known as rapping.

During its folk phase in the mid-1970s, these DJ performances were only preserved on recordings in the form of *mix tapes*, homemade tapes made at the dances. Hip hop officially went to vinyl in 1979 with the Sugarhill Gang's "Rapper's Delight," released by the Sugarhill record label. Sugarhill became the important independent label for New York hip hop, much as the Sub Pop label promoted Northwest *grunge*. Clocking in at over 17 minutes in length, largely improvised, and done in a single take, "Rapper's Delight" was not necessarily the best representation of the genre at the time, but it made hip hop an instant international phenomenon. Soon came vinyl recordings by Grandmaster Flash, the Furious Five, and Kurtis Blow (Kurt Walker).

In the meantime hip hop was moving out of the clubs and streets of the Bronx and Queens and into the more affluent New York borough of Manhattan. It first appeared at the trendy Mudd Club, then the Negril, the Danceteria, and the Roxy (the old Negril). New wave music celebrities such as Talking Heads and

Run-D.M.C., the rap group that combined elements of hip hop and guitar-dominated heavy metal.

Blondie were impressed by the emerging style and used their influence to showcase it to the world. Blondie recorded "Rapture," released in 1981, which included a rap tribute to Fab Five Freddy.

The next step in hip hop's development was a technological one. Inspired by techno new wave bands Yellow Magic Orchestra and Kraftwerk, Afrika Bambaataa sought to develop a black electronic music. "Planet Rock" was released in 1982 and inspired several electro groups and several substyles in the 1980s and 1990s: Detroit techno, Miami bass, and to some extent, Chicago house. "The Adventures of Grandmaster Flash on the Wheels of Steel," from 1981, was the first hip hop record to employ *sampling,* using digital snippets from many disparate recordings and mixing them together. "The Message" was one of the first hip hop records to use a drum machine and synthesizer bass.

Beyond its technical aspects, "The Message" offered another hip hop innovation. The genre had previously been considered light party music with bragging dance lyrics; but "The Message" was the first real venture into lyrics on social issues. Rapper Melle Mel delivered a scathing commentary on inner-city life.

Run-D.M.C. would take hip hop to the next level of recognition and popularity. Its members successfully married the honesty of real street hip hop with rock elements, including a prominent use of guitar on their big hits "Rock Box" and "King of Rock." Their record sales were unprecedented in hip hop. As rappers they crossed over to mainstream television, appearing on *American Bandstand,* MTV, and Live Aid. Over the years the group adopted more R&B and funk elements and, after a couple of members had a bout with substance abuse, added Christian themes to their music.

Analysis of "King of Rock" (*King of Rock*, CD format, Profile 1205) (remastered and reissued on Profile/Arista 16407)

Run-D.M.C. was a pioneering rap group that successfully fused rap with heavy metal riffs and distorted electric metal-style guitar. *King of Rock* was the group's second highly successful album, paving the way for their mainstream crossover

Listening Guide   23.3
"King of Rock" 4 beats per measure

TIME	FORM	EVENT DESCRIPTION
:00	Section 1	Solo voice over bass drum and snare; voices shout on every beat (4 measures)
:10	Section 2	Higher solo voice enters; guitar riff introduced with an intermittent drum beat (4 measures)
:19	Section 3	Drum solo, 2, measures; distorted guitar solo over guitar riff with full drums, 8 measures (10 measures)
:44	Section 4	Solo voices trade off 4 measures each; guitar growls and screams long notes, 2 measures (10 measures)
1:08	Section 5	Solo voices trade off more frequently, usually two beats apart, 6 measures; drum solo, 4 measures (10 measures)
1:32	Section 6	Voices, 4 measures; guitar riff, 4 measures (8 measures)
1:52	Section 7	Alternating voices, 4 measures; drum solo of bass drum and cymbal, 2 measures (6 measures)
2:06	Section 8	Voice with drums, 4 measures; voice with guitar riff, 4 measures (8 measures)
2:25	Section 9	Guitar solo (4 measures)
2:35	Section 10	Alternating voices over guitar riff (12 measures)
3:05	Section 11	Guitar solo over riff (4 measures)
3:15	Section 12	Voices, 6 measures; guitar solo over drum, 2 measures; solo over guitar riff, 2 measures (10 measures)
3:39	Section 13	Alternating voices (12 measures)
4:10	End	

third album, *Raising Hell,* featuring their collaboration with metal band Aerosmith on a cover of the latter's "Walk This Way." The lyric of the song "King of Rock" features heavy band bragging in the tradition of first-generation rappers like Grandmaster Flash but with a tougher edge that paved the way for political rappers of the future.

"King of Rock" features a slow, grinding drum beat and a two-measure metal guitar riff. It has no traditional verse/chorus form or other clearly contrasting sections marked by a change of harmony or melody, but there is a consistent form of a sort. In general, a *section* of the song is defined by a rap of four to eight measures, followed by an instrumental response of some kind. Changes of sound and texture between sections are achieved in a number of ways. Sometimes only the drums are heard, guitar solos come in and out, sometimes over the basic riff melody and sometimes not. The voices sometimes appear in a solo presentation; at other times, the rap lyric is passed from one vocalist to another, then done together in rapid succession. One solo voice is high and light; the other is deeper and more robust.

Run-D.M.C. was a product of Def Jam Records, the next important hip hop label after Sugarhill. White co-owner Rick Rubin, a former punker, was out to have hip hop appeal to as many people as possible, including young whites. To that end Rubin signed an all-white rap group, the Beastie Boys. Beginning their career in New York as a punk act, the Beastie Boys kept the snotty attitude of punk in their hip hop and again proved how closely related hip hop and punk were aesthetically. Their 1986 *Licensed to Ill* album was the first hip hop record to top the *Billboard* charts, despite the controversy that they were cultural pirates and their stage antics were vulgar and testosterone-driven.

Def Jam's next triumph was Public Enemy. Carrying the street-life topic of "The Message" several steps further, Public Enemy addressed police brutality, gang violence, drug addiction, and the ambivalence toward the black community by every institution, from public emergency services to record companies. Underneath Chuck D and Flavor Fav's virtuoso raps were sampled funk groove loops, synthesizer hits, and grating shrieking noises. The macho attitude was definitely in place. Chuck D used as his musical sources anything his girlfriend hated; Def Jam cofounder Russell Simmons called it *black punk rock.* It all seemed to come together in the 1988 album *It Takes a Nation of Millions to Hold Us Back.* Using a production team called the Bomb Squad, the music was dense and intense, used intricate technology, and was deeply funky. It was faster and more shrieking than the slow and low productions of earlier Def Jam productions. It was also perhaps the first album-oriented performance by a hip hop group, with each piece being unified thematically. It was the first real grown-up rap.

West Coast Hip Hop

West Coast hip hop began much later than its New York counterpart. The MTV program *Yo! MTV Raps* spread the gospel of East Coast hip hop most effectively. Early West Coast artists like Ice-T first cut their teeth on hip hop by improvising over East Coast hip hop recordings. Ice-T helped to identify a distinctive West Coast style with his 1986 "Six 'n the Morning," inspired by Philadelphia *gun rap,* and soon developing the West Coast's signature *gansta rap,* dealing more flagrantly with topics of drugs and gang violence.

From Compton, California, came the group N.W.A. (Niggaz with Attitude). Its 1989 *Straight Out of Compton* album was the height of rap rebellion, profanity, violent stories, and hostility toward women. The group's lead rapper, Ice Cube, soon left to pursue a career as a solo artist, utilizing Public Enemy's Bomb Squad for his debut album. The formation of *gansta rap* found its most profound context in 1991. Los Angeles police officers were caught on an amateur videotape beating black motorist Rodney King. When they were acquitted a year later, riots exploded in the city. Ice-T released "Cop Killer," but public outcry was so severe that he eventually deleted it from future copies of the album *Body Count.*

Not every hip hop artist was moving toward obscene or violent subjects. MC Hammer, of Oakland, California, had grown up with church music and wanted to create a style around lighter topics and an entertaining, dance-oriented presentation modeled after the Jackson Five and others of earlier years. His 1990 "U Can't Touch This" was a hooklike rap over a sample of funk star Rick James's "Superfreak," and the phrase "U Can't Touch This" took its place among short-lived trendy popular phrases along with Wendy's "Where's the Beef?" and Steve Martin's "Well, excuuuuse me." Many considered Hammer a sellout, certainly the first time a rapper was seen on a television commercial endorsing KFC chicken. Nevertheless, Hammer brought a nonthreatening brand of hip hop to a large segment of the public fearful of angrier, less family-oriented presentations.

Hammer certainly didn't initiate any widespread reforms regarding wholesomeness in hip hop. A Miami group, 2 Live Crew, released their controversial *As Nasty as They Wanna Be* in 1989, the first recording ever to be officially designated by a court as obscene. Though the ruling was overturned, it brought up issues of First Amendment rights, exposure of such material to young people, and the music industry's liability in releasing such material. Written off as a party-oriented, sexual-bragging "booty band," 2 Live Crew may never have gained such notoriety had it not been for the public alarm and official legal reaction surrounding *As Nasty as They Wanna Be.*

Then there was Snoop Doggy Dogg, a former drug dealer from the Long Beach Crips gang and an artist for Death Row Records. He appeared on Dr. Dre's album *The Chronic,* released in 1992. The album moved from the stripped-down street sound to more funk grooves and the use of real guitars, pianos, bass, and drum machine figures more like a real drummer would play. Just prior to the release of his *Doggystyle* album in 1993, Snoop Doggy Dogg was arrested on first-degree murder charges (later released). It added to the reality of his lyrics and ultimately enhanced his career. Other hip hop artists involved with crime activities included Tupac Shakur and Biggie Smalls. Tupac was convinced that Biggie had tried to have him killed, and he was indeed shot to death in 1996. Smalls met the same fate a year later. Following their deaths, not necessarily due to them, gangsta rap began to fade. However, controversial rap has lived on in new substyles such as *thug rap* and with performers such as Eminem.

Marshall Mathers (hence M & M, or Eminem) spent his youth migrating with his mother between Kansas City and Detroit to live with relatives. He grew up with hip hop, aspiring to become a great hip hop artist. Dr. Dre discovered the white youth through his "Slim Shady" EP and his second place title at the 1997 Rap Olympics in Los Angeles. Eminem's 1999 *Slim Shady LP,* on the Interscope label, went triple platinum. *The Marshall Mathers LP* may have been the fastest-selling rap album ever. He is the most significant white rapper to date, a popular phenomenon respected within the hip hop industry. He has continued his association with Dr. Dre, appearing as one of many guests on *Dr. Dre 2001.*

Eminem has also been one of the most controversial rap artists to date. His lyrics have reached such violent and hateful proportions as to be viewed as almost cartoonish. Of particular concern were his attacks on homosexuals, creating an equal backlash from the gay community. As the gay controversy reached its peak, Eminem appeared in performance with Elton John, rock elder statesman and homosexual, at the 43rd Grammy awards show on February 1, 2001. This was not a first for Sir Elton, previously performing with the group Guns 'N Roses in 1992. The band's song "One in a Million" from its EP *GNR Lies* was hostile toward gays. The song John and Eminem performed, "Stan," was not about gay issues but about an obsessed fan. The symbolism of the performance was not altogether clear. The intent seemed to lean toward showing the sensitive side of Eminem and that his venomous persona was just an act. Not that it seemed to set Eminem on any path of reform. He has admitted that he would never let his own daughter listen to any of his music.

Hip hop and rap has spread out to encompass many value systems and communities. It began as a music of pride and escapism, then to an expression of social outrage, and even to a depiction, and sometimes advocation, of illicit behavior. *Screwed* music originated in Houston, Texas, and is named after its creator DJ Screw, born Robert Earl Davis, a local hip hop producer. His innovation, dating back to 1989, was to slow tracks down, like a tape running at too low a speed. Often the reference in Screw's tape production was to codeine cough syrup, referred to as "Barr," "drank," or "lean." It glorified the use of the substance, which consumers would either drink straight or mix with soda, wine, or anything else they wanted to taste. In 2001 illegal use of codeine as a party drug was on the rise, with a pint fetching as much as 500 dollars. The music and the practice of getting high on codeine has spread beyond Houston. Ironically, DJ Screw died in November 2000 at the age of 29 from a codeine overdose.

Women Rappers

It would seem that hip hop was male-dominated in its early years. Its macho posturing and disrespect toward women, however exaggerated, was pervasive. Yet women were intrigued by the genre and wanted a piece of the action, either to show they could be just as tough as the men, to offer a rebuttal to some of the male domination in the songs, or just to pursue hip hop as a new creative vehicle in popular music.

One of the first significant women in hip hop was Queen Latifah. Born Dana Owens in 1970, Latifah started with a loose hip hop coalition called Native Tongues Posse and a group called Ladies Fresh. Her 1989 debut album *All Hail the Queen* yielded the single "Ladies First." It was recorded with England-born rapper Monie Love (born Simone Johnson in 1970) and was the most significant feminist hip hop recording to date. There had been a number of "answer" recordings from women rap artists earlier in the decade, but nothing that inspired pride in the female audience and challenged the role of women in hip hop the way "Ladies First" did. Latifah has since expanded her career as an actress and talk-show host.

Salt-N-Pepa has been the most enduring of all female rap groups. The girl trio format is reminiscent of 1960s groups like the Supremes, the Ronettes, and the like, and those acts are certainly evident in Salt-N-Pepa's repertoire and stylistic makeup. They first emerged in 1986 with *Hot, Cold, and Vicious,* one of the many female hip hop rebuttals to lyrics by male rappers. With their sexy image, light party lyrics, and accessible music style, it was believed that the group would be a quickly passing fad, but it has shown its staying power. After signing with Polygram Records, the group released *Very Necessary* in 1993. The album, particularly its single "Shoop," reached number four on the pop charts. "Whatta Man," a duet with the vocal group En Vogue, reached number three on both the pop and R&B charts in 1994. Like Queen Latifah, the members have since pursued acting careers. In 2001 another female trio, Destiny's Child, peaked in popular success.

RETRO SWING

In the wake of the early 1990s grunge movement, an unlikely trend welled up from the alternative underground. The infectious dance rhythm of 1930s and 40s Swing Era had won the affections of later generations in fitful spurts over a period of many years, but in the 1990s it was claimed by teenage and 20-something postpunkers. Some confident speculation can be made as to the origins of this particular movement. A pioneer of the jump swing revival was the British new waver Joe Jackson. He was a contemporary of Elvis Costello and just as determined to prove his stylistic eclecticism, recording albums of reggae and 1940s jump blues in the style of R&B king Louis Jordan. His top 10 1981 album *Jumpin' Jive* proved a huge hit with the new wave underground, and he followed it up with a tour backed by a swing big band. Sequel albums followed, *Night and Day* and *Body and Soul,* but with the 1986 album *Big World* the swing infatuation began to fade. His effort was gone but not forgotten.

There were other protoretro swing efforts as well. The western swing revival band Asleep at the Wheel (AATW) began in Virginia, moved to San Francisco at the end of the psychedelic era, and then, in 1974, moved to Austin, Texas, a bastion of Texas culture yet extremely eclectic. AATW's early repertoire was a mix of jump blues, western swing, honky tonk, and rockabilly, but through it all the band demonstrated a consistent swing that has maintained a large following ever since. Another Austin act, singer Lyle Lovett, demonstrated his eclecticism with the introduction of "Large Band" on his third album in 1989. Also emphasizing the swing/rockabilly connection was the Stray Cats. The group was a trio of Americans, including New York–born guitarist Brian Setzer. The band exported itself to the British new wave scene soon after its formation in 1979. After building a sizable following in England, it returned to the United States to enjoy the early years of MTV. The novelty of the 1950s throwback image soon faded, and the group disbanded by 1984; but Setzer was to return 10 years later with equal success as a solo act he built in Los Angeles.

To some postpunks there was a delight in reviving and glorifying the "cheesy" styles of past entertainment or giving a rather gothic spin to the elegance of early twentieth-century popular dance music. Novelty was found in venerable martini-sipping, Las Vegas crooner lounge acts like Frank Sinatra, Dean Martin, and other members of the Rat Pack. From among these classic performers that were still living, Generation X youth targeted veteran pop singer Tony Bennett. Bennett was a logical choice. His son Danny had taken over his father's management in the 1980s, pursuing the seemingly implausible tactic of trying to market Tony to a younger audience. But compared with his crooner contemporaries, the elder Bennett's voice is strident, loud, and coarse—more likely to appeal to postpunks. Additionally, Bennett has adamantly resisted musical fashion, committing himself to repertoire that he personally believed in. This fiercely independent sentiment would also endear him to the nonconformist attitude of the postpunk aesthetic. Tony Bennett made a triumphant appearance on MTV's *Unplugged* broadcast series in 1993 (the same year Nirvana made its appearance on the show), doing the same songs the same way he had always done them. He was gracious to his audience, as he always was, and totally himself. A best-selling album and video followed. Another veteran singer, Mel Tormé, also enjoyed a newfound fame with young people, and appeared as host and performer on several MTV programs.

In the Dallas alternative enclave of Deep Ellum (the city's old blues district), there were acts like Café Noir that featured what they called "symphonic gypsy swing" and a singer, Randy Erwin, who specialized in movie cowboy yodeling and song as well as French salon music. In Chapel Hill, North Carolina, the Squirrel Nut Zippers (named after an old candy bar) was formed by a group of young friends fascinated by early jazz. The group really didn't hit until the release of its second album *Hot* in 1997, which included the single "Hell." In true postpunk tradition, the group's members were deliberately inept at their instruments, particularly the horn players, who resurrected their old high school chops to play saxophone, trumpet, and trombone in the band. While no one could ever decide if the band's music was tribute or parody, retro swing played by young postpunkers in vintage clothing was hip.

Brian Setzer, retro swing artist and former member of the group Stray Cats, in September 1997.

The satirical nouveau lounge aesthetic and retro swing found new energy in the 1986 independent comedy film *Swingers,* in which one of the characters, Trent, exemplified the exaggerated barfly masher parodied by the movement. The film also featured the music of the retro swing band Big Bad Voodoo Daddy, a zoot-suit clad, hipster-lingo band formed in Los Angeles in 1992 that had made the lounge circuit courting Generation X. Former Stray Cat Brian Setzer, also in L.A., founded his Brian Setzer Orchestra, which he fronted with his guitar and vocals. His *Dirty Boogie* album, released in 1998, featured the hit single "Jump, Jive, and Wail." The Setzer recording exploded in popularity when it appeared in a trendy television commercial for the Gap, a young people's clothing retailer. "Jump, Jive, and Wail" was a cover of a late 1950s recording by Louis Prima.

Prima, who died in 1978, possessed every aspect of the retro swing aesthetic. He was a trumpet player of Italian ancestry, born in New Orleans in 1911. He composed and originally featured the classic jungle-drum showcase "Sing, Sing, Sing," popularized to a greater extent by Gene Krupa and Benny Goodman on their classic 1937 recording. In the late 1950s Prima was one of the most popular and energetic lounge acts in Las Vegas. With fellow singer Keely Smith and the wailing R&B tenor sax sound of Sam Butera, Prima created a successful blend of swing, R&B, Dixieland, and Italian-American popular music. Prima was also the voice of the orangutan King Louie in Disney's animated movie of Rudyard Kipling's *The Jungle Book* in 1967. The retro swing movement brought about a great reissue effort of Prima's classic recordings as well as recordings by Louis Jordan and other jump swing stars of the past.

Similar bands followed. The group called the Cherry Poppin' Daddies was formed in the university area of Eugene, Oregon. Lead singer and founder Steve Perry (not the lead singer with the rock band Journey) said he began his fascination with early swing when his mother gave him the *Smithsonian Collection of Classic Jazz* recordings set as a gift. At the height of the grunge movement in the Northwest, the group confounded young fans with their repertoire of ska and retro swing. (Revival of Jamaican ska has also been an important part of the alternative music scene, particularly as a context for using horns in a rock band.) The band also maintained a strong postpunk element. Its very name is morally challenging and misogynistic, although the aggressively feminist team hosts of the ABC morning talk program *The View* seemed to have no problem in inviting the Cherry Poppin' Daddies on as a guest act and enthusiastically invoking its name in the introduction. Its lyrics were perfunctorily angry, obscene, and nonconformist. The Daddies' 1997 MCA release *Zoot Suit Riot* was a compilation of the most swing-oriented tracks from earlier recordings and went multiplatinum. The title track owed much of its character to "Sing, Sing, Sing" and from the early Harlem swing style of bandleader and singer Cab Calloway, particularly his 1932 theme song "Minnie the Moocher."

Listening Guide   23.4
"Zoot Suit Riot" 4 beats per measure

TIME	FORM	EVENT DESCRIPTION
:00	Intro	Drum solo (6 measures); guitar solo (2 measures)
:11	Horn riff 1	Eight measures played twice (16 measures)
:32	Verse 1	Vocal (16 measures)
:53	Chorus 1	Vocal answered by shouts from the band (8 measures)
1:03	Chorus 2	Same as Chorus 1
1:13	Horn riff 2	(8 measures)
1:24	Verse 2	Vocal (16 measures)
1:45	Chorus 3	See :53 time-line description (8 measures)
1:56	Interlude 1	Horns play short upbeat notes, 2 measures; saxes answer, 1 measure; vocal responds, 1 measure; this 4-measure phrase played four times (16 measures)
2:15	Breakdown	Drum solo similar to intro, 4 measures; call-and-response between vocal and horn section, 16 measures (20 measures)
2:42	Verse 3	Uses only the last half of the verse (8 measures)
2:52	Chorus 4	See :53 time-line description (8 measures)
3:02	Chorus 5	Vocalist is freer with melody, more intense (8 measures)
3:13	Interlude 2	See 1:56 time-line description (16 measures)
3:34	Ending	Drum solo and guitar solo similar to intro; horns play a loud chord at the end, with growl/plunger trumpet solo (8 measures)
3:52	End	

Analysis of "Zoot Suit Riot" (*Zoot Suit Riot*, CD format, Uptown/Universal 53081)

The Cherry Poppin' Daddies was one of a legion of bands following the neoswing craze of the late 1990s. "Zoot Suit Riot" was one of the movement's biggest hits. It owes a great debt to two songs from the swing era: Louis Prima's "Sing, Sing, Sing" and Cab Calloway's "Minnie the Moocher." The sound and feel of the rhythm section borrow more from jump blues bands of the 1940s and 1950s.

The song opens with a drum solo played on the tom-toms reminiscent of Gene Krupa's famous drum solo with Benny Goodman's band in the 1930s. It is followed by a guitar solo that is more in the style of early rockabilly guitar. The horn section plays one of two riff passages they present in the course of the song.

The vocalist sings with a style and sound that is almost a throwback to old radio singers of the 1930s. The song's chorus features the vocal soloist answered by vocal shouts from the band, a common practice among swing bands of the past. After a couple of verse/chorus cycles, the horns play an interlude with a vocal response. The drums' tom-tom solo then returns without any chords from the other instruments. This type of section is often called a *breakdown* by musicians, meaning the song has broken down to only a vamp or drum beat over which someone will improvise a solo. In this case the vocal soloist does a call-and-response banter with the horn section, reminiscent of Cab Calloway's "hi-de-ho" call-and-response section of "Minnie the Moocher." The vocalist returns with a truncated verse and a double chorus. The horn interlude is repeated; then the drum solo and guitar break heard in the song's introduction wraps up the performance. A horn section chord is held at the very end, over which a trumpet soloist plays an improvisation, growling through the horn and using a plunger mute in the manner of Cootie Williams, trumpet soloist with the Duke Ellington Orchestra.

Suddenly, big bands were back. Old swing dance palaces came back to life, filled with kids in 1930s swing-cat clothing. Old Harlem swing dance patriarchs were opening dance schools. Ballroom dance salons and schools, heretofore ghettos for elderly singles gathering to tango and fox-trot, were packed every weekend. As far as the music was concerned, it didn't seem to matter to the young participants that the music didn't really swing, have any subtlety, or possess many able improvisers. This was aggressive, hard-driving music with a healthy dose of punk that glorified the raw and the incompetent. However, it was only a phase. By the end of the 1990s retro swing had run its course and, probably much to the relief of the precraze purveyors of true classic swing and R&B, faded away.

LATIN POP

Latin music has always been woven into the fabric of American popular music. Whether it was music from Spain, Cuba, the Caribbean, Central and South America, or Mexico, it was never far from the surface.

Latin pop was a phenomenon that really began in the 1980s. Various substyles of Latin music, already enjoying a loyal following within their own somewhat isolated cultural enclaves, began to show influence of higher production and technology taken from mainstream American popular music, including the use of synthesizers, drum machines, and an urban, discolike format and sound. Likewise, Latino people in the United States were becoming more urbane, prosperous, and influential. There were burgeoning Latin dance club scenes throughout the major urban centers of the United States, particularly New York and Miami. Spanish-language television, such as Univision, and radio found huge audiences and big profits within the American market. U.S. Latinos were increasingly becoming the mainstream, and Latino artists and music producers were ready and willing to win a larger non-Latino audience.

The first great insurgence of Latin pop in the 1980s was accomplished by Gloria Estefan in Miami. She was born Gloria Fajardo in Havana, Cuba, in 1957 but grew up in Miami after her family fled the coup led by Fidel Castro. She met her husband Emilio Estefan in a Miami wedding band, later dubbed the Miami Sound Machine. The group pursued a blend of dance pop and salsa and eventually moved out of the "International" record category into mainstream pop by releasing the English-language *Primitive Love* on the Epic label in 1985. "Conga" and "Bad Boy" were top 10 hits that everyone could dance to, and the hit ballad "Words Get in the Way" showed Gloria's beautiful ballad voice and crossed her over firmly into the adult contemporary market. (She also recorded this ballad in Spanish.) Two years later, the group, now billed as Gloria Estefan and the Miami Sound Machine, released the triple-platinum *Let It Loose*, featuring the dance hits "Rhythm Is Gonna Get You" and "1-2-3."

In 1990 Estefan's tour bus was involved in a serious accident in which her back was broken, keeping her out of the scene for a year. By 1993 she returned to her

Latino roots with *Mi Tierra*, a Spanish-language album that won a Grammy in the tropical Latin category. She has continued to conquer both the Latin and adult contemporary audiences to the present.

Closely associated with Gloria Estefan's career was Jon Secada. Also a native of Havana (b. 1962), Secada earned his bachelor's and master's degrees in vocal jazz performance at the University of Miami. (The University of Miami contributed many jazz- and pop-trained musicians to Estefan's band and to the Latin pop industry over the years.) He was an important contributor to Estefan's *Into the Light*, her 1991 comeback album after her bus accident. He launched his solo career in 1992. Like Estefan, he presented a smooth mix of R&B, Latin, dance pop, and adult contemporary ballads.

Enrique Iglesias is the son of Julio Iglesias, who, in the 1970s, was one of the most popular vocalists in the world and almost unknown to American audiences. Julio then recorded a duet album with, among others, Willie Nelson, and conquered the adult market in the United States as well. Enrique, in turn, became the most popular Latin singles artist during 1996.

One of the most significant footnotes in the history of Latin pop is the incredible success of Los del Rio's dance hit "Macarena" in 1996. The duo of Antonio Romeo Monge and Rafael Ruiz, having performed and recorded Spanish pop for years, wrote and released the song in 1993. A success in Spain, it was made into a dance mix for the United States by the Bayside Boys, a stage name for the Miami Bayside Productions team of Carlos De Yarza and Mike Triay. The remix, with some English portions, was released in 1995 and reached number one by 1996. Taking its place in dance history with the twist or the hustle, the accompanying dance step swept the world. People could be found doing the Macarena at ball games, wedding receptions, and clubs. Gymnastics teams at the Olympics were doing it on television.

As much as Gloria Estefan, Jon Secada, and Enrique Iglesias opened doors for Latino artists into the mainstream, no one could claim as much credit for the 1990s Latin explosion as Ricky Martin. Enrique Martin Morales was born in San Juan, Puerto Rico, in 1971. He began his career in the Latino boy band Menudo, which enjoyed moderate success in the United States but widely appealed to Latino youth around the world. In the early 1990s Martin slowly and methodically built his adult career as an actor, appearing on the soap opera *General Hospital* and on Broadway in the musical *Les Miserables*. Beginning in 1995 his music began incorporating a harder rock style blended with a mixture of Latin styles. The real breakthrough came with his first English language album release, *Ricky Martin*, in 1999. Riding on the blockbuster single, "Livin' la Vida Loca," Martin blew the gates off Latin music and made it a mainstream sensation. Combining good looks, an extremely positive, sexy yet wholesome stage show, dance, and accessible music, Martin created a wave that many other Latin artists would ride to unprecedented success.

One of the first to share the newfound popularity was Marc Anthony, already a longtime, hardworking songwriter, singer, and producer.

Latin pop sensation Ricky Martin performing in Los Angeles on June 16, 2001.

He was born in New York City to Puerto Rican parents. As a young musician he had little interest in pursuing Latino music despite his musical upbringing. That all changed when he became involved in the 1990 Atlantic album *When the Night Is Over*, performing with Latin legends Little Louie Vega, Eddie Palmieri, and the great Tito Puente. Anthony began involving himself more with Latin music, later collaborating with actor, political activist, and Latin musician Ruben Blades. He made his first English-language album in 1999, featuring "I Need to Know." At the first Latin Grammy awards, "I Need to Know" won song of the year.

Jennifer Lopez, like Marc Anthony, was a native New Yorker of Puerto Rican descent. Her childhood efforts were in music theater, but her real success came in television and film acting. One milestone for her music and acting career came in 1997 when she was selected to portray Tejano singing star Selena in a made-for-television movie biography. (Selena Perez had a following of almost religious proportion in the Mexican-American community in Texas. She was about to break into the mainstream with an English-language album in 1995 when, tragically, the manager of her San Antonio boutique murdered her. The album, *Dreaming of You*, was released posthumously. It was the first Tejano album to reach *Billboard*'s number-one position and went double platinum.)

In the late 1990s Lopez became involved romantically and professionally with Sean "Puffy" Combs, a major rap music producer. It was a controversial relationship for many reasons, including a 1999 shooting incident in a New York club that took Combs to trial. In any event Lopez was compelled to return to her musical roots. She appeared in music videos for other artists and those featuring herself, and she developed a blend of music she calls *Latin soul*, releasing the albums *On the 6* and *J. Lo.* Already the highest-paid Latino actress, she, at the time of this writing, seems on her way to pop music superstardom as well.

Another Latin female sensation is Christina Aguilera, born in New York in 1980. Her style has been more teen pop, and her career has been compared to teen pop idol Britney Spears. (Both were veterans of the New Mickey Mouse Club as kids.) By 1999 she had sold over 10 million recordings but seemed linked to the world of Latin pop only by her Venezuelan ancestry. However, she wanted to cash in on the Latin pop craze and, in 2000, released the Spanish-language *Mi Reflejo*. On closer inspection, however, it proves to be a recycling of the songs on her 1999 debut album done in Spanish (which she had to learn phonetically since she doesn't speak Spanish).

The Latin explosion of the late 1990s also marked the comeback of legendary guitarist Carlos Santana. Santana was born in Mexico in 1947 but moved with his family to San Francisco while in high school. He became involved with the San Francisco psychedelic scene of the late 1960s and appeared at Woodstock in 1969. He enjoyed tremendous success at the time with a cover version of Tito Puente's "Oyé Como Va." Extremely influenced by the music of jazz saxophonist John Coltrane (as were other 1960s rock groups), he associated himself with a number of notable jazz artists during the 1970s and 1980s. In 1987 he did his first musical score for the film biography of Ritchie Valens, an early Latino rock star who popularized the adapted Mexican folk song "La Bamba" before dying in a plane crash with Buddy Holly in 1959. After a five-year recording hiatus, Santana released *Supernatural* on the Arista label in 1999. The album featured songs co-written by many popular artists of the day. The single "Smooth" was done in collaboration with Rob Thomas of the postgrunge band Matchbox 20. The album sold 10 million copies and won Santana eight Grammys at the 2000 awards show, including best single. He tied Michael Jackson's 1983 record for the most Grammys won on a single night.

TEEN POP

One thing pop music can always rely on is the preteen and early-teenage market. While youngsters inevitably outgrow the music aimed at this age group, there is always another group of adolescents coming in behind them, just as impressionable and easily manipulated by the commercial music machine. It is, in fact, the next phase of manipulation after pushing toys and junk food.

Teen idols in popular music have a long history in rock. The first notable point was the manufacturing of teen idols in the late 1950s—notable because it was a deliberate effort by the pop music industry to groom young, cute music celebrities to target mainstream adolescents. Paul Anka, Frankie Avalon, Connie Francis, and Annette Funicello were pawns of the image brokers and music moguls who sought to create high-production, palatable music and an entertainer with a persona that young people with disposable income can identify. Very often, wardrobe, the ability to dance, and lyrics predominate over any musical substance.

The tradition continued with kid acts like Motown's Jackson Five, the Monkees, and the Osmonds through the 1960s. However, the era that spawned the phenomenon often labeled as teen pop by rock historians encompasses the late 1980s to the first decade of the 2000s. Inextricably linked to Disney and a perfunctory Christmas album, teen girls Tiffany and Debbie Gibson kicked things off, but teen pop reached its first real peak with the New Kids on the Block (NKOTB), a quintet of boys from the Boston area. They were produced by Maurice Starr, who was looking for a white follow-up to his earlier teen pop group New Edition. NKOTB's first album premiered in 1986, but the group's second album, *Hangin' Tough,* introduced an updated, tougher image and musical style that better connected with the preteens of the day. Of course, there was the requisite number of love ballads to show the macho boys' tender side to infatuated girl fans. In the tradition of the Jacksons the group featured intricate and exhausting dance routines. From 1988 to 1990 NKOTB consistently achieved hit status. Typically, as the boys aged they wanted their music to evolve, to successfully transition to an adult act, and to distance themselves from ridicule by music critics and the more mature milieu in the music business. It ultimately failed, and members have since pursued solo careers on their own.

A quick successor was Boyz II Men, a young, black male vocal quartet. The product of producer Michael Bivens, the group created a timeless style that blended smooth vocal group harmony reminiscent of 1950s doo-wop, 1960s R&B, and a bit of hip hop. Formed in 1988, they found their first real success in 1992, a year after the release of their debut album, *Cooleyhighharmony,* and their success has continued ever since.

In the mid-1990s a dynasty was created by boy-band producer Louis J. Pearlman. Pearlman was the owner of a plane-leasing company that sometimes shuttled teen acts to their concerts. After witnessing the acts and the reaction of their ever-renewable fans, Pearlman decided he could replicate the formula successfully and repeatedly.

His first product certainly proved he was up to the task. The Backstreet Boys, like the New Kids on the Block before them, was comprised of white, middle-class young men. Stylistically, they combined the current popular styles of hip hop, techno dance pop, and sweet ballads. As far as image, the group carefully blended a combination of different looks, guaranteeing sex appeal to any girl's personal tastes in boys.

The group's first album, on the Jive/Zomba label, was released in Europe in 1995. It was a big success in England and moved on to Canada the next year. The American version of the album combined some of the European release tracks with new material and was released in 1997. It continued to produce hit singles for two years, and the album sold over 13 million copies. At the height of their success, the group became embroiled in a bitter legal battle with Pearlman and other members of their management team. The Backstreet Boys and its clone 'N Sync became incensed over the percentage of profits taken in by Pearlman. There was also a concern over both acts being signed with Jive Records; the Backstreet Boys felt they would not be supported as well by the label.

When the dust settled, Pearlman remained the Backstreet Boys' manager and work began on their follow-up album, *Millennium*. It was released in early 1999 and debuted at number one, with first-week sales topping one million units. Relentlessly following one top-selling album after another, they released a Christmas album and *Black and Blue* by the fall of 2000. The success of the Backstreet Boys has led to numerous copycat boy bands such as 'N Sync and 98°. In 1999 the ABC network created a television series in the fashionable reality TV format called *Making the Band*. Borrowing ideas from MTV's *The Real World* and VH1's *Behind the Music*, it was a behind-the-scenes docudrama on the recruiting, training, and marketing of a boy band, O-Town, by teen pop mogul Lou Pearlman.

Between New Kids on the Block and the Backstreet Boys came grunge rock from the Northwest, putting light American teen rock in peril. The style took refuge in the United Kingdom, where both British and American acts flourished for a time. The U.K. had tremendous success with the boy band Take That. The group of cute boys, whether by design or not, had an ambiguous appeal to both young girls and homosexual males. (The same has been said of pretty-boy Latin pop sensation Ricky Martin.) However, the real British sensation that went on to conquer the United States was the Spice Girls. The underlying musical trait of the Spice Girls was dance pop, but their image was further removed from that of the teen appeal boy bands. They combined characteristics of Madonna with an old-time British floozie image and added some alternative rock angry feminism and a lot of good humor. Reminiscent of the disco era's the Village People, each Spice Girl was given a distinct identity: the sexy Spice, the scary Spice, the posh Spice, the sporty Spice, and the baby Spice. It didn't seem to matter that their musical ability was in question (members were occasionally caught forgetting to turn on their mics in live shows), they had a naughty-girl image that appealed to young female audiences everywhere. Their hit single "Wannabe" debuted in the United States in 1997. Phenomenal success led to a film and album *Spice World*. In 1998 Geri Halliwell left the group, and other members eventually married, had children, and pursued solo careers. However, four of the members reconvened, got Janet Jackson producers Terry Lewis and Jimmy Jam, and released the album *Forever* in the United States in 2000.

Back in the United States, the Tulsa, Oklahoma, brother-group Hanson made a different offering from the typical boy bands of the era. They were a family band, reminiscent of the Jackson Five, the Cowsills, and the fictitious television Partridge family. They were naturally and extraordinarily talented, playing their

Teen pop star Britney Spears performing in Pittsburgh, Pennsylvania, on August 21, 2000.

own instruments, doing their own singing, and writing their own material. Of course, they were also cute, especially the younger brother, drummer Zac. They produced the hit single "MMMBop," marking their stylistic crossover from fifties and sixties rock influences to a newer hip hop and soul influence. After a couple of years as teen pop sensations, they dropped out of the limelight to produce an album with more musical substance and appeal to a more mature audience. The album, *This Time Around,* reflects yet newer musical influences and promises that the Hansons may successfully make the transition to serious critical acceptance as mature musicians.

In the wake of the Spice Girls came a series of female teen pop solo acts—coincidently, veterans of the Disney cable channel's New Mickey Mouse Club. By far the most successful was Britney Spears, born in Louisiana in 1981. After working in commercials and stage shows, Spears did two seasons on the Mickey Mouse Club show then, in 1999, signed with Jive Records. Her first album, . . . *Baby One More Time,* spawned a series of hit singles. Spears's image connoted many things to many people. On the one hand, she was the girl next door, seemingly very young and innocent. Her song lyrics certainly seemed wholesome enough. On the other hand, she exuded an underage sex appeal that bordered on pedophilia. She bared her midriff, sang with a moaning vocal style that was semiorgasmic, and used some dance moves that were semierotic. Parents weren't certain if they wanted her as a role model for their daughters or not. But Spears seemed to know exactly what she was doing. An emblem to teenage girls and an object of fantasy for males of all ages, her appeal was widespread.

Britney Spears opened the floodgate for other teen pop divas. In addition to Christina Aguilera, the next contender was Jessica Simpson, a failed Mickey Mouse auditionee and contemporary Christian singer who finally found her mark with Sony and touring with boy band 98°. While disposable bubblegum pop has always been a sure thing, it would seem that, at the end of the twentieth century, teen pop had entered its golden era.

MUSIC TELEVISION IN THE NINETIES

MTV not only continued to shape the popular music business but went on to be a powerful force in nonmusic entertainment and, eventually, politics. It premiered a trivia game show, *Remote Control,* in 1987, the first reality show, *The Real World,* in 1992, and the cartoon rock losers *Beavis and Butthead* in 1993.

After early controversy about excluding black music and artists in the first part of the 1980s, MTV turned out to be the major catalyst for many hip hop artists. *Yo! MTV Raps* premiered in 1987, followed shortly by *Club MTV*. By the 1990s hip hop was the dominant video act on MTV. Music television programming further diversified with the initiation of MTV sibling networks, MTV2 and the Box. MTV also began a series of intimate, live, studio concerts called *Unplugged*, in which prominent rock stars played mostly acoustic instruments and shed the trappings of dazzling stage props and theatrics. There were defining moments in this series. Two programs of note among many: Nirvana's appearance and the unlikely appearance of pop crooner Tony Bennett.

MTV was not only a reflection of Generation X's musical tastes but an important vehicle for others to communicate with that generation. Bill Clinton realized this and became the first U.S. "rock president." President George Bush, Ronald Reagan's vice president and successor, was increasingly out of touch with the culture and concerns of the country's young voters. Antagonistic toward the morals of many rock acts, Bush preferred country music, actually appearing in the audience of a Country Music Association Awards broadcast. Meanwhile, Arkansas governor Bill Clinton became the Democratic nominee to block Bush's reelection. Clinton was younger, loved jazz and rock, fooled around with tenor saxophone, and offered himself openly to young Americans. His first great coup was an appearance on Arsenio Hall's talk show during his presidential campaign. To the shock and delight of his audience, he appeared with the house band, saxophone in hand, and clad in a dark suit and sunglasses reminiscent of the Blues Brothers. He then conducted studio town hall forums with young people broadcast on MTV, even though the network had shown little interest in news and politics prior to that time. Clinton won the election by a landslide, was overwhelmingly elected for a second term, and was beloved by the MTV generation in spite of his personal calamities during his tenure in office. The Clinton decade of the 1990s clearly demonstrates the power of MTV and its hold on popular culture.

In 1998 MTV created a program that rekindled the folksy success formula that sustained Dick Clark's *American Bandstand* for 30 years. *Total Request Live (TRL),* like *American Bandstand,* made the young audience the real star. Boys and girls not only got to pick the music to be played but got to interact with the stars. Teen pop acts, in particular, found *TRL* to be as important a marketing tool as radio airplay.

In 1999 MTV broadcast *Woodstock '99,* an ill-fated attempt to recapture the peaceful and legendary rock megaconcert of 30 years before. Many problems arose, and MTV was there to capture them. There were a number of great current acts, but the crass commercialism, overpriced concessions, and general inconvenience to the fans led to a violent uprising and vandalism.

MP3: THE TECHNOLOGY AND THE THREAT

As the general population entered the world of digital imaging and the Internet in the 1990s, there was a revolution in the way that people communicated and exchanged information. This includes the exchange of the recorded music that people may or may not have purchased. For decades magnetic tape media—reel-to-reel, cassettes, and eight-track—has allowed the duplication of music, but always with a loss of audio quality compared to its source. With the introduction of digital recording and playback, most commonly on compact discs and minidiscs, consumers were suddenly able to replicate recordings with no degradation of sound. The drawback is that the digital information needed to reproduce a high-quality stereo recording can be massive, requiring equally massive storage media and computer memory. For a time the recording industry felt safer from piracy because CDs and digital audio in general was more immune to duplication by the consumer.

Over time, this safe situation became less and less the case. Technological innovation progressed, and a culminating point was the development of MP3 compression technology. Compression is the procedure of squeezing a digital file to a smaller size for economical storage and quicker transportation from one digital point to another. One of these compression technologies is called MPEG (Motion Picture Experts Group). This format is used widely for digital video, such as DVDs, digital satellite television transmission, and the emerging high-definition television broadcast platform. The MPEG audio subsystem of compression is called *MPEG audio layer 3*, or *MP3*. The way in which MP3 compresses digital audio is significant and distinctive from previous techniques. It trims the digital information of the frequencies that are beyond the range of human hearing and retains the integrity of the remaining frequencies. The goal of the MP3 format is to compress a CD-quality song by a factor of 10 to 14 without losing the CD quality of the sound.

From the industry's point of view, the idea of any recording duplication technology available on the consumer level was to allow that consumer, who had already legally purchased a recorded product, to transfer it to another medium for his or her own personal convenience of use. For instance, transferring an LP or CD to a cassette tape would allow someone to listen to his or her favorite music on a cassette player in a car or on a portable playback system. MP3 compression was intended for just such a purpose, with MP3 players like those from the company Diamond Rio. It boasts superiority over cassettes and even portable CD players in that it has no moving parts (digital information is stored on computer chips), and because MP3 files are so much smaller than CD digital files, more music can be downloaded into the player. Owners of laptop computers could put small MP3 copies of their CDs on their machines, making virtual jukeboxes of their favorite music to listen to on planes or buses. However, with sizable personal libraries of MP3 music "ripped" from commercial recordings abounding, it was only a matter of time before people began using the accommodating size of MP3 files to swap them over the Internet.

Internet services like MP3.com tried to make online transportation of MP3 files legitimate by offering the files from its site with the blessing of artists and the industry. It looked like a promising way to introduce deserving, overlooked artists and independent music producers to the masses without running the gauntlet of major label acceptance and distribution. Most of the exchange of MP3s, however, took place between the common users of the Internet and involved illegal copies of copyrighted material. This was particularly prevalent among young people. It was only a matter of time before someone would offer a formal means to expedite this arguably illicit sharing.

In January 1999 student Shawn Fanning dropped out of Boston's Northeastern University to go commercial with his MP3 file-sharing software. It was an innovative way for computer users to exchange music, called a *peer-to-peer network*. Rather than pointing to a central computer server system that stores music files in one place, Fanning's software allowed users to search each other's computers for audio files. The inventory seemed limitless. By May Napster was founded. This protocol created a formidable new threat to the music recording industry, and in December of 1999 the Recording Industry of America sued Napster. Back in April the popular metal band Metallica, with drummer Lars Ulrich as its spokesman, was the first major artist to sue Napster. Hip hop artist Dr. Dre actually went after the consumers, mostly university students. Since universities have such a heavy concentration of young people with high-speed campus computer network access, they were the epicenter of the music trading activity. In July 2000 Napster was ordered to block any exchange of copyrighted material, but the fight was not yet over. On October 2 a three-judge panel weighed the validity of the earlier injunction, and BMG offered Napster a compromise: 50 million dollars to develop a legal file-sharing system. Ultimately, on February 12, 2001, the Ninth Circuit court decided that Napster did indeed violate copyright law and ordered it to be shut down.

Napster became the sacrificial lamb for the concept of peer-to-peer MP3 file exchange, but other software using the same protocol have continued with less aggression from the industry. Programs such as Freenet and Gnutella will fill in the gap, and if they are stamped out, others will continue the music-sharing underground. For better or worse, music is in the hands of the consumer to do with as they wish. No longer are major labels, with their powers of promotion, production, distribution, and price setting, a prerequisite for launching an artist's or group's career. Yet without centralized control there are drawbacks. Just as there is no one to sue, there is also no standard bearer, either for the performance of the software and network or for the quality of the music available to the public. In 2001 even MP3.com (not a peer-to-peer product) had to admit that there were deplorable recordings on its site, and some sites featured "worst of MP3.com" offerings. In other words, MP3 files offered for free were music that no one would steal in the first place.

EPILOGUE: DEFINING THE NEW MILLENNIUM

In discussing the popular music history of each new decade, the narrative always begins by establishing the well-heeled styles and artists carried over from the previous decade and the identification of some musical or cultural trigger within the first year or so that sparks the identity for the next decade. Perhaps we would generalize the 1960s as the Vietnam Era, the 1970s as the "Me" era, and so on.

The transition to the twenty-first century was fraught with paranoia and fear of great disaster. There had been established fears of diseases such as AIDS and Ebola. Suddenly, our digital world was also open to danger of disease. Numerous computer viruses distributed via shared data and the Internet created intermittent pandemonium. Then, as the year 2000 approached, computer experts began expressing concern that computers, some constructed and programmed as many as 30 years earlier, would shut down when their internal calendars changed over to the year 2000. Business and the public, in anticipation of an apocalyptic event, took extraordinary measures. The world braced itself as New Year's Day came and went—a false alarm.

The presidential election of November 2000 will go down as the most controversial in America's history. In a tight race, Vice President Al Gore lost to Texas Governor George W. Bush, a victory darkened by the questionable handling of crucial ballots in Florida. The decade was off to a grim start indeed. But it turned out that all the technical and political disturbances were only a rehearsal for the devastating event that will, without doubt, define the 2000s. On Tuesday morning, September 11, 2001, terrorists hijacked four commercial passenger jet liners. In suicide attacks, two jets crashed into each of the World Trade Center towers in New York City, one crashed into the side of the Pentagon in Washington, D.C., and the fourth, assumed to have targeted another Washington location, crashed in a field in Pennsylvania.

The United States was stunned, frightened, and angered. Popular culture and entertainment also took a terrible blow. For the first few days after the attack, every network was running nonstop news, even MTV. Suddenly, everything and everyone concerned with entertainment seemed frivolous and unimportant. Comedic entertainers had no idea when or if to be funny again. After a few days, entertainers slowly began easing back into their jobs. Late-night hosts David Letterman, Jay Leno, and Conan O'Brien gently presented themselves on the air, making it all up as they went along.

After a time, musical artists once again found their place in the scheme of things. The tragic events of September 11 proved that, in times of trouble, music helps everyone cope, either voicing their indignation or creating a diversion from the horror of the situation. In the many stories told by people touched by the attacks, they often spoke of music that helped them deal with their situation. Musicians found that what they had to offer victims was as important and healing as anything offered by physicians, rescue workers, or disaster relief organizations. Soon after September 11, actors and musicians did a telethon entitled *America: A Tribute to Heroes,* broadcast commercial free on almost every broadcast and cable network. Live concerts were given in New York and Nashville.

As the world soberly proceeds into the new millennium, popular music will, as always, reflect our values, our circumstances, our technology, and our hopes and needs. We can only hope that, after the time of this writing, we'll find popular music later in the 2000s reflecting a brighter day of harmony among humankind and the joy of all who make the music and hear it.

Additional Listening

Refer to the citations in the body of the text.

Review Questions

1. What is the punk aesthetic reflected in Northwest grunge music? Who were specific early punk and postpunk groups that influenced the new music?
2. How did disc jockeys shape the character of early hip hop music?
3. Is there a distinction between East Coast and West Coast rap?
4. Who were early artists that influenced retro swing? How did retro swing fuse early swing with a punk sensibility?
5. What innovations were made to Latin pop music to help it cross over to a mainstream audience?
6. What was the design of the boy band that led to new heights of popularity in teen pop?
7. What is the design of the MP3 technology and how did it and Napster team up to pose a threat to music producers?

Notes

1. Katherine Charlton, *Rock Music Styles: A History*, 3rd ed. (Madison, WI: Mc Graw-Hill, 1998), p. 250.

Photo Credits

Index